Adobe
After Effects CC
2015 release

WITHDRAWN

Bē
Ash Thorp

CLASSROOM IN A BOOK®

WHERE ARE THE LESSON FILES?

Purchasing this Classroom in a Book gives you access to the lesson files you'll need to complete the exercises in the book.

You'll find the files you need on your **Account** page at peachpit.com on the **Lesson & Update Files** tab.

For complete instructions, see "Accessing the Classroom in a Book files" in the Getting Started section of this book.

The example below shows how the files appear on your Account page. The files are packaged as ZIP archives, which you will need to expand after downloading. You can download the lessons individually or as a single large ZIP file if your network connection is fast enough.

CONTENTS

GETTING STARTED

Adobe After Effects CC provides a comprehensive set of 2D and 3D tools for compositing, animation, and effects that motion-graphics professionals, visual effects artists, web designers, and film and video professionals need. After Effects is widely used for digital post-production of film, video, DVD, and the web. You can composite layers in various ways, apply and combine sophisticated visual and audio effects, and animate both objects and effects.

About Classroom in a Book

Adobe After Effects CC Classroom in a Book (2015 release) is part of the official training series for Adobe graphics and publishing software, developed with the support of Adobe product experts. The lessons are designed to let you learn at your own pace. If you're new to Adobe After Effects, you'll learn the fundamental concepts and features you'll need to master the program. And if you've been using Adobe After Effects for a while, you'll find that Classroom in a Book teaches many advanced features, including tips and techniques for using the latest version.

Although each lesson provides step-by-step instructions for creating a specific project, there's room for exploration and experimentation. You can follow the book from start to finish, or do only the lessons that match your interests and needs. Each lesson concludes with a review section summarizing what you've covered.

Prerequisites

Before beginning to use *Adobe After Effects CC Classroom in a Book (2015 release)*, make sure that your system is set up correctly and that you've installed the required software and hardware. You should have a working knowledge of your computer and operating system. You should know how to use the mouse and standard menus and commands, and also how to open, save, and close files. If you need to review these techniques, see the printed or online documentation included with your Microsoft® Windows® or Apple® Mac® OS software.

To complete the lessons in this book, you'll need to have both Adobe After Effects CC (2015 release) and Adobe Bridge CC installed. The exercises in this book are based on After Effects CC (2015.1 release).

Installing After Effects and Bridge

You must purchase the Adobe After Effects CC software separately. For system requirements and complete instructions on installing the software, visit www.adobe.com/support. Note that After Effects CC requires a 64-bit operating system and OpenGL 3.3 support. You must also have Apple QuickTime 7.6.6 or later installed on your system.

Some of the lessons in this book use Adobe Bridge. After Effects and Bridge use separate installers. You must install these applications from Adobe Creative Cloud (creative.adobe.com) onto your hard disk. Follow the onscreen instructions.

Optimizing performance

Creating movies is memory-intensive work for a desktop computer. After Effects CC (2015 release) requires a minimum of 4GB of RAM. The more RAM that is available to After Effects, the faster the application will work for you. For information about optimizing memory, cache, and other settings for After Effects, see "Improve performance" in After Effects Help.

Restoring default preferences

The preferences files control the way the After Effects user interface appears on your screen. The instructions in this book assume that you see the default interface when they describe the appearance of tools, options, windows, panels, and so forth. Therefore, it's a good idea to restore the default preferences, especially if you are new to After Effects.

Each time you quit After Effects, the panel positions and certain command settings are recorded in the preferences files. To restore the original default settings, press Ctrl+Alt+Shift (Windows) or Command+Option+Shift (Mac OS) while starting After Effects. (After Effects creates new preferences files if they don't already exist the next time you start the program.)

Restoring the default preferences can be especially helpful if someone has already customized After Effects on your computer. If your copy of After Effects hasn't been used yet, these files won't exist, so this procedure is unnecessary.

Important: If you want to save the current settings, you can rename a preferences file instead of deleting it. When you are ready to restore those settings, change the name back, and make sure that the file is located in the correct preferences folder.

1 Locate the After Effects preferences folder on your computer:

- **For Windows:** .../Users/<*user name*>/AppData/Roaming/Adobe/ AfterEffects/13.6

- **For Mac OS:** .../Users/<*user name*>/Library/Preferences/Adobe/ After Effects/13.6

2 Rename any preferences files you want to preserve, and then restart After Effects.

Accessing the Classroom in a Book files

The lessons in *Adobe After Effects CC Classroom in a Book (2015 release)* use specific source files, such as image files created in Adobe Photoshop® and Adobe Illustrator®, audio files, and prepared QuickTime movies. In order to work through the projects in this book, you will need to download the lesson files from your Account page at peachpit.com. You can download the files for individual lessons or download them all in a single file.

If you purchased an eBook from peachpit.com or adobepress.com, the files will automatically appear on your Account page, under the Lesson & Update Files tab.

If you purchased an eBook from a different vendor or a print book, use the unique code in the back of this book to gain access to the lesson files.

To access the *Classroom in a Book* files, follow these steps:

1 On a Mac or PC, go to www.peachpit.com/redeem, and enter the code found at the back of your book. **This code is not the same as the book's ISBN.**

2 Click Redeem Code, and sign in or create an account. You will be taken to your Account page.

You only need to enter the code once. After you redeem the code, you'll be able to access your lesson files at peachpit.com any time you want without entering the code again.

3 Click the Lesson & Update Files tab of your Account page to see a list of downloadable files.

4 Click the lesson file links to download them to your computer.

The files are compressed into ZIP archives to speed download time and protect the contents from damage during transfer. You must uncompress (or "unzip") the files to restore them to their original size and format before you use them with the book. Modern Mac and Windows systems are set up to open ZIP archives by simply double-clicking.

Note: In Mac OS 10.7 and later, the user library folder is hidden by default. To see it, in the Finder, choose Go > Go To Folder. In the Go To Folder dialog box, type **~/Library**, and then click Go.

◆ **Warning:** Once the code has been used, it cannot be used again.

5 On your hard drive, create a new folder in a convenient location and give it the name "Lessons," following the standard procedure for your operating system:

- In Windows, right-click, and choose New > Folder. Then enter the new name for your folder.

- In Mac OS, in the Finder, choose File > New Folder. Type the new name, and drag the folder to the location you want to use.

6 Drag the unzipped Lessons folder (which contains folders named Lesson01, Lesson02, and so on) that you downloaded onto your hard drive to your new Lessons folder. When you begin each lesson, navigate to the folder with that lesson number to access all the assets you need to complete the lesson.

● **Note:** If for any reason you need to download fresh copies of the lesson files, you can download them from your account again at any time.

About copying the sample movies and projects

You will create and render one or more QuickTime movies in some lessons in this book. The files in the Sample_Movie folders are examples that you can use to see the end results of each lesson and to compare them with your own results.

The files in the End_Project_File folders are samples of the completed project for each lesson. Use these files for reference if you want to compare your work in progress with the project files used to generate the sample movies. These end-project files vary in size from relatively small to a couple of megabytes, so you can either download them all now if you have ample storage space, or download just the end-project file for each lesson as needed, and then delete it when you finish that lesson.

Web Edition

● **Note:** Registering to access the Web Edition does not automatically provide access to your lesson files, and vice versa. You must follow the instructions for each to claim the full benefits of your purchase.

This book comes with a free Web Edition that provides many benefits and can be accessed from any device with a connection to the Internet.

Your Web Edition contains the complete text of the book, plus hours of instructional video keyed to the text as well as interactive quizzes. In addition, the Web Edition will be updated when Adobe adds significant feature updates between major Creative Cloud releases.

Accessing the free Web Edition

You must register your book purchase on peachpit.com in order to access the free Web Edition:

1 Go to www.peachpit.com/register, and then sign in or create a new account.

2 Enter the book's ISBN: 9780134308128.

3 Answer the questions as proof of purchase. The Web Edition will appear under the Digital Purchases tab on your Account page.

4 Click the Launch link to access the product.

How to use these lessons

Each lesson in this book provides step-by-step instructions for creating one or more specific elements of a real-world project. The lessons build on each other in terms of concepts and skills, so the best way to learn from this book is to proceed through the lessons in sequential order. In this book, some techniques and processes are explained and described in detail only the first few times you perform them.

Many aspects of the After Effects application can be controlled by multiple techniques, such as a menu command, a button, dragging, and a keyboard shortcut. Only one or two of the methods are described in any given procedure, so that you can learn different ways of working even when the task is one you've done before.

The organization of the lessons is also design-oriented rather than feature-oriented. That means, for example, that you'll work with layers and effects on real-world design projects over several lessons, rather than in just one lesson.

Additional resources

Adobe After Effects CC Classroom in a Book (2015 release) is not meant to replace documentation that comes with the program or to be a comprehensive reference for every feature. Only the commands and options used in the lessons are explained in this book. For comprehensive information about program features and tutorials, refer to these resources:

- **Adobe After Effects Learn & Support:** helpx.adobe.com/after-effects.html is where you can find and browse tutorials, help, and support on Adobe.com.

- **After Effects Forums:** forums.adobe.com/community/aftereffects_general_ discussion lets you tap into peer-to-peer discussions, and questions and answers about After Effects.

- **Adobe *Create* Magazine:** create.adobe.com offers thoughtful articles on design and design issues, a gallery showcasing the work of top-notch designers, tutorials, and more.

- **Resources for educators:** www.adobe.com/education and edex.adobe. com offer a treasure trove of information for instructors who teach classes on Adobe software. Find solutions for education at all levels, including free curricula that use an integrated approach to teaching Adobe software and can be used to prepare for the Adobe Certified Associate exams.

Also check out these useful links:

- **Adobe Add-ons:** creative.adobe.com/addons is a central resource for finding tools, services, extensions, code samples, and more to supplement and extend your Adobe products.
- **Adobe After Effects CC product home page:** www.adobe.com/products/aftereffects

Adobe Authorized Training Centers

Adobe Authorized Training Centers offer instructor-led courses and training on Adobe products. A directory of AATCs is available at training.adobe.com/trainingpartners.

1 GETTING TO KNOW THE WORKFLOW

Lesson overview

In this lesson, you'll learn how to do the following:

- Create a project and import footage.

- Create compositions and arrange layers.

- Navigate the Adobe After Effects interface.

- Use the Project, Composition, and Timeline panels.

- Apply basic keyframes and effects.

- Preview your work.

- Customize the workspace.

- Adjust preferences related to the user interface.

- Find additional resources for using After Effects.

 This lesson will take about an hour to complete. Download the Lesson01 project files from the Lesson & Update Files tab on your Account page at www.peachpit.com, if you haven't already done so. As you work on this lesson, you'll preserve the start files. If you need to restore the start files, download them from your Account page.

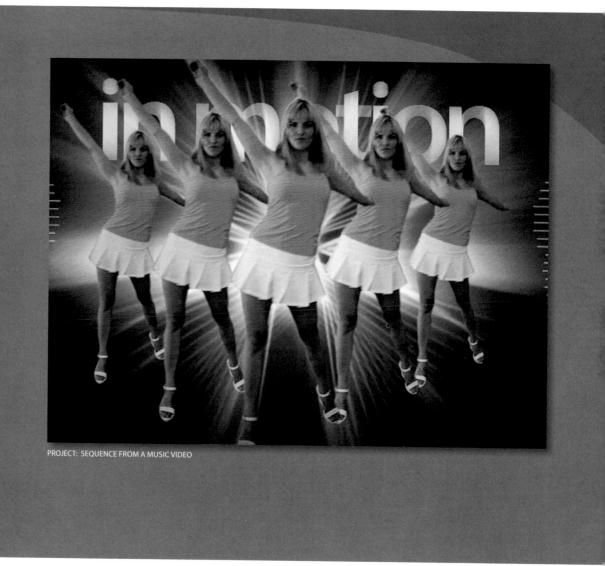

PROJECT: SEQUENCE FROM A MUSIC VIDEO

Whether you use After Effects to animate a simple
DVD title sequence or to create complex special
effects, you generally follow the same basic workflow.
The After Effects interface facilitates your work and
adapts to each stage of production.

About the After Effects work area

After Effects offers a flexible, customizable work area. The main window of the program is called the *application window*. Panels are organized in this window in an arrangement called a *workspace*. The default workspace contains stacked panels as well as panels that stand alone, as shown below.

A. Application window **B.** Workspace bar **C.** Tools panel **D.** Project panel **E.** Composition panel **F.** Timeline panel
G. Stacked panels **H.** Time graph

You customize a workspace by dragging the panels into the configuration that best suits your working style. You can drag panels to new locations, change the order of stacked panels, move panels into or out of a group, place panels alongside each other, stack panels, and undock a panel so that it floats in a new window above the application window. As you rearrange panels, the other panels resize automatically to fit the window.

When you drag a panel by its tab to relocate it, the area where you can drop it—called a *drop zone*—becomes highlighted. The drop zone determines where and how the panel is inserted into the workspace. Dragging a panel to a drop zone either docks it, groups it, or stacks it.

If you drop a panel along the edge of another panel, group, or window, it will dock next to the existing group, resizing all groups to accommodate the new panel.

If you drop a panel in the middle of another panel or group, or along the tab area of a panel, it will be added to the existing group and be placed at the top of the stack. Grouping a panel does not resize other groups.

You can also open a panel in a floating window. To do so, select the panel, and then choose Undock Panel or Undock Frame from the panel menu. Or, drag the panel or group outside the application window.

Getting started

A basic After Effects workflow follows six steps: importing and organizing footage, creating compositions and arranging layers, adding effects, animating elements, previewing your work, and rendering and outputting the final composition so that it can be viewed by others. In this lesson, you will create a simple animated video using this workflow, and along the way, you'll learn your way around the After Effects interface.

First, you'll preview the final movie to see what you'll create in this lesson.

1 Make sure the following files are in the Lessons/Lesson01 folder on your hard disk, or download them from your Account page at www.peachpit.com now:

 • In the Assets folder: bgwtext.psd, dancers.mov, gc_adobe_dance.mp3, pulsating_radial_waves.mov, vertical_waveforms.mov

 • In the Sample_Movie folder: Lesson01.mov

2 Open and play the Lesson01.mov sample movie in QuickTime Player to see what you will create in this lesson. When you're done, quit QuickTime Player. You may delete this sample movie from your hard disk if you have limited storage space.

Creating a project and importing footage

When you begin each lesson of this book, it's a good idea to restore the default preferences for After Effects. (For more information, see "Restoring default preferences" on page 2.) You can do this with a simple keyboard shortcut.

1 Start After Effects, and then immediately hold down Ctrl+Alt+Shift (Windows) or Command+Option+Shift (Mac OS) to restore default preferences settings. When prompted, click OK to delete your preferences.

2 Close the Start window.

> **Tip:** Restoring default preferences can be tricky in Windows, especially if you're working on a fast system. Press the keys after you double-click the application icon but before After Effects begins to list the files it's activating. Alternatively, you can choose Edit > [your Creative Cloud account username] > Clear Settings, and then restart the application.

After Effects opens to display an empty, untitled project.

Tip: To quickly
maximize a panel,
position the pointer
over it and press the
accent grave key (`) —
the unshifted character
under the tilde (~) on
standard US keyboards.
Press the ` key again to
return the panel to its
original size.

An After Effects project is a single file that stores references to all the footage
you use in that project. It also contains *compositions*, which are the individual
containers used to combine footage, apply effects, and, ultimately, drive the output.

When you begin a project, often the first thing you'll do is add footage to it.

3 Choose File > Import > File.

4 Navigate to the Assets folder in your
 Lessons/Lesson01 folder. Shift-click
 to select the dancers.mov, gc_adobe_
 dance.mp3, pulsating_radial_waves.
 mov, and vertical_waveforms.mov
 files (all the files except bgwtext.
 psd). Then click Import or Open.

A *footage item* is the basic unit in an After Effects project. You can import many types of footage items, including moving-image files, still-image files, still-image sequences, audio files, layered files from Adobe Photoshop and Adobe Illustrator, other After Effects projects, and projects created in Adobe Premiere® Pro. You can import footage items at any time.

As you import assets, After Effects reports its progress in the Info panel.

Because one of the footage items for this project is a multilayer Photoshop file, you'll import it separately as a composition.

5 Double-click in the lower area of the Project panel to open the Import File dialog box.

6 Navigate to the Lesson01/Assets folder again, and select the bgwtext.psd file. Choose Composition from the Import As menu, and then click Import or Open.

▶ **Tip:** You can also choose File > Import > Multiple Files to select files located in different folders, or drag and drop files from Explorer or the Finder. You can use Adobe Bridge to search for, manage, preview, and import footage.

After Effects opens an additional dialog box that displays options for the file you are importing.

7 In the bgwtext.psd dialog box, choose Composition from the Import Kind menu to import the layered Photoshop file as a composition. Select Editable Layer Styles in the Layer Options area, and then click OK.

The footage items appear in the Project panel.

8 In the Project panel, click to select different footage items. Notice that a thumbnail preview appears at the top of the Project panel. You can also see the file type and size, as well as other information about each item, in the Project panel columns.

When you import files, After Effects doesn't copy the video and audio data itself into your project. Instead, each footage item in the Project panel contains a reference link to the source files. When After Effects needs to retrieve image or audio data, it reads it from the source file. This keeps the project file small, and allows you to update source files in another application without modifying the project.

If you move a file or if After Effects can't access its location, it will report that the file is missing. To find missing files, choose File > Dependencies > Find Missing Footage. You can also type **Missing Footage** into the Search box in the Project panel to look for the missing assets.

Tip: You can locate missing fonts or effects the same way. Choose File > Dependencies, and then choose Find Missing Fonts or Find Missing Effects. Or just type **Missing Fonts** or **Missing Effects** into the Search box in the Project panel.

To save time and minimize the size and complexity of a project, you'll usually import a footage item once even if you're using it multiple times in a composition. However, you may sometimes need to import a source file more than once, such as if you want to use it at two different frame rates.

After you've imported footage, it's a good time to save the project.

9 Choose File > Save. In the Save As dialog box, navigate to the Lessons/Lesson01/ Finished_Project folder. Name the project **Lesson01_Finished.aep**, and then click Save.

Creating a composition and arranging layers

The next step of the workflow is to create a composition. You create all animation, layering, and effects in a composition. An After Effects composition has both spatial dimensions and a temporal dimension (time).

Compositions include one or more layers, arranged in the Composition panel and in the Timeline panel. Any item that you add to a composition—such as a still image, moving-image file, audio file, light layer, camera layer, or even another composition—becomes a new layer. Simple projects may include only one composition, while elaborate projects may include several compositions to organize large amounts of footage or intricate effects sequences.

To create a composition, you'll drag the footage items into the Timeline panel, and After Effects will create layers for them.

1 In the Project panel, Ctrl-click (Windows) or Command-click (Mac OS) to select the bgwtext composition as well as the dancers, gc_adobe_dance, vertical_ waveforms, and pulsating_radial_waves footage items.

2 Drag the selected footage items into the Timeline panel. The New Composition From Selection dialog box appears.

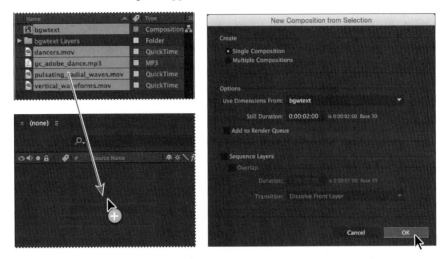

After Effects bases the dimensions of the new composition on the selected footage. In this example, all of the footage is sized identically, so you can accept the default settings for the composition.

3 Click OK to create the new composition.

The footage items appear as layers in the Timeline panel, and After Effects displays the composition, named bgwtext 2, in the Composition panel.

When you add a footage item to a composition, the footage becomes the source for a new layer. A composition can have any number of layers, and you can also include a composition as a layer in another composition, which is called *nesting*.

Some of the assets are longer than others, but you want them all to appear only as long as the dancers are on the screen. You'll change the length of the entire composition to 1:15 to match the dancers.

4 Choose Composition > Composition Settings.

5 In the Composition Settings dialog box, type **1:15** for the Duration, and then click OK.

The Timeline panel displays the same duration for each of the layers.

In this composition, there are five footage items, and therefore five layers in the Timeline panel. Depending on the order in which the elements were selected when you imported them, your layer stack may differ from the one shown on the previous page. The layers need to be in a specific order as you add effects and animations, however, so you'll rearrange them now.

About layers

Layers are the components you use to build a composition. Any item that you add to a composition—such as a still image, moving-image file, audio file, light layer, camera layer, or even another composition—becomes a new layer. Without layers, a composition consists only of an empty frame.

Using layers, you can work with specific footage items in a composition without affecting any other footage. For example, you can move, rotate, and draw masks for one layer without disturbing any other layers in the composition, or you can use the same footage in more than one layer and use it differently in each instance. In general, the layer order in the Timeline panel corresponds to the stacking order in the Composition panel.

● **Note:** You may need to click a blank area of the Timeline panel or press F2 to deselect layers before you can select an individual layer.

6 Click an empty area of the Timeline panel to deselect the layers, and then drag bgwtext to the bottom of the layer stack, if it is not already there. Drag the other four layers so that they're in the order shown at right.

From this point forward in the workflow, you should be thinking about layers, not footage items. You'll change the column title accordingly.

7 Click the Source Name column title in the Timeline panel to change it to Layer Name.

8 Choose File > Save to save your project so far.

About the Tools panel

As soon as you create a composition, the tools in the Tools panel in the upper left corner of the After Effects application window become available. After Effects includes tools that enable you to modify elements of your composition. Some of these tools—the Selection tool and the Hand tool, for example—will be familiar to you if you use other Adobe applications, such as Photoshop. Others will be new.

A. Selection *B.* Hand *C.* Zoom *D.* Rotation *E.* Camera tools *F.* Pan Behind *G.* Mask and Shape tools *H.* Pen tools *I.* Type tools *J.* Brush *K.* Clone Stamp *L.* Eraser *M.* Roto Brush and Refine Edge tools *N.* Puppet tools

When you hover the pointer over any button in the Tools panel, a tool tip identifies the tool and its keyboard shortcut. A small triangle in the lower right corner of the button indicates that one or more additional tools are hidden behind it. Click and hold the button to display the hidden tools, and then select the tool you want to use.

Adding effects and modifying layer properties

Now that your composition is set up, you can start having fun—applying effects, making transformations, and adding animation. You can add any combination of effects and modify any of a layer's properties, such as size, placement, and opacity. Using effects, you can alter a layer's appearance or sound, and even generate visual elements from scratch. The easiest way to start is to apply any of the hundreds of effects included with After Effects.

Note: This exercise is just the tip of the iceberg. You will learn more about effects and animation presets in Lesson 2, "Creating a Basic Animation Using Effects and Presets," and throughout the rest of this book.

Preparing the layers

You'll apply the effects to duplicates of selected layers—the dancers layer and the vertical_waveforms layer. Working with duplicates lets you apply an effect to one layer and then use it in conjunction with the unmodified original.

1 Select the first layer, dancers.mov, in the Timeline panel, and then choose Edit > Duplicate. A new layer with the same name appears at the top of the stack, so the first two layers are now both named dancers.mov.

► **Tip:** You can make the Layer Name column wider in order to see the full layer name, if you need to.

2 Select the second layer, and rename it to avoid confusion: Press Enter (Windows) or Return (Mac OS) to make the name editable, and type **dancers_with_effects.mov**. Then press Enter or Return again to accept the new name.

► **Tip:** Use the keyboard shortcut Ctrl+D (Windows) or Command+D (Mac OS) to duplicate the layer quickly.

3 Select the vertical_waveforms layer, and make one duplicate. Rename it **vertical_duplicate.mov**.

4 Drag, if necessary, to rearrange the layers in the Timeline panel so that they're in the order shown.

Adding a Radial Blur effect

The Radial Blur effect creates blurs around a specific point in a layer, simulating the effects of a zooming or rotating camera. You'll add a Radial Blur effect to the dancers.

1 Select the dancers_with_effects layer in the Timeline panel. Notice that layer handles appear around the layer in the Composition panel.

● **Note:** If you double-click a layer in the Timeline panel, it appears in the Layer panel. To return to the Composition panel, click the Composition tab.

2 Click the Effects & Presets panel (in the panel stack at the right side of the application window) to open it, and type **radial blur** in the search box.

After Effects searches for effects and presets that contain the letters you type, and displays the results interactively. Before you have finished typing, the Radial Blur effect—located in the Blur & Sharpen category—appears in the panel.

3 Drag the Radial Blur effect onto the dancers_with_effects layer in the Timeline panel.

After Effects applies the effect and automatically opens the Effect Controls panel in the upper left area of the workspace.

Now you'll customize the settings.

4 In the Effect Controls panel, choose Zoom from the Type menu.

Tip: You can also type the x and y values directly into the coordinate fields in the Effect Controls panel, or you can position the pointer over the fields to see the double-arrow icon (⇹), and then drag right or left to increase or decrease the values, respectively.

5 In the Composition panel, move the center point of the blur by dragging the center cross-hairs icon (⊕) until it's roughly centered in the image. As you drag the cross-hairs, the Center value updates in the Effect Controls panel. The left and right values are x and y coordinates, respectively. Center the blur at approximately 325, 235.

6 Click the number next to Amount, type **130** to increase the amount of blur, and press Enter or Return.

Adding an exposure effect

To punch up the brightness of this layer, you will apply the Exposure color-correction effect. This effect lets you make tonal adjustments to footage. It simulates the result of modifying the exposure setting (in f-stops) of the camera that captured the image.

1 Click the *x* in the search box in the Effects & Presets panel to clear it, and then locate the Exposure effect by doing one of the following:

- Type **Exposure** in the search box.

- Click the triangle next to Color Correction to expand the list of color-correction effects in alphabetical order.

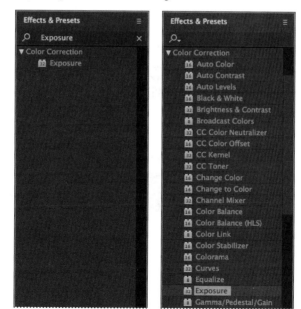

2 Drag the Exposure effect in the Color Correction category onto the dancers_ with_effects layer name in the Timeline panel. After Effects adds the Exposure settings to the Effect Controls panel under the Radial Blur effect.

3 In the Effect Controls panel, click the triangle next to the Radial Blur effect to hide those settings so that you can see the Exposure settings more easily.

4 For Master Exposure, type **1.60**. This will make everything brighter in the layer, simulating an overexposed image.

Transforming layer properties

The dancers look smashing, so you can turn your attention to the vertical waveforms that are part of the background. You'll reposition the duplicate layer you created earlier to create an edgy effect.

1 Select the vertical_duplicate layer (layer 5) in the Timeline panel.

2 Click the triangle to the left of the layer number to expand the layer, and then expand the layer's Transform properties: Anchor Point, Position, Scale, Rotation, and Opacity.

3 If you can't see the properties, scroll down the Timeline panel using the scroll bar at the right side of the panel. Better yet, select the vertical_duplicate layer name again, and press P.

This keyboard shortcut displays only the Position property, which is the only property you want to change for this exercise. You'll move this layer to the left approximately 200 pixels.

4 Change the x coordinate for the Position property to **0**. Leave the y coordinate at 243.

▶ **Tip:** With any layer selected in the Timeline panel, you can display any single Transform property by pressing a keyboard shortcut: P displays Position; A displays Anchor Point; S displays Scale; R displays Rotation; T displays Opacity.

5 Select the vertical_waveforms layer (layer 4), and press P to display its Position property.

You will move this layer to the right.

6 Change the x coordinate for the vertical_waveforms Position property to **712**. Leave the y coordinate at 243. Now you can see the two waveforms in the Composition panel, emerging from either side.

Now you will reduce the opacity of the waveforms.

7 Select the vertical_waveforms layer in the Timeline panel, and press T to reveal its Opacity property. Set it to **75%**.

▶ **Tip:** To change the Opacity property for multiple layers at once, select the layers, press T, and change the property for one of the selected layers.

8 Select the vertical_duplicate layer in the Timeline panel, press T to reveal its Opacity property, and set it to **75%**.

While you're at it, you'll reduce the opacity of the dancers_with_effects layer, too.

9 Select the dancers_with_effects layer in the Timeline panel, press T to reveal its Opacity property, and set it to **75%**.

10 Hide the properties for all layers, and then choose File > Save to save your work so far.

Animating the composition

So far, you've started a project, created a composition, imported footage, and applied some effects. It all looks great, but how about some movement? You've applied only static effects.

In After Effects, you can change any combination of a layer's properties over time using conventional keyframing, expressions, or keyframe assistants. You'll explore many of these methods throughout the lessons of this book. For this project, you'll animate the Position property of a text layer using keyframes, and then use an animation preset so that the letters appear to rain down on the screen.

Preparing the text composition

In this exercise, you'll work with a separate composition—the one you imported from a layered Photoshop file.

About the Timeline panel

Use the Timeline panel to animate layer properties and set In and Out points for a layer. (In and Out points are the points at which a layer begins and ends in the composition.) Many of the Timeline panel controls are organized in columns of related functions. By default, the Timeline panel contains a number of columns and controls, as shown here:

A. *Current time* **B.** *Composition name* **C.** *Timeline panel menu* **D.** *Audio/Video Switches column* **E.** *Source Name/Layer Name column* **F.** *Layer switches* **G.** *Time graph/Graph Editor area*

Understanding the time graph

The time graph portion of the Timeline panel (the right side) contains a time ruler, markers to indicate specific times, and duration bars for the layers in your composition.

Before delving too deeply into animation, it will help to understand at least some of these controls. The duration of a composition, a layer, or a footage item is represented visually in the time graph. On the time ruler, the current-time indicator marks the frame you are viewing or editing, and the frame appears in the Composition panel.

A. *Time navigator start and end brackets* **B.** *Work area start and end brackets* **C.** *Time zoom slider* **D.** *Time ruler* **E.** *Composition marker bin* **F.** *Composition button*

The work area start and end brackets indicate the part of the composition that will be rendered for previews or final output. When you work on a composition, you may want to render only a portion of it by specifying a segment of the composition time ruler as a work area.

A composition's current time appears in the upper left corner of the Timeline panel. To move to a different time, drag the current-time indicator in the time ruler—or click the current-time field in the Timeline panel or Composition panel, type a new time, and click OK.

For more information about the Timeline panel, see After Effects Help.

Note: If the Project tab isn't visible, choose Window > Project to open the Project panel.

1 Select the Project tab to display the Project panel, and then double-click the bgwtext composition to open it as a composition in its own Timeline panel.

This composition is the layered Photoshop file you imported. Two layers—Title Here and Background—appear in the Timeline panel. The Title Here layer contains placeholder text that was created in Photoshop.

At the top of the Composition panel is the Composition Navigator bar, which displays the relationship between the main composition (bgwtext 2) and the current composition (bgwtext), which is nested within the main composition.

You can nest multiple compositions within each other; the Composition Navigator bar displays the entire composition path. Arrows between the composition names indicate the direction in which information flows.

Before you can replace the text, you need to make the layer editable.

Note: If you see a warning about missing fonts or layer dependencies, click OK.

2 Select the Title Here layer (layer 1) in the Timeline panel, and then choose Layer > Convert To Editable Text.

A T icon appears next to the layer name in the Timeline panel, indicating that it is now an editable text layer. The layer is also selected in the Composition panel, ready for you to edit.

The blue lines at the top, bottom, and sides of the Composition panel indicate title-safe and action-safe zones. Television sets enlarge a video image and allow some portion of its outer edges to be cut off by the edge of the screen. This is known as *overscan*. The amount of overscan is not consistent between television sets, so you should keep important parts of a video image, such as action or titles, within margins called *safe zones*. Keep your text inside the inner blue guides to ensure that it is in the title-safe zone, and keep important scene elements inside the outer blue guides to ensure that they are in the action-safe zone.

Animating text with animation presets

You'll start by replacing the placeholder text with real text. Then you'll animate it.

1 Select the Horizontal Type tool (T) in the Tools panel, and drag over the placeholder text in the Composition panel to select it. Then type **in motion**.

● **Note:** After Effects offers robust character and paragraph formatting controls, but the default settings—whatever typeface appears when you type—should be fine for this project. You'll learn more about type in Lesson 3, "Animating Text."

2 Select the Title Here layer in the Timeline panel again, and make sure you're at the first frame of the animation by doing one of the following:

• Drag the current-time indicator all the way to the left of the time ruler, to 0:00.

• Press the Home key on your keyboard.

3 Select the Effects & Presets tab to display the Effects & Presets panel. Then type **bubble** in the search box.

4 Select the Zoom-Bubble effect in the Transitions-Movement category, and drag it onto the **in motion** text in the Composition panel.

After Effects adds the effect and displays its settings in the Effect Controls panel. You can change effect settings in this panel or in the Timeline panel. You'll add keyframes in the Timeline panel.

About timecode and duration

The primary concept related to time is *duration*, or length. Each footage item, layer, and composition in a project has its own duration, which is reflected in the beginning and ending times displayed in the time rulers in the Composition, Layer, and Timeline panels.

The way you view and specify time in After Effects depends on the display style, or unit of measure, that you use to describe time. By default, After Effects displays time in Society of Motion Picture and Television Engineers (SMPTE) timecode: hours, minutes, seconds, and frames. Note that the figures are separated by semicolons in the After Effects interface, representing drop-frame timecode (which adjusts for the real-time frame rate), but this book uses a colon to represent non-drop-frame timecode.

To learn when and how to change to another system of time display, such as frames, or feet and frames of film, see After Effects Help.

5 In the Timeline panel, expand the Title Here layer, and then expand Effects > Zoom-bubble to reveal the Transition Completion setting.

● **Note:** Don't select the Transition Completion property, as that will select both keyframes, and you want to change only the value of the second one.

The stopwatch icon (⏱) next to Transition Completion is selected, and the value is 0%. A diamond appears in the Transition Completion bar for the layer in the time graph, indicating the keyframe that After Effects created when you added the effect.

6 Go to 1:00 in the timeline by clicking the Current Time field in the Timeline panel and typing **100**, and then pressing Enter or Return, or by dragging the current-time indicator to 1:00.

7 Change the Transition Completion value to **100%**.

Even though this is a simple animation, you'll learn good animation practices right away by adding ease-in controls using the Easy Ease feature. Easing into (and out of) animations keeps the motion from appearing to be too sudden or robotic.

8 Right-click or Control-click the keyframe at 1:00, and choose Keyframe Assistant > Easy Ease In.

Tip: To see greater detail in the Timeline panel, move the time zoom slider at the bottom of the panel.

Keyframes are used to create and control animation, effects, audio properties, and many other kinds of changes that occur over time. A keyframe marks the point in time where you specify a value, such as spatial position, opacity, or audio volume. Values between keyframes are *interpolated*. When you use keyframes to create a change over time, you must use at least two keyframes—one for the state at the beginning of the change, and one for the state at the end of the change.

9 Manually preview the effect by moving the current-time indicator from 0 to 1:00.

Changing preset settings in the Effect Controls panel

You'll add another animation preset to the type layer, but this time, you'll adjust its settings in the Effect Controls panel.

1 Go to the beginning of the time ruler by doing one of the following:

 • Drag the current-time indicator to the left in the time ruler so that it's positioned at 0:00.

 • Click the Current Time field in the Timeline panel or Composition panel, and type **00**. If you clicked in the Current Time field in the Composition panel, click OK to close the Go To Time dialog box.

2 Type **channel blur** in the search box in the Effects & Presets panel.

3 Drag the Channel Blur effect onto the type in the Composition panel.

After Effects adds the Channel Blur effect to the Timeline panel and displays its settings in the Effect Controls panel.

4 In the Effect Controls panel, click the triangles next to Zoom-bubble, Spherize, and Transform to hide their settings so you can focus on the Channel Blur settings.

5 Set the Red Blurriness, Green Blurriness, Blue Blurriness, and Alpha Blurriness values to **50**.

6 Click the stopwatch icon next to each of the settings you changed to create initial keyframes.

7 From the Blur Dimensions menu, choose Vertical.

8 Go to 1:00 in the timeline.

9 Change the values as follows:

- Red Blurriness: **75**

- Green Blurriness: **25**

- Blue Blurriness: **0**

- Alpha Blurriness: **0**

Previewing your work

You're probably eager to see the results of your work. You can preview your composition using the Preview panel, which is in the stacked panels on the right side of the application window in the default workspace. To preview your composition, click the Play/Stop button in the Preview panel, or press the spacebar on your keyboard.

1 In the bgwtext Timeline panel, collapse the Title Here layer, and deselect both layers.

2 Make sure that the Video switch (●) is selected for the layers that you want to preview—in this case, the Title Here and Background layers.

3 Press the Home key to go to the beginning of the time ruler.

► **Tip:** Click the pasteboard of the Composition panel if you want to hide the motion path for this preview.

▶ **Tip:** Verify that the
work area brackets
include all the frames
you want to preview.

4 Do one of the following:

- Click the Play/Stop button (▶) in the Preview panel.

- Press the spacebar.

5 To stop the preview, do one of the following:

- Click the Play/Stop button in the Preview panel.

- Press the spacebar.

You've previewed a simple animation, so it probably played back in real time.

When you press the spacebar or click the Play/Stop button, After Effects caches the composition and allocates enough RAM to play the preview (with audio) as fast as the system allows, up to the frame rate of the composition. The number of frames played depends on the amount of RAM available to the application. Often, the preview will play in real time only after After Effects has cached all the included frames.

In the Timeline panel, the preview plays either the span of time you specify as the work area, or from the beginning of the time ruler. In the Layer and Footage panels, the preview plays only untrimmed footage. Before you preview, check which frames are designated as the work area.

Now you'll preview the entire composition—the animated text plus graphic effects.

6 Click the bgwtext 2 tab in the Timeline panel to bring it forward.

7 Make sure that the Video switch (●) is turned on for all of the layers in the com-
position (except the audio layer), and press F2 to deselect all layers.

8 Drag the current-time indicator to the beginning of the time ruler, or press
the Home key.

9 To start the preview, click the Play/Stop button (▶) in the Preview panel, or press the spacebar.

A green progress bar indicates which frames are cached to RAM. When all of the frames in the work area are cached, the preview plays back in real time.

The more detail and precision you want to preview, the more RAM is required. You can control the amount of detail shown by changing the resolution, magnification, and preview quality of your composition. You can also limit the number of layers previewed by turning off the Video switch for certain layers, or limit the number of frames previewed by adjusting the composition's work area.

10 Press the spacebar to stop the preview.

11 Choose File > Save to save your project.

Optimizing performance in After Effects

How you configure After Effects and your computer determines how quickly After Effects renders projects. Complex compositions can require a large amount of memory to render, and the rendered movies can take a large amount of disk space to store. Search for "Improve Performance" in After Effects Help for tips that can help you configure your system, After Effects preferences, and your projects for better performance.

Rendering and exporting your composition

When you're finished with your masterpiece—as you are now—you can render and export it at the quality settings you choose, and create movies in the formats that you specify. You will learn about exporting compositions in subsequent lessons, especially in Lesson 14, "Rendering and Outputting."

Customizing workspaces

In the course of this project, you may have resized or repositioned some panels or opened new ones. As you modify a workspace, After Effects saves those modifications, so the next time you open the project, the most recent version of a workspace is used. However, you can choose to restore the original workspace at any time by choosing Window > Workspace > Reset "Essentials" To Saved Layout.

Alternatively, if you find yourself frequently using panels that aren't part of the Essentials workspace, or if you like to resize or group panels for different types of projects, you can save time by customizing the workspace to suit your needs. You can save any workspace configuration, or use any of the preset workspaces that come with After Effects. These predefined workspaces are suitable for different types of workflows, such as animation or effects work.

Using predefined workspaces

Take a minute to explore the predefined workspaces in After Effects.

1 If you closed the Lesson01_Finished.aep project, open it—or any other project—to explore the workspaces.

2 Click Animation in the Workspace bar, which is next to the Tools panel. Click the double arrows to see workspaces that don't fit in the Workspace bar.

After Effects opens the following panels at the right side of the application window: Info, Preview, Effects & Presets, Motion Sketch, Wiggler, Smoother, and Audio.

You can also change workspaces using the Workspace menu.

3 Choose Window > Workspace > Paint.

Different panels open. The Composition panel is replaced by the Layer panel, for easy access to the tools and controls you need to paint in your compositions.

Saving a custom workspace

You can save any workspace, at any time, as a custom workspace. Once saved, new and edited workspaces appear in the Window > Workspace submenu and in the Workspace bar at the top of the application window. If a project with a custom workspace is opened on a system other than the one on which it was created, After Effects looks for a workspace with a matching name. If After Effects finds a match (and the monitor configuration matches), it uses that workspace; if it can't find a match (or the monitor configuration doesn't match), it opens the project using the current local workspace.

1 Close a panel by choosing Close Panel from its panel menu.

2 Choose Window > Effects & Presets to open that panel.

The Effects & Presets panel is added to the panel stack.

3 Choose Window > Workspace > Save As New Workspace. Enter a name for the workspace, and click OK to save it, or click Cancel if you don't want to save it.

4 Click Essentials in the Workspace bar.

Controlling the brightness of the user interface

You can brighten or darken the After Effects user interface. Changing the brightness preference affects panels, windows, and dialog boxes.

1 Choose Edit > Preferences > Appearance (Windows) or After Effects CC> Preferences > Appearance (Mac OS).

2 Drag the Brightness slider to the left or right, and notice how the screen changes.

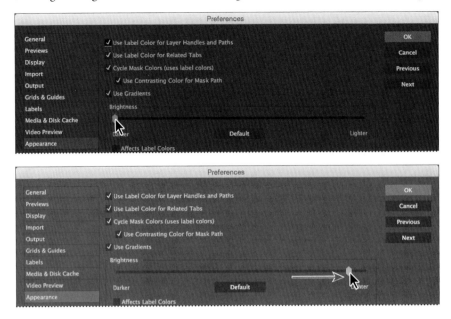

3 Click OK to save the new brightness setting or Cancel to leave your preferences unchanged. You can click Default to restore the default brightness setting.

Finding resources for using After Effects

For complete and up-to-date information about using After Effects panels, tools, and other application features, visit the Adobe website. To search for information in After Effects Help and support documents, as well as on other websites relevant to After Effects users, simply enter a search term in the Search Help box in the upper right corner of the application window. You can narrow the results to view only Adobe Help and support documents.

The Start window that appears when you open the application provides access to video tutorials and other information to help you get the most out of After Effects.

For additional resources, such as tips and techniques and the latest product information, check out the After Effects Help And Support page at helpx.adobe.com/after-effects.html.

Congratulations! You've finished Lesson 1. Now that you're acquainted with the After Effects workspace, you can continue to Lesson 2 to learn how to create and animate compositions using effects and preset animations, or you can proceed to another lesson in this book.

Review questions

1 What are the basic components of the After Effects workflow?

2 What is a composition?

3 How can you find missing footage?

4 How can you preview your work in After Effects?

5 How can you customize an After Effects workspace?

Review answers

1 Most After Effects workflows include these steps: importing and organizing footage, creating compositions and arranging layers, adding effects, animating elements, previewing your work, and rendering and exporting the final composition.

2 A composition is where you create all animation, layering, and effects. An After Effects composition has both spatial and temporal (time) dimensions. Compositions include one or more layers—video, audio, still images—arranged in the Composition panel and in the Timeline panel. Simple projects may include only one composition, while elaborate projects may include several compositions to organize large amounts of footage or intricate effects sequences.

3 To locate missing footage, choose File > Dependencies > Find Missing Footage. Or type **Missing Footage** into the Search field in the Properties panel.

4 You can manually preview your work in After Effects by moving the current-time indicator, or you can press the spacebar or click the Play/Stop button in the Preview panel to preview your composition from the current-time indicator to the end of the composition. After Effects allocates enough RAM to play the preview (with audio) as fast as the system allows, up to the frame rate of the composition.

5 You can customize an After Effects workspace by dragging the panels into the configuration that best suits your working style. You can drag panels to new locations, move panels into or out of groups, place panels alongside each other, stack panels, and undock a panel so that it floats above the application window. As you rearrange panels, the other panels resize automatically to fit the application window. You can save custom workspaces by choosing Window > Workspace > Save As New Workspace.

2 CREATING A BASIC ANIMATION USING EFFECTS AND PRESETS

Lesson overview

In this lesson, you'll learn how to do the following:

- Use Adobe Bridge to preview and import footage items.
- Work with the layers of an imported Adobe Illustrator file.
- Apply drop-shadow and emboss effects.
- Apply a text animation preset.
- Adjust the time range of a text animation preset.
- Precompose layers.
- Apply a dissolve transition effect.
- Adjust the transparency of a layer.
- Render an animation for broadcast use.

 This lesson will take about an hour to complete. Download the Lesson02 project files from the Lesson & Update Files tab on your Account page at www.peachpit.com, if you haven't already done so. As you work on this lesson, you'll preserve the start files. If you need to restore the start files, download them from your Account page.

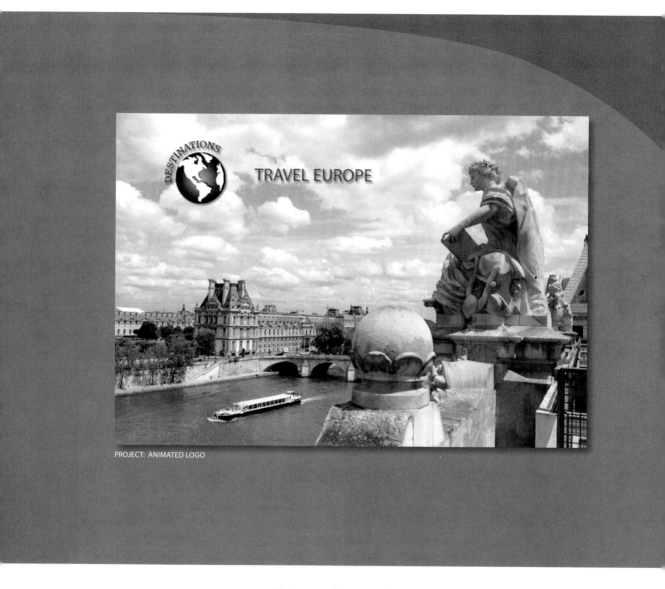

PROJECT: ANIMATED LOGO

Hit the ground running with a variety of effects and animation presets in After Effects. You can use them to create great-looking animations quickly and easily.

Getting started

In this lesson, you will become more familiar with the Adobe After Effects project workflow. You'll learn new ways to accomplish basic tasks as you create a simple identification graphic for a fictional travel show called "Travel Europe" on the fictional Destinations cable network. You will animate the travel show ID so that it fades to become a watermark that can appear in the lower right corner of the screen during other TV programs. Then you'll export the ID for use in broadcast output.

First, take a look at the final project files to see what you'll be doing.

1 Make sure the following files are in the Lessons/Lesson02 folder on your hard disk, or download them from your Account page at www.peachpit.com now:

 • In the Assets folder: destinations_logo.ai, ParisRiver.jpg

 • In the Sample_Movie folder: Lesson02.mov

2 Open and play the Lesson02.mov sample movie in QuickTime Player to see what you will create in this lesson. When you are done, quit QuickTime Player. You may delete this sample movie from your hard disk if you have limited storage space.

When you begin the lesson, restore the default application settings for After Effects. See "Restoring default preferences" on page 2 for more information.

3 Start After Effects, and then immediately hold down Ctrl+Alt+Shift (Windows) or Command+Option+Shift (Mac OS) to restore default preferences settings. When prompted, click OK to delete your preferences.

4 Close the Start window.

After Effects opens to display a blank, untitled project.

5 Choose File > Save As > Save As.

6 In the Save As dialog box, navigate to the Lessons/Lesson02/ Finished_Project folder.

7 Name the project **Lesson02_Finished.aep**, and then click Save.

Importing footage using Adobe Bridge

In Lesson 1, you chose File > Import > File to import footage. However, After Effects offers another, more powerful, more flexible way to import footage for a composition: Adobe Bridge. You can use Adobe Bridge to organize, browse, and locate the assets you need to create content for print, web, television, DVD, film, and mobile devices. Adobe Bridge keeps native Adobe files (such as PSD and PDF files) as well as non-Adobe application files available for easy access. You can drag assets into your layouts, projects, and compositions as needed; preview your assets; and even add metadata (file information) to assets to make files easier to locate.

Adobe Bridge is not automatically installed with After Effects CC. You'll need to install it separately. If Bridge is not installed, you'll be prompted to install it when you choose File > Browse In Bridge.

In this exercise, you will jump to Adobe Bridge to import the still image that will serve as the background of your composition.

1 Choose File > Browse In Bridge. If you receive a message about enabling an extension to Adobe Bridge, click Yes.

Adobe Bridge opens, displaying a collection of panels, menus, and buttons.

2 Click the Folders tab in the upper left corner of Adobe Bridge.

3 In the Folders panel, navigate to the Lessons/Lesson02/Assets folder. Click the arrows to open nested folders. You can also double-click folder thumbnail icons in the Content panel.

▶ **Tip:** You can use Adobe Bridge separately to manage your files. To open Adobe Bridge directly, choose Adobe Bridge from the Start menu (Windows) or double-click the Adobe Bridge icon in the Applications / Adobe Bridge folder (Mac OS).

● **Note:** We're using the Essentials workspace, which is the default workspace in Bridge.

The Content panel updates interactively. For example, when you select the Assets folder in the Folders panel, thumbnail previews of the folder's contents appear in the Content panel. Adobe Bridge displays previews of image files such as those in PSD, TIFF, and JPEG formats, as well as Illustrator vector files, multipage Adobe PDF files, QuickTime movie files, and more.

▶ **Tip:** To prioritize different information in Adobe Bridge, change the workspace: Choose Window > Workspace, and then select a workspace. See Adobe Bridge Help to learn about customizing Adobe Bridge.

4 Drag the thumbnail slider at the bottom of the Adobe Bridge window to enlarge the thumbnail previews.

5 Select the ParisRiver.jpg file in the Content panel, and notice that it appears in the Preview panel as well. Information about the file, including its creation date, bit depth, and file size, appears in the Metadata panel.

6 Double-click the ParisRiver.jpg thumbnail in the Content panel to place the file in your After Effects project. Alternatively, you can drag the thumbnail into the Project panel in After Effects.

7 Return to After Effects, if you're not already there.

You can close Adobe Bridge if you'd like. You won't be using it again during this lesson.

Creating a new composition

Following the After Effects workflow you learned in Lesson 1, the next step to building the travel show ID is to create a new composition. In Lesson 1, you created the composition based on footage items that were selected in the Project panel. You can also create an empty composition, and then add your footage items to it.

1 Create a new composition by doing one of the following:

- Click the Create A New Composition button (▣) at the bottom of the Project panel.

- Choose Composition > New Composition.

- Press Ctrl+N (Windows) or Command+N (Mac OS).

2 In the Composition Settings dialog box, do the following:

- Name the composition **Destinations**.

- Choose NTSC D1 from the Preset pop-up menu. NTSC D1 is the resolution for standard-definition television in the United States and some other countries. This preset automatically sets the width, height, pixel aspect ratio, and frame rate for the composition to NTSC standards.

- In the Duration field, type **300** to specify 3 seconds.

- Click OK.

After Effects displays an empty composition named Destinations in the Composition panel and in the Timeline panel. Now, you'll add the background.

3 Drag the ParisRiver.jpg footage item from the Project panel to the Timeline panel to add it to the Destinations composition.

4 With the ParisRiver layer selected in the Timeline panel, choose Layer > Transform > Fit To Comp to scale the background image to the dimensions of the composition.

Importing the foreground element

Your background is now in place. The foreground object you'll use is a layered vector graphic that was created in Illustrator.

1 Choose File > Import > File.

2 In the Import File dialog box, select the destinations_logo.ai file in the Lessons/ Lesson02/Assets folder. (The file appears as destinations_logo if file extensions are hidden.)

3 Select Composition from the Import As menu, and then click Import or Open.

The Illustrator file is added to the Project panel as a composition named destinations_logo. A folder named destinations_logo Layers also appears. This folder contains the three individual layers of the Illustrator file. Click the triangle to open the folder and see its contents if you like.

4 Drag the destinations_logo composition file from the Project panel into the Timeline panel above the ParisRiver layer.

You should now see both the background image and the logo in the Composition panel and in the Timeline panel.

Working with imported Illustrator layers

The destinations_logo graphic was created in Illustrator; your job in After Effects is to add text and animate it. To work with the layers of the Illustrator file independently of the background footage, you'll open the destinations_logo composition in its own Timeline and Composition panels.

1 Double-click the destinations_logo composition in the Project panel. The composition opens in its own Timeline and Composition panels.

2 Select the Horizontal Type tool (T) in the Tools panel, and click in the Composition panel.

3 Type **TRAVEL EUROPE**, all capital letters, and then select all of the text you just entered.

4 In the Character panel, select a sans serif typeface such as Myriad Pro, and change the font size to **24** pixels. Click the eyedropper in the Character panel, and click the rotated "Destinations" text on the logo to select the green color. After Effects applies it to the text you typed. Leave all other options in the Character panel at their defaults.

You'll learn more about working with text in Lesson 3, "Animating Text."

Note: If the Character panel isn't open, choose Window > Character. You may need to expand the width of the panel to see the eyedropper.

5 Select the Selection tool (⬆), and then drag the text in the Composition panel to position it as it appears in the following figure. Notice that when you switch to the Selection tool, the generic Text 1 layer name in the Timeline panel changes to TRAVEL EUROPE, the text you typed.

Tip: Choose View > Show Grid to make the nonprinting grid visible to help you position objects. Choose View > Show Grid again to hide the grid later.

Applying effects to a layer

Now you will return to the main composition, Destinations, and apply an effect to the destinations_logo layer. This will apply the effect to all of the layers nested in the destinations_logo composition.

1 Click the Destinations tab in the Timeline panel, and then select the destinations_logo layer.

The effect you create next will be applied only to the logo elements, not to the background image of the river.

2 Choose Effect > Perspective > Drop Shadow.

A soft-edged shadow appears behind the nested layers of the destinations_logo layer—the logo graphic, the rotated type, and the words *travel Europe*—in the Composition panel. You can customize the effect using the Effect Controls panel, which appears in front of the Project panel when you apply an effect.

Applying and controlling effects

You can apply or remove an effect at any time. Once you've applied effects to a layer, you can temporarily turn off one or all of the effects in the layer to concentrate on another aspect of your composition. Effects that are turned off do not appear in the Composition panel, and typically aren't included when the layer is previewed or rendered.

By default, when you apply an effect to a layer, the effect is active for the duration of the layer. However, you can make an effect start and stop at specific times, or make the effect more or less intense over time. You'll learn more about creating animation using keyframes or expressions in Lesson 5, "Animating a Multimedia Presentation," and Lesson 6, "Animating Layers."

You can apply and edit effects on adjustment layers just as you do with other layers. Note, however, that when you apply an effect to an adjustment layer, the effect is applied to all layers below it in the Timeline panel.

Effects can also be saved, browsed, and applied as animation presets.

3 In the Effect Controls panel, reduce the drop shadow's Distance to **3** and increase its Softness to **4**. You can set these values by clicking the field and typing the number or by dragging the blue value.

The drop shadow is nice, but the logo will stand out even more if you apply an emboss effect. You can use either the Effect menu or the Effects & Presets panel to locate and apply effects.

4 Click the Effects & Presets tab to open the panel. Then click the triangle next to Stylize to expand the category.

5 With the destinations_logo layer selected in the Timeline panel, drag the Color Emboss effect into the Composition panel.

The Color Emboss effect sharpens the edges of objects in the layer without suppressing the original colors. The Effect Controls panel displays the Color Emboss effect and its settings below the Drop Shadow effect.

6 Choose File > Save to save your work.

Applying an animation preset

You've positioned the logo and applied some effects to it. It's time to add some animation! You will learn several ways to animate text in Lesson 3; for now, you'll use a simple animation preset that will fade the words *travel Europe* onto the screen next to the logo. You'll need to work in the destinations_logo composition so that you can apply the animation to only the TRAVEL EUROPE text layer.

1 Click the destinations_logo tab in the Timeline panel, and select the TRAVEL EUROPE layer.

2 Move the current-time indicator to 1:10, which is the point at which you want the text to start fading in.

3 In the Effects & Presets panel, choose Animation Presets > Text > Blurs.

4 Drag the Bullet Train animation preset onto the TRAVEL EUROPE layer in the Timeline panel or over the words *travel Europe* in the Composition panel. Don't worry about the text disappearing—you're looking at the first frame of the animation, which happens to be blank.

5 Click a blank area of the Timeline panel to deselect the TRAVEL EUROPE layer, and then drag the current-time indicator to 2:00 to manually preview the text animation. The text appears, letter by letter, until the words *travel Europe* are fully onscreen at 2:00.

Precomposing layers for a new animation

The travel show ID is coming along nicely, and you're probably eager to preview the complete animation. Before you do, however, you'll add a dissolve to all of the logo elements except the words *travel Europe*. To do this, you need to precompose the other three layers of the destinations_logo composition: rotated type, Globe logo, and crop area.

Precomposing is a way to nest layers within a composition. Precomposing moves the layers to a new composition, which takes the place of the selected layers. When you want to change the order in which layer components are rendered, precomposing is a quick way to create intermediate levels of nesting in an existing hierarchy.

1 Shift-click to select the rotated type, Globe logo, and crop area layers in the destinations_logo Timeline panel.

2 Choose Layer > Pre-compose.

3 In the Pre-compose dialog box, name the new composition **Dissolve_logo**. Make sure the Move All Attributes Into The New Composition option is selected. Then click OK.

The three layers are replaced in the destinations_logo Timeline panel with a single layer, Dissolve_logo. This new, precomposed layer contains the three layers that you selected in step 1. You can apply the dissolve effect to it without affecting the TRAVEL EUROPE text layer and its Bullet Train animation.

4 Make sure the Dissolve_logo layer is selected in the Timeline panel, and press the Home key or drag the current-time indicator to go to 0:00.

Tip: To locate the Dissolve – Vapor preset quickly, type **vap** in the search box in the Effects & Presets panel.

5 In the Effects & Presets panel, choose Animation Presets > Transitions – Dissolves, and then drag the Dissolve – Vapor animation preset onto the Dissolve_logo layer in the Timeline panel or onto the Composition panel.

The Dissolve – Vapor animation preset includes three components—a master dissolve, a box blur, and a solid composite, all of which appear in the Effect Controls panel. The default settings are fine for this project.

6 Choose File > Save.

Previewing the effects

It's time to preview all of the effects together.

1 Click the Destinations tab in the Timeline panel to switch to the main composition. Press the Home key or drag the current-time indicator to make sure you're at the beginning of the time ruler.

2 Make sure the Video switch (👁) is selected for both layers in the Destinations Timeline panel.

3 Click the Play button (▶) in the Preview panel, or press the spacebar, to watch the preview. Press the spacebar to stop playback at any time.

Adding transparency

Many TV stations display logos semitransparently in the corner of the frame to emphasize the brand. You'll reduce the opacity of the ID so that it can be used this way.

1 Still in the Destinations Timeline panel, go to 2:24.

2 Select the destinations_logo layer, and press T to display its Opacity property. By default, the Opacity is 100%—fully opaque. Click the stopwatch icon (⏱) to set an Opacity keyframe at this point in time.

3 Press the End key or drag the current-time indicator to go to the end of the time ruler (2:29), and change the Opacity to **40%**. After Effects adds a keyframe.

The logo appears, the words *travel Europe* fly in, and it all fades to 40% opacity.

4 Click the Play button (▶) in the Preview panel, press the spacebar, or press 0 on your numeric keypad to preview your composition. Press the spacebar to stop playback when you're done.

5 Choose File > Save to save your project.

Rendering the composition

Note: For more about output formats and rendering, see Lesson 14, "Rendering and Outputting."

You're ready to prepare your travel show ID for output. When you create output, the layers of a composition and each layer's masks, effects, and properties are rendered frame by frame into one or more output files or, in the case of an image sequence, into a series of consecutive files.

Making a movie from your final composition can take a few minutes or many hours, depending on the composition's frame size, quality, complexity, and compression method. When you place your composition in the Render Queue, it becomes a render item that uses the render settings assigned to it.

After Effects provides a variety of formats and compression types for rendering output; the format you choose depends on the medium from which you'll play your final output or on the requirements of your hardware, such as a video-editing system.

You'll render and export the composition so that it can be broadcast on television.

Note: For output to final-delivery formats, you can use Adobe Media Encoder, which is installed when you install After Effects. You'll learn about Adobe Media Encoder in Lesson 14, "Rendering and Outputting."

1 Do one of the following to add the composition to the Render Queue:

 • Select the Destinations composition in the Project panel, and choose Composition > Add To Render Queue. The Render Queue panel opens automatically.

 • Choose Window > Render Queue to open the Render Queue panel, and then drag the Destinations composition from the Project panel onto the Render Queue panel.

Tip: The keyboard shortcut for the Maximize Panel Group command is the accent grave character (`), which shares a key with the tilde character (~).

2 Choose Panel Group Settings > Maximize Panel Group from the Render Queue panel menu so that the panel fills the application window.

3 Click the triangle to expand the Render Settings options. By default, After Effects renders compositions with Best Quality and Full Resolution. The default settings are fine for this project.

4 Click the triangle to expand the Output Module options. By default, After Effects uses lossless compression to encode the rendered composition into a movie file, which is fine for this project. But you need to identify where to save the file.

5 Click the blue words *Not Yet Specified* next to the Output To pop-up menu.

6 In the Output Movie To dialog box, accept the default movie name (Destinations), select the Lessons/Lesson02/Finished_Project folder for the location, and then click Save.

7 Back in the Render Queue panel, click the Render button.

After Effects displays a progress bar in the Render Queue panel as it encodes the file, and issues an audio alert when all items in the Render Queue have been rendered and encoded.

8 When the movie is complete, choose Panel Group Settings > Restore Panel Group Size from the Render Queue panel menu to restore your workspace.

9 If you want to see your final product, double-click the Destinations.avi or Destinations.mov file in the Lessons/Lesson02/Finished_Project folder to open it in Windows Media Player or QuickTime, and then play the file.

10 Close the project file, and then quit After Effects.

Congratulations. You've created a travel show ID suitable for broadcast.

Review questions

1 How do you use Adobe Bridge to preview and import files?

2 What is *precomposing*?

3 How do you customize an effect?

4 How do you modify the transparency of a layer in a composition?

Review answers

1 Choose File > Browse In Bridge to jump from After Effects to Adobe Bridge. If Bridge isn't installed, you'll be prompted to download and install it. In Bridge, you can search for and preview image assets. When you locate the asset you want to use in an After Effects project, double-click it, or drag it to the Project panel.

2 *Precomposing* is a way to nest layers within a composition. Precomposing moves the layers to a new composition, which takes the place of the selected layers. When you want to change the order in which layer components are rendered, precomposing is a quick way to create intermediate levels of nesting in an existing hierarchy.

3 After you apply an effect to a layer in a composition, you can customize its properties in the Effect Controls panel. This panel opens automatically when you apply the effect, or you can open it at any time by selecting the layer with the effect and choosing Window > Effect Controls.

4 To modify the transparency of a layer, reduce its opacity. Select the layer in the Timeline panel, press T to reveal its Opacity property, and enter a value lower than 100%.

3 ANIMATING TEXT

Lesson overview

In this lesson, you'll learn how to do the following:

- Create and animate text layers.
- Stylize text using the Character and Paragraph panels.
- Apply and customize text animation presets.
- Preview animation presets in Adobe Bridge.
- Install fonts using Adobe Typekit.
- Animate text using keyframes.
- Animate layers using parenting.
- Edit and animate imported Adobe Photoshop text.
- Use a text animator group to animate selected characters on a layer.

This lesson will take approximately two hours to complete. Download the Lesson03 project files from the Lesson & Update Files tab on your Account page at www.peachpit.com, if you haven't already done so. As you work on this lesson, you'll preserve the start files. If you need to restore the start files, download them from your Account page.

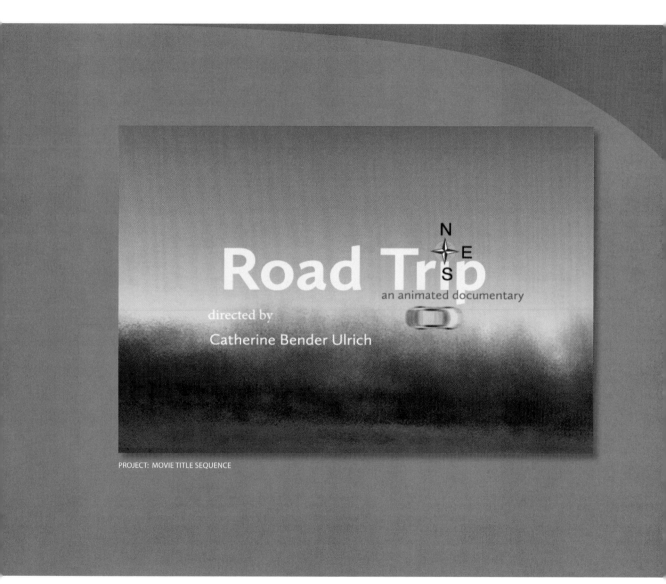

PROJECT: MOVIE TITLE SEQUENCE

Your type doesn't need to sit still while your audience is reading it. In this lesson, you'll learn several ways to animate type in After Effects, including timesaving methods unique to text layers.

Getting started

Adobe After Effects offers many ways to animate text. You can animate text layers by manually creating keyframes in the Timeline panel, using animation presets, or using expressions. You can even animate individual characters or words in a text layer. In this lesson, you'll employ several different animation techniques, including some that are unique to text, while you design the opening title credits for an animated documentary called *Road Trip*. You'll also take advantage of Adobe Typekit to install a font for use in your project.

As in other projects, you'll begin by previewing the movie you're creating, and then you'll open After Effects.

1 Make sure the following files are in the Lessons/Lesson03 folder on your hard disk, or download them from your Account page at www.peachpit.com now:

 • In the Assets folder: background_movie.mov, car.ai, compass.swf, credits.psd

 • In the Sample_Movie folder: Lesson03.mov

2 Open and play the Lesson03.mov sample movie to see the title credits you will create in this lesson. When you're done, quit QuickTime Player. You may delete this sample movie from your hard disk if you have limited storage space.

As you start the application, restore the default settings for After Effects. See "Restoring default preferences" on page 2.

3 Start After Effects, and then immediately hold down Ctrl+Alt+Shift (Windows) or Command+Option+Shift (Mac OS) to restore default preferences settings. When prompted, click OK to delete your preferences.

4 Close the Start window.

After Effects opens to display a blank, untitled project.

5 Choose File > Save As > Save As, and navigate to the Lessons/Lesson03/ Finished_Project folder.

6 Name the project **Lesson03_Finished.aep**, and then click Save.

Importing the footage

You need to import two footage items to begin this lesson.

1 Double-click an empty area of the Project panel to open the Import File dialog box.

2 Navigate to the Lessons/Lesson03/Assets folder on your hard disk, Ctrl-click (Windows) or Command-click (Mac OS) to select both the background_ movie.mov and compass.swf files, and then click Import or Open.

After Effects can import several file formats including Adobe Photoshop and Adobe Illustrator files, as well as QuickTime and AVI movies. This makes After Effects an incredibly powerful application for compositing and motion graphics work.

Creating the composition

Now, you'll create the composition.

1 Press Ctrl+N (Windows) or Command+N (Mac OS) to create a new composition.

2 In the Composition Settings dialog box, name the composition **Road_Trip_Title_Sequence**, choose NTSC DV from the Preset menu, and set the Duration to **10:00**, which is the length of the background movie. Then click OK.

3 Drag the background_movie.mov and compass.swf footage items from the Project panel to the Timeline panel. Arrange the layers so that compass.swf is above background_movie.mov in the layer stack.

4 Choose File > Save.

You're ready to add the title text to the composition.

About text layers

In After Effects, you can add text with flexibility and precision. The Tools, Character, and Paragraph panels contain a wide range of text controls. You can create and edit horizontal or vertical text directly on the screen in the Composition panel, and quickly change the font, style, size, and color of the text. You can apply changes to individual characters and set formatting options for entire paragraphs, including alignment, justification, and word-wrapping. In addition to all of these style features, After Effects provides tools for easily animating specific characters and properties, such as text opacity and hue.

After Effects uses two types of text: point text and paragraph text. Use *point text* to enter a single word or line of characters; use *paragraph text* to enter and format text as one or more paragraphs.

In many ways, text layers are just like any other layers in After Effects. You can apply effects and expressions to text layers, animate them, designate them as 3D layers, and edit the 3D text while viewing from multiple angles. As with layers imported from Illustrator, text layers are continuously rasterized, so when you scale the layer or resize the text, it retains crisp, resolution-independent edges. The two main differences between text layers and other layers are that you cannot open a text layer in its own Layer panel and you can animate the text in a text layer using special text-animator properties and selectors.

Installing a font using Typekit

Hundreds of fonts are available through Adobe Typekit, which is included with an Adobe Creative Cloud membership. You'll use Typekit to install a font that will work well for the title text. When you install a Typekit font on your system, it's available in any application.

1 Choose File > Add Fonts From Typekit.

After Effects opens the Adobe Typekit page in your default browser.

2 Make sure you're signed in to Creative Cloud. If not, click Sign In at the top of the screen, and then enter your Adobe ID.

You can browse fonts on the Adobe Typekit website, but because there are so many, it's often more efficient to filter them or to search for a specific font. You'll filter fonts to see those that meet your requirements.

3 Make sure the My Library tab is selected so you'll see all the fonts.

4 Choose Sort By Name from the pop-up menu in the upper right corner. Then, on the right side of the page, click the Sans Serif button in the Classification area and both the Web and Sync buttons in the Availability area. In the Properties area, select the buttons for medium weight, medium width, low contrast, and standard capitalization.

Typekit displays several fonts that meet the requirements you specified. You'll preview the fonts to see which one looks best.

5 Type **Road Trip** in the sample text field, and move the slider to decrease the sample text size so you can see the full title.

Using your own text as the sample text lets you get a feel for how a font will work in your project. Calluna Sans will work nicely.

► **Tip:** If you click the font name without clicking +Use Fonts, you'll see sample text for all the fonts in the selected family, as well as additional information about the font.

6 Hover your mouse over Calluna Sans until you see a green overlay. Then click +Use Fonts. (If you don't see Calluna Sans, click +Load More until you do, or choose a different font.)

7 Click Sync Selected Fonts. If the Creative Cloud application isn't running on your computer, click Launch The Creative Cloud Application to start it.

The selected fonts are automatically added to your system and are then available in any application, including After Effects.

Creating and formatting point text

When you enter point text, each line of text is independent—the length of a line increases or decreases as you edit the text, but it doesn't wrap to the next line. The text you enter appears in a new text layer. The small line through the I-beam marks the position of the text baseline.

1 In the Tools panel, select the Horizontal Type tool (T).

2 Click anywhere in the Composition panel, and type **Road Trip**. Then press Enter on the numeric keypad to exit text-editing mode and to select the text layer in the Composition panel. Or, you can select the layer name to exit text-editing mode.

● **Note:** If you press Enter or Return on the regular keyboard instead of on the numeric keypad, you'll begin a new paragraph.

Using the Character panel

The Character panel provides options for formatting characters. If text is high-lighted, changes you make in the Character panel affect only the highlighted text. If no text is highlighted, changes you make in the Character panel affect the selected text layers and the text layers' selected Source Text keyframes, if any exist. If no text is highlighted and no text layers are selected, changes you make in the Character panel become the new defaults for the next text entry.

1 Choose Window > Workspace > Text to display only those panels you need while working with text.

2 Select the Road Trip text layer in the Timeline panel.

3 In the Character panel, choose Calluna Sans from the Font Family menu.

4 Choose Bold from the Font Style menu.

5 Set the Font Size to **90** pixels.

6 Leave all other options at their default settings.

▶ **Tip:** To open the panels individually, choose Window > Character or Window > Paragraph. To open both panels, select the Horizontal Type tool, and then click the Toggle The Character And Paragraph Panels button in the Tools panel.

▶ **Tip:** To select a font quickly, begin typing its name in the Font Family box. The Font Family menu jumps to the first font on your system that matches the letters you've typed. If a type layer is selected, the text in the Composition panel takes on the newly selected font.

Using the Paragraph panel

Use the Paragraph panel to set options that apply to an entire paragraph, such as alignment, indentation, and leading. For point text, each line is a separate paragraph. You can use the Paragraph panel to set formatting options for a single paragraph, multiple paragraphs, or all paragraphs in a text layer. You just need to make one adjustment in the Paragraph panel for this composition's title text.

1 In the Paragraph panel, click the Center Text button (≣). This aligns horizontal text to the center of the layer, not to the center of the composition.

● **Note:** Your screen may look different, depending on where you started typing.

2 Leave all other options at their default settings.

Positioning the type

To precisely position layers, such as the text layer you're working on now, you can display rulers, guides, and grids in the Composition panel. These visual reference tools don't appear in the final rendered movie.

1 Make sure the Road Trip text layer is selected in the Timeline panel.

2 Choose Layer > Transform > Fit To Comp Width. This scales the layer to fit to the width of the composition.

Now you can position the text layer using a grid.

3 Choose View > Show Grid and then View > Snap To Grid.

4 Using the Selection tool (⬈), drag the text up in the Composition panel until the base of the letters sits on the horizontal gridline in the center of the composition. Press Shift after you start dragging to constrain the movement and help you position the text.

5 When the layer is in position, choose View > Show Grid again to hide the grid.

This project isn't destined for broadcast TV, so it's okay that the title extends beyond the title-safe and action-safe areas of the composition at the beginning of the animation.

6 Click Essentials in the Workspace bar at the top of the application window to return to the Essentials workspace. (Click the double arrows to see Essentials if it doesn't fit in the Workspace bar.)

7 Choose File > Save to save your project.

Using a text animation preset

Now you're ready to animate the title. The easiest way to do that is to use one of the many animation presets that come with After Effects. After applying an animation preset, you can customize it and save it to use again in other projects.

1 Press the Home key or go to 0:00 to make sure the current-time indicator is at the beginning of the time ruler.

After Effects applies animation presets from the current time.

2 Select the Road Trip text layer.

Browsing animation presets

Note: If Bridge isn't installed, you'll be prompted to install it when you choose Browse In Bridge. For more information, see page 2.

You already applied an animation preset using the Effects & Presets panel in Lesson 2, "Creating a Basic Animation Using Effects and Presets." But what if you're not sure which animation preset you want to use? To help you choose the right animation preset for your projects, you can preview them in Adobe Bridge.

1 Choose Animation > Browse Presets. Adobe Bridge opens, displaying the contents of the After Effects Presets folder.

2 In the Content panel, double-click the Text folder, and then the Blurs folder.

3 Click to select the first preset, Blur By Word. Adobe Bridge plays a sample of the animation in the Preview panel.

4 Select a few other presets, and watch them in the Preview panel.

5 Preview the Evaporate preset, and then double-click its thumbnail preview. Alternatively, you can right-click (Windows) or Control-click (Mac OS) the thumbnail and choose Place In After Effects CC 2015.

Note: Leave Adobe Bridge open in the background. You'll use it again later in the lesson.

After Effects applies the preset to the selected layer, which is the Road Trip layer, but nothing appears to change in the composition. This is because at 0:00, the first frame of the animation, the letters haven't yet evaporated.

Previewing a range of frames

Now, preview the animation. Although the composition is 10 seconds long, you need to preview only the first few seconds, since that is where the text animation occurs.

1 In the Timeline panel, move the current-time indicator to 3:00, and press N to set the end bracket of the work area.

2 Press the spacebar to watch a preview of the animation.

The letters appear to evaporate into the background. It looks great—but you want the letters to fade in and remain onscreen, not disappear. You'll customize the preset to suit your needs.

3 Press the spacebar to stop the preview, and then press the Home key to move the current-time indicator back to 0:00.

Customizing an animation preset

After you apply an animation preset to a layer, all of its properties and keyframes are listed in the Timeline panel. You'll use those properties to customize the preset.

1 Select the Road Trip text layer in the Timeline panel, and press U.

The U key, sometimes referred to as the *Überkey*, is a valuable keyboard shortcut that reveals all the animated properties of a layer.

2 Click the Offset property name to select both of its keyframes.

▶ **Tip:** If you press U twice (UU), After Effects displays all modified properties for the layer, instead of only the animated properties. Press the U key again to hide all the layer's properties.

The Offset property specifies how much to offset the start and end of the selection.

3 Choose Animation > Keyframe Assistant > Time-Reverse Keyframes.

The Time-Reverse Keyframes command switches the order of the two Offset keyframes so that the letters are invisible at the beginning of the composition, and then emerge into view.

4 Drag the current-time indicator from 0:00 to 3:00 to manually preview the animation you edited.

The letters now fade into, rather than disappear from, the composition.

5 Press U to hide the layer's properties.

6 Press the End key to move the current-time indicator to the end of the time ruler, and then press N to set the end bracket of the work area.

7 Choose File > Save to save your project.

Animating with scale keyframes

The text layer was scaled to nearly 200% when you applied the Fit To Comp Width command to it earlier in this lesson. Now, you'll animate the layer's scale so that the type gradually shrinks down to its original size.

1 In the Timeline panel, move the current-time indicator to 3:00.

2 Select the Road Trip text layer, and press the S key to reveal its Scale property.

3 Click the stopwatch icon (⏱) to add a Scale keyframe at the current time (3:00).

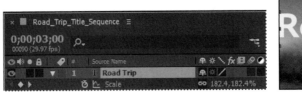

4 Move the current-time indicator to 5:00.

5 Reduce the layer's Scale values to **100, 100%**. After Effects adds a new Scale keyframe at the current time.

Previewing the scale animation

Now you'll preview the change.

1 Move the current-time indicator to 5:10, and press N to set the end of the work area. The scale animation ends shortly before 5:10.

2 Press the spacebar to preview the animation from 0:00 to 5:10. The movie title fades in and then scales to a smaller size.

3 Press the spacebar to stop playback after you've viewed the animation.

Adding Easy Ease

The beginning and end of the scale animation are rather abrupt. In nature, nothing comes to an absolute stop. Instead, objects ease into and out of starting and stopping points.

1 Right-click (Windows) or Control-click (Mac OS) the Scale keyframe at 3:00, and choose Keyframe Assistant > Easy Ease Out. The keyframe becomes a left-pointing icon.

2 Right-click (Windows) or Control-click (Mac OS) the Scale keyframe at 5:00, and choose Keyframe Assistant > Easy Ease In. The keyframe becomes a right-pointing icon.

3 Watch another preview. Press the spacebar to stop it when you're done.

4 Choose File > Save.

Animating using parenting

The next task is to make it appear as if the virtual camera is zooming away from the composition. The text scale animation you just applied gets you halfway there, but you need to animate the scale of the compass as well. You could manually animate the compass layer, but it's easier to take advantage of parenting relationships in After Effects.

1 Press the Home key, or drag the current-time indicator to the beginning of the time ruler.

2 In the Timeline panel, click the Parent pop-up menu for the compass layer, and choose 1. Road Trip.

This sets the Road Trip text layer as the parent of the compass layer, which in turn becomes the child layer.

Note: When you move the compass layer, its parent becomes 2. Road Trip, because Road Trip is now the second layer.

As the child layer, the compass layer inherits the Scale keyframes of its parent layer (Road Trip). Not only is this a quick way to animate the compass, but it also ensures that the compass scales at the same rate and by the same amount as the text layer.

3 In the Timeline panel, move the compass layer above the Road Trip text layer.

4 Move the current-time indicator to 9:29, so you can clearly see the compass in the Composition panel.

5 In the Composition panel, drag the compass so that its anchor point is over the dot in the letter *i* in the word *trip*. Alternatively, you can select the compass layer in the Timeline panel, press P to reveal its Position property, and then enter **124, −62**.

6 Move the current-time indicator from 3:00 to 5:00 to manually preview the scaling. Both the text and the compass scale down in size, so that it appears that the camera is moving away from the scene.

7 Press the Home key to return to 0:00, and drag the work area end bracket to the end of the time ruler.

8 Select the Road Trip layer in the Timeline panel, and press S to hide its Scale property. If you entered Position values for the compass, select the compass layer, and press P to hide the Position property, too. Then choose File > Save.

About parent and child layers

Parenting assigns one layer's transformations to another layer, called a *child layer*. Creating a parenting relationship between layers synchronizes the changes in the parent layer with the corresponding transformation values of the child layers, except opacity. For example, if a parent layer moves 5 pixels to the right of its starting position, then the child layer also moves 5 pixels to the right of its starting position. A layer can have only one parent, but a layer can be a parent to any number of 2D or 3D layers within the same composition. Parenting layers is useful for creating complex animations such as linking the movements of a marionette or depicting the orbits of planets in the solar system.

For more on parent and child layers, see After Effects Help.

Animating imported Photoshop text

If all text animations involved just two short words, such as *road trip*, life would be easy. But in the real world, you may often have to work with longer blocks of text, and they can be tedious to enter manually. Fortunately, you can import text from Photoshop or Illustrator. You can preserve text layers, edit them, and animate them in After Effects.

Importing text

Some of the remaining text for this composition is in a layered Photoshop file, which you'll import now.

1 Double-click an empty area in the Project panel to open the Import File dialog box.

2 Select the credits.psd file in the Lessons/Lesson03/Assets folder. Choose Composition – Retain Layer Sizes from the Import As menu, and then click Import or Open.

3 In the Credits.psd dialog box, select Editable Layer Styles, and click OK.

After Effects can import Photoshop layer styles, retaining the appearance of the layers you're importing. The imported file is added as a composition to the Project panel; its layers are added in a separate folder.

4 Drag the credits composition from the Project panel into the Timeline panel, placing it at the top of the layer stack.

Because you imported the credits.psd file as a composition with layers intact, you can work on it in its own Timeline panel, editing and animating its layers independently.

Editing imported text

The text you imported isn't currently editable in After Effects. You'll change that so that you can control the type and apply animations. And if you have a sharp eye, you've noticed some typos in the imported text. So, first you'll clean up the type.

1 Double-click the credits composition in the Project panel to open it in its own Timeline panel.

2 Shift-click to select both layers in the credits Timeline panel, and choose Layer > Convert To Editable Text. (Click OK if you see a warning about missing fonts.)

Now the text layers can be edited, and you can fix the typos.

3 Deselect both layers, and then double-click layer 2 in the Timeline panel to select the text and automatically switch to the Horizontal Type tool (T).

4 Type an *e* between the *t* and *d* in the word *animated.* Then change the *k* to a *c* in *documentary.*

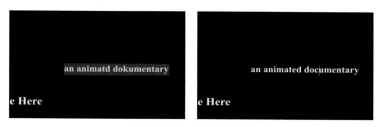

Note: The layer name does not change in the Timeline panel when you correct the spelling in the layer. This is because the original layer name was created in Photoshop. To change a layer's name, select it in the Timeline panel, press Enter or Return, type the new name, and press Enter or Return again.

5 Switch to the Selection tool (▸) to exit text-editing mode.

6 Shift-click to select both layers in the Timeline panel.

7 If the Character panel isn't open, choose Window > Character to open it.

8 Choose the same typeface you used for the words *Road Trip*: Calluna Sans. Leave all other settings as they are.

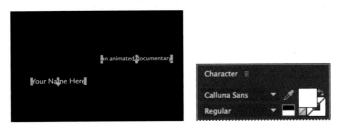

9 Click an empty area of the Timeline panel to deselect both layers. Then select layer 2 again.

10 In the Character panel, click the Fill Color box. Then, in the Text Color dialog box, select a shade of green, and click OK. We used R=66, G=82, B=42.

Animating the subtitle

You want the letters of the subtitle—*an animated documentary*—to fade onscreen from left to right under the movie title. The easiest way to do this is to use another text animation preset.

1 Go to 5:00 in the timeline. At that point, the title and the compass have finished scaling to their final size.

2 Select the subtitle layer (layer 2) in the Timeline panel.

3 Press Ctrl+Alt+Shift+O (Windows) or Command+Option+Shift+O (Mac OS) to jump to Adobe Bridge.

4 Navigate to the Presets/Text/Animate In folder.

5 Select the Fade Up Characters animation preset, and watch it in the Preview panel. This effect works well to reveal the text gradually.

6 Double-click the Fade Up Characters preset to apply it to the subtitle layer in After Effects.

7 With the subtitle layer selected in the Timeline panel, press UU to see the properties modified by the animation preset. You should see two keyframes for Range Selector 1 Start: one at 5:00, and one at 7:00.

You still have a lot of animation to do in this composition, so you will speed up the effect by 1 second.

8 Go to 6:00, and then drag the second Range Selector 1 Start keyframe to 6:00.

9 Drag the current-time indicator across the time ruler between 5:00 and 6:00 to see the letters fade in.

10 When you're done, select the subtitle layer, and press U to hide the modified properties. Then choose File > Save to save your work.

Animating type tracking

Next, you'll animate the appearance of the director's name in the composition using a text animation tracking preset. By animating tracking, you can make words seem to expand outward as they appear onscreen from a central point.

Customizing placeholder text

Currently, the director's name is simply a layer with placeholder text—*Your Name Here*. Before you animate it, change it to your own name.

1 Still working in the credits timeline in the Timeline panel, select the Your Name Here layer.

2 Select the Horizontal Type tool (T), and then replace *Your Name Here* in the Composition panel with your own name. Use a first, middle, and last name so that you have a nice long string of text to animate. Click the layer name when you're done. The layer name doesn't change, because it was named in Photoshop.

Note: It doesn't matter where the current-time indicator is located when you edit the text of this layer. Currently, the text is onscreen for the duration of the composition. That will change once you animate it.

Applying a tracking preset

Now you will animate the director's name with a tracking preset so that it starts to appear onscreen shortly after the words *an animated documentary* are fully visible in the composition.

1 Go to 7:10.

2 Select the Your Name Here layer in the Timeline panel.

▶ **Tip:** If you're tired of jumping to Adobe Bridge and don't care to preview the preset, simply type **Increase Tracking** in the search box of the Effects & Presets panel. Then double-click the effect to apply it to the selected layer in the Timeline panel.

3 Jump to Adobe Bridge, and go to the Presets/Text/Tracking folder. Double-click the Increase Tracking preset to apply it to the Your Name Here layer in After Effects.

4 Drag the current-time indicator across the time ruler between 7:10 and 9:10 to manually preview the tracking animation.

Customizing the tracking animation preset

The text expands, but you want the letters to be so close initially that they're on top of each other, and then to expand to a reasonable, readable distance apart. The animation should also occur faster. You'll adjust the Tracking Amount to achieve both goals.

1 Select the Your Name Here layer in the Timeline panel, and press UU to reveal the properties that were modified.

2 Go to 7:10.

3 Under Animator 1, change the Tracking Amount to −5 so that the letters are squeezed together.

4 Click the Go To Next Keyframe arrow (▶) for the Tracking Amount property, and then change the value to **0**.

5 Drag the current-time indicator across the time ruler between 7:10 and 8:10. The letters expand as they appear onscreen, and stop animating at the last keyframe.

Animating text opacity

You'll take the animation of the director's name a little further by having it fade onscreen as the letters expand. To do this, you'll animate the layer's Opacity property.

1 Select the Your Name Here layer in the credits timeline.

2 Press T to reveal only the layer's Opacity property.

3 Go to 7:10, and set the Opacity to **0%**. Then click the stopwatch icon (⏱) to set an Opacity keyframe.

4 Go to 7:20, and set the Opacity to **100%**. After Effects adds a second keyframe.

Now the letters of the director's name should fade in as they expand onscreen.

5 Drag the current-time indicator across the time ruler between 7:10 and 8:10 to see the letters of the director's name fade in as they spread out.

6 Right-click (Windows) or Control-click (Mac OS) the ending Opacity keyframe, and choose Keyframe Assistant > Easy Ease In.

7 Choose File > Save.

Using a text animator group

Text animator groups let you animate individual letters within a block of text in a layer. You'll use a text animator group to animate only the characters in your middle name without affecting the tracking and opacity animation of the other names in the layer.

1 In the Timeline panel, go to 8:10.

2 Hide the Opacity property for the Your Name Here layer. Then expand the layer to see its Text property group name.

3 Next to the Text property name, click the Animate pop-up menu, and choose Skew.

A property group named Animator 2 appears in the layer's Text properties.

About text animator groups

A text animator group includes one or more *selectors* and one or more *animator properties*. A selector is like a mask—it specifies which characters or section of a text layer you want an animator property to affect. Using a selector, you can define a percentage of the text, specific characters in the text, or a specific range of text.

Using a combination of animator properties and selectors, you can create complex text animations that would otherwise require painstaking keyframing. Most text animations require you to animate only the selector values—not the property values. Consequently, text animators use a small number of keyframes even for complex animations.

For more about text animator groups, see After Effects Help.

4 Select Animator 2, press Enter or Return, and rename it **Skew Animator**. Then press Enter or Return again to accept the new name.

Now you're ready to define the range of letters that you want to skew.

5 Expand the Skew Animator's Range Selector 1 properties.

Each animator group includes a default range selector. Range selectors constrain the animation to particular letters in the text layer. You can add additional selectors to an animator group, or apply multiple animator properties to the same range selector.

6 While watching the Composition panel, drag the Skew Animator's Range Selector 1 Start value up (to the right) until the left selector indicator (⤵) is just before the first letter of your middle name (the *B* in *Bender*, in this example).

7 Drag the Skew Animator's Range Selector 1 End value down (to the left) until its indicator (⤵) is just after the last letter of your middle name (the *r* in *Bender*, in this example) in the Composition panel.

Now, any properties that you animate with the Skew Animator will affect only the middle name that you selected.

Skewing the range of text

Now, make that middle name shake and shimmy by setting Skew keyframes.

1 Drag the Skew Animator's Skew value left and right, and notice that only the middle name sways. The other names in the line of text remain steady.

2 Set the Skew Animator's Skew value to **0**.

3 Go to 8:05, and click the stopwatch icon (⏱) for Skew to add a keyframe to the property.

4 Go to 8:08, and set the Skew value to **50**. After Effects adds a keyframe.

5 Go to 8:15, and change the Skew value to **–50**. After Effects adds another keyframe.

6 Go to 8:20, and change the Skew value to **0** to set the final keyframe.

7. Click the Skew property name to select all of the Skew keyframes. Then choose Animation > Keyframe Assistant > Easy Ease to add an Easy Ease to all keyframes.

8. Drag the current-time indicator across the time ruler from 7:10 to 8:20 to see how the director's name fades in and expands onscreen, and the middle name rocks side to side while the other names are unaffected.

9. Hide the properties for the Your Name Here layer in the Timeline panel.

10. Select the Road_Trip_Title_Sequence tab to open its timeline.

11. Press Home, or go to 0:00, and then preview the entire composition.

12. Press the spacebar to stop playback, and then choose File > Save to save your work.

▶ **Tip:** To quickly remove all text animators from a text layer, select the layer in the Timeline panel, and choose Animation > Remove All Text Animators. To remove only one animator, select its name in the Timeline panel, and press Delete.

Animating a layer's position

You've used several text animation presets to dazzle your audience. But for a simpler effect, you can animate the Transform properties for a text layer, just as you can any other layer.

Currently, your name appears onscreen, but there's no context for it. You'll add the words "directed by," animating them so that they move into position as your name is appearing onscreen.

1. In the Road_Trip_Title_Sequence Timeline panel, go to 9:29, the end of the project.

At this point, all the other text is onscreen, so you can position the "directed by" line accurately.

2 Select the Horizontal Type tool.

3 Make sure no layers are selected, and then click in the Composition panel. Make sure you're clicking in an area that doesn't overlap an existing text layer.

4 Type **directed by**.

5 Select the directed by layer. Then, in the Character panel, choose Minion Pro from the Font Family menu.

6 Choose Regular for the Font Style, and set the Font Size to 20 pixels.

7 In the Character panel, click the Fill Color box. Then, in the Text Color dialog box, select white, and click OK. Leave all other options at their default settings.

8 Select the Selection tool, and then drag the directed by layer so that the text is centered over your name.

9 Press P to display the layer's Position property. Click the stopwatch icon to create an initial keyframe for the layer.

10 Go to 7:00, the point where "documentary" has just finished appearing and your name hasn't yet started to appear.

11 Drag the directed by layer off the left edge of the Composition window. Press the Shift key as you drag to create a straight path.

12 Preview the animation, and then hide the Position property.

It's simple, but effective. The text moves in from the left side and stops in its final position above your name. To make the text's entrance a little more interesting, you'll add a car graphic that will appear to be dragging the text onscreen.

Timing layer animations

You'll animate a simple car graphic so that the text appears to trail behind the car onscreen. The words should follow the car and come to rest above your name, while the car continues to fly off screen. The timing will require some adjustment, in order to keep the text and the car in sync.

First, you'll import the car graphic and add it to your composition.

1 Double-click an empty area in the Project panel to open the Import File dialog box.

2 In the Lessons/Lesson03/Assets folder, select the car.ai file, choose Composition – Retain Layer Sizes from the Import As menu, and then click Import or Open.

3 Drag the car composition from the Project panel to the top of the layer stack in the Road_Trip_Title_Sequence Timeline panel.

4 Go to 6:25, just before the directed by text begins moving.

5 Select the car layer, and press P to reveal its Position property.

6 Drag the car off the left of the Composition window, so that it overlaps the directed by text.

7 Click the stopwatch icon for the layer's Position property to create an initial keyframe.

8 Go to 9:29, the end of the composition.

9 Drag the car off the right side of the Composition window. The car shouldn't be visible on the screen. Hold down the Shift key as you drag to create a straight path.

10 Manually preview the animation from 6:25 to 9:29.

The text trails the car, but the car picks up speed too quickly so it's not obvious that it's dragging the text. You'll need to make an adjustment to its timing to slow the car down until the text is in place.

11 Go to 8:29.

12 Move the car immediately to the right of the text.

13 Preview the animation again.

The timing is better, but now the car overlaps the text at the beginning. One more adjustment should do the trick.

14 Go to 7:19.

15 Pull the car forward, just ahead of the text.

16 Preview the animation again.

Now the car is clearly pulling the text, and it speeds up to roll off the screen before the composition finishes. If you'd like to more precisely control the animation, you can add more keyframes.

17 Hide the properties for all layers, and then choose File > Save to save your work.

Adding motion blur

Motion blur is the blur that occurs as an object moves. You'll apply motion blur to finesse the composition and make the movement look more natural.

1 In the Timeline panel, click the Motion Blur switch (⊘) for each layer *except* the background_movie and credits layers.

Now you'll apply motion blur to the layers in the credits composition.

2 Switch to the credits Timeline panel, and enable motion blur for both layers.

3 Switch back to the Road_Trip_Title_Sequence Timeline panel, and select the Motion Blur switch for the credits layer. Then click the Enable Motion Blur button (⊘) at the top of the Timeline panel so that you can see the motion blur in the Composition panel.

4 Preview the entire, completed animation.

5 Choose File > Save.

Give yourself a pat on the back. You just completed some hard-core text animations. If you'd like to export the composition as a movie file, see Lesson 14, "Rendering and Outputting," for instructions.

Review questions

1 What are some similarities and differences between text layers and other types of layers in After Effects?

2 How can you preview a text animation preset?

3 How can you assign one layer's transformations to another layer?

4 What are text animator groups?

Review answers

1 In many ways, a text layer is just like any other layer in After Effects. You can apply effects and expressions to text layers, animate them, designate them as 3D layers, and edit the 3D text while viewing it in multiple views. However, text layers are like shape layers in that you can't open them in their own Layer panels, and in that they are synthetic layers that consist entirely of vector graphics. You can animate the text in a text layer using special text animator properties and selectors.

2 You can preview text animation presets in Adobe Bridge by choosing Animation > Browse Presets. Adobe Bridge opens and displays the contents of the After Effects Presets folder. Navigate to folders containing categories of text animation presets, such as Blurs or Paths, and watch samples in the Preview panel. Then double-click a preset to add it to the currently selected layer in the After Effects Timeline panel.

3 You can use parenting relationships in After Effects to assign one layer's transformations to another layer (except opacity transformations). When a layer is made a parent to another layer, the other layer is called the *child layer*. Creating a parenting relationship between layers synchronizes the changes in the parent layer with corresponding transformation values of the child layers.

4 Text animator groups enable you to animate the properties of individual characters in a text layer over time. Text animator groups contain one or more *selectors*, which are like masks: They let you specify which characters or section of a text layer you want an animator property to affect. Using a selector, you can define a percentage of the text, specific characters in the text, or a specific range of text.

4 WORKING WITH SHAPE LAYERS

Lesson overview

In this lesson, you'll learn how to do the following:

- Create custom shapes.

- Customize a shape's fill and stroke.

- Use path operations to transform shapes.

- Animate shapes.

- Repeat shapes.

- Snap layers into alignment.

- Use an expression to animate properties in time with audio.

 This lesson will take approximately an hour to complete. Download the Lesson04 project files from the Lesson & Update Files tab on your Account page at www.peachpit.com, if you haven't already done so. As you work on this lesson, you'll preserve the start files. If you need to restore the start files, download them from your Account page.

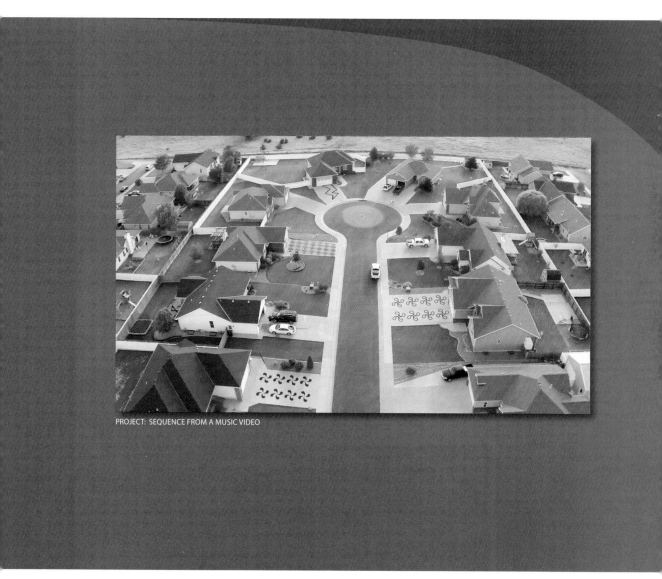

PROJECT: SEQUENCE FROM A MUSIC VIDEO

Shape layers make it easy to create expressive backgrounds and intriguing results. You can animate shapes, apply animation presets, and add Repeaters to intensify their impact.

Getting started

Shape layers are created automatically when you draw a shape with any of the drawing tools. You can customize and transform an individual shape or its entire layer to create interesting results. In this lesson, you will use shape layers to build dynamic and whimsical designs on the street and driveways of a neighborhood.

First, you'll preview the final movie and set up the project.

1 Make sure the following files are in the Lessons/Lesson04 folder on your hard disk, or download them from your Account page at www.peachpit.com now:

 • In the Assets folder: Beat.aif, drop.aep, Melody.aif, tracking.aep, Tracking.mp4

 • In the Sample_Movie folder: Lesson04.mov

2 Open and play the Lesson04.mov sample movie to see what you will create in this lesson. When you are done, quit QuickTime Player. You may delete this sample movie from your hard disk if you have limited storage space.

As you start After Effects, restore the default application settings. See "Restoring default preferences" on page 2.

3 Start After Effects, and then immediately hold down Ctrl+Alt+Shift (Windows) or Command+Option+Shift (Mac OS) to restore default preferences settings. When prompted, click OK to delete your preferences.

4 Close the Start window.

After Effects opens to display a blank, untitled project.

5 Choose File > Save As > Save As, and then navigate to the Lessons/Lesson04/ Finished_Project folder.

6 Name the project **Lesson04_Finished.aep**, and then click Save.

Creating the composition

Next, you'll import the files you need and create the composition. You'll import two footage items and two saved project files.

1 Double-click an empty area of the Project panel to open the Import File dialog box.

2 Navigate to the Lessons/Lesson04/Assets folder on your hard disk, Ctrl-click (Windows) or Command-click (Mac OS) to select the Beat.aif and Melody.aif files, and then click Import or Open.

3 Choose File > New > New Folder to create a new folder in the Project panel.

4 Name the folder **Audio**, press Enter or Return to accept the name, and then drag the two audio files you imported into the Audio folder. Then expand the folder so you can see its contents.

5 Double-click an empty area of the Project panel to open the Import File dialog box again.

6 Navigate to the Lessons/Lesson04/ Assets folder. Ctrl-click (Windows) or Command-click (Mac OS) to select the drop.aep and tracking. aep project files, and then click Import or Open. The video files and other elements you will need later are imported with the projects.

Now you're ready to create the composition.

7 Press Ctrl+N (Windows) or Command+N (Mac OS) to create a new composition.

8 In the Composition Settings dialog box, name the composition **Spiral**, select the HDTV 1080 24 preset, and set the Duration to **10:00**. Then click OK.

After Effects opens the new composition in both the Timeline and Composition panels.

▶ **Tip:** To specify 10 seconds, type **10.** in the Duration box. The period indicates that there are no units in that position. To specify 10 minutes, type **10..** in the box.

Adding a shape layer

After Effects includes five shape tools: Rectangle, Rounded Rectangle, Ellipse, Polygon, and Star. When you draw a shape directly in the Composition panel, After Effects adds a new shape layer to the composition. You can apply stroke and fill settings to a shape, modify its path, and apply animation presets. Shape attributes are all represented in the Timeline panel, and you can animate each setting over time.

The same drawing tools can create both shapes and masks. Masks are applied to layers to hide or reveal areas or as input into effects; shapes have their own layers. When you select a drawing tool, you can specify whether the tool draws a shape or a mask.

Drawing a shape

You'll begin by drawing a rectangle with a fill and stroke.

1 Select the Rectangle tool (▢).

2 Choose Fit from the Magnification Ratio pop-up menu at the bottom of the Composition panel so that you can see the entire composition.

3 Using the Info panel to guide you, position the cursor at approximately 950, 540, which is near the center of the Composition panel. (You may need to widen the Info panel to see the X and Y coordinates.)

4 Drag down and to the right to create a rectangle. Again, watch the Info panel. The bottom (B) value should be approximately 40 pixels and the right side (R) value should be about 400 pixels. The shape appears in the Composition panel, and After Effects adds a shape layer named Shape Layer 1 to the Timeline panel.

5 Select the Shape Layer 1 layer name, press Enter or Return, change the layer name to **Spiral**, and press Enter or Return to accept the change.

Applying a fill and stroke

You can change the color of a shape by modifying its Fill settings in the Tools panel. Clicking the word *Fill* opens the Fill Options dialog box, where you can select the kind of fill, its blending mode, and its opacity. Clicking the Fill Color box opens the Adobe Color Picker if the fill is solid, or the Gradient Editor if the fill is a gradient.

Similarly, you can change the stroke color and width of a shape by modifying its Stroke settings in the Tools panel. Click the word *Stroke* to open the Stroke Options dialog box; click the Stroke Color box to select a color.

1 Select Rectangle 1 in the Timeline panel.

2 Click the Fill Color box (next to *Fill*) to open the Shape Fill Color dialog box.

3 Change the color to a light blue (we used R=0, G=170, B=255), and click OK.

4 Click the Stroke Color box in the Tools panel, change the stroke color to the same light blue color, and then click OK.

5 Choose File > Save to save your work so far.

Twisting a shape

The rectangle is fine, but it isn't very exciting. In After Effects, you can easily modify a basic shape into something more complex and interesting. You'll use the Twist path operation to transform this rectangle into a spiral shape.

As you work with the Twist path operation, keep in mind that it rotates a path more sharply in the center than at the edges. Positive values twist clockwise; negative values twist counterclockwise.

1 In the Timeline panel, open the Add pop-up menu next to Contents in the Spiral layer, and choose Twist.

2 Expand Twist 1.

3 Change the Angle to **220**.

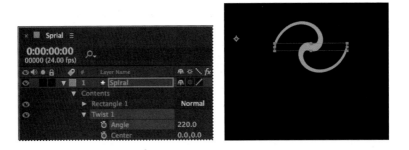

The rectangle changes dramatically. Next, you'll change the center point of the twist to create a larger spiral.

● **Note:** If the center of your spiral looks different from ours, you probably drew a slightly larger or smaller rectangle. You can delete what you have and start over with a fresh composition or try adjusting the x-axis value for Center.

4 In the Timeline panel, change the x-axis value for Center to **−220**.

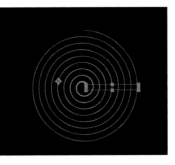

The spiral is a bit thin. You'll change the stroke width to thicken it.

5 Select the Spiral layer in the Timeline panel, and then change the Stroke Width value in the Tools panel to **20** px.

The center of the spiral has a rounded cap, but the end is square. You'll change the end so that they match.

6 Expand Stroke 1 to see its properties.

7 Choose Round Join from the Line Join menu.

The spiral looks great. Now you just need to center it, so that it looks natural when it rotates, and then you'll set up its rotation and add motion blur.

8 Press A to reveal the Anchor Point property for the layer. Then adjust the x-axis and y-axis values until the anchor point is centered in the black center (negative space) of the spiral, just above the center end cap. (The exact values will vary depending on how you created the initial shape.)

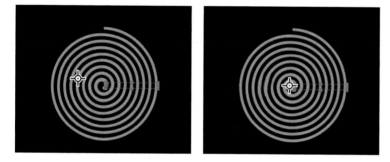

9 Make sure the current-time indicator is at the beginning of the timeline. Then press R to reveal the Rotation property for the layer. Click the stopwatch icon (⏱) to create an initial keyframe.

10 Press the End key, or move the current-time indicator to the end of the timeline. Change the Rotation value to **1x+0.0°**. With this setting, the shape will rotate once during its ten-second cycle.

11 Click the Motion Blur switch for the layer, and then click the Enable Motion Blur button (⊘) at the top of the Timeline panel.

12 Press the spacebar to preview your animation, and press the spacebar again to stop the preview. Choose File > Save to save your work so far.

Creating custom shapes

You can use the five shape tools to create a wide variety of shapes. However, the real power in using shape layers is that you can draw any shape and manipulate it in a myriad of ways.

Drawing a shape with the Pen tool

You'll use the Pen tool to draw a shape that resembles a lightning bolt. In order to position it properly in the final project, you'll create a separate composition for this shape.

1 Press Ctrl+N (Windows) or Command+N (Mac OS) to create a new composition.

2 In the Composition Settings dialog box, name the composition **Bolt**, select the HDTV 1080 24 preset, set the duration to **10:00**, and then click OK.

3 Select the Pen tool (✒) in the Tools panel.

4 In the Composition panel, draw a shape that resembles a lightning bolt, as in the illustration. When you create the first vertex, After Effects automatically adds a shape layer to the Timeline panel.

> ▶ **Tip:** Your lightning bolt doesn't need to look exactly like ours, but you can use the one in the illustration as a guide. Click an initial vertex at the bottom of the shape, and then click to create each additional point. If you're not familiar with the Pen tool, you may find the display distracting, as the fill seems to jump around as you draw; ignore the preview until you've clicked each vertex and completed the shape.

5 Select Shape Layer 1, press Enter or Return, and change the layer's name to **Bolt**. Press Enter or Return to accept the new name.

6 With the Bolt layer selected, click the Fill Color box in the Tools panel, and select a yellow color (we used R=255, G=237, B=0). Then click the Stroke Color box in the Tools panel, and select black (R=0, G=0, B=0).

7 Change the Stroke Width to **10** px.

Creating a self-animating shape

Wiggle Paths turns a smooth shape into a series of jagged peaks and valleys. You'll use it to make the lightning bolt more electrifying. Because the operation is self-animating, you need to change only a few properties for the entire shape to move on its own.

1 Expand the Bolt layer in the Timeline panel, and choose Wiggle Paths from the Add pop-up menu.

2 Expand Wiggle Paths 1. Then change the Size to **15** and the Detail to **30**.

3 Change Wiggles/Second to **24** to speed up the movement.

4 Click the Motion Blur switch for the layer, and then click the Enable Motion Blur button at the top of the Timeline panel. Then hide the layer properties.

5 Move the current-time indicator across the time ruler to see the shape move.

Duplicating shapes

You could draw a shape multiple times, but it's easier to duplicate the shape automatically. The Repeater path operation lets you multiply a shape and transform its properties to achieve different results.

You'll use the Repeater path operation to duplicate a shape that was created in Adobe Illustrator and then pasted into the Path property of a shape layer in the Drop.aep project file.

● **Note:** Choose Fit from the Magnification Ratio pop-up menu in the Composition window if you don't see the full shape.

1 In the Project panel, expand the drop.aep folder, and then double-click the Drop composition to open it.

The Drop composition opens in the Timeline panel and the Composition panel.

2 Expand the Drop layer and its Contents folder if its properties aren't visible. Then select Shape 1, and choose Repeater from the Add pop-up menu.

You're selecting Shape 1 because you want to add the Repeater to the individual shape, not the entire layer.

3 Expand Repeater 1.

4 Change the number of copies to **4**.

The Repeater creates three copies of the shape, for a total of four. You'll rotate the shapes and then reposition them to create a pinwheel.

5 Expand Transform: Repeater 1.

6 Change the Rotation to **90°**.

● **Note:** There are multiple Transform properties in the Timeline panel, applying to different path operators. Make sure you're selecting the appropriate Transform property for the object or layer you want to affect. In this case, you want to affect only the Repeater.

Because you applied the rotation to the Repeater rather than to the shape, each drop rotates around the layer's anchor point to a different degree. When you change the Transform properties for the Repeater, the change is multiplied by the number of copies created. In this case, the first shape retains the original value of 0, the second shape rotates 90 degrees, the third shape rotates 180 degrees, and the fourth shape rotates 270 degrees. The same concept applies to each of the Transform properties.

7 In the Transform: Repeater 1 properties, change the Position to **0, 0**.

The shapes overlap because the anchor point is located in the center of each shape.

8 Change the Anchor Point value to **15, 45**.

The shapes align to form a pinwheel. Now you'll make the pinwheel rotate.

9 Make sure the current-time indicator is at the beginning of the time ruler. Then, expand the Transform: Shape 1 category, and click the stopwatch icon next to the Rotation value to create an initial keyframe.

10 Press the End key or move the current-time indicator to the end of the time ruler, and change the Rotation value to **2x+0.0°**.

11 Drag the current-time indicator across the time ruler to see the pinwheel rotate.

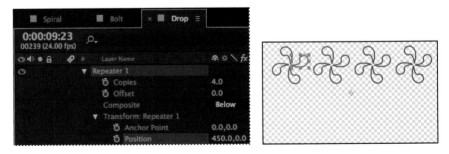

You used the Repeater path operation to duplicate an individual shape. Now you'll use it to copy all the contents of the layer, turning one pinwheel into eight.

12 In the Timeline panel, hide all the properties under Shape 1. Then select the Drop layer, and choose Repeater from the Add pop-up menu.

13 Expand the new Repeater 1 category, and change the number of copies to **4**.

Because you applied the Repeater to the entire layer, the full pinwheel was copied.

14 Expand the Transform: Repeater 1 category, and change the Position values to **450, 0**.

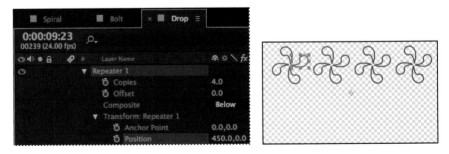

There are now four pinwheels across the top of the Composition window.

15 Select the Drop layer, and choose Repeater from the Add pop-up menu again to create the Repeater 2 category.

16 Expand the Repeater 2 category, and change the number of copies to **2**. Then expand the Transform: Repeater 2 category, and change the Position values to **0, 575**.

By applying another Repeater to the entire layer, you copied the full row of pinwheels.

17 Hide all the properties for the layer.

18 Click the Motion Blur switch for the layer, and then click the Enable Motion Blur button (⊘) at the top of the Timeline panel.

19 Press the spacebar to preview eight pinwheels rotating in unison; press the spacebar again to stop the preview. Then choose File > Save to save your work so far.

Duplicating and modifying a composition

You'll use the Drop composition as a starting point for a similar composition that uses different fill and stroke options.

1 In the Project panel, select the Drop composition, and choose Edit > Duplicate to create a copy of the composition.

2 Double-click the Drop 2 composition in the Project panel to open it. Then, in the Timeline panel, expand the Drop layer, and the Contents category.

3 Select Shape 1, and then choose Fill from the Add pop-up menu.

4 Expand Fill 1, click the Color box, and choose any fill color you like

5 Expand Stroke 1, click the Color box, and choose the stroke color you like.

6 Move the current-time indicator across the time ruler to preview the rotating pinwheels.

7 Hide all the properties for the layer.

8 Choose File > Save to save your work so far.

Positioning layers with snapping

You've created and manipulated shapes in a variety of ways. Now you'll create a checkerboard pattern. Positioning the layers will be easy with the snapping feature in After Effects.

Creating a new composition

This checkerboard background includes multiple layers, so you'll create a new composition for it.

1 Press Ctrl+N (Windows) or Command+N (Mac OS) to create a new composition.

2 In the Composition Settings dialog box, name the composition **Checkerboard**, choose HDTV 1080 24 from the Preset menu, and type **10:00** for Duration. Then click OK.

After Effects opens the new Checkerboard composition in the Timeline and Composition panels. You'll start by adding two solid layers—the building blocks of the checkerboard background.

3 Choose Layer > New > Solid to create a solid layer.

4 In the Solid Settings dialog box, do the following, and then click OK:

- Name the layer **Dark Red**.

- Change both the Width and Height to **200** px.

- Choose Square Pixels from the Pixel Aspect Ratio menu.

- Select a dark red color. (We used R=145, G=0, B=0.)

5 With the Dark Red layer selected in the Timeline panel, press R to display the Rotation property for the layer. Then change the Rotation to **45** degrees.

6 Select the Selection tool (![arrow]). Then, in the Composition panel, drag the layer up so that only the bottom half of the diamond appears in the composition.

7 Press Ctrl+Y (Windows) or Command+Y (Mac OS) to create another solid layer.

8 In the Solid Settings dialog box, name the layer **Light Red**, and change the color to a light red (we used R=180, G=75, B=75). Then click OK.

The default width and height for the new solid layer match the settings you used previously, so the Light Red layer has the same dimensions as the Dark Red layer.

9 With the Light Red layer selected in the Timeline panel, press R to display the Rotation property. Then change the Rotation to **45** degrees.

Snapping layers into position

You've created two layers, but they have no relationship to each other in the composition. You'll use the Snapping option in After Effects to quickly align the layers. When the Snapping option is enabled, the layer feature that is closest to your pointer when you click becomes the snapping feature. As you drag the layer near other layers, features on other layers are highlighted, showing you where the snapping feature would snap if you released the mouse button.

Note: You can snap two shape layers together, but not two shapes within a single layer. Also, a layer must be visible to snap to it. 2D layers can snap to 2D layers, and 3D layers can snap to 3D layers.

1 Select Snapping in the options section of the Tools panel, if it's not already selected.

2 Using the Selection tool, select the Light Red layer in the Composition panel.

When you select a layer in the Composition panel, After Effects displays the layer handles and anchor point. You can use any of these points as the snapping feature for a layer.

Tip: If the Snapping option isn't selected, you can temporarily enable it: Click a layer and start dragging, and then press Ctrl (Windows) or Command (Mac OS) as you drag the layer.

3 Click near the corner handle on the left side of the Light Red layer, and drag it near the lower right edge of the Dark Red layer until it snaps into place, with the sides abutted. Be careful not to drag the corner itself, or you'll resize the layer.

As you drag the layer, a box appears around the left corner handle you selected, indicating that it is the snapping feature.

4 In the Timeline panel, select both of the layers, and press R to hide the Rotation property for both layers.

▶ **Tip:** Instead of choosing Edit > Duplicate, you can press Ctrl+D (Windows) or Command+D (Mac OS) to duplicate layers.

5 With both layers still selected, choose Edit > Duplicate to copy them.

6 In the Composition panel, drag the two new layers down to the left, and then down to the right, so that the new Dark Red layer abuts the original Light Red layer. Remember that the snapping feature is determined by where you initially click when you begin to drag.

7 Repeat steps 5–6 until you have a column of diamonds filling the screen.

8 Choose Edit > Select All to select the layers in the Timeline panel.

9 Press Ctrl+D (Windows) or Command+D (Mac OS) to duplicate the layers. Then move them to the left in the Composition panel until they snap into place.

▶ **Tip:** If you need to generate a checkerboard more quickly, use the Checkerboard effect. For more information, see After Effects Help.

10 Repeat step 9 until the Composition panel is full. Pull the duplicate layers to the left or right as necessary. Remember to click near an appropriate snapping feature as you begin dragging each time.

11 Choose File > Save to save your work.

Adding compositions to a 3D project

You've created several compositions, all of which need to stay in position as the camera moves through the scene. You'll integrate the compositions using the 3D Camera Tracker effect, which lets you add 3D layers to a clip with the same movement and perspective changes as the original.

You'll work extensively with the 3D Camera Tracker effect in Lesson 12. For this project, we've set the effect up so that all you need to do is to position layers and parent them to a null object to attach them to the 3D scene. A null object is an invisible layer that has all the properties of a visible layer, so that it can be a parent to any layer in the composition. In this case, the null object tracks the camera movement.

1 In the Project panel, double-click the Tracking composition (in the tracking.aep folder) to open it. Choose Fit from the Magnification Ratio pop-up menu at the bottom of the Composition panel so that you can see the entire composition.

The Tracking composition includes the background video you'll use to place the shapes you've created.

2 Select the Spiral composition in the Timeline panel, and then select the 3D switch (⬡) for the Spiral layer.

3 Select the Tracking composition in the Timeline panel again. Then drag the Spiral composition from the Project panel to the Timeline panel, placing it at the top of the layer stack.

4 Select the 3D switch for the Spiral layer, and then select the Collapse Transformations switch (✳) for the layer, too.

The Collapse Transformations switch ensures that transformations in a nested composition aren't flattened; instead, when the project is rendered, transformations in the nested composition will be performed at the same time transformations are performed for the containing composition.

5 In the Timeline panel, click the Parent pop-up menu for the Spiral layer, and choose 2. Track Null 1. This sets the Track Null 1 layer as the parent of the Spiral layer, which in turn becomes the child layer.

6 With the Spiral layer selected, press P to reveal its Position property. Change the value to **0, 0, 0**. This moves the spiral to the same location as the Null object.

7 Move the current-time indicator to 5:00 so you can clearly see the Spiral layer's position in the image. Then press Shift+R to reveal the Rotation properties, and change the Orientation values to **0, 0, 0**.

The spiral is almost in the right place, but you want to position it perfectly in the cul-de-sac. You'll tweak its position.

8 Change the Position for the layer to **−35, −225, 0**.

9 Press the spacebar to preview the spiral rotating in the cul-de-sac. Press the spacebar again to stop the preview. Hide the Spiral layer's properties to keep the Timeline panel tidy.

You've placed the first composition. You'll repeat the process to place the others.

10 Drag the Bolt composition from the Project panel to the top of the Timeline panel, and select the 3D switch for the Bolt layer.

11 Select 3. Track Null 1 from the Parent menu for the Bolt layer. Then press the P key, press Shift+R, and press Shift+S to reveal the Position, Rotation, and Scale properties for the layer.

Pressing the Shift key as you press keyboard shortcuts lets you view multiple layer properties at the same time.

12 Change the Position values to **−650, −1200, 0**. Change the Orientation to **0, 0, 345**. Change the Scale to **85%**. Finally, select the Motion Blur switch for the Bolt layer, and then hide the layer's properties.

● **Note:** You may need to adjust the Position, Orientation, and Scale values, depending on how you drew the lightning bolt.

Next, you'll use the same process to integrate the Drop composition.

13 Go to 2:00 so you can see the driveway where this composition will be placed. Drag the Drop composition from the Project panel to the top of the stack in the Timeline panel, and select the 3D switch for the layer.

14 Select 4. Track Null 1 from the Parent menu for the Drop layer. Then press P, Shift+R, and Shift+S to reveal the Position, Rotation, and Scale properties.

15 Change the Position values to **730, 2275, 0**; the Orientation values to **5, 8, 2**; and the Scale to **45%**. Then select the Motion Blur switch for the layer, and hide the layer's properties.

You'll place the Drop2 composition in the lower left driveway, visible as the camera begins to pan.

16 Go to the beginning of the time ruler. Drag the Drop2 composition from the Project panel to the top of the Timeline panel, select the 3D switch, and select 5. Track Null 1 from the Parent menu.

17 Press P, Shift+R, and Shift+S. Change the Position values to **−1025, 3575, 0**; the Orientation to **0, 352, 0**; and the Scale to **35%**. Select the Motion Blur switch for the layer, and hide the layer's properties.

Finally, you'll add the Checkerboard composition. You'll need to scale it a little differently so that it fits into the driveway.

18 Go to 4:00 in the time ruler. Drag the Checkerboard composition from the Project panel to the top of the Timeline panel, select its 3D switch, and choose 6. Track Null 1 from the Parent menu.

19 Press P, Shift+R, and Shift+S. Change the Position values to **−922, 814, 10** and the Orientation to **1, 355, 2**. Then click the link icon for the Scale property to unlink the values, and change the values to **42%, 35%, 42%**. Select the Motion Blur switch for the layer, and hide the layer's properties.

Adding the finishing touches

The layers work pretty well with the underlying video, but they'll blend more convincingly if you change the blending modes. You'll also add the audio file.

1 Click the Toggle Switches/Modes button at the bottom of the Timeline panel.

2 Choose Multiply from the Mode menu for all the layers except the Checkerboard layer; choose Overlay for the Checkerboard layer. (You won't be able to change the mode for the Spiral layer, because Collapse Transformations is selected.)

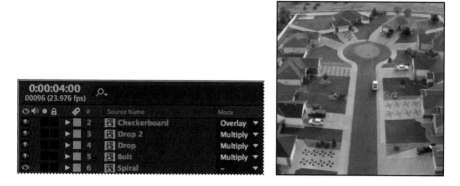

3 Drag the Melody.aif clip from the Project panel to the bottom of the layer stack in the Timeline panel.

4 Press the spacebar to enjoy your creation! When you're done previewing the project, save your work.

Extra credit

Animating layers to match audio

Currently, the spiral shape turns in a slow circle. The movie will be more compelling if the size of the spiral is animated to match the beat of the music. You can scale the spiral in time with the amplitude of an audio file. First, you need to create keyframes from the audio information.

1 Select the Spiral composition in the Timeline panel. Drag the Beat.aif file from the Project panel into the Timeline panel, and place it beneath the Spiral layer.

2 Right-click or Control-click the Beat.aif layer, and choose Keyframe Assistant > Convert Audio To Keyframes.

After Effects adds the Audio Amplitude layer. The new layer is a null object layer, meaning it has no size or shape and won't appear in a final render. Null objects let you parent layers or drive effects.

3 Select the Audio Amplitude layer, and press E to display the effects properties for the layer.

Three categories of effects properties are available for the layer: Left Channel, Right Channel, and Both Channels. You'll work with the Both Channels category.

4 Expand the Both Channels category.

When you converted the audio to keyframes, After Effects created keyframes that specify the amplitude of the audio file in each frame of the layer. You'll sync the scale of the spiral to those values.

5 Select the Spiral layer, and press S to reveal the Scale property for the layer.

6 Alt-click (Windows) or Option-click (Mac OS) the Scale stopwatch to add an expression. The words *transform.scale* appear in the time ruler for the layer.

7 With the transform.scale expression selected in the time ruler, click the pick whip icon (◉) on the Expression:Scale line, and drag it to the Slider property name in the Audio Amplitude layer.

When you release the mouse, the pick whip snaps, and the expression in the shape layer time ruler now reads *temp = thisComp.layer("Audio Amplitude").effect("Both Channels")("Slider"); [temp, temp, temp].* (You may need to click the expression to see the full thing.) This expression means that the Scale values for the shape layer will depend on the Slider values of the Audio Amplitude layer.

Note: *You'll learn more about expressions in Lesson 6.*

8 Choose Edit > Deselect All to deselect the layers. Then move the current-time indicator through the time ruler to see the spiral resize with the audio's amplitude.

The scale definitely changes, but sometimes the spiral disappears. You'll modify the expression so that the spiral remains visible.

9 In the time ruler, click the expression to make it active. Click an insertion point at the end of the first line, between the closing parentheses and the semicolon. Type **+90**, and then click an empty area of the Timeline panel to accept the change.

10 Preview the composition, and watch the spiral pulse to the beat of the audio file.

11 Return to the Tracking composition in the Timeline panel. Then press the spacebar, and watch the spiral pulse as the camera moves through the scene. Save your work.

Review questions

1 What is a shape layer, and how do you create one?

2 How can you quickly create multiple copies of a shape?

3 How can you snap one layer to another?

4 What does the Twist path operation do?

Review answers

1 A shape layer is simply a layer that contains a vector graphic called a shape. To create a shape layer, draw a shape directly in the Composition panel using any of the drawing tools or the Pen tool.

2 To quickly duplicate a shape multiple times, apply a Repeater operation to the shape layer. The Repeater path operation creates copies of all paths, strokes, and fills included in the layer.

3 To snap one layer to another in the Composition panel, select Snapping in the options section of the Tools panel. Then click next to the handle or point you want to use as a snapping feature, and drag the layer close to the point to which you want to align it. After Effects highlights the points to which it will align when you release the mouse button. Note that you cannot snap shape layers.

4 The Twist path operation rotates a path more sharply in the center than it does at the edges. Entering a positive value twists clockwise; entering a negative value twists counterclockwise.

5 ANIMATING A MULTIMEDIA PRESENTATION

Lesson overview

In this lesson, you'll learn how to do the following:

- Create a complex animation with multiple layers.

- Adjust the duration of a layer.

- Animate with Position, Scale, and Rotation keyframes.

- Use parenting to sync the animation of layers.

- Use Bezier curves to smooth a motion path.

- Animate a precomposed layer.

- Apply effects to a solid layer.

- Fade out audio.

 This lesson will take about an hour to complete. Download the Lesson05 project files from the Lesson & Update Files tab on your Account page at www.peachpit.com, if you haven't already done so. As you work on this lesson, you'll preserve the start files. If you need to restore the start files, download them from your Account page.

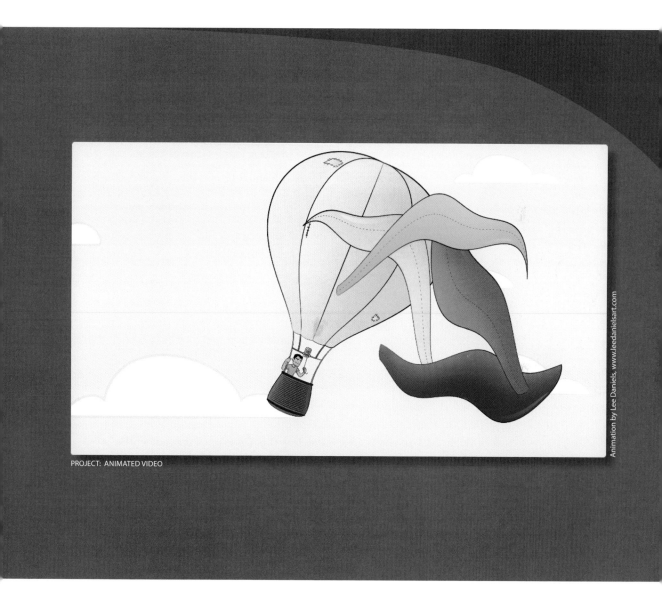

PROJECT: ANIMATED VIDEO

Adobe After Effects projects typically use a variety of imported footage, arranged in a composition, which is edited and animated using the Timeline panel. In this lesson, you'll become more familiar with animation fundamentals as you build a multi-media presentation.

Getting started

In this project, you will animate a hot air balloon floating through the sky. All seems peaceful until a gust of wind blows the balloon's colorful canvas off to cover the clouds.

1 Make sure the following files are in the Lessons/Lesson05 folder on your hard disk, or download them from your Account page at www.peachpit.com now:

 • In the Assets folder: Balloon.ai, Fire.mov, Sky.ai, Soundtrack.wav

 • In the Sample_Movie folder: Lesson05.mov

2 Open and play the Lesson05.mov sample movie to see what you will create in this lesson. When you're done, quit QuickTime Player. You may delete the sample movie from your hard disk if you have limited storage space.

As you start After Effects, restore the default application settings. See "Restoring default preferences" on page 2.

3 Start After Effects, and then immediately hold down Ctrl+Alt+Shift (Windows) or Command+Option+Shift (Mac OS) to restore default preferences settings. When prompted, click OK to delete your preferences.

4 Close the Start window.

5 Choose File > Save As > Save As.

6 In the Save As dialog box, navigate to the Lessons/Lesson05/Finished_Project folder. Name the project **Lesson05_Finished.aep**, and then click Save.

Importing the footage

Next, you'll import the footage you need for the project, including the balloon.ai composition.

1 Double-click an empty area of the Project panel to open the Import File dialog box.

2 Navigate to the Lessons/Lesson05/Assets folder on your hard disk, and select the Sky.ai file.

3 Choose Footage from the Import As menu, and then click Import or Open.

4 In the Sky.ai dialog box, make sure Merged Layers is selected, and then click OK.

5 Double-click an empty area of the Project panel, navigate to the Lessons/Lesson05 /Assets folder, and select the Balloon.ai file.

6 Choose Composition - Retain Layer Sizes from the Import As menu, and click Import or Open.

7 Press Ctrl+I (Windows) or Command+I (Mac OS) to open the Import File dialog box again.

8 Navigate to the Lessons/Lesson05/Assets folder, and select the Fire.mov file.

9 Make sure Footage is chosen in the Import As menu, and click Import or Open.

Using Creative Cloud Libraries in After Effects

Easily access images, videos, colors, and other assets you've created in After Effects and other Adobe applications. Through Creative Cloud Libraries, you can also use Looks, shapes, and other assets you create with Adobe Capture CC and other mobile apps.

Even Adobe Stock images and videos are available in the Libraries panel: Search and browse assets within the panel, download watermarked versions to see how they work with your projects, and license the ones you want to keep—all without leaving After Effects.

The same search bar you use to search Adobe Stock makes it easier to find specific items in your Creative Cloud Libraries, too.

To learn more about all the ways you can use Creative Cloud Libraries, see After Effects Help.

Creating the composition

You'll create the composition and add the sky.

1 Choose Composition > New Composition.

2 In the Composition Settings dialog box, do the following:

 - Name the composition **Balloon Scene**.
 - Choose HDTV 1080 25 from the Preset menu.
 - Make sure Square Pixels is chosen from the Pixel Aspect Ratio menu.
 - Choose Quarter for the Resolution.
 - Set Duration to **20** seconds.
 - Click OK.

3 Drag the Sky.ai footage item from the Project panel into the Timeline panel.

The balloon will float across the Sky.ai image. The far right of the image contains the canvas-wrapped clouds that appear at the end of the scene. The wrapped clouds shouldn't be visible earlier in the movie.

4 In the Composition window, drag the Sky layer so that its lower left corner is even with the lower left corner of the composition.

Adjusting anchor points

The anchor point is the point about which transformations, such as scaling or rotation, are performed. By default, a layer's anchor point is at the center of the layer.

You'll change the anchor points for the character's arm and head so that you can better control the character's movements as he tugs on the cord to ignite the fire, and as he looks up and down.

1 Double-click the Balloon composition in the Project panel to open it in the Composition panel and the Timeline panel.

The Balloon composition includes layers for the canvas colors, the balloon itself, and the character's eyes, head, forearm, and upper arm.

2 Choose 50% from the Magnification Ratio pop-up menu at the bottom of the Composition panel so you can see the balloon's detail more clearly.

3 Select the Hand tool (🖐) in the Tools panel, and then pan so that the character is centered in the Composition panel.

4 Select the Selection tool (➤) in the Tools panel.

5 Select the Upper arm layer in the Timeline panel.

6 Select the Pan Behind tool (✛) in the Tools panel (or press Y to activate it).

With the Pan Behind tool, you can move the anchor point without moving the entire layer in the Composition window.

7 Move the anchor point to the character's shoulder.

8 Select the Forearm layer in the Timeline panel, and then move its anchor point to the elbow.

9 Select the Head layer in the Timeline panel, and move its anchor point to the character's neck.

10 Select the Selection tool in the Tools panel.

11 Choose File > Save to save your work so far.

Parenting layers

This composition includes several layers that need to move together. For example, as the balloon floats, the character's arm and head should move along with it. As you've seen in previous lessons, a parenting relationship synchronizes changes in the parent layer with corresponding changes in the child layer. You'll establish parenting relationships among the layers in this composition, and you'll add the fire video as well.

1 In the Timeline panel, press Ctrl (Windows) or Command (Mac OS) as you select the Head and Upper arm layers.

2 In the Parent column for either of the selected layers, choose 7. Balloon from the pop-up menu.

This establishes both the Head and Upper arm layers as child layers of the Balloon layer. When the Balloon layer moves, the other two layers will move with it.

The eyes not only need to move with the balloon, they need to move with the head, so you'll create that parenting relationship next.

3 In the Parent column for the Eyes layer, choose 6. Head from the pop-up menu.

The forearm should move with the upper arm as well.

4 In the Parent column for the Forearm layer, choose 9. Upper arm from the pop-up menu.

Now you need to ensure that the fire video travels with the balloon.

5 Drag the Fire.mov file from the Project panel to the Timeline panel, positioning it directly below the canvas layers so that the fire will appear to go inside the balloon, rather than outside it. (The Fire layer should be between the Yellow Canvas layer and the Eyes layer.)

The fire video is positioned in the center of the composition, so you'll need to zoom out a bit to see it.

6 Choose 25% from the Magnification Ratio pop-up menu so that you can see the outline of the selected video.

7 In the Composition window, drag the fire video over the burner. To see the flame in action so you can position it correctly, drag the current-time marker across the first second of the time ruler.

8 When you're satisfied with the Fire layer's position, choose 8. Balloon from the pop-up menu in the Fire layer's Parent column.

9 Choose File > Save to save your work so far.

Precomposing layers

Sometimes it's easier to work with a set of layers in a composition. Precomposing layers moves them to a new composition, nested inside the original composition. You'll precompose the canvas layers so that you can work with them separately when you animate them sailing off the balloon.

1 In the Balloon Timeline panel, Shift-click the Green Canvas and Yellow Canvas layers to select all four canvas layers.

2 Choose Layer > Pre-compose.

3 In the Pre-compose dialog box, name the composition **Canvas**, select Move All Attributes Into The New Composition, and click OK.

The four layers you selected in the Timeline panel are replaced by a single Canvas composition layer.

4 Double-click the Canvas layer in the Timeline panel to edit the composition.

5 Choose Composition > Composition Settings.

6 In the Composition Settings dialog box, deselect Lock Aspect Ratio, change the Width value to **5000** px, and click OK.

7 Shift-select all four layers in the Timeline panel, and then drag them to the far left side of the Composition panel. You may need to change the magnification.

Increasing the width of the composition and then moving the canvas to the far left side will give you room to animate the canvas layers later.

8 Switch to the Balloon Timeline panel.

You moved the canvas to the far left side of the Canvas composition, revealing the uncovered balloon in the Balloon composition. At the beginning of the animation, though, the canvas should be *on* the balloon. You'll reposition the Canvas layer.

9 Choose Fit from the Magnification Ratio pop-up menu in the Composition panel so you can see the full balloon.

10 Select the Canvas layer in the Timeline panel, and then drag the layer so that it covers the bare balloon in the Composition panel.

11 In the Parent column of the Canvas layer, choose 5. Balloon from the pop-up menu so that the canvas will follow the balloon.

Keyframing a motion path

Now that all the initial pieces are set up, you're ready to animate the balloon and the character using position and rotation keyframes.

Copying layers into a composition

You've worked with the balloon, character, and fire layers in the Balloon composition. Now, you'll copy those layers into the Balloon Scene composition.

1 In the Balloon Timeline panel, Shift-click the Canvas and Upper arm layers to select all the layers in the composition.

2 Press Ctrl+C (Windows) or Command+C (Mac OS) to copy all the layers.

3 Switch to the Balloon Scene Timeline panel.

4 Press Ctrl+V (Windows) or Command+V (Mac OS) to paste the layers.

5 Click an empty area in the Timeline panel to deselect all layers.

The layers appear in the same order they were when you copied them, and they retain all the properties they had in the Balloon composition, including parenting relationships.

Placing initial keyframes

The balloon will enter the scene from the bottom, drift through the sky, and eventually depart from the upper right corner of the frame. You'll keyframe the balloon's starting and ending points first.

1 Select the Balloon/Balloon.ai layer, and press S to reveal its Scale property.

2 Press Shift+P to display its Position property, and then press Shift+R to display the Rotation property.

3 Change the Scale property to **60**%.

The balloon and all of its child layers scale to 60%.

4 Choose 25% from the Magnification Ratio pop-up menu in the Composition panel so that you can see the pasteboard around the composition.

5 In the Composition panel, drag the balloon and its child layers offscreen, below the scene. (We used Position values 844.5, 2250.2.)

6 Drag the Rotation value to rotate the balloon so it tilts to the right. (We used 19 degrees.)

7 Click the stopwatch icons (🕒) for the Position, Scale, and Rotation properties to create initial keyframes.

8 Go to 14:20.

9 Scale the balloon to about one-third its original size. We used 39.4%.

10 Drag the balloon off the upper right corner of the frame, tilted slightly to the left. We used the following values: Position 2976.5, −185.8; Rotation −8.1 degrees.

11 Move the current-time indicator across the timeline to see the animation so far.

Customizing a motion path

The balloon moves through the scene, but its path isn't very interesting, and it isn't onscreen long. You'll customize the path between its starting point and end point. You can use the values we used or create your own path, as long as the balloon stays fully visible on the screen until a little after 11 seconds, and then slowly makes its way offscreen.

1 Go to 3:00.

2 Drag the balloon straight up so that the character and the basket are fully visible, and then rotate it slightly to the left. (We used Position: 952.5, 402.2; Rotation: −11.1 degrees.)

3 Go to 6:16.

4 Shift the balloon's rotation the other direction. (We used 9.9 degrees.)

5 Move the balloon to the left side of the scene. (We used Position: 531.7, 404.)

6 Go to 7:20.

7 Change the scale to 39.4%.

8 Set additional Rotation keyframes to create swirling motions. If you're using our values, do the following:

- At 8:23, change the Rotation value to **−6.1**.
- At 9:16, change the Rotation value to **22.1**.
- At 10:16, change the Rotation value to **−18.3**.
- At 11:24, change the Rotation value to **11.9**.
- At 14:19, change the Rotation value to **−8.1**.

9 Set additional Position keyframes to move the balloon. If you're using our values, do the following:

- At 9:04, change the Position to **726.5**, **356.2**.
- At 10:12, change the Position to **1396.7**, **537.1**.

10 Press the spacebar key to preview the balloon's current path, and then press the spacebar to stop the preview. Save your work so far.

Using Bezier handles to smooth a motion path

The basic path is in place, but you can smooth it out a bit. Each keyframe includes Bezier handles that you can adjust to change the angle of the curve. You'll learn more about Bezier curves in Lesson 7.

1 Make sure the Balloon/Balloon.ai layer is selected in the Timeline panel.

2 Move the current-time indicator to a position where you can clearly see the motion path in the Composition panel.

3 Click a keyframe point in the Composition panel to reveal its Bezier handles, if they aren't already shown.

4 Drag a Bezier handle to change the curve for that keyframe.

5 Continue to drag Bezier handles for the keyframe points until you achieve the path you want. Our final path is shown below in the image on the right.

6 Preview the balloon on the path by moving the current-time indicator across the time ruler. Make any adjustments you want. You can also make adjustments later, after you've animated the canvas and sky.

7 Hide the properties for the Balloon layer, and save your work so far.

Animating additional elements

The balloon swoops and swirls through the sky, and its child layers go with it. But the character is currently static in his balloon. You'll animate his arm tugging on the cord to ignite the burner.

1 Go to 3:08.

2 Choose 100% from the Magnification Ratio pop-up menu in the Composition window so that you can see the character clearly. Use the Hand tool to adjust the image in the Composition window if you need to.

3 Shift-select the Forearm/Balloon.ai layer and the Upper arm/Balloon.ai layer.

4 Press R to reveal the Rotation property for both layers.

5 Click the stopwatch icon next to one of the Rotation properties to create an initial keyframe for each.

6 Go to 3:17, the point at which the character will tug the cord to ignite the burner.

7 Deselect the layers.

8 Change the Rotation property for the Forearm layer to **−35** and the Rotation property for the Upper arm layer to **46**.

The character tugs the cord down. You may need to deselect the layers so you can see the action clearly in the Composition window.

9 Go to 4:23.

10 Change the Rotation property for the Forearm layer to **−32.8**.

11 Click the Add Or Remove Keyframe At Current Time icon for the Rotation property for the Upper arm layer.

12 Go to 5:06.

13 Change the Rotation value for both layers to **0**.

14 Deselect both layers, and then manually preview from 3:00 to 5:07 to see the character tug the cord. You may need to zoom out to see the animation.

Duplicating keyframes to repeat an animation

Now that you've created the initial movements, you can easily repeat them at different times in the timeline. You'll duplicate the tugging arm, and then create corresponding head and eye movements.

1 Select the Rotation property for the Forearm layer to select all its keyframes.

2 Press Ctrl+C (Windows) or Command+C (Mac OS) to copy the keyframes.

3 Go to 7:10, the point at which the character tugs the cord again.

4 Press Ctrl+V (Windows) or Command+V (Mac OS) to paste the keyframes.

5 Repeat steps 1–4 to copy the Upper arm Rotation property keyframes.

6 Hide the properties for all layers.

7 Select the Head layer, and press R to reveal its Rotation property.

8 Go to 3:08, and click the stopwatch icon to create an initial keyframe.

9 Go to 3:17, and change the Rotation property to **−10.3**.

10 Go to 4:23, and click the Add Or Remove Keyframe At Current Time icon to add a keyframe at the current value.

11 Go to 5:06, and change the Rotation property to **0**.

12 Select the Rotation property to select all of its keyframes, and press Ctrl+C (Windows) or Command+C (Mac OS) to copy them.

13 Go to 7:10, and press Ctrl+V (Windows) or Command+V (Mac OS) to paste them.

14 Press R to hide the Rotation property for the Head layer.

Now the character tilts his head up each time he tugs the cord. You'll also animate the position of his eyes to create a subtle change each time he tilts his head.

15 Select the Eyes layer, and press P to reveal the Position property.

16 Go to 3:08, and click the stopwatch icon to create an initial keyframe at the current value (62, 55).

17 Go to 3:17, and change the Position value to **62.4**, **53**.

18 Go to 4:23, and create a keyframe at the current value.

19 Go to 5:06, and change the Position value to **62**, **55**.

20 Select the Position property to select all its keyframes, and then copy them.

21 Go to 7:10, and paste the keyframes.

22 Hide all layer properties, and then deselect all layers.

23 Choose Fit from the Magnification Ratio pop-up menu in the Composition window so that you can see the entire scene. Then preview the animation.

24 Save your work.

Positioning and duplicating a video

When the character tugs the cord, flame should emerge from the burner. You'll use the four-second Fire.mov video to represent the flame each time the cord is tugged.

1 Go to 3:10.

2 Drag the Fire.mov video in the Timeline panel so that it starts at 3:10.

3 Select the Fire.mov layer, and choose Edit > Duplicate.

4 Go to 7:10.

5 Press the left bracket key ([) on your keyboard to move the In point of the duplicate Fire.mov layer to 7:10.

Applying an effect

Now that the balloon and character are taken care of, you'll create the gust of wind that blows the canvas off the balloon. The Fractal Noise and Directional Blur effects will work well.

Adding a solid-color layer

You need to apply the effects on their own layer, which will be a solid-color layer. You'll create a new composition for the layer.

1 Press Ctrl+N (Windows) or Command+N (Mac OS) to create a new composition.

2 In the Composition Settings dialog box, do the following:

- Name the composition **Wind**.
- Make sure the width is **1920** px.
- Make sure the height is **1080** px.
- Make sure the duration is **20** seconds.
- Make sure the Frame Rate is 25 fps to match the Balloon Scene composition.
- Click OK.

3 Right-click in the Timeline panel, and choose New > Solid.

4 In the Solid Settings dialog box, do the following:

 • Name the layer **Wind**.

 • Select black for the color.

 • Click the Make Comp Size button.

 • Click OK.

About solid-color layers

You can create solid images of any color or size (up to 30,000 x 30,000 pixels) in After Effects. After Effects treats solids as it does any other footage item: You can modify the mask, transform properties, and apply effects to a solid layer. If you change settings for a solid that is used by more than one layer, you can apply the changes to all layers that use the solid or to only the single occurrence of the solid. Use solid layers to color a background or to create simple graphic images.

Applying the effects

You're ready to apply the effects to the solid layer. The Fractal Noise effect will create the gust of wind. The Directional Blur effect will create a blur in the direction the canvas flies.

1. In the Effects & Presets panel, search for the Fractal Noise effect; it's in the Noise & Grain category. Double-click the Fractal Noise effect to apply it.

2. In the Effect Controls panel, do the following:

 - Choose Smeary for the Fractal Type.

 - Choose Soft Linear for the Noise Type.

 - Set the Contrast to **700**.

 - Set the Brightness to **59**.

 - Expand the Transform properties, and set the Scale to **800**.

3. Click the stopwatch next to Offset Turbulence to create an initial keyframe at the beginning of the time ruler.

4. Go to 2:00, and change the x value for Offset Turbulence to **20,000** px.

5. Hide the Fractal Noise properties in the Effect Controls panel.

6. In the Effects & Presets panel, search for the Directional Blur effect, and then double-click it to apply it.

7. In the Effect Controls panel, set the Direction to **90** degrees and the Blur Length to **236**.

You've created a sense of motion. Now you need to add the Wind composition to the Balloon Scene composition.

8 Switch to the Balloon Scene Timeline panel.

9 Drag the Wind composition from the Project window into the Balloon Scene Timeline above all the other layers.

10 Go to 8:10, and then press the left bracket key ([) so that the Wind layer starts at 8:10.

Finally, you'll apply a blending mode and adjust the opacity to make the effect of the wind more subtle.

11 Click Toggle Switches/Modes at the bottom of the Timeline panel to view the Mode column.

12 Choose Screen from the Wind layer's Mode pop-up menu.

13 Press T to reveal the Opacity property for the Wind layer, and then click the stopwatch to create an initial keyframe at the beginning of the layer (8:10).

14 Go to 8:20, and change the opacity to **35**%.

15 Go to 10:20, and change the opacity to **0**%.

16 Press T to hide the Opacity property, and then save your work so far.

Animating precomposed layers

Earlier, you precomposed the four canvas layers, creating a composition called Canvas. You then positioned the Canvas composition layer to match the balloon, and parented the two. Now, you'll animate the canvas layers so that they blow off the balloon when the gust of wind occurs.

1 Double-click the Canvas layer to open the Canvas composition in the Composition panel and the Timeline panel.

2 Go to 9:10, which is about a second after the wind effect begins.

3 Shift-select all four layers, and then press R to display their Rotation properties; press Shift+P to display the Position properties, too.

4 With all layers still selected, click the stopwatch icons for the Position and Rotation properties in one of the layers to create initial keyframes for all of them.

5 Go to 9:24.

6 With all layers still selected, drag a Rotation value until the canvas is nearly horizontal (about 81 degrees). All four canvas layers become nearly horizontal.

7 Press F2 or click an empty area in the Timeline panel to deselect all areas so you can adjust their Rotation values separately.

8 Adjust each Rotation value, using positive and negative numbers so that there is some variation in their appearance. (We used these values: Green: +100, Red: −74, Blue: +113, Yellow: −103.)

9 Go to 10:12.

10 Move all the canvas layers off the screen to the right. Vary their motion paths to make them more interesting. You can add intermediate rotation and position keyframes (between 10:06 and 10:12), edit Bezier curves, or just drag the canvas layers off the edge. If you edit the Bezier curves, make changes only to the keyframes on the right side of the motion path (at 10:12) so you don't disturb the original balloon formation.

11 Move the current-time indicator across the time ruler to preview the animation, and then make any adjustments you want.

12 Hide the properties for all layers, and save your work.

Adding an adjustment layer

You'll add a warp effect to the canvas. You can use an adjustment layer to apply an effect to all the layers beneath it at once.

1 Click an empty area in the Timeline panel to deselect all layers.

2 Choose Layer > New > Adjustment Layer.

A new adjustment layer is automatically added to the top of the layer stack.

3 In the Effects & Presets panel, navigate to the Wave Warp effect in the Distort category, and then double-click the effect.

4 Go to 9:12.

5 In the Effect Controls panel, change Wave Height to **0** and Wave Width to **1**. Then click the stopwatch icons to create initial keyframes for each of them.

6 Go to 9:16.

7 Change the Wave Height value to **90** and the Wave Width value to **478**.

Trimming a layer

You don't need the Wave Warp effect until the canvas flies off the balloon, but even if the values are 0, After Effects will have to calculate the effect for the entire layer. So you'll trim the layer to speed up the time it takes to render the file.

1 Go to 9:12.

2 Press Alt+[(Windows) or Option+[(Mac OS) to set the In point to **9:12**.

3 Return to the Balloon Scene Timeline panel.

4 Press the spacebar to preview the movie. Press the spacebar again to stop the preview.

5 Save your work so far.

> **Note:** Press [to move the In point of a clip without changing its duration. Press Alt+[or Option+[to trim a clip to a new In point, shortening its duration.

Animating the background

The movie should end with the revelation that the canvas from the balloons has been draped on the clouds. But right now, the canvas flies off and the balloon floats away. You need to animate the sky so that the canvas-covered clouds are centered at the end of the scene.

1 In the Balloon Scene Timeline panel, go to the beginning of the time ruler (0:00).

2 Select the Sky layer, and press P to display its Position property.

3 Click the stopwatch icon to create an initial keyframe.

4 Go to 16:00, and drag the Sky layer until the wrapped clouds are in the center of the frame. (Our values are −236.4, 566.7.)

5 Go to 8:00, and move the wrapped clouds completely off the screen, far off to the right.

6 Right-click the first keyframe, and choose Keyframe Assistant > Easy Ease Out.

7 Right-click the middle keyframe, and choose Keyframe Assistant > Easy Ease, and then right-click the last keyframe, and choose Keyframe Assistant > Easy Ease In.

8 Move the current-time indicator through the time ruler to see how the canvas' departure matches up with the appearance of the canvas-colored clouds. The canvas should be completely offscreen before the canvas-colored clouds appear.

9 Move the middle keyframe forward and backward in the time ruler to adjust the sky animation so that it matches the progress of the canvas and the balloon. The bare balloon should float in front of at least a few of the canvas-colored clouds before it disappears.

10 Press the spacebar to preview the entire video. Press the spacebar again to stop the preview.

11 Adjust the motion paths and rotations for the balloon, canvas pieces, or the sky as necessary.

12 Hide the properties for all layers, and save the project.

Adding an audio track

Give yourself a hand—you've done a lot of animating in this project. But you're not quite done. You'll add a soundtrack that matches the lighthearted mood of the video, and fade it out. You'll also shorten the composition, since the last few seconds are static.

1 Double-click an empty area of the Project panel to open the Import File dialog box.

2 Navigate to the Lessons/Lesson05/Assets folder, and double-click the Soundtrack.wave file.

3 Drag the Soundtrack.wav item from the Project panel into the Balloon Scene Timeline panel, placing it at the bottom of the layer stack.

4 Preview the movie. The music changes just as the canvas flies off the balloon.

5 Go to 18:00, and press N to move the work area end point to the current time.

6 Choose Composition > Trim Comp to Work Area.

7 Go to 16:00. Expand the Soundtrack.wav layer and the Audio properties.

8 Click the stopwatch icon to create an initial keyframe for Audio Levels value.

9 Go to 18:00, and change the Audio Levels value to **–40** dB.

10 Preview the animation, and then save it.

Congratulations. You've just created a complex animation, practicing all kinds of After Effects techniques and capabilities along the way.

Supported audio file formats

You can import any of the following types of audio files into After Effects:

- Adobe Sound Document (ASND; multitrack files import as merged single track)
- Advanced Audio Coding (AAC, M4A)
- Audio Interchange File Format (AIF, AIFF)
- MP3 (MP3, MPEG, MPG, MPA, MPE)
- Video for Windows (AVI, WAV; requires QuickTime on Mac OS)
- Waveform (WAV)

Editing audio files in Adobe Audition

You can make some very simple changes to audio in After Effects. For more substantial edits, use Adobe Audition. Audition is available with a full Adobe Creative Cloud membership.

You can use Audition to change the length of an audio file, alter its pitch, or change its tempo. You can apply effects, record new audio, mix multitrack sessions, and more.

To edit an audio clip you've used in After Effects, select the file in the Project panel, and choose Edit > Edit In Adobe Audition. Then, make your changes in Audition, and save the file. The changes you made are automatically reflected in your After Effects project.

Review questions

1 How does After Effects display an animation of the Position property?

2 What is a solid-color layer, and what can you do with it?

3 What types of audio can you import into an After Effects project?

Review answers

1 When you animate the Position property, After Effects displays the movement as a motion path. You can create a motion path for the position of the layer or for the anchor point of a layer. A position motion path appears in the Composition panel; an anchor-point motion path appears in the Layer panel. The motion path appears as a sequence of dots, where each dot marks the position of the layer at each frame. A box in the path marks the position of a keyframe.

2 You can create solid images of any color or size (up to 30,000 x 30,000 pixels) in After Effects. After Effects treats solids as it does any other footage item: You can modify the mask, transform properties, and apply effects to the solid layer. If you change settings for a solid that is used by more than one layer, you can apply the changes to all layers that use the solid or to only the single occurrence of the solid. Use solid layers to color a background or create simple graphic images.

3 You can import any of the following types of audio files into After Effects: Adobe Sound Document (ASND; multitrack files import as merged single track), Advanced Audio Coding (AAC, M4A), Audio Interchange File Format (AIF, AIFF), MP3 (MP3, MPEG, MPG, MPA, MPE), Video for Windows (AVI, WAV; requires QuickTime on Mac OS), and Waveform (WAV).

6 ANIMATING LAYERS

Lesson overview

In this lesson, you'll learn how to do the following:

- Animate a layered Adobe Photoshop file.

- Duplicate an animation using the pick whip.

- Work with imported Photoshop layer styles.

- Apply a track matte to control the visibility of layers.

- Animate a layer using the Corner Pin effect.

- Apply the Lens Flare effect to a solid layer.

- Use time remapping and the Layer panel to dynamically retime footage.

- Edit Time Remap keyframes in the Graph Editor.

 This lesson will take approximately an hour to complete. Download the Lesson06 project files from the Lesson & Update Files tab on your Account page at www.peachpit.com, if you haven't already done so. As you work on this lesson, you'll preserve the start files. If you need to restore the start files, download them from your Account page.

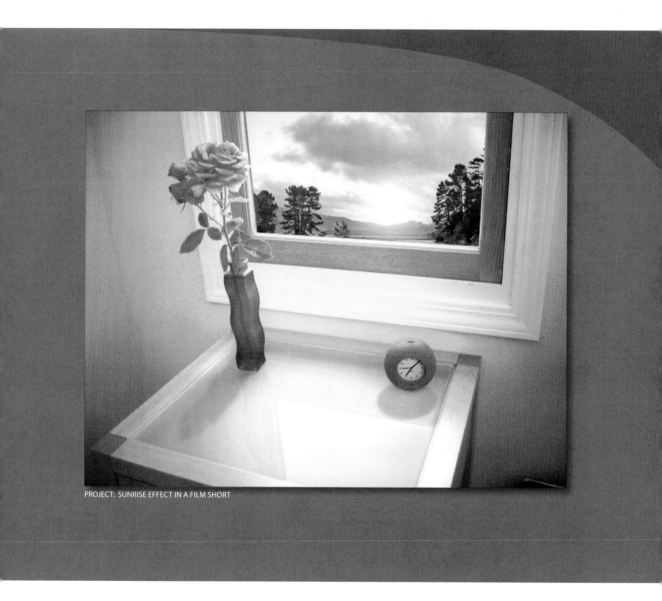

PROJECT: SUNRISE EFFECT IN A FILM SHORT

Animation is all about making changes over time —
changes to an object or image's position, opacity, scale,
and other properties. This lesson provides more practice
animating the layers of a Photoshop file, including
dynamically remapping time.

143

Getting started

Adobe After Effects provides several tools and effects that let you simulate motion video using a layered Photoshop file. In this lesson, you will import a layered Photoshop file of the sun appearing through a window, and then animate it to simulate the motion of the sun rising behind the panes of glass. This is a stylized animation in which the motion is first accelerated, and then slows down as clouds and birds move through the window frame at the end.

First, you'll preview the final movie and set up the project.

1 Make sure the following files are in the Lessons/Lesson06 folder on your hard disk, or download them from your Account page at www.peachpit.com now:

 • In the Assets folder: clock.mov, sunrise.psd

 • In the Sample_Movies folder: Lesson06_regular.mov, Lesson06_retimed.mov

2 Open and play the Lesson06_regular.mov file to see the straightforward time-lapse animation you will create in this lesson.

3 Open and play the Lesson06_retimed.mov file to see the same animation after time has been remapped, which you will also do in this lesson.

4 When you're done, quit QuickTime Player. You may delete the sample movies from your hard disk if you have limited storage space.

When you begin the lesson, restore the default application settings for After Effects. See "Restoring default preferences" on page 2.

5 Start After Effects, and then immediately hold down Ctrl+Alt+Shift (Windows) or Command+Option+Shift (Mac OS) to restore default preferences settings. When prompted, click OK to delete your preferences file. Then, close the Start window.

After Effects opens to display an empty, untitled project.

6 Choose File > Save As > Save As.

7 In the Save As dialog box, navigate to the Lessons/Lesson06/Finished_ Project folder.

8 Name the project **Lesson06_Finished.aep**, and then click Save.

Importing the footage

You need to import one source item for this lesson.

1 Double-click an empty area of the Project panel to open the Import File dialog box.

2 Navigate to the Lessons/Lesson06/Assets folder on your hard disk, and select the sunrise.psd file.

3 Choose Composition – Retain Layer Sizes from the Import As menu, so the dimensions of each layer will match the layer's content.

4 Click Import or Open.

5 In the Sunrise.psd dialog box, make sure Composition – Retain Layer Sizes is selected in the Import Kind menu, and click OK.

Before continuing, take a moment to study the layers of the file you just imported.

6 In the Project panel, expand the sunrise Layers folder to see the Photoshop layers. Resize the Name column to make it wider and easier to read, if necessary.

Each of the elements you'll animate in After Effects—the shadows, birds, clouds, and sun—is on a separate layer. In addition, there is one layer representing the initial, predawn lighting conditions in the room (Background), and a second layer that represents the final, bright daylight conditions in the room (Background Lit). Similarly, there are two layers for the two lighting conditions outside the window: Window and Window Lit. The Window Pane layer includes a Photoshop layer style that simulates a pane of glass.

After Effects preserves the layer order, transparency data, and layer styles from the source Photoshop document. It also preserves other features, such as adjustment layers and type, which you don't happen to be using in this project.

Preparing layered Photoshop files

Before you import a layered Photoshop file, name its layers carefully to reduce preview and rendering time, and to avoid problems importing and updating the layers:

- Organize and name layers. If you change a layer name in a Photoshop file after you have imported it into After Effects, After Effects retains the link to the original layer. However, if you delete an imported layer, After Effects will be unable to find the original layer and will list it as missing in the Project panel.

- To avoid confusion, make sure that each layer has a unique name.

Creating the composition

For this lesson, you'll use the imported Photoshop file as the basis of the composition.

1 Double-click the sunrise composition in the Project panel to open it in the Composition panel and in the Timeline panel.

2 Choose Composition > Composition Settings.

3 In the Composition Settings dialog box, change the Duration to **10:00** to make the composition 10 seconds long, and then click OK.

About Photoshop layer styles

Adobe Photoshop provides a variety of layer styles—such as shadows, glows, and bevels—that change the appearance of a layer. After Effects can preserve these layer styles when you import Photoshop layers. You can also apply layer styles in After Effects.

Though layer styles are referred to as *effects* in Photoshop, they behave more like blending modes in After Effects. Layer styles follow transformations in the standard render order, whereas effects precede transformations. Another difference is that each layer style blends directly with the underlying layers in the composition, whereas an effect is rendered on the layer to which it's applied, the result of which then interacts with the underlying layers as a whole.

The layer style properties are available for the layer in the Timeline panel.

To learn more about working with layer styles in After Effects, see After Effects Help.

Simulating lighting changes

The first part of the animation involves lightening the dark room. You'll use Opacity keyframes to animate the light.

1 In the Timeline panel, click the Solo switch (●) for both the Background Lit and Background layers.

Soloing the layers isolates them to speed animating, previewing, and rendering.

Currently, the lit background is on top of the regular (darker) background, obscuring it and making the initial frame of the animation light. However, you want the animation to start dark, and then lighten. To accomplish this, you will make the Background Lit layer initially transparent, and then animate its opacity so that it appears to lighten the background over time.

2 Go to 5:00.

3 Select the Background Lit layer in the Timeline panel, and press T to reveal its Opacity property.

4 Click the stopwatch icon (⏱) to set an Opacity keyframe. Note that the Opacity value is 100%.

5 Press the Home key, or drag the current-time indicator to 0:00. Then set the Opacity for the Background Lit layer to **0%**. After Effects adds a keyframe.

Now, when the animation begins, the Background Lit layer is transparent, which allows the dark Background layer to show through.

6 Click the Solo switches (●) for the Background Lit and Background layers to restore the view of the other layers, including Window and Window Lit. Make sure to leave the Opacity property for the Background Lit layer visible.

7 Expand the Window Pane layer's Transform properties. The Window Pane layer has a Photoshop layer style that creates a bevel on the window.

8 Go to 2:00, and click the stopwatch next to the Opacity property for the Window Pane layer to create a keyframe at the current value, 30%.

9 Press the Home key or drag the current-time indicator to the beginning of the time ruler, and change the Opacity property to **0%**.

10 Hide the Window Pane properties.

11 Click the Play/Pause button (▶) in the Preview panel, or press the spacebar, to preview the animation.

The interior of the room transitions gently from dimly to brightly lit.

12 Press the spacebar to stop playback at any time after 5:00.

13 Choose File > Save.

About expressions

When you want to create and link complex animations, such as multiple car wheels spinning, but want to avoid creating tens or hundreds of keyframes by hand, you can use *expressions* instead. With expressions, you can create relationships between layer properties and use one property's keyframes to dynamically animate another layer. For example, if you set rotation keyframes for a layer and then apply the Drop Shadow effect, you can use an expression to link the Rotation property's values with the Drop Shadow effect's Direction values; that way, the drop shadow changes with the layer as it rotates.

Expressions are based on the JavaScript language, but you don't need to know JavaScript to use them. You can create expressions by using simple examples and modifying them to suit your needs, or by chaining objects and methods together.

You work with expressions in the Timeline panel or the Effect Controls panel. You can use the pick whip to create expressions, or you can enter and edit expressions manually in the expression field—a text field in the time graph under the property.

For more about expressions, see After Effects Help.

Duplicating an animation using the pick whip

Now you need to lighten the view through the window. To do this, you'll use the pick whip to duplicate the animation you just created. You can use the pick whip to create expressions that link the values of one property or effect to another.

1 Press the Home key, or move the current-time indicator to the beginning of the time ruler.

2 Select the Window Lit layer, and press T to reveal its Opacity property.

3 Alt-click (Windows) or Option-click (Mac OS) the Opacity stopwatch for the Window Lit layer to add an expression for the default Opacity value, 100%. The words *transform.opacity* appear in the time ruler for the Window Lit layer.

4 Click the pick whip icon (◎) on the Window Lit Expression: Opacity line, and drag it to the Opacity property name in the Background Lit layer. When you release the mouse, the pick whip snaps, and the expression in the Window Lit layer time ruler now reads "`thisComp.layer("Background Lit").transform.opacity`." This means that the Opacity value for the Background Lit layer (0%) replaces the previous Opacity value (100%) for the Window Lit layer.

5 Drag the current-time indicator from 0:00 to 5:00. Notice that the Opacity values for the two layers match.

6 Go to the beginning of the time ruler, and then press the spacebar to preview the animation again. Notice that the sky outside the window lightens as the room inside the window does.

7 Press the spacebar to stop playback.

8 Hide the Window Lit and Background Lit layers' properties to keep the Timeline panel tidy for your next task.

9 Choose File > Save to save your project.

Animating movement in the scenery

The scenery outside the window is unrealistically static. For one thing, the sun should actually rise. In addition, shifting clouds and flying birds would bring this scene to life.

Animating the sun

To make the sun rise in the sky, you'll set keyframes for its Position, Scale, and Opacity properties.

1 In the Timeline panel, select the Sun layer, and expand its Transform properties.

2 Go to 4:07, and click the stopwatch icons (⏱) to set keyframes for the Position, Scale, and Opacity properties at their default values.

3 Go to 3:13.

4 Still working with the Sun layer, set its Scale to **33, 33%** and its Opacity to **10%**. After Effects adds a keyframe for each property.

5 Press the End key, or move the current-time indicator to the end of the composition.

6 For the Position property of the Sun layer, set the y value to **18**, and then set the Scale values to **150**, **150%**. After Effects adds two keyframes.

You've just set keyframes that instruct the sun to move up and across the sky, and to become slightly larger and brighter as it rises.

7 Hide the Sun layer's properties.

Animating the birds

Next, you'll animate the motion of the birds flying by. To create the animation faster, you'll take advantage of the Auto-Keyframe option. When Auto-Keyframe is enabled, After Effects automatically creates a keyframe whenever you change a value.

1 Select the Birds layer in the Timeline panel, and press P to reveal its Position property.

2 From the Timeline panel menu, choose Enable Auto-Keyframe.

A red stopwatch icon appears at the top of the Timeline panel to remind you that Auto-Keyframe is selected.

3 Go to 4:20, and set the Position values for the Birds layer to **200**, **49**. After Effects automatically adds a keyframe.

Note: While the Auto-Keyframe option can make your life easier, it can also create more keyframes than you intended. Choose Enable Auto-Keyframe only when you need it for a specific task, and remember to disable it when you're done with that task!

4 Go to 4:25, and set the Position values of the Birds layer to **670, 49**. After Effects adds a keyframe.

5 Select the Birds layer, and press P to hide its Position property.

Animating the clouds

Next, you'll animate the clouds drifting across the sky.

1 Select the Clouds layer in the Timeline panel, and expand its Transform properties.

2 Go to 5:22, and click the stopwatch icon (⏱) for the Position property to set a Position keyframe at the current value (406.5, 58.5).

3 Still at 5:22, set the Opacity for the Clouds layer to **33%**.

After Effects automatically adds a keyframe, because Auto-Keyframe is still enabled.

4 Choose Enable Auto-Keyframe from the Timeline panel menu to deselect it.

5 Go to 5:02, and set the Clouds layer Opacity value to **0%**.

After Effects adds a keyframe, even though you disabled Auto-Keyframe. After Effects adds a keyframe whenever you change the value for a property that already has a keyframe in the timeline.

6 Go to 9:07, and set the Clouds layer Opacity value to **50%**. After Effects adds a keyframe.

7 Press the End key, or move the current-time indicator to the last frame of the composition.

8 Set the Position of the Clouds layer to **456.5**, **48.5**. After Effects adds a keyframe.

Previewing the animation

Now, see how it all comes together.

1 Press the Home key, or go to 0:00.

2 Press F2 or click an empty area in the Timeline panel to deselect everything, and then press the spacebar to preview the animation.

The sun rises in the sky, the birds fly by (very quickly), and the clouds drift. So far, so good! However, there's a fundamental problem: These elements all overlap the window frame—the birds even appear to be flying inside the room. You'll solve this next.

3 Press the spacebar to stop playback.

4 Hide the properties for the Clouds layer, and then choose File > Save.

Adjusting the layers and creating a track matte

To solve the problem of the sun, birds, and clouds overlapping the window frame, you must first adjust the hierarchy of the layers within the composition. Then you'll use an alpha track matte to allow the outside scenery to show through the window, but not appear to be inside the room.

Precomposing layers

You'll start by precomposing the Sun, Birds, and Clouds layers into one composition.

1 Shift-click to select the Sun, Birds, and Clouds layers in the Timeline panel.

2 Choose Layer > Pre-compose.

3 In the Pre-compose dialog box, name the new composition **Window Contents**. Make sure the Move All Attributes Into The New Composition option is selected, and select Open New Composition. Then click OK.

A new Timeline panel named Window Contents appears. It contains the Sun, Birds, and Clouds layers you selected in step 1 above. The Window Contents composition also appears in the Composition window.

4 Click the sunrise Timeline panel to see the contents of the main composition. Notice that the Sun, Birds, and Clouds layers have been replaced by the Window Contents layer, which refers to the Window Contents composition.

Creating the track matte

Now, you will create the track matte to hide the outside scenery behind all areas of the image except the windowpane. To do that, you'll duplicate the Window Lit layer and use its alpha channel.

About track mattes and traveling mattes

When you want one layer to show through a hole in another layer, set up a *track matte*. You'll need two layers—one to act as a matte, the other to fill the hole in the matte. You can animate either the track matte layer or the fill layer. When you animate the track matte layer, you create a *traveling matte*. If you want to animate the track matte and fill layers using identical settings, you can precompose them.

You define transparency in a track matte using values from either its alpha channel or the luminance of its pixels. Using luminance is handy when you want to create a track matte from a layer without an alpha channel, or a layer imported from a program that can't create an alpha channel. In both alpha-channel mattes and luminance mattes, pixels with higher values are more transparent. In most cases, you use a high-contrast matte so that areas are either completely transparent or completely opaque. Intermediate shades should appear only where you want partial or gradual transparency, such as along a soft edge.

After Effects preserves the order of a layer and its track matte after you duplicate or split the layer. Within the duplicated or split layers, the track matte layer remains on top of the fill layer. For example, if your project contains layers X and Y, where X is the track matte and Y the fill layer, duplicating or splitting both of these layers results in the layer order XYXY.

<p style="text-align:center">A B C</p>

Anatomy of a traveling matte
A. Track matte layer: a solid with a rectangular mask, set to Luma Matte. The mask is animated to travel across the screen.
B. Fill layer: a solid with a pattern effect.
C. Result: The pattern is seen in the track matte's shape and added to the image layer, which is below the track matte layer.

1 In the sunrise Timeline panel, select the Window Lit layer.

2 Choose Edit > Duplicate.

3 Drag the duplicate layer, Window Lit 2, up in the layer stack so that it's above the Window Contents layer.

4 Click Toggle Switches/Modes in the Timeline panel to display the TrkMat column, so you can apply the track matte.

5 Select the Window Contents layer, and choose Alpha Matte "Window Lit 2" from the TrkMat pop-up menu.

The alpha channel of the layer above (Window Lit 2) is used to set transparency for the Window Contents layer, so the scenery outside the window shows through the transparent areas of the windowpane.

6 Press the Home key or move the current-time indicator to the beginning of the time ruler, and then press the spacebar to preview the animation. Press the spacebar again when you're done.

7 Choose File > Save to save your project.

Adding motion blur

The birds will look more authentic if they include motion blur. You'll add the motion blur and then set the shutter angle and phase, which control the intensity of the blur.

1 Switch to the Window Contents Timeline panel.

2 Go to 4:22—the middle of the birds' animation. Then select the Birds layer, and choose Layer > Switches > Motion Blur to turn on motion blur for the layer.

3 Click the Enable Motion Blur button () at the top of the Timeline panel to display the motion blur for the Birds layer in the Composition panel.

4 Choose Composition > Composition Settings.

5 In the Composition Settings dialog box, click the Advanced tab, and reduce the Shutter Angle to **30** degrees.

The Shutter Angle setting imitates the effect of adjusting a shutter angle on a real camera, which controls how long the camera aperture is open, gathering light. Larger values create more motion blur.

6 Change the Shutter Phase to **0** degrees, and then click OK.

Animating the shadows

It's time to turn your attention to the shadows cast on the table by the clock and the vase. In a realistic time-lapse image, those shadows would shorten as the sun rises.

There are a few ways to create and animate shadows in After Effects. For example, you could use 3D layers and lights. In this project, however, you'll use the Corner Pin effect to distort the Shadows layer of the imported Photoshop image. Using the Corner Pin effect is like animating with the Photoshop Free Transform tool—the effect distorts an image by repositioning each of its four corners. You can use it to stretch, shrink, skew, or twist an image, or to simulate perspective or movement that pivots from the edge of a layer, such as a door opening.

1 Switch to the sunrise Timeline panel, and make sure you're at the beginning of the time ruler.

● **Note:** If you don't see the controls, choose View Options from the Composition panel menu. In the View Options dialog box, select the Handles and Effect Controls options, and then click OK.

2 Select the Shadows layer in the Timeline panel, and then choose Effect > Distort > Corner Pin. Small circles appear around the corner points of the Shadows layer in the Composition panel.

You'll start by setting the four corners of the Shadows layer to correspond to the four corners of the glass tabletop. Begin about midway into the animation, when the sun is high enough to start affecting the shadow.

▶ **Tip:** The lower right corner of the Shadows layer is offscreen. To adjust that corner, switch to the Hand tool (🖐), and drag up in the Composition panel so that you can see some of the pasteboard below the image. Then switch back to the Selection tool (▶), and drag the lower right corner-pin handle to the approximate location of the lower right corner of the glass tabletop.

3 Go to 6:00, and then drag each of the four corner-pin handles to the respective corners of the glass tabletop. Notice that the x and y coordinates update in the Effect Controls panel.

If you have trouble getting the shadows to look right, you can manually enter the values shown in the figure that follows step 4.

4 Set a keyframe for each corner at 6:00 by clicking the stopwatch icon (⏱) for each position in the Effect Controls panel.

5 Press the End key, or move the current-time indicator to the last frame of the composition.

6 Using the Selection tool (▶), shorten the shadows: Drag the two lower corner-pins about 25% closer to the back edge of the tabletop. You may also need to move the two upper corners in slightly so that the bases of the shadows still align properly with the vase and the clock. Your corner-pin values should be similar to those in the figure below; you can enter the values directly if you prefer not to drag the corners. After Effects adds keyframes.

7 If necessary, select the Hand tool (✋), and drag the composition down to center it vertically in the Composition panel. Then switch back to the Selection tool, and deselect the layer.

8 Go to 0:00, and then press the spacebar to preview the entire animation, including the corner-pin effect. When you're done, press the spacebar again.

9 Choose File > Save to save your project.

Adding a lens flare effect

In photography, when bright light (such as sunlight) reflects off the lens of a camera, it causes a flare effect. Lens flares can be bright, colorful circles and halos, depending on the type of lens in the camera. After Effects offers a few lens flare effects. You'll add one now to enhance the realism of this time-lapse photography composition.

1 Go to 5:10, where the sun is shining brightly into the lens of the camera.

2 With no layers selected in the Timeline panel, choose Layer > New > Solid.

3 In the Solid Settings dialog box, name the layer **Lens Flare,** and click the Make Comp Size button. Then set the Color to black by clicking the swatch and setting all the RGB values to 0 in the Solid Color dialog box. Click OK to return to the Solid Settings dialog box.

4 Click OK to create the Lens Flare layer.

5 With the Lens Flare layer selected in the sunrise Timeline panel, choose Effect > Generate > Lens Flare.

The Composition panel and the Effect Controls panel display the visual and numeric default Lens Flare settings, respectively; you'll customize the effect for this composition.

6 Drag the Flare Center cross-hairs icon (⊕) in the Composition panel to the center of the sun. You cannot see the sun in the Composition panel; the x, y coordinates, which you can read in the Effect Controls or Info panel, are approximately 455, 135.

Tip: You can also enter the Flare Center values directly in the Effect Controls panel.

7 In the Effect Controls panel, change the Lens Type to 35mm Prime, a more diffuse flare effect.

8 Make sure you're still at 5:10. In the Effect Controls panel, click the stopwatch icon (⏱) for the Flare Brightness property to set a keyframe at the default value of 100%.

9 Adjust the brightness of the lens flare to peak when the sun is highest:

 • Go to 3:27, and set the Flare Brightness value to **0%**.

 • Go to 6:27, and set the Flare Brightness value to **0%**, also.

 • Go to 6:00, and set the Flare Brightness to **100%**.

10 With the Lens Flare layer selected in the Timeline panel, choose Layer > Blending Mode > Screen to change the blending mode.

Tip: You can also choose Screen from the Mode pop-up menu in the Timeline panel.

11 Press the Home key or move the current-time indicator to the beginning of the time ruler, and then press the spacebar to preview the Lens Flare effect. When you're done, press the spacebar again.

12 Choose File > Save to save your project.

Adding a video animation

● **Note:** You'll learn more about 3D layers in Lessons 11, "Using 3D Features," and 12, "Working with the 3D Camera Tracker."

The animation now looks very much like a time-lapse photo—except the clock isn't working yet! The hands of the clock should be spinning quickly to show the progress of time. To show this, you will add an animation that was created specifically for this scene. The animation was created in After Effects as a set of 3D layers that are lit, textured, and masked to blend into the scene.

1 Bring the Project panel forward. Close the sunrise Layers folder, and then double-click an empty area in the panel to open the Import File dialog box.

2 In the Lessons/Lesson06/Assets folder, select the clock.mov file, and click Import or Open.

The QuickTime movie clock.mov now appears at the top of the Project panel.

3 Click in the sunrise Timeline panel to make it active, and then go to the beginning of the time ruler. Drag the clock.mov footage item from the Project panel to the top of the layer stack in the Timeline panel.

4 Preview the animation by pressing the spacebar. Press the spacebar again to stop playback when you're done.

5 Choose File > Save to save the project.

Rendering the animation

To prepare for the next task—retiming the composition—you need to render the sunrise composition and export it as a movie.

1 Select the sunrise composition in the Project panel, and then choose Composition > Add To Render Queue.

The Render Queue panel opens. Depending on the size of your screen, you may need to maximize the panel to see all the settings.

2 (Optional) Choose Panel Group Settings > Maximize Panel Group from the Render Queue panel menu to make the panel larger.

3 Accept the default Render Settings in the Render Queue panel. Then click the blue, italicized words *Not Yet Specified* next to the Output To pop-up menu.

4 Navigate to the Lessons/Lesson06/Assets folder, and name the file **Lesson06_ retime.avi** (Windows) or **Lesson06_retime.mov** (Mac OS). Then click Save.

5 Expand the Output Module group, and then choose Import from the Post-Render Action menu. After Effects will import the movie file after it's rendered.

6 Hide the Output Module section.

7 Click the Render button in the Render Queue panel.

After Effects displays a progress bar as it renders and exports the composition, and plays an audio alert when it is finished. It also imports the resulting movie file into the project.

8 When After Effects has finished rendering and exporting the composition, choose Panel Group Settings > Restore Panel Group Size from the Render Queue panel menu if you maximized the panel earlier, and then close the Render Queue panel.

Retiming the composition

▶ **Tip:** You can get even finer control with the Timewarp effect, which you'll use in Lesson 13, "Advanced Editing Techniques."

So far, you have created a straightforward time-lapse simulation. That's fine, but After Effects offers more ways to play with time using the time-remapping feature. Time remapping lets you dynamically speed up, slow down, stop, or reverse footage. You can also use it to do things like create a freeze-frame result. The Graph Editor and the Layer panel are a big help when remapping time, as you'll see in the following exercise, when you retime the project so that the time-lapse speed changes over the course of the movie.

For this exercise, you'll use the movie that you just imported as the basis of a new composition, which will be easier to remap than the original.

1 Drag the Lesson06_retime movie onto the Create A New Composition button (■) at the bottom of the Project panel.

After Effects creates a new composition named Lesson06_retime, and displays it in the Timeline and Composition panels. Now you can remap all of the elements of the project at once.

2 With the Lesson06_retime layer selected in the Timeline panel, choose Layer > Time > Enable Time Remapping.

After Effects adds two keyframes, at the first and last frames of the layer, visible in the time ruler. A Time Remap property also appears under the layer name in the Timeline panel; this property lets you control which frame is displayed at a given point in time.

3 Double-click the Lesson06_retime layer name in the Timeline panel to open it in the Layer panel.

The Layer panel provides a visual reference of the frames you change when you remap time. It displays two time rulers: The time ruler at the bottom of the panel displays the current time. The Source Time ruler, just above the time ruler, has a remap-time marker that indicates which frame is playing at the current time.

4 Drag the current-time indicator across the time ruler in the Timeline panel, and notice that the source-time and current-time markers in the two Layer panel rulers are synchronized. That will change as you remap time.

5 Go to 4:00, and change the Time Remap value to **2:00**.

This remaps time so that frame 2:00 plays at 4:00. In other words, the composition now plays back at half-speed for the first four seconds of the composition.

6 Press the spacebar to preview the animation. The composition now runs at half-speed until 4:00, and at a faster speed thereafter. Press the spacebar again when you have finished previewing the animation.

Viewing time remapping in the Graph Editor

Using the Graph Editor, you can view and manipulate all aspects of effects and animations, including effect property values, keyframes, and interpolation. The Graph Editor displays changes in effects and animations as a two-dimensional graph, with playback time represented horizontally (from left to right). In layer bar mode, in contrast, the time ruler represents only the horizontal time element, without a graphical display of changing values.

1 Make sure the Time Remap property is selected for the Lesson06_retime layer in the Timeline panel.

2 Click the Graph Editor button (⬚) to display the Graph Editor.

The Graph Editor displays a time-remap graph that shows a white line connecting the keyframes at 0:00, 4:00, and 10:00. The angle of the line is shallow up to 4:00, and then becomes steeper. The steeper the line, the faster the playback time.

Using the Graph Editor to remap time

When remapping time, you can use the values in the time-remap graph to determine and control which frame of the movie plays at which point in time. Each Time Remap keyframe has a time value associated with it that corresponds to a specific frame in the layer; this value is represented vertically on the time-remap graph. When you enable time remapping for a layer, After Effects adds a Time Remap keyframe at the start and end points of the layer. These initial Time Remap keyframes have vertical time values equal to their horizontal position.

By setting additional Time Remap keyframes, you can create complex motion effects. Every time you add a Time Remap keyframe, you create another point at which you can change the playback speed or direction. As you move the keyframe up or down in the time-remap graph, you adjust which frame of the video is set to play at the current time.

You'll have some fun with the timing of this project.

1 In the time-remap graph, drag the middle keyframe vertically from 2 up to 10 seconds.

2 Drag the last keyframe down to 0 seconds.

3 Go to 0:00, and then press the spacebar to preview the results. Watch the time ruler and Source Time ruler in the Layer panel to see which frames are playing at any given point in time.

▶ **Tip:** Watch the Info panel as you drag to see more information as you adjust the keyframe.

The animation progresses rapidly over the first four seconds of the composition, and then plays in reverse for the rest of the composition.

4 Press the spacebar to stop the preview.

Having fun yet? Keep going.

5 Ctrl-click (Windows) or Command-click (Mac OS) the last keyframe to delete it. The composition is still in fast-forward mode for the first 4 seconds, but now it holds on a single frame (the last frame) for the rest of the composition.

6 Press the Home key or move the current-time indicator to the beginning of the time ruler, and then press the spacebar to preview the animation. Press the spacebar again when you're done.

● **Note:** Pressing Ctrl or Command temporarily activates the Add Vertex tool.

7 Ctrl-click (Windows) or Command-click (Mac OS) the dotted line at 6:00 to add a keyframe at 6:00 with the same value as the keyframe at 4:00.

8 Ctrl-click (Windows) or Command-click (Mac OS) at 10:00 to add another keyframe, and then drag it down to 0 seconds.

The animation progresses rapidly, holds for two seconds on the last frame, and then runs in reverse.

9 Go to the beginning of the composition, and then press the spacebar to preview the change. Press the spacebar again when you're done.

Adding an Easy Ease Out

Soften the shift in time that occurs at 6 seconds with an Easy Ease Out.

1 Click to select the keyframe at 6:00, and then click the Easy Ease Out button () at the bottom of the Graph Editor. This slows the shift into reverse—the footage runs slowly in reverse at first, and then gradually speeds up.

▶ **Tip:** You can refine the amount of ease on this transition further by dragging the Bezier handle that appears out of the right side of the keyframe at 6:00. If you drag it to the right, the transition is softer; if you drag it down or to the left, the transition is more pronounced.

2 Choose File > Save to save your work so far.

Scaling the animation in time

Finally, use the Graph Editor to scale the entire animation in time.

1 Click the Time Remap property name in the Timeline panel to select all of the Time Remap keyframes.

2 Make sure the Show Transform Box button () at the bottom of the Graph Editor is selected; a free-transform selection box should be visible around all of the keyframes.

3 Drag one of the upper transform handles from 10 seconds to 5 seconds.

The entire graph shifts, reducing the top keyframe values and slowing playback.

4 Press the Home key or move the current-time indicator to the beginning of the time ruler, and then press the spacebar to preview the change. Press the spacebar again when you're done.

5 Choose File > Save.

Congratulations. You've completed a complex animation, including shifts in time. You can render and export the time-remap project if you'd like. Follow the instructions in "Rendering the animation" in this lesson, or see Lesson 14, "Rendering and Outputting," for detailed instructions on rendering and exporting a composition.

Review questions

1 Why would you import a layered Photoshop file as a composition?

2 What is the pick whip, and how do you use it?

3 What is a track matte, and how do you use it?

4 How do you remap time in After Effects?

Review answers

1 When you import a layered Photoshop file into After Effects as a composition, After Effects preserves the layer order, transparency data, and layer styles from the source Photoshop document. It also preserves other features, such as adjustment layers and type.

2 The pick whip creates expressions that link the values of one property or effect to another layer. The pick whip is also a way to create parenting relationships. To use the pick whip, simply drag the pick whip icon from one property to another.

3 When you want one layer to show through a hole in another layer, you can use a track matte. To create a track matte, you need two layers: one to act as a matte, and another to fill the hole in the matte. You can animate either the track matte layer or the fill layer. When you animate the track matte layer, you create a traveling matte.

4 There are several ways to remap time in After Effects. Time remapping lets you dynamically speed up, slow down, stop, or reverse footage. When remapping time, you can use the values in the time-remap graph in the Graph Editor to determine and control which frame of the movie plays at which point in time. When you enable time remapping for a layer, After Effects adds a Time Remap keyframe at the start and end points of the layer. By setting additional Time Remap keyframes, you can create complex motion effects. Every time you add a Time Remap keyframe, you create another point at which you can change the playback speed or direction.

7 WORKING WITH MASKS

Lesson overview

In this lesson, you'll learn how to do the following:

- Create a mask using the Pen tool.

- Change a mask's mode.

- Edit a mask shape by controlling vertices and direction handles.

- Feather a mask edge.

- Replace the contents of a mask shape.

- Adjust the position of a layer in 3D space to blend it with the rest of a shot.

- Create a reflection effect.

- Modify a mask using the Mask Feather tool.

- Create a vignette.

 This lesson will take approximately an hour to complete. Download the Lesson07 project files from the Lesson & Update Files tab on your Account page at www.peachpit.com, if you haven't already done so. As you work on this lesson, you'll preserve the start files. If you need to restore the start files, download them from your Account page.

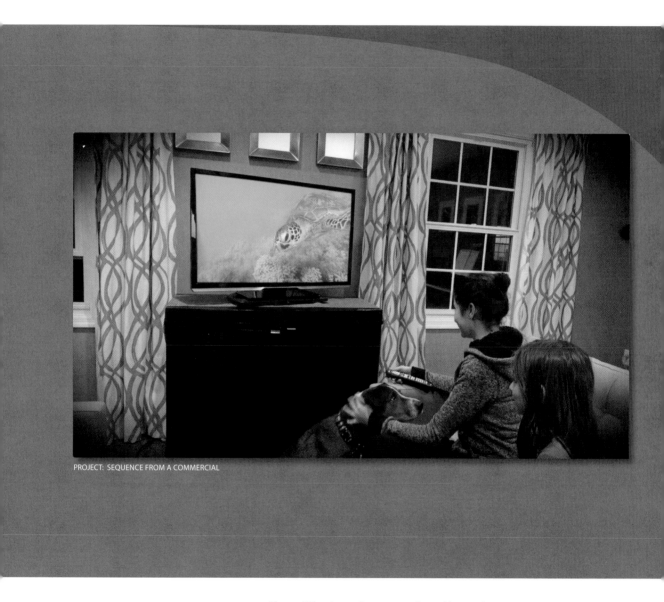

PROJECT: SEQUENCE FROM A COMMERCIAL

There will be times when you won't need (or want) everything in a shot to be included in the final composite. Use masks to control what appears.

About masks

A mask in Adobe After Effects is a path, or outline, that is used to modify layer effects and properties. The most common use of masks is to modify a layer's alpha channel. A mask consists of segments and vertices: *Segments* are the lines or curves that connect vertices. *Vertices* define where each segment of a path starts and ends.

A mask can be either an open or a closed path. An open path has a beginning point that is not the same as its end point; for example, a straight line is an open path. A closed path is continuous and has no beginning or end, such as a circle. Closed-path masks can create transparent areas for a layer. Open paths cannot create transparent areas for a layer, but are useful as parameters for an effect. For example, you can use an effect to generate a running light around a mask.

A mask belongs to a specific layer. Each layer can contain multiple masks.

You can draw masks in common geometric shapes—including polygons, ellipses, and stars—with the shape tools, or you can use the Pen tool to draw an arbitrary path.

Getting started

In this lesson, you will create a mask for the screen of a television and replace the screen's original content with a movie. Then you'll adjust the positioning of the new footage so that it fits the perspective of the shot. Finally, you'll polish the scene by adding a reflection, creating a vignette effect, and adjusting the color.

Begin by previewing the movie and setting up the project.

1 Make sure the following files are in the Lessons/Lesson07 folder on your hard disk, or download them from your Account page at www.peachpit.com now:

 • In the Assets folder: Turtle.mov, Watching_TV.mov

 • In the Sample_Movie folder: Lesson07.mov

2 Open and play the Lesson07.mov sample movie to see what you will create in this lesson. When you are done, quit QuickTime Player. You may delete the sample movie from your hard disk if you have limited storage space.

When you begin the lesson, restore the default application settings for After Effects. See "Restoring default preferences" on page 2.

3 Start After Effects, and then immediately hold down Ctrl+Alt+Shift (Windows) or Command+Option+Shift (Mac OS) to restore default preferences settings. When prompted, click OK to delete your preferences. Close the Start window.

After Effects opens to display a new, untitled project.

4 Choose File > Save As > Save As, and navigate to the Lessons/Lesson07/ Finished_Project folder.

5 Name the project **Lesson07_Finished.aep**, and then click Save.

Creating the composition

You'll import two footage items for this exercise. Then, you'll create the composition based on the aspect ratio and duration of one of the footage items.

1 Double-click an empty area of the Project panel to open the Import File dialog box.

2 Navigate to the Lessons/Lesson07/Assets folder, Shift-click to select the Turtle.mov and Watching_TV.mov files, and then click Import or Open.

3 Select the Watching_TV.mov footage item in the Project panel, and drag it to the Create A New Composition button (■) at the bottom of the panel.

After Effects creates a composition named Watching_TV, and opens it in the Composition and Timeline panels.

4 Choose File > Save to save your work so far.

Creating a mask with the Pen tool

The TV screen is currently blank. To fill it with the video of a sea turtle, you need to mask the screen.

1 Press the Home key, or move the current-time indicator to the beginning of the time ruler.

2 Zoom in to the Composition panel until the TV screen nearly fills the view. You may need to use the Hand tool (✋) to reposition the view in the panel.

3 Make sure the Watching_TV.mov layer is selected in the Timeline panel, and then select the Pen tool (✒) in the Tools panel.

> **Tip:** You can also create a mask using the mocha shape plug-in, which comes with After Effects, and then import it into After Effects. To learn more about using the plug-in, see After Effects Help.

The Pen tool creates straight lines or curved segments. The TV appears to be rectangular, so you'll try using straight lines first.

4 Click the upper left corner of the TV screen to place the first vertex.

5 Click the upper right corner of the TV screen to place the second vertex. After Effects connects the two points with a segment.

6 Click to place a third vertex in the lower right corner of the TV screen, and then click to place a fourth vertex in the lower left corner of the screen.

7 Move the Pen tool over the first vertex (in the upper left corner). When a circle appears next to the pointer (as in the middle image below), click to close the mask path.

Editing a mask

The mask looks pretty good, but instead of masking the information *inside* the monitor, the mask has removed everything *outside* the monitor. You need to invert the mask. You'll also use Bezier curves to create a more accurate mask.

Inverting the mask

For this project, you need everything inside the mask to be transparent and everything outside the mask to be opaque. You'll invert the mask now.

> **Tip:** Pressing the M key twice in quick succession displays all mask properties for the selected layer.

1 Select the Watching_TV layer in the Timeline panel, and press the M key to see the Mask Path property for the mask.

There are two ways to invert this mask: by choosing Subtract from the Mask Mode pop-up menu, or by selecting the Inverted option.

2 Select the Inverted option for Mask 1.

The mask inverts.

3 Press F2, or click an empty area of the Timeline panel, to deselect the Watching_TV layer.

About mask modes

Blending modes for masks (mask modes) control how masks within a layer interact with one another. By default, all masks are set to Add, which combines the transparency values of any masks that overlap on the same layer. You can apply one mode to each mask, but you cannot change a mask's mode over time.

The first mask you create interacts with the layer's alpha channel. If that channel doesn't define the entire image as opaque, then the mask interacts with the layer frame. Each additional mask that you create interacts with masks located above it in the Timeline panel. The results of mask modes vary depending on the modes set for the masks higher up in the Timeline panel. You can use mask modes only between masks in the same layer. Using mask modes, you can create complex mask shapes with multiple transparent areas. For example, you can set a mask mode that combines masks and sets the opaque area to the regions where the masks intersect.

Original masks

None

Add

Subtract

Intersect

Lighten

Darken

Difference

If you look closely at the TV, you will probably see portions of the screen still appearing around the edges of the mask.

These errors will certainly call attention to changes being made to the layer, and they need to be fixed. To fix them, you'll change the straight lines to subtle curves.

Creating curved masks

Curved or freeform masks use Bezier curves to define the shape of the mask. Bezier curves give you the greatest control over the shape of the mask. With them, you can create straight lines with sharp angles, perfectly smooth curves, or a combination of the two.

1 In the Timeline panel, select Mask 1, the mask for the Watching_TV layer. Selecting Mask 1 makes the mask active and also selects all the vertices.

2 In the Tools panel, select the Convert Vertex tool (⋏), which is hidden behind the Pen tool.

3 In the Composition panel, click any of the vertices. The Convert Vertex tool changes the corner vertices to smooth points.

4 Switch to the Selection tool (▶), click anywhere in the Composition panel to deselect the mask, and then click the first vertex that you created.

Two direction handles extend off the smooth point. The angle and length of these handles control the shape of the mask.

5 Drag the right handle of the first vertex around the screen. Notice how this changes the shape of the mask. Notice also that the closer you drag the handle to another vertex, the less the shape of the path is influenced by the direction handle of the first vertex, and the more it is influenced by the direction handle of the second vertex.

Click the vertex. Drag the handle.

6 Once you are comfortable moving the handles, position the handle of the upper left vertex as in the preceding figure. As you have seen, you can create very fluid shapes.

Breaking direction handles

By default, the direction handles of any smooth point are connected to one another. As you drag one handle, the opposite handle moves as well. However, you can break this connection to get greater control over the shape of the mask, and you can create sharp points or long, smooth curves.

1 Select the Convert Vertex tool (⌐) in the Tools panel.

2 Drag the right direction handle of the upper left vertex. The left direction handle remains stationary.

3 Adjust the right direction handle until the top segment of the mask shape more closely follows the curve of the TV in that corner. It doesn't have to be perfect.

4 Drag the left direction handle of the same vertex until the left segment of the shape more closely follows the curve of the TV in that corner.

Drag the right direction handle of the upper left vertex, and then the left direction handle, to follow the curve of the TV screen.

Tip: If you make a mistake, press Ctrl+Z (Windows) or Command+Z (Mac OS) to undo your last action. You can also change the zoom level and use the Hand tool to reposition the image in the Composition panel as you work.

▶ **Tip:** Again, you may need to adjust your view in the Composition panel as you work. You can drag the image with the Hand tool. To temporarily switch to the Hand tool, press and hold the spacebar.

5 For each of the remaining corner points, click with the Convert Vertex tool, and then repeat steps 2–4 until the mask's shape more closely matches the curvature of the TV. If you need to shift a corner point, use the Selection tool.

6 When you're done, deselect the Watching_TV layer in the Timeline panel to check the edge of your mask. You should not see any of the TV screen.

7 Choose File > Save to save your work.

Creating a Bezier mask

You used the Convert Vertex tool to change a corner vertex to a smooth point with Bezier handles, but you could have created a Bezier mask in the first place. To do so, click in the Composition panel with the Pen tool where you want to place the first vertex. Then click where you want to place the next vertex, and drag in the direction you want to create a curve. When you are satisfied with the curve, release the mouse button. Continue to add points until you've created the shape you want. Close the mask by either clicking on the first vertex or double-clicking the last vertex. Then switch to the Selection tool to refine the mask.

Feathering the edges of a mask

The mask looks good, but you need to soften the edges a bit.

1 Choose Composition > Composition Settings.

2 Click the Background Color box, and choose white for the background color (R=**255**, G=**255**, B=**255**). Then click OK to close the Color Picker, and OK again to close the Composition Settings dialog box.

The white background allows you to see that the edge of the TV screen looks a little too sharp and unrealistic. To address this, you'll feather, or soften, the edges.

3 Select the Watching_TV layer in the Timeline panel, and press the F key to display the Mask Feather property for the mask.

4 Increase the Mask Feather amount to **1.5**, **1.5** pixels.

5 Hide the properties for the Watching_TV layer, and then choose File > Save to save your work.

Replacing the content of the mask

You are now ready to replace the background with the video of a sea turtle and blend it with the overall shot.

1 In the Project panel, select the Turtle.mov file, and drag it to the Timeline panel, placing it below the Watching_TV layer.

2 Choose Fit Up To 100% from the Magnification Ratio pop-up menu at the bottom of the Composition panel so that you can see the whole composition.

3 Select the Selection tool (![selection tool]), and then drag the Turtle layer in the Composition panel until the anchor point is centered in the TV screen.

Zooming and panning by touch

If you're using a touch-enabled device, such as a Microsoft Surface, Wacom Cintiqu Touch, or multi-touch trackpad, you can use your fingers to zoom and pan. Touch gestures let you zoom and pan in the Composition, Layer, Footage, and Timeline panels.

To zoom: Pinch two fingers closer together to zoom in, or move them further apart to zoom out.

To pan: Move two fingers in unison to pan up, down, left, or right in the panel's current view.

Repositioning and resizing the clip

The sea turtle clip is too big for the TV screen, so you'll resize it as a 3D layer, which will give you more control over its shape and size.

1 With the Turtle layer selected in the Timeline panel, click the 3D switch (![3D switch]) for the layer.

2 Press the P key to show the Position property for the Turtle layer.

The Position property for a 3D layer has three values: From left to right, they represent the x, y, and z axes of the image. The z axis controls the depth of the layer. You can see these axes represented in the Composition panel.

Note: You'll learn more about 3D layers in Lessons 11, "Using 3D Features," and 12, "Working with the 3D Camera Tracker."

3 Position the pointer in the Composition panel over the red arrow so that a small *x* appears. The red arrow controls the x (horizontal) axis of the layer.

4 Drag left or right as necessary to center the clip horizontally in the monitor screen.

5 Position the pointer in the Composition panel over the green arrow so that a small *y* appears. Then drag up or down as necessary to position the clip vertically in the monitor screen.

6 Position the pointer in the Composition panel over the blue cube where the red and green arrows meet so that a small *z* appears. Then drag down and to the right to increase the depth of field, so that the Turtle layer appears smaller.

7 Continue to drag the x, y, and z axes until the entire clip fits into the TV screen, as shown in the following image. Our final x, y, and z values are approximately **390**, **162**, **825**.

Tip: You can also enter the Position values directly in the Timeline panel instead of dragging in the Composition panel.

Rotating the clip

The video clip fits better, but you need to rotate it slightly to improve the perspective.

1 Select the Turtle layer in the Timeline panel, and press the R key to reveal its Rotation properties.

Again, since this is a 3D layer, you can control rotation on the x, y, and z axes.

2 Change the X Rotation value to **1** degree and the Y Rotation value to **−40** degrees. This swivels the layer to match the perspective of the TV screen.

3 Change the Z Rotation value to **1** degree to align the layer with the TV screen.

Your composition should now resemble the preceding image.

4 Hide the properties for the Turtle layer, and then choose File > Save to save your work.

Adding a reflection

The masked image looks convincing, but you can make it look even more realistic by adding a reflection to the TV screen.

1 Click an empty area in the Timeline panel to deselect all layers, and then choose Layer > New > Solid.

2 In the Solid Settings dialog box, name the layer **Reflection**, click the Make Comp Size button, change the Color to white, and then click OK.

Instead of trying to exactly re-create the shape of the Watching_TV layer's mask, it is easier to copy it to the Reflection layer.

3 Select the Watching_TV layer in the Timeline panel, and press the M key to display the Mask Path property for the mask.

4 Select Mask 1, and then choose Edit > Copy or press Ctrl+C (Windows) or Command+C (Mac OS).

5 Select the Reflection layer in the Timeline panel, and then choose Edit > Paste or press Ctrl+V (Windows) or Command+V (Mac OS).

This time, you want to keep the area inside the mask opaque and make the area outside the mask transparent.

6 Select the Watching_TV layer, and then press U to hide the mask properties.

7 Select the Reflection layer in the Timeline panel, and press the F key to reveal the Mask 1 Mask Feather property for the layer.

8 Change the Mask Feather value to **0** (zero).

9 Deselect the Inverted option. The Reflection layer now obscures the Turtle layer.

10 Zoom in to see the screen, and then select the Mask Feather tool (⌀), hidden beneath the Convert Vertex tool (⌐) in the Tools panel.

When you feather a mask, the width of the feather is the same all the way around the mask. The Mask Feather Tool lets you vary the feathering width at points you define on the closed mask.

11 Click the Reflection layer in the Timeline panel to select it. Then click the lower left vertex to create a feather point.

12 Click the feather point again, and without releasing the mouse button, drag that feather point inward so that only the center of the screen is reflected, and so that the feather point is centered, as in the image below.

Currently the feather extends evenly across the mask. You'll add more feather points for greater flexibility.

13 Click in the center of the top of the mask to create another feather point. Then drag the feather point down slightly, into the mask.

14 Right-click or Control-click the feather point you just created, and choose Edit Radius. Change the Feather Radius to **0**, and click OK.

This is a good start, but the sides slope in too sharply. You'll add more feather points to change the angle.

15 Add another feather point by clicking the left edge of the matte, about one-third of the way from the top.

16 Add a similar feather point on the right side.

The shape of the reflection is good, but it's obscuring the image. You'll change the opacity to reduce its effect.

17 Select the Reflection layer in the Timeline panel, and then press the T key to reveal the Opacity property. Change its value to **10%**.

18 Press T to hide the Opacity property, and then press F2 or click an empty area in the Timeline panel to deselect all layers.

Applying a blending mode

To create unique interactions between layers, you may want to experiment with blending modes. Blending modes control how each layer blends with, or reacts to, layers beneath it. Blending modes for layers in After Effects are identical to blending modes in Adobe Photoshop.

1 From the Timeline panel menu, choose Columns > Modes to display the Mode pop-up menu.

2 Choose Add from the Reflection layer's Mode pop-up menu.

This creates a hard glare on the TV screen image and boosts the colors underneath.

3 Choose File > Save to save your work.

Creating a vignette

A popular effect in motion graphic design is to apply a vignette to the composition. This is often done to simulate light variations of a glass lens. It creates an interesting look that focuses the attention on the subject and sets the shot apart.

1 Zoom out to see the whole image.

2 Choose Layer > New > Solid.

3 In the Solid Settings dialog box, name this layer **Vignette**, click the Make Comp Size button, change the Color to black (R=**0**, G=**0**, B=**0**), and then click OK.

In addition to the Pen tool, After Effects provides tools that let you easily create square and elliptical masks.

4 In the Tools panel, select the Ellipse tool (⬭), hidden behind the Rectangle tool (▭).

5 In the Composition panel, position the cross-hairs pointer in the upper left corner of the image. Drag to the opposite corner to create an elliptical shape that fills the image. Adjust the shape and position using the Selection tool, if necessary.

6 Expand the Mask 1 property in the Vignette layer to display all of the mask properties for the layer.

7 Choose Subtract from the Mask 1 Mode pop-up menu.

8 Increase the Mask Feather amount to **200, 200** pixels.

Your composition should now resemble the following figure.

Even with this large feather amount, the vignette is a bit intense and constricting. You can give the composition more breathing room by adjusting the Mask Expansion property. The Mask Expansion property represents, in pixels, how far from the original mask edge you are expanding or contracting the adjusted edge.

9 Increase Mask Expansion to **90** pixels.

10 Hide the properties for the Vignette layer, and then choose File > Save.

Using the Rectangle and Ellipse tools

The Rectangle tool, as the name suggests, creates a rectangle or square. The Ellipse tool creates an ellipse or circle. You create mask shapes with these tools by dragging them in the Composition or Layer panel.

If you want to draw a perfect square or circle, press the Shift key as you drag with the Rectangle tool or the Ellipse tool. To create your mask from the center, press Ctrl (Windows) or Command (Mac OS) after you start to drag. Press Ctrl+Shift or Command+Shift after you start to drag to create a perfect square or circle mask from a center anchor point.

Be careful! If you use these tools without a layer selected, you'll draw a shape, not a mask.

Adjusting the timing

The sea turtle video shouldn't appear until the girl turns on the TV. You'll adjust the Turtle layer's start point and animate the mask accordingly.

1 Go to 2:00, and then drag the Turtle layer so that it begins at 2:00.

2 Select the Watching_TV layer, and press MM to see the mask properties.

3 Click the stopwatch icon next to Mask Expansion to create a keyframe at 2:00.

4 Go to 1:23, and change the Mask Expansion value to **−150** pixels to reveal the blank TV screen.

5 Go to the beginning of the time ruler, and click the Add Or Remove Keyframe At Current Time icon to add a keyframe for the mask expansion property.

6 Hide the properties for all layers, and press the spacebar to preview your movie.

Tips for creating masks

If you have worked with Adobe Illustrator or Photoshop, or similar applications, you're probably familiar with masks and Bezier curves. If not, here are a few additional tips to help you create them effectively:

- Use as few vertices as possible.

- You can close a mask by clicking the starting vertex. To open a closed mask, click a mask segment, choose Layer > Mask And Shape Path, and deselect Closed.

- To add points to an open path, press Ctrl (Windows) or Command (Mac OS), and click the last point on the path with the Pen tool. When the point is selected, you can continue adding points.

Trimming the work area

Tip: Alternatively, you can change the duration of the movie to 11:17. To do so, choose Composition > Composition Settings, and then type **11.17** in the Duration box.

The Turtle clip is shorter than the Watching_TV clip. Currently, the girls are watching a blank screen at the end of the movie. You'll move the work area end point to the end of the Turtle layer so only that portion of the movie will render.

1 Go to 11:17, the last frame of the Turtle layer.

2 Press N to move the work area end point to the current time.

3 Choose File > Save to save your work.

In this lesson, you have worked with the mask tools to hide, reveal, and adjust portions of a composition to create a stylized inset shot. Next to keyframes, masks are probably the most-used feature of After Effects.

Review questions

1 What is a mask?

2 Name two ways to adjust the shape of a mask.

3 What is a direction handle used for?

4 What is the difference between an open mask and a closed mask?

5 How is the Mask Feather tool useful?

Review answers

1 A mask in After Effects is a path, or outline, that is used to modify layer effects and properties. The most common use of masks is to modify a layer's alpha channel. A mask consists of segments and vertices.

2 You can adjust the shape of a mask by dragging individual vertices or by dragging a segment.

3 A direction handle is used to control the shape and angle of a Bezier curve.

4 An open mask can be used to control effects or the placement of text; it does not define a region of transparency. A closed mask defines a region that will affect the alpha channel of a layer.

5 The Mask Feather tool lets you vary the width of feathering at different points on a mask. With the Mask Feather tool, click to add a Feather point, and then drag it.

8 DISTORTING OBJECTS WITH THE PUPPET TOOLS

Lesson overview

In this lesson, you'll learn how to do the following:

- Place Deform pins using the Puppet Pin tool.

- Define areas of overlap using the Puppet Overlap tool.

- Stiffen parts of an image using the Puppet Starch tool.

- Animate the position of Deform pins.

- Record animation using the Puppet Sketch tool.

This lesson will take approximately an hour to complete. Download the Lesson08 project files from the Lesson & Update Files tab on your Account page at www.peachpit.com, if you haven't already done so. As you work on this lesson, you'll preserve the start files. If you need to restore the start files, download them from your Account page.

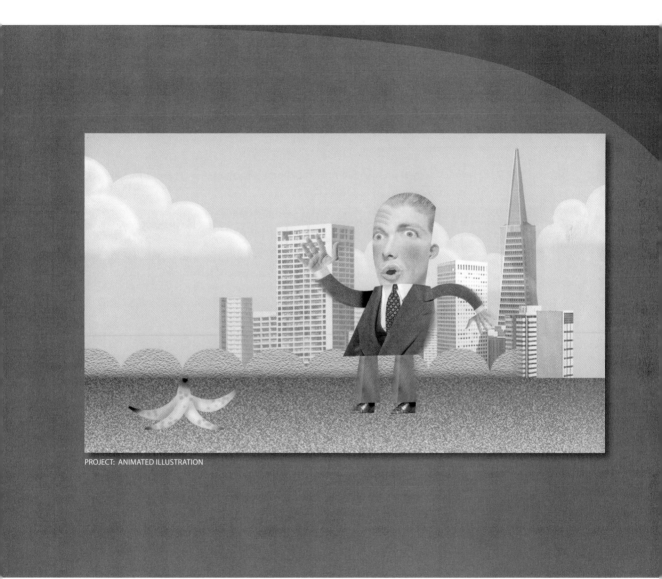

PROJECT: ANIMATED ILLUSTRATION

Pull, squash, stretch, and otherwise deform objects on the screen using the Puppet tools. Whether you're creating realistic animations, fantastic scenarios, or modern art, the Puppet tools will expand your creative freedom.

Getting started

Using the Puppet tools in After Effects, you can add natural motion to raster images and vector graphics. Three tools create pins to define the point of deformation, areas of overlap, and areas that should remain more rigid. An additional tool, the Puppet Sketch tool, lets you record animation in real time. In this lesson, you'll use the Puppet tools to animate a character slipping on a banana peel.

Start by previewing the final movie and then setting up the project.

1 Make sure the following files are in the Lessons/Lesson08 folder on your hard disk, or download them from your Account page at www.peachpit.com now:

 • In the Assets folder: backdrop.psd, banana.psd, man.psd

 • In the Sample_Movie folder: Lesson08.mov

2 Open and play the Lesson08.mov file to see what you will create in this lesson. When you are done, quit QuickTime Player.

When you begin this lesson, restore the default application settings for After Effects. See "Restoring default preferences" on page 2.

3 Start After Effects, and then immediately hold down Ctrl+Alt+Shift (Windows) or Command+Option+Shift (Mac OS). When prompted, click OK to delete your preferences. Close the Start window.

After Effects opens to display a blank, untitled project.

4 Choose File > Save As > Save As.

5 In the Save As dialog box, navigate to the Lessons/Lesson08/Finished_Project folder.

6 Name the project **Lesson08_Finished.aep**, and then click Save.

Importing footage

You'll import three Adobe Photoshop files, which you'll use to create the scene.

1 Choose File > Import > File.

2 Navigate to the Lessons/Lesson08/Assets folder. Shift-click to select the backdrop.psd, banana.psd, and man.psd files, and then click Import or Open. The footage items appear in the Project panel.

3 Click the Create A New Folder button (▪) at the bottom of the Project panel.

4 Name the new folder **Assets**, and then drag the footage items into the folder.

5 Expand the Assets folder to see its contents.

Creating the composition

As with any project, you need to create a new composition.

1 Choose Composition > New Composition.

2 Name the composition **Walking Man**.

3 Choose NTSC DV from the Preset pop-up menu. The preset automatically sets the width, height, pixel aspect ratio, and frame rate for the composition.

4 In the Duration field, type **500** to specify 5 seconds, and then click OK.

After Effects opens the new composition in the Timeline and Composition panels.

Adding the background

It's easier to animate a character in context, so first you'll add the background to the composition.

1 Press the Home key, or move the current-time indicator to the beginning of the composition.

2 Drag the backdrop.psd file to the Timeline panel.

3 Click the Lock icon (🔒) for the layer to prevent accidental changes to it.

Scaling an object

Next, you'll add the banana peel. At its default size, it's large enough to do real damage to anyone who slips on it. You'll scale it to a more proportional size for the scene.

1 Drag the banana.psd file from the Project panel to the top layer in the Timeline panel.

2 Select the banana.psd layer in the Timeline panel, and press S to display its Scale property.

3 Change the Scale value to **15%**.

4 Press P to display the layer's Position property.

5 Change the Position to **160, 420**. The banana peel moves to the left side of the composition.

6 Hide the properties for the banana.psd layer.

Adding the character

The last element in the scene is the character himself. You'll add him to the composition and then scale and position him appropriately.

1 Drag the man.psd footage item from the Project panel to the Timeline panel at the top of the layer stack.

2 Select the man.psd layer, and press S to display its Scale property.

3 Change the Scale value to **15%**.

4 Press P to display the Position property, and change the Position to **575, 300**.

Note: In the original drawing, the character had already slipped on the banana peel and was falling. To make it easier to animate, the character has been modified to be more upright. Sometimes you can make your work easier by making some adjustments before animation.

5 Press P again to hide the Position property for the layer.

6 Choose File > Save to save your work so far.

About the Puppet tools

The Puppet tools turn raster and vector images into virtual marionettes. When you move the string of a marionette, the body part attached to that string moves; pull the string attached to the hand, and the hand goes up. The Puppet tools use pins to indicate where strings would be attached.

The Puppet effect deforms parts of an image based on the positions of pins that you place and animate. These pins determine which parts of the image should move, which parts should remain rigid, and which parts should be in front when areas overlap.

There are three kinds of pins, each placed by a different tool:

- The Puppet Pin tool (⚲) places and moves Deform pins, which deform a layer.

- The Puppet Overlap tool (⚲) places Overlap pins, which indicate the parts of an image that should be in the front when areas overlap.

- The Puppet Starch tool (⚲) places Starch pins, which stiffen parts of the image so that they are distorted less.

● **Note:** The mesh is calculated at the frame where the Deform pins are applied. If you add more pins anywhere in the timeline, they are placed based on the original position of the mesh.

As soon as you place a pin, the area within an outline is automatically divided into a mesh of triangles. Each part of the mesh is associated with the pixels of the image, so as the mesh moves, so do the pixels. When you animate a Deform pin, the mesh deforms more in the area closest to the pin, while keeping the overall shape as rigid as possible. For example, if you animate a pin in a character's hand, the hand and arm will be deformed, but most of the character will remain in place.

Adding Deform pins

Deform pins are the main component of the Puppet effect. Where you place these pins and how you position them determine how the objects move on the screen. You'll place Deform pins and display the mesh that After Effects creates to determine the area of influence for each pin.

When you select the Puppet Pin tool, the Tools panel displays the Puppet tool options. Each pin has its own properties in the Timeline panel, and After Effects automatically creates an initial keyframe for each pin.

1 Select the Puppet Pin tool (✖) in the Tools panel.

2 In the Composition panel, place a Deform pin in the character's right arm, near the wrist. You may find it helpful to zoom in to see the character more clearly.

⬤ **Note:** Be careful! The character's right arm is on the left side of the image, and vice versa. Pin the character according to *his* left and right, not yours!

A yellow dot representing the Deform pin appears in the Composition panel. If at this point you were to use the Selection tool (➤) to move the Deform pin, the entire character would move with it. You need more pins to keep the other parts of the mesh in place.

3 Using the Puppet Pin tool, place another Deform pin in the left arm near the wrist.

Now you can move the right hand with the Selection tool. The more pins you place, the smaller the area of influence for each pin, and the less each area will stretch. If you experimented, undo any stretching by pressing Ctrl+Z (Windows) or Command+Z (Mac OS).

4 Place additional Deform pins in the man's right and left legs (near the ankles), torso (near the bottom of the tie), and forehead.

5 In the Timeline panel, expand the Mesh 1 > Deform properties. Each Deform pin is listed. To keep track of each pin, you'll rename them.

6 Select Puppet Pin 1, press Enter or Return, and rename the pin **Right Arm**. Press Enter or Return again to accept the new name.

7 Rename the remaining pins (Puppet Pin 2 through Puppet Pin 6) **Left Arm**, **Right Leg**, **Left Leg**, **Torso**, and **Head**, respectively.

8 Select Show in the options section of the Tools panel to display the distortion mesh.

Tip: You can extend the mesh beyond the outline of the layer in order to ensure a stroke is included in the deformation. To expand the mesh, increase the Expansion property in the options section of the Tools panel.

9 Change the Triangles value in the options section of the Tools panel to **300**.

The Triangles setting determines how many triangles are included in the mesh. Increasing the number of triangles results in a smoother animation, but also increases rendering time.

Defining areas of overlap

Note: You must select the Show option separately for each Puppet tool. You can also place pins without viewing the mesh.

Normal human movement requires the arms to swing, so as the character walks across the screen, portions of his right arm and leg will be behind other areas of his body. You'll use the Puppet Overlap tool to define the areas that should appear in front when areas overlap.

1 Zoom in, and use the Hand tool (🖑) to position the man in the Composition window so that you can see his torso and legs clearly.

2 Select the Puppet Overlap tool (🖎), which is hidden behind the Puppet Pin tool in the Tools panel.

3 Select Show in the options area of the Tools panel to view the distortion mesh.

4 In the options area of the Tools panel, change In Front to **100%**.

Tip: If the mesh doesn't appear when you select Show, click outside the path shape in the Composition panel.

The In Front value determines the apparent proximity to the viewer; setting the value to 100% prevents those parts of the body that are overlapped from showing through.

5 Click intersections in the mesh to place Overlap pins on the right side of the character's torso and left leg, which are the areas that should remain in the front. As you add a pin, you may want to adjust its Extent value in the options area of the Tools panel. The Extent value determines how far the overlap influence extends for the pin; the affected area appears lighter in the Composition panel. Use this image as a guide.

Stiffening an area

The character's arms and legs should move as he walks, but his torso should stay fairly firm. You'll use the Puppet Starch tool to add Starch pins where you want the character to be stiffer.

1 Select the Puppet Starch tool (￼), which is hidden behind the Puppet Overlap tool in the Tools panel.

2 Select Show in the options area of the Tools panel to display the distortion mesh.

3 Place Starch pins on intersections to stiffen the lower half of the torso, as in the image at right.

4 Hide the properties for the man.psd layer in the Timeline panel.

5 Choose File > Save to save your work so far.

Note: The Amount value determines how rigid the area will be. Typically, a low value is fine; higher values make the area more rigid. You can also use negative numbers to reduce the rigidity of another pin.

Animating pin positions

The Deform, Overlap, and Starch pins are in place. Now you can change the Deform pin positions to animate the character. The Overlap pins keep the front areas in the front, and the Starch pins keep specific areas (in this case, the torso) from moving too much.

Creating a walking cycle

Initially, the character should be walking across the screen. To create a realistic walking cycle, keep in mind that as humans walk, wave patterns develop in the motion path. You'll create a wave pattern in the pin positions. However, the values will vary slightly to add a bit of randomness, and to keep the character from looking too much like a robot.

1 Select the man.psd layer in the Timeline panel, and then press U to display all the keyframes for the layer.

2 Press Home, or move the current-time indicator to the beginning of the timeline.

Squash and stretch

As the character moves, his body squashes and stretches. Squash and stretch is a traditional animation technique that adds realism and weight to objects. It's an exaggeration of the effect that occurs in real life when a moving object comes into contact with a stationary object, such as the ground. When squashing and stretching are applied correctly, the volume of the character doesn't change.

The easiest way to understand the principle of squash and stretch is to view an animation of a bouncing ball. As the ball lands, it partially flattens, or squashes. As it bounces up, it stretches.

To see squash and stretch in action, open the Squash_and_stretch.aep project file in the Lesson08/End_Project_Files folder.

3 In the Timeline panel, change the position of the Deform pins as follows:

- Head: **845, 295**
- Torso: **821.5, 1210**
- Left Leg: **1000.5, 1734**
- Right Leg: **580.5, 1734**
- Left Arm: **1384.5, 1214.7**
- Right Arm: **478.5, 1108**

Note: After Effects automatically creates keyframes when you place Deform pins, so you don't need to click the stopwatch for each pin before setting its initial position.

Note: All the values listed here depend on where the deform pins were placed. You may need to adjust the values for keyframes to compensate for changes in the deform pin positions..

4 To complete the walking cycle, move the pins to the positions at the times indicated in the chart below. Where the chart says "Add keyframe," click the Add Or Remove Keyframe At Current Time button (◈) in the Timeline panel to create a keyframe at the pin's current position.

Note: To add a keyframe, click the diamond (between two arrows) on the left side of the Timeline panel.

TIME	HEAD	TORSO	LEFT LEG	RIGHT LEG	LEFT ARM	RIGHT ARM
0:07	593, 214	570.5, 1095	604, 1614.5			
0:15	314, 295	312.5, 1210	118.5, 1748.3	Add keyframe (◈)	886.5, 1208	−325.5, 1214.7
0:18	−6, 217	37.5, 1098.3		352.5, 1618.6		
1:00	−286, 295	−253.5, 1210	Add keyframe (◈)	−561.5, 1734	−121.5, 1234.7	Add keyframe (◈)
1:07	−614, 218.3	−530, 1094	−70.3, 1628.8			
1:15	−883, 300.7	−803.5, 1213.3	−1003.5, 1728.7	Add keyframe (◈)	Add keyframe (◈)	−1309.5, 1101.3
1:23	−1153, 212.7	−1055.5, 1099.7	−789.3, 1609.4			
2:00	−1412, 319.3	−1283.5, 1213	−1003.4, 1728.7	−1545.5, 1740.7	−1147.5, 1241.3	Add keyframe (◈)
2:08	−1622, 246	−1505.5, 1099.7	−996, 1617	−1926.5, 1677.1		

▶ **Tip:** The Timeline panel measures time in seconds and frames, depending on the frames-per-second (fps) rate. So 1:15 equals 1 second and 15 frames. At 29.97 fps, 1:15 is frame 45.

Animating a slip

The character steps on a banana peel, loses his balance, and falls. The falling movements occur more quickly than the walking cycle. To surprise the viewer, you'll animate the character to fall off the screen.

1 Choose File > Save to save the work you've just done.

2 Move the current-time indicator to 2:11, and then change the position of the Left Leg pin to **–2281, 1495.3**.

3 At 2:15, move the Deform pins to the following positions:

 • Head: **–1298, 532.7**

 • Torso: **–1667.5, 1246.3**

 • Left Leg: **–2398.8, 1282.7**

 • Right Leg: **–2277.5, 874**

 • Left Arm: **–1219.5, 1768**

 • Right Arm: **–1753.5, 454.7**

4 At 2:20, make the character fall off the screen by moving the Deform pins to the following positions:

 • Head: **–1094, 2452.7**

 • Torso: **–1643.5, 3219.7**

 • Left Leg: **–2329.5, 2682**

 • Right Leg: **–2169.5, 2234**

 • Left Arm: **–1189.5, 3088**

 • Right Arm: **–1597.5, 2654.7**

5 Hide the properties for the man.psd layer, and save your work so far.

Moving an object

Of course, when the man slips on the banana peel, the banana peel moves, too. It should slide out from beneath the man's feet and fly off the screen. You didn't add any pins to the banana, and you don't need them. Instead, you'll move the entire layer, using its Position and Rotation properties.

1 Move the current-time indicator to 2:00.

2 Select the banana.psd layer in the Timeline panel, and press P to display its Position property.

3 Press Shift+R to also display the layer's Rotation property.

▶ **Tip:** To view multiple layer properties at the same time, press the Shift key while you press the keyboard shortcut for the additional layer property.

4 Click the stopwatch icons (⏱) next to Position and Rotation to create initial keyframes for each property.

5 Move to 2:06, and change the Position to **80**, **246** and the Rotation to **19** degrees.

6 Move to 2:15, and change the Position to **–59**, **361**, so that the banana peel moves completely off the screen.

7 At 2:15, change the Rotation to **42** degrees, so that the peel continues to rotate slightly as it moves off the screen.

8 Choose Fit Up To 100% in the Magnification pop-up menu at the bottom of the Composition panel so you can see the entire composition. Then press the spacebar to preview your animation. If necessary, adjust the Position property for the Deform pins in the Timeline panel. Then choose File > Save.

▶ **Tip:** To make the animation appear more natural, you can use roving keyframes. Roving keyframes aren't linked to a specific time; they change according to the keyframes near them. To make a keyframe a roving keyframe, right-click or Control-click it, and choose Rove Across Time.

Recording animation

Changing the Position property for each pin at each keyframe worked, but you probably found the process to be slow and tedious. If you were creating a much longer animation, you'd quickly tire of entering precise numbers for each keyframe. Instead of manually animating keyframes, you can use the Puppet Sketch tool to drag the objects into position in real time. After Effects starts recording the motion as soon as you begin dragging a pin, and it stops recording when you release the mouse button. The composition moves forward through time as you move the pin. When you stop recording, the current-time indicator returns to the point at which you began recording, so that you can record the path for another pin during the same time period.

Experiment with this method of animation as you re-create the slipping motion using the Puppet Sketch tool.

▶ **Tip:** By default, the motion is played back at the speed at which it was recorded. To change the ratio of recording speed to playback speed, click Record Options in the Tools panel, and change the Speed value before recording.

1 Choose File > Save As > Save As, and name the project **Motionsketch.aep**. Save it in the Lesson08/Finished_Project folder.

2 Move the current-time indicator to 2:08.

3 In the Timeline panel, expand the man.psd layer, and then expand Effects.

4 Delete all keyframes after 2:08.

The walking cycle remains, but you've removed the keyframes that animate the character slipping and falling.

5 Select the Puppet Pin tool (⚲) in the Tools panel.

6 In the Timeline panel, select Puppet to see the pins in the Composition panel.

7 Select a pin in the Composition panel, and press Ctrl (Windows) or Command (Mac OS) to activate the Puppet Sketch tool (a clock icon appears next to the pointer).

8 Continue to hold down Ctrl or Command as you drag the pin into a new position. Release the mouse button when you've finished. The current-time indicator returns to 2:08.

9 Press Ctrl or Command, and drag another pin into position. Use the outline of the character to guide you.

10 Continue using the Puppet Sketch tool to move all the pins through the animation until you're satisfied with the movement.

11 Preview the final animation.

Now you've used all the Puppet tools to create a realistic, engaging animation. Remember that you can use the Puppet tools to deform and manipulate many kinds of objects, not just drawn art. And watch out for banana peels!

Review questions

1 What's the difference between the Puppet Pin tool and the Puppet Overlap tool?

2 When would you use the Puppet Starch tool?

3 Describe two methods of animating pin positions.

Review answers

1 The Puppet Pin tool creates Deform pins, which define the position of a portion of the image as the image is deformed. The Puppet Overlap tool creates Overlap pins, which determine which areas of an object remain in front when two areas overlap.

2 Use the Puppet Starch tool to add Starch pins to an area that you want to remain more rigid while other areas of the object are distorted.

3 You can manually animate pin positions by changing the value of the Position property for each pin in the Timeline panel. To animate pin positions more quickly, use the Puppet Sketch tool: With the Puppet Pin tool selected, press Ctrl or Command, and drag a pin to record its movement.

9 USING THE ROTO BRUSH TOOL

Lesson overview

In this lesson, you'll learn how to do the following:

- Extract a foreground object from the background using the Roto Brush tool.

- Correct the segmentation boundary across a span of frames.

- Touch up a matte with the Refine Edge Tool.

- Freeze a matte across a clip.

- Animate properties for creative effects.

- Track a face in footage.

 This lesson will take approximately an hour to complete. Download the Lesson09 project files from the Lesson & Update Files tab on your Account page at www.peachpit.com, if you haven't already done so. As you work on this lesson, you'll preserve the start files. If you need to restore the start files, download them from your Account page.

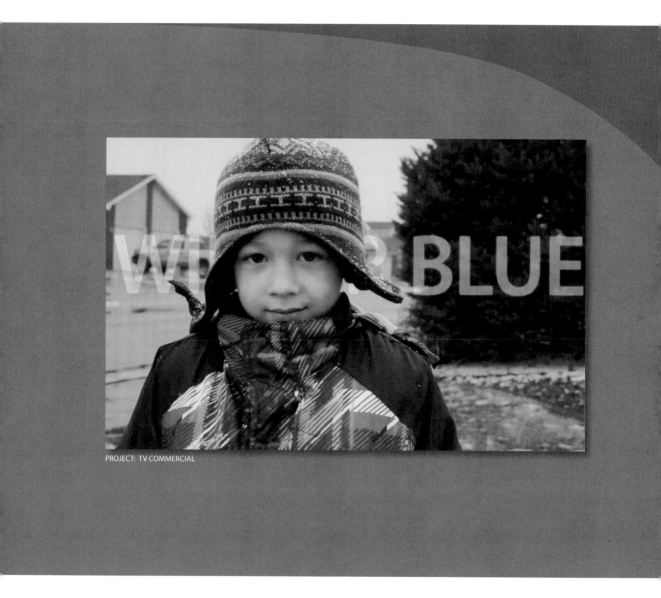

PROJECT: TV COMMERCIAL

With the Roto Brush tool, you can quickly separate a foreground object from a background across many frames. You can achieve professional results in a fraction of the time you'd spend performing the same task with traditional rotoscoping.

About rotoscoping

When you draw or paint on the frames of a movie, you're *rotoscoping*. For example, a common use of rotoscoping is to trace an object, using the path as a mask to separate it from the background so you can work with it separately. Traditionally in After Effects, you drew masks, animated the mask paths, and then used the masks to define a matte. (A *matte* is a mask used to hide part of an image so that another image can be superimposed.) While effective, this is a time-intensive, tedious process, especially if the object moves a great deal or the background is complex.

If a background or foreground object is a consistent, distinct color, you could use color keying to separate the object from the background. If the subject was shot against a green or blue background (green screen or blue screen), keying is usually much easier than rotoscoping.

The Roto Brush tool in After Effects is much faster than conventional rotoscoping, and for movies with complex backgrounds, it's much easier than keying. You use the Roto Brush tool to define the foreground and background elements. Then, After Effects creates a matte, and tracks the movement of the matte over time. The Roto Brush tool does much of the work for you, leaving only a little cleanup work to be done.

Getting started

In this lesson, you'll use the Roto Brush tool to isolate a young boy from a wet winter background so you can color-treat the background without affecting the boy. To finish up the project, you'll add an animated title.

First, you'll preview the final movie and set up your project.

1 Make sure the following files are in the Lessons/Lesson09 folder on your hard disk, or download them from your Account page at www.peachpit.com now:

 • In the Assets folder: boy.mov, Facetracking.mov

 • In the Sample_Movie folder: Lesson09.mov

2 Open and play the Lesson09.mov file to see what you will create in this lesson. When you're done, quit QuickTime Player.

When you begin this lesson, restore the default application settings for After Effects. See "Restoring default preferences" on page 2.

3 Start After Effects, and then immediately hold down Ctrl+Alt+Shift (Windows) or Command+Option+Shift (Mac OS). When prompted, click OK to delete your preferences. Close the Start window.

After Effects opens to display an empty, untitled project.

4 Choose File > Save As > Save As.

5 In the Save As dialog box, navigate to the Lessons/Lesson09/ Finished_Project folder.

6 Name the project **Lesson09_Finished.aep**, and then click Save.

Creating the composition

You need to import one footage item for this lesson.

1 Choose File > Import > File.

2 Navigate to the Lessons/Lesson09/Assets folder, select the boy.mov file, and then click Import or Open.

3 Drag the boy.mov clip onto the Create A New Composition button (▣) at the bottom of the Project panel.

After Effects creates a composition named boy, based on the settings in the boy.mov file. The composition is three seconds long, with a frame size of 1920 x 1080. The movie file was shot at a rate of 29.97 frames per second.

4 Choose File > Save to save the project so far.

Using Adobe Premiere Pro with After Effects

You can work with a clip in both Adobe Premiere Pro and After Effects, moving easily between the two applications as you edit your project.

To edit an Adobe Premiere Pro clip in After Effects, do the following:

1 Right-click or Control-click the clip in Adobe Premiere Pro, and choose Replace With After Effects Composition.

After Effects starts, and opens the Adobe Premiere Pro clip.

2 Save the project when you're prompted by After Effects. Then, work in the composition just as you'd work in any other After Effects project.

3 When you're finished, save the project, and return to Adobe Premiere Pro.

Your changes are automatically reflected in the timeline.

Creating a segmentation boundary

You use the Roto Brush tool to specify which parts of the clip are in the foreground and which are in the background. You add strokes to distinguish the two, and then After Effects creates a segmentation boundary between the foreground and background.

Creating a base frame

To use the Roto Brush tool to isolate a foreground object, you start by adding strokes to a base frame to identify foreground and background areas. You can start on any frame in the clip, but in this exercise, you'll use the first frame as the base frame. Then you'll add the strokes that identify the boy as the foreground object.

1 Move the current-time indicator across the time ruler to preview the footage.

2 Press the Home key to move the current-time indicator to the beginning of the time ruler.

3 Select the Roto Brush tool () in the Tools panel.

You use the Roto Brush tool in the Layer panel, so you'll open it now.

4 Double-click the boy.mov layer in the Timeline panel to open the clip in the Layer panel.

5 Choose Fit from the Magnification Ratio pop-up menu at the bottom of the Layer panel if you don't see the entire image.

By default, the Roto Brush tool creates green foreground strokes. You'll start by adding strokes to the foreground—the boy. Generally, it's most efficient to start with broad strokes and then use smaller brushes to refine the border.

6 Choose Window > Brushes to open the Brushes panel. Set up a hard round 100-pixel brush. (You may need to resize the Brushes panel to see the options.)

When you're drawing strokes to define the foreground object, follow the skeletal structure of the subject. Unlike traditional rotoscoping, you don't need to define a precise boundary around the object. Start with broad strokes, and work down to small regions as After Effects determines where the boundary is supposed to be.

7 Draw a green stroke from the boy's head down toward the bottom of the clip.

A magenta outline identifies the boundaries After Effects created for the foreground object. After Effects recognized only about half of the boy, because you initially sampled only a small area of the subject. You'll help After Effects find the boundary by adding some more foreground strokes.

8 Still using a large brush, draw a green stroke from left to right across the boy's coat, including the black strip on the right.

9 Use a smaller brush to add any neglected areas to the foreground.

It can be tricky to get some areas without accidentally adding background as well. It's okay if you haven't captured every detail in the foreground. You'll use background strokes to remove any extraneous areas of the matte.

10 Press Alt (Windows) or Option (Mac OS) to switch to the red background stroke brush.

11 Add red strokes to background areas you want to exclude from the matte. Switch back and forth between the foreground and background brushes to fine-tune the matte. Don't forget to deselect the area under the boy's hat where the background shows through. In fact, one click may be all it takes to exclude that area from the matte.

Don't worry about being exact about your brush strokes. Just make sure the matte is within 1 to 2 pixels of the edge of the foreground object. You'll have an opportunity to refine the matte later. However, After Effects uses the information on the base frame to adjust the matte for the rest of the span, so you want the matte to be accurate.

12 Click the Toggle Alpha button () at the bottom of the Layer panel. The selected area is white against a black background, so you can see the matte clearly.

13 Click the Toggle Alpha Overlay button (■) at the bottom of the Layer panel. The foreground area appears in color, and the background has a red overlay.

14 Click the Toggle Alpha Boundary button (■) at the bottom of the Layer panel to see the outline around the boy again.

As you use the Roto Brush tool, the Alpha Boundary is the best way to see how accurate your boundary is, because you can see everything in the frame. However, the Alpha and Alpha Overlay options let you see your matte without the distraction of the background.

Refining the boundary across the initial span

You used the Roto Brush tool to create a base frame, which includes a segmentation boundary that divides the foreground from the background. After Effects applied the segmentation boundary across a span of frames. The Roto Brush span appears below the time ruler at the bottom of the Layer panel. As you move forward and backward through the footage, the segmentation boundary moves with the foreground object (in this case, the boy).

1 Extend the span range by dragging the end of the span to 1:00 in the Layer panel.

You'll step through the frames in the span and make adjustments to the segmentation boundary as necessary.

▶ **Tip:** To move forward one frame, press the 2 key on your keyboard; to move back one frame, press the 1 key.

2 Press the 2 key on your main keyboard (not the numeric keypad) to move forward one frame.

Working from the base frame, After Effects tracks the edge of the object and attempts to follow its movement. Depending on how complex your foreground and background elements are, the boundary may or may not conform exactly to the area you hoped it would. In this case, you may notice changes to the segmentation boundary along the boy's right sleeve (the left edge of the clip) as more of the coat is revealed in the frame. Likewise, the flaps of the cap and the edges of the hood need some adjustment, which means you need to refine the segmentation.

● **Note:** As it propagates the segmentation boundary for a frame, After Effects caches that frame. Cached frames have a green bar in the time ruler. If you jump ahead to a frame further along the span, After Effects may take longer to calculate the boundary.

3 Using the Roto Brush tool, paint foreground and background strokes to refine the matte for this frame. If the matte is accurate, you don't need to paint any strokes.

If you make a stroke you don't like, you can always undo the stroke and try again. As you move through the span, each change you make affects the frames after it. The more you refine your selection, the better the overall results will be. You may find it useful to move forward a few frames to see how changes affect the boundary.

4 Press the 2 key again to move forward to the next frame.

5 Use the Roto Brush tool to add to the foreground or subtract from the background as necessary to refine the boundary.

6 Repeat steps 4 and 5 until you reach 1:00.

Adding new base frames

After Effects creates an initial Roto Brush span of 40 frames (20 in each direction). As you move through the frames, the span range may increase automatically, or you can drag to extend the span. However, the further you move from the base frame, the longer After Effects takes to propagate, or calculate, the segmentation for each frame, especially if the shot is complex. If the scene changes significantly, it may be better to create multiple base frames for your footage than to have one really long span. The scene in this project remains fairly consistent, so you could extend the span and make additional adjustments as needed. However, you'll create additional base frames to gain experience using the tools, learn to connect spans, and see how the segmentation shifts as you move further from a base frame.

You've reached 1:00 in the refining process. Now you'll add a new base frame to the project.

1 Go to 1:20 in the Layer panel. This frame isn't included in the initial span, so the segmentation boundary disappears.

2 Use the Roto Brush tool to add foreground and background strokes, defining the segmentation boundary.

A new base frame (represented by a gold rectangle) is added to the time ruler, and the Roto Brush span extends several frames behind and ahead of the new base frame. Depending on how far the initial span propagated, there may be a gap between the two spans. If so, you'll connect the two.

3 If necessary, drag the left edge of the new span to the edge of the previous span.

4 Press 1 to move backward one frame (from the new base frame), and then refine the segmentation boundary.

5 Continue to move backward through the span, refining the segmentation boundary until you reach the frame at 1:00.

6 Move back to the base frame at 1:20, and then press 2 to move forward, correcting the segmentation boundary for each frame if necessary.

7 When you reach the end of the span, drag the right edge to the end of the clip, and continue to refine each frame in the footage as needed. Pay special attention to the left earflap of the cap when it crosses in front of the tree. The dark areas overlap, making it more difficult to get a consistent edge. Remember that you are trying to get the segmentation boundary as close to the edge of the foreground object as possible.

8 When you have completed refining the segmentation boundary for the entire clip, choose File > Save to save your work so far.

Fine-tuning the matte

Roto Brush does a pretty good job, but there may be stray bits of background in the matte, or foreground areas that weren't included. You'll clean those up by refining the edge.

Adjusting the Roto Brush & Refine Edge effect

When you use the Roto Brush tool, After Effects applies the Roto Brush & Refine Edge effect to the layer. You can modify the effect using settings in the Effect Controls panel. You'll use those settings to further refine the edge of the matte.

1 Press the spacebar to play the clip in the Layer panel; press the spacebar again to end the preview when you've seen the whole clip.

As you preview the clip, you may notice that the segmentation boundary area jumps around quite a bit. You'll use the Reduce Chatter setting to make it smoother.

2 In the Effect Controls panel, increase the Feather amount to **10**, and increase Reduce Chatter to **20%**.

The Reduce Chatter value determines how much influence the current frame has when performing a weighted average across adjacent frames. Depending on how tight your matte was, you may need to increase Reduce Chatter to 50%.

3 Preview the clip again. Notice how much smoother the edge of the matte has become.

Using the Refine Edge tool

The boy's coat and face have hard edges, but his cap is fuzzy, and the Roto Brush tool didn't pick up the nuanced edge. The Refine Edge tool lets you include fine details such as wisps of hair in designated areas of the segmentation boundary.

Though it might be tempting to use the Refine Edge tool immediately after creating the base frame, it's best to wait until you've refined the segmentation boundary across the entire clip. Because of the way After Effects propagates the segmentation boundary, using the Refine Edge tool too early results in a matte that is difficult to use.

1 Zoom in so that you can see the edges of the cap clearly. Enlarge the Layer panel if necessary, and use the Hand tool to move the layer so you can see the entire cap.

2 Select the Refine Edge tool (✍), hidden beneath the Roto Brush tool in the Tools panel, and then move to the beginning of the clip in the Layer panel.

The cap is relatively soft, so a small brush size will work well. For a fuzzier object, you might have better results with a much larger brush. The brush needs to overlap the stray edges that emerge from the object.

3 Change the brush size to **10** pixels.

When you use the Refine Edge tool, draw strokes across or along the edges of the matte.

4 In the Layer panel, move the Refine Edge tool over the edge of the cap, straddling the segmentation boundary and including the fuzzy variations. You can use multiple strokes to move the tool around the entire cap.

When you release the mouse, After Effects switches to the Refine Edge X-ray view so that you can see how the Refine Edge tool changes the matte, capturing the detail in the edges.

5 Move to the second base frame in the Layer panel (1:20), and then repeat steps 1–4 to complete the rotoscoping process.

● **Note:** Use the Refine Edge tool only after you have cleaned up the matte across the entire clip.

6 Zoom out to see the entire scene, resize the Layer panel if you enlarged it, and then choose File > Save to save your work.

Refine Soft Matte and Refine Hard Matte effects

After Effects includes two related effects for refining mattes: Refine Soft Matte and Refine Hard Matte. The Refine Soft Matte effect does the same thing as Refine Edge Matte, except it applies the effect to the entire matte at a constant width. If you need to capture subtle variations across an entire matte, use this effect.

The Refine Hard Matte effect performs the same edge refinements as the Roto Brush when Fine-Tune Roto Brush Matte is turned on in the Roto Brush & Refine Edge effect in the Effect Controls panel.

Freezing your Roto Brush tool results

You've put a fair amount of time and effort into creating the segmentation boundary across the entire clip. After Effects has cached the segmentation boundary so it can recall it without having to make the calculations again. To keep that data easily accessible, you'll *freeze* it. This reduces the processing demands on your system so you can work faster in After Effects.

Once the segmentation is frozen, you cannot edit it unless you unfreeze it. Refreezing the segmentation is time-consuming, so it's best to refine the segmentation boundary as much as possible before freezing.

1 Click the Freeze button in the lower right area of the Layer panel.

Depending on your system, this may take a while.

The Freezing Roto Brush dialog box displays a progress bar as it freezes the Roto Brush and Refine Edge tool data. Freezing may take a few minutes, depending on your system. As After Effects freezes the information for each frame, the cache line turns blue. When it has finished freezing, a blue warning bar appears above the time ruler in the Layer panel, reminding you that the segmentation is frozen.

2 Click the Toggle Alpha Boundary button () in the Layer panel to see the matte. Then click the Toggle Transparency Grid button (▒). Move the time marker across the time ruler to see the subject without the distractions of the background.

3 Click the Toggle Alpha Boundary button again to see the boundary.

4 Choose File > Save.

After Effects saves the frozen segmentation information with the project.

Changing the background

There are many reasons to isolate a foreground image from a background. Often, you want to replace the background entirely, moving the subject to a different setting. But rotoscoping is also useful if you simply want to change the foreground or background without modifying the other. In this lesson, you'll make the background blue to enhance the theme of winter and help the subject stand out.

1 Close the Layer panel to return to the Composition panel, and then move the current-time indicator to the beginning of the timeline.

The Composition panel displays the composition, which includes only the boy layer, consisting only of the foreground you isolated from the clip.

2 Hide the properties for the boy layer, if they're visible.

3 Click the Project tab to display the Project panel. Then drag another copy of the boy.mov clip from the Project panel to the Timeline panel, and place it below the original boy layer.

4 Click the new layer, press Enter or Return, and rename the layer **Background**. Then press Enter or Return again.

5 With the Background layer selected, choose Effect > Color Correction > Hue/Saturation.

6 In the Effect Controls panel, do the following:

• Select Colorize.

• Change Colorize Hue to −**122** degrees.

• Change Colorize Saturation to **29**.

• Change Colorize Lightness to −**13**.

7 Choose File > Increment And Save.

If you save incrementally, you can return to earlier versions of your project to make adjustments later. This can be very useful if you're experimenting or want to try alternative effects. The Increment And Save feature preserves the previously saved version of the project and creates a new project with the same name, with an increasing number added to the filename.

Adding animated text

You're nearly done. All you need to do is to add the animated title between the boy and the background.

1 Deselect all layers, and then move the current-time indicator to the beginning of the time ruler.

2 Choose Layer > New > Text.

A new text layer appears in the Timeline panel at the top of the layer stack, and a cursor appears in the Composition panel.

3 Type **WINTER BLUES** in the Composition panel.

4 Select all the text in the Composition panel, and then do the following in the Character panel:

- Choose Myriad Pro for the font.
- Choose Black or Semibold for the font style.
- Type **300** px for the font size.
- Choose Optical from the Kerning menu.
- Select white for the fill color.
- Select black for the stroke color.
- Make sure the stroke width is 1 px and Stroke Over Fill is selected.

5 Select the text layer in the Timeline panel to deselect the text. Then press T to reveal the layer's Opacity property. Change the Opacity to **40%**.

6 Click the Effects & Presets tab to open the panel, and then type **Glow** in the search box. Double-click the Glow preset under Stylize.

The text gains some texture. The default settings are fine.

7 Drag the WINTER BLUES layer in the Timeline panel down to position it between the boy.mov and Background layers. Then move the current-time indicator to the beginning of the time ruler, if it's not already there.

You'll animate the text so that it moves left behind the boy while he crosses to the right of the frame.

8 With the WINTER BLUES layer selected, press P to reveal its Position property. Change the Position to **1925, 540**. Click the stopwatch icon for the Position property to set a keyframe.

The text moves offscreen, so it's not visible when the movie begins.

9 Move the current-time indicator to 3:01 (the end of the clip), and change the Position to **−1990, 540**.

The text moves to the left. After Effects creates a keyframe.

10 Deselect all layers in the Timeline panel, and move the current-time indicator to the beginning of the time ruler. Press the spacebar to preview the clip.

11 Choose File > Save to save your work.

Outputting your project

Render your movie to complete the project.

1 Choose File > Export > Add To Render Queue.

2 In the Render Queue panel, click the blue words *Best Settings*.

3 In the Render Settings dialog box, choose Half from the Resolution pop-up menu, and make sure Use Comp's Frame Rate is selected in the Frame Rate area. Then click OK.

4 Click the blue text next to Output Module. Then, at the bottom of the Output Module Settings dialog box, choose Audio Output Off, and click OK.

5 Click the blue text next to Output To. In the Output Movie To dialog box, navigate to the Lesson09/Finished_Project folder, and click Save.

6 Click Render in the top right corner of the Render Queue panel.

Congratulations! You've separated a foreground object from the background, including tricky details, modified the background, and animated some text to complete the movie. You're ready to use the Roto Brush tool on your own projects.

Extra credit

Tracking faces

The face-tracking feature in After Effects makes it easier to track a face or specific facial features, such as lips or eyes. Previously, tracking a face required roto brushing or complex keying.

● **Note:** If you open the Lesson09_extra_credit.aep file, you may need to relink the Facetracking.mov asset.

1 Open a new project. Double-click in the Project panel to open the Import File dialog box, and then navigate to the Lessons/Lesson09/Assets folder. Select the Facetracking.mov file, and click Import or Open.

2 Drag the Facetracking.mov clip onto the Create A New Composition button at the bottom of the Project panel.

3 Select the Facetracking.mov layer in the Timeline panel. Then, select the Ellipse tool, hidden by the Rectangle tool in the Tools panel.

4 Drag an elliptical mask roughly covering the face.

5 Right-click the Mask 1 layer, and choose Track Mask.

6 In the Tracker panel, choose Face Tracking (Outline Only) from the Method menu.

The Face Tracking (Outline Only) option tracks the entire face. The Face Tracking (Detailed Features) option tracks the outline plus the lips, eyes, and other distinctive facial features. You can export detailed facial data for use in Character Animator, or you can use it in After Effects to apply effects or to match it with another layer, such as an eye patch or a hat.

(continued on next page)

Extra credit (continued)

7 Click the Track Forward button in the Tracker panel.

The Tracker tracks the face, changing the mask's shape and position as the face moves.

8 Press the Home key to return to the beginning of the timeline, and then move the current-time indicator across the time ruler to see how the mask moves with the face.

9 In the Effects & Presets panel, search for **Bright**. Then drag the Brightness and Contrast effect onto the Facetracking.mov layer in the Timeline panel.

10 Expand Effects > Brightness & Contrast > Compositing Options in the Timeline panel.

11 Click the + icon next to Compositing Options. Choose Mask 1 from the Mask Reference 1 menu, and increase Brightness to **50**.

The masked area of the face brightens, but nothing else does. This setting is too bright, and the edge of the mask is too abrupt. You'll make it more subtle.

13 Reduce the Brightness to **20**.

14 Expand the Mask 1 properties. Change the Mask Feather property to **70**, **70** pixels.

15 Save the project, and close it.

You can use the face tracker to blur a face, brighten it, or add any other effect. You can also invert the mask to affect everything but the face.

Review questions

1 When should you use the Roto Brush tool?

2 What is the segmentation boundary?

3 When should you use the Refine Edge tool?

Review answers

1 Use the Roto Brush tool any time you would have used traditional rotoscoping. It's particularly useful for removing a foreground element from the background.

2 The segmentation boundary is the boundary between the foreground and background. The Roto Brush tool adjusts the segmentation boundary as you progress through the frames in the Roto Brush span.

3 Use the Refine Edge tool when you need to rotoscope objects with fuzzy or wispy edges. The Refine Edge tool creates partial transparency for areas of fine detail, such as hair. Use the Refine Edge tool only after you've adjusted the segmentation boundary across the entire clip.

10 PERFORMING COLOR CORRECTION

Lesson overview

In this lesson, you'll learn how to do the following:

- Use a transition to move from one clip to another.
- Use the Levels effect to correct the color in a shot.
- Use the mask tracker to track part of a scene.
- Remove an area using the Keylight (1.2) effect.
- Use the Auto Levels effect to remove a color cast.
- Key out an area using the Color Range effect.
- Correct colors using Synthetic Aperture Color Finesse 3.
- Use the CC Toner effect to create a mood.
- Copy an object in the scene with the Clone Stamp tool.

 This lesson will take approximately an hour to complete. Download the Lesson10 project files from the Lesson & Update Files tab on your Account page at www.peachpit.com, if you haven't already done so. As you work on this lesson, you'll preserve the start files. If you need to restore the start files, download them from your Account page.

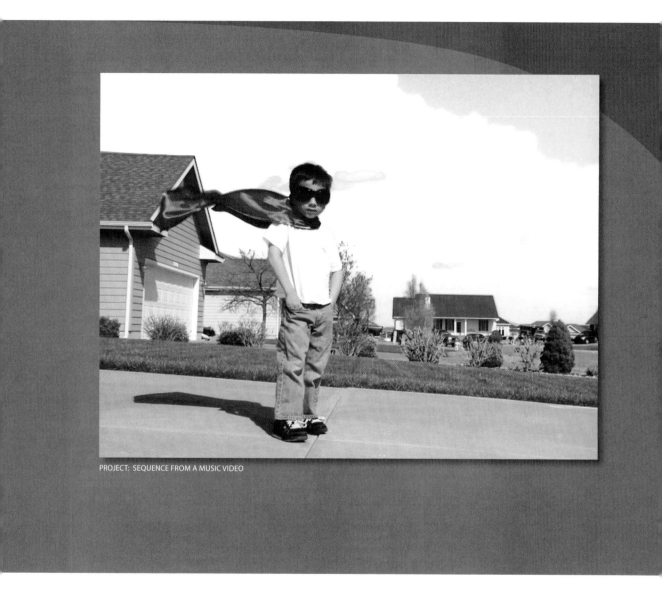

PROJECT: SEQUENCE FROM A MUSIC VIDEO

Most shots require some degree of color correction and color grading. With Adobe After Effects, you can remove color casts, brighten images, and change the mood of a clip easily.

Getting started

As the term implies, color correction is a way of altering or adapting the color of a captured image. Strictly speaking, *color correction* is the act of adjusting the color in a shot to correct errors in white balance and exposure, and to ensure color consistency from one shot to another. However, you can use the same color-correction tools and techniques to perform *color grading*, which is the subjective manipulation of color to focus attention on a key element in a shot or create a color palette for a specific visual look.

In this lesson, you will correct the color of a video clip that was shot without the proper white-balance setting. First, you'll combine two clips from a longer video of a young superhero taking off and flying through the sky. Then, you'll apply a variety of color-correction effects to clean up and enhance the image. You'll also use mask tracking and motion tracking to replace the sky with more dramatic clouds.

First, you'll preview the final movie and set up your project.

1 Make sure the following files are in the Lessons/Lesson10 folder on your hard disk, or download them from your Account page at www.peachpit.com now:

- In the Assets folder: storm_clouds.jpg, superkid_01.mov, superkid_02.mov

- In the Sample_Movie folder: Lesson10.mov

● **Note:** This lesson includes the SA Color Finesse 3 effect, which requires registration. If you open the Lesson10_end file, you may be prompted to register the effect.

2 Open and play the Lesson10.mov file to see what you will create in this lesson. When you're done, quit QuickTime Player. You may delete the sample movie from your hard disk if you have limited storage space.

When you begin this lesson, restore the default application settings for After Effects. See "Restoring default preferences" on page 2.

3 Start After Effects, and then immediately hold down Ctrl+Alt+Shift (Windows) or Command+Option+Shift (Mac OS). When prompted, click OK to delete your preferences. Close the Start window.

After Effects opens to display an empty, untitled project.

4 Choose File > Save As > Save As.

5 In the Save As dialog box, navigate to the Lessons/Lesson10/Finished_Project folder.

6 Name the project **Lesson10_Finished.aep**, and then click Save.

Creating the composition

You'll create a new composition based on the two superkid movie files.

1 Choose File > Import > File.

2 Navigate to the Lessons/Lesson10/Assets folder, Shift-click to select the storm_
 clouds.jpg, superkid_01.mov, and superkid_02.mov files, and then click Import
 or Open.

3 In the Project panel, deselect the assets you imported. Then Shift-click to select
 the superkid_01.mov and superkid_02.mov files, and drag the files onto the
 Create A New Composition button (▣) at the bottom of the Project panel.

4 In the New Composition From Selection dialog box, do the following:

 • Make sure Single
 Composition is selected.

 • In the Options area,
 choose superkid_01.mov
 from the Use Dimensions
 From menu.

 • Select Sequence Layers.

 • Select Overlap.

 • For Duration, enter **0:18**.

 • Choose Dissolve
 Front Layer from the
 Transition menu.

 • Click OK.

Note: You can add transitions after you've created a composition by selecting the layers, choosing Animation > Keyframe Assistant > Sequence Layers, and then selecting the options.

When Sequence Layers is selected, After Effects places the layers in sequence rather
than placing them both to start at 0:00. You specified an overlap of 18 frames and a
cross-dissolve transition so that the first clip dissolves into the second.

After Effects creates a new composition named for the superkid_01.mov file, and
displays it in the Composition and Timeline panels.

5 Select the superkid_01 composition in the Project panel, press Enter or Return,
 and rename the composition **Taking Flight**. Press Enter or Return again to accept
 the change.

6 Press the spacebar to preview the clips, including the transition, and then press
 the spacebar again to stop the preview.

7 Choose File > Save to save your work so far.

Previewing your project on a video monitor

If possible, perform color correction on a video monitor instead of a computer monitor. The gamma values between a computer monitor and a broadcast monitor vary greatly. What may look good on a computer screen may be too bright and washed out on a broadcast monitor. Always be sure your video or computer monitor is properly calibrated before performing color correction. For instructions on calibrating a computer monitor, see After Effects Help.

Mercury Transmit is a software interface that Adobe digital video applications use to send video frames to external video displays. Video device manufacturers AJA, Blackmagic Design, Bluefish444, and Matrox provide plug-ins that route the video frames from Mercury Transmit to their hardware. The same Mercury Transmit plug-ins work in Adobe Premiere Pro, Prelude, SpeedGrade, and After Effects. Mercury Transmit can also use monitors connected to your computer's video card and FireWire-connected DV devices without an additional plug-in.

1 With a video monitor connected to your computer system, start After Effects.

2 Choose Edit > Preferences > Video Preview (Windows) or After Effects CC > Preferences > Video Preview (Mac OS). Then select Enable Mercury Transmit.

3 Choose a device from the list. Devices with names such as AJA Kona 3G or Blackmagic Playback represent video devices connected to your computer. Adobe Monitor devices are the computer monitors connected to your video card. Adobe DV requires a DV device connected to a FireWire port on your computer.

4 To change the options for your video device, click Setup next to its name. More options may be available in the device's control panel or management application.

5 Click OK to close the Preferences dialog box.

Adjusting color balance with levels

After Effects provides several tools for color correction. Some may do the job with a single click, but understanding how to adjust colors manually gives you the greatest freedom to achieve the look you want. You'll use the Levels effect to adjust the shadows, remove the blue cast, and make the image pop a little more. You'll work on the clips individually, starting with the second clip.

Note: An additional color-correction tool, called Adobe SpeedGrade, is available with Adobe Creative Cloud membership. To learn about SpeedGrade, see creative.adobe.com/products/speedgrade.

1 Go to 4:00 in the time ruler.

2 Select the superkid_02.mov layer in the Timeline panel.

3 Press Enter or Return, rename the layer **Wide Shot**, and then press Enter or Return to accept the new name.

4 With the Wide Shot layer selected, choose Effect > Color Correction > Levels (Individual Controls).

The Levels (Individual Controls) effect may be a little intimidating at first, but it can give you great control over your shot. It remaps the range of input color or alpha channel levels onto a new range of output levels, functioning much the same as the Levels adjustment in Adobe Photoshop.

The Channel menu specifies the channel to be modified, and the histogram shows the number of pixels with each luminance value in the image. When the selected channel is RGB, you can adjust the overall brightness and contrast of the image.

To remove a color cast, you must first know which areas of the image are supposed to be gray (or white or black). In this shot, the driveway is gray, the shirt is white, and the shoes and goggles are black.

Note: You may need to resize the Info panel to see the values.

5 Open the Info panel. Then, move the cursor over the white frame of the garage. As you move the cursor, the RGB values change in the Info panel.

Tip: For an even more accurate number, sample multiple areas of the image that are gray or white, average those values, and then use those numbers to determine the adjustments.

In one area of the garage, the RGB values are R=186, G=218, B=239. To determine what the values should be, divide 255 (the highest possible RGB value) by the highest value in the sample. That gives you 255 divided by 239 (the blue value), or 1.08. To equalize the colors so that blue is no longer prominent, multiply 1.08 by the original red and green values (186 and 218, respectively). The new values (rounded) are 200 for red and 233 for green.

6 In the Effect Controls panel, expand the Red and Green properties.

7 For the Red Input White value, enter **200**; for the Green Input White value, enter **233**.

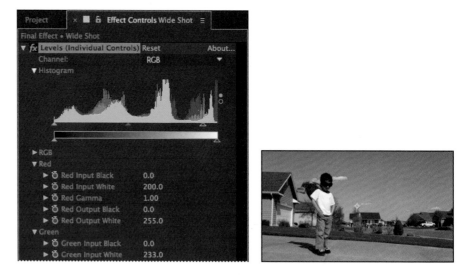

The blue cast is gone, and the image appears warmer.

For each channel, the Input settings increase the value, while the Output settings decrease the value. For example, lowering the Red Input White value adds red to the highlights in the shot, and increasing the Red Output White value adds red to the shadows or dark areas in the shot.

Performing the math lets you zero in on the appropriate settings quickly. If you prefer, you could experiment with the settings to find the best values for the footage you're using.

8 Hide the Levels (Individual Controls) properties in the Effect Controls panel.

Adjusting color balance with Color Finesse 3

You used the Levels effect to adjust the color balance in the second clip. Now you'll use Synthetic Aperture Color Finesse 3 to do the same for the first clip. Synthetic Aperture Color Finesse 3 is a third-party plug-in that installs with After Effects. It offers a number of ways to correct and enhance an image, along with a variety of tools to measure the results. The clip is in pretty good shape, but some fine-tuning will result in a better project.

● **Note:** Synthetic Aperture Color Finesse 3 is a powerful color-correction plug-in. Once you're familiar with it, you can use it to perform a wide variety of color corrections.

1 Press the Home key, or move the current-time indicator to the beginning of the time ruler.

2 Select the superkid_01.mov layer in the Timeline panel, press Enter or Return, rename the layer **Close Shot**, and press Enter or Return to accept the new name.

3 With the Close Shot layer selected, choose Effect > Synthetic Aperture > SA Color Finesse 3. Register if prompted to do so.

Experienced users may find the simplified interface controls the most efficient way to adjust the color of an image, but the full interface is helpful to truly master the effect. You'll use the full interface.

4 In the SA Color Finesse 3 area of the Effect Controls panel, click Full Interface.

SA Color Finesse 3 opens in its own window. The upper left area of the window provides different scopes that measure the results in different ways. You make adjustments using controls in the bottom area of the window.

▶ **Tip:** In other applications, the RGB Waveform scope may be called the RGB Parade scope.

5 In the upper left area of the window, click RGB WFM to select the RGB Waveform scope.

The RGB Waveform scope displays the luminance range in each of the RGB channels, measured from 0 to 100%. Generally, luminance shouldn't exceed 100%, but in this clip, the luminance of the blue channel does, which means some areas of detail are clipped. Leveling the luminance values will improve the overall image.

6 On the far left side of the lower area of the window, click the RGB tab to activate the controls. (Click the tab itself; if you just check the box, the controls aren't activated.)

7 Click Master to activate the color controls for the entire image.

Tip: When you change a value on a tab, a check mark appears next to the tab to indicate you've adjusted the controls. called the RGB Parade scope.

In this shot, the green channel appears to have the most even luminance, so you'll use it as a baseline to adjust the other two channels.

8 Move the Master Gamma slider to **1.08**—the same value you used to adjust the color balance in the second clip using the Levels effect.

The Master Gamma slider adjusts the midtone values in the overall image without affecting the black and white values. Increasing the value to 1.08 brightens the image slightly.

9 Click the Highlights tab to activate it.

Sliders on the Highlights tab adjust the bright portions of the image.

On all the tabs, Gamma sliders affect the midtones for a channel. Pedestal correction adds a fixed offset to the channel's pixel values; you can use it to boost an image's overall brightness, but doing so will also make the blacks brighter. Gain adjusts an image's "brightness" by multiplication so that lighter pixels are affected more than darker pixels, effectively raising the white point.

10 Increase the Red Pedestal to **.04**. Then lower the Blue Gamma value to **.84**, and decrease the Blue Pedestal value to **−.08**.

Increasing the Red Pedestal value bumped up the peak luminance values for the red channel, and decreasing the Blue Pedestal value lowered the peak luminance value for the blue channel. The luminance peaks for each channel are now close to 100.

Note: We're providing the values to use for this clip, but you can also experiment with the sliders to balance the colors. As you become more familiar with the controls, you'll know intuitively which changes to make.

11 Click the Midtones tab to activate it. Then increase the Red Gamma to **1.23** and the Blue Gamma to **1.12**.

Sliders on the Midtones tab affect only the midtones of the image. The large gray range of colors in each channel are now more similar.

12 Click the Shadows tab to activate it. Then increase the Red Pedestal value to **.02** and the Red Gain to **1.07**. Lower the Blue Gamma value to **.91**.

Sliders on the Shadows tab affect the darker areas of the image, which appear at the bottom of the RGB waveform.

13 Click OK in the lower right corner to accept the changes and close the SA Color Finesse 3 window.

● **Note:** To learn more about SA Color Finesse 3, within the plug-in's interface, choose Help > View Color Finesse User's Guide or Help > View Color Finesse Online Knowledge Base.

Before After

14 Choose File > Save to save your work.

Replacing the background

These shots were taken on a clear day with few clouds. To add a little drama, you'll key out the sky and replace it with storm clouds. You'll start by using the rigid mask tracker to mask the sky, and then key out the sky color. Then you'll replace it with another image.

Using the mask tracker

The mask tracker transforms a mask so that it follows the motion of an object or objects in a movie. It's similar to the face tracker you used in the Extra Credit project in Lesson 9. You can use it to mask a moving object so that you can apply a special effect to it, for example. In this case, you'll use it to track the sky as it shifts in a handheld camera. There is a great deal of blue in this clip in shadows, the cape, and other areas, so it would be difficult to key out the sky without first isolating it.

1 Go to 2:22—the last frame in the first clip before the transition begins.

2 Select the Close Shot layer in the Timeline panel. Then select the Pen tool (✐) from the Tools panel.

3 In the Composition panel, draw a mask that follows the roofline of the buildings. Complete the mask above the image in the Composition panel. It's okay if the mask cuts off the boy's head, because his head doesn't contain blue and won't be keyed out.

4 With the Close Shot layer selected in the Timeline panel, press the M key to display the Mask properties.

5 Choose None from the Mask Mode menu.

Mask modes (blending modes for masks) control how masks within a layer interact with one another. By default, all masks are set to Add, which combines the transparency values of any masks that overlap on the same layer. While Add is chosen, areas outside the mask disappear. Choosing None from the Mask Mode menu reveals the entire clip in the Composition panel, not just the masked area, so it's easier to edit.

6 Right-click or Control-click Mask 1, and choose Track Mask.

After Effects opens the Tracker panel. The mask tracker does not alter the shape of the mask to follow a shape; the mask remains the same shape but the tracker can change its position, rotation, or scale based on the motion in the clip. You'll use it to track the edges of the buildings without having to manually adjust and track the mask. Because the scene was shot without a tripod, you'll track the position, scale, and rotation of the mask.

● **Note:** You'll learn more about tracking objects in Lesson 13, "Advanced Editing Techniques." For help working with track points, see "Moving and resizing the track points" on page 324.

7 In the Tracker panel, choose Position, Scale & Rotation from the Method menu. Click the Track Selected Masks Backward button to begin tracking backward from 2:22.

Note: If the mask requires adjustment on more than a few frames, delete it and draw the mask again.

8 When the tracking is complete, scrub through the clip to see the mask. If it slips out of place, adjust the mask on individual frames. You can shift the entire mask or reposition individual points, but don't delete any points, as that will change the mask for all the frames that follow.

Keying out the sky with Keylight (1.2)

Now that you've masked the sky, you'll key out the blue in the area that you masked. First, you'll duplicate the layer, and apply mask modes to isolate the mask.

1 Select the Close Shot layer and choose Edit > Duplicate.

After Effects adds an identical layer, named Close Shot 2, above the Close Shot layer.

2 Select the Close Shot layer, and choose Subtract from its Mask Mode menu.

3 Select the Close Shot 2 layer, press M to display its Mask properties, and choose Add from its Mask Mode menu.

When you apply the Subtract mask mode, the influence of the mask is subtracted from the masks above it in the stacking order. The Add mask mode adds the mask to the masks above it. In this case, you're ensuring that only the sky will be selected in the Close Shot 2 layer. If you zoom in to the Composition window while no layers are selected, you can see a faint line where the two layers intersect.

4 Select the Close Shot layer, and press the M key twice to show all of the mask properties for the layer. Reduce the Mask Expansion value to −**1.0**.

The Mask Expansion setting determines how far, in pixels, from the mask path the influence of the mask on the alpha channel extends. You've shrunk the mask on the Close Shot layer so that the two masks don't overlap.

5 Hide the properties for the Close Shot layer.

6 Select the Close Shot 2 layer, and choose Effect > Keying > Keylight (1.2).

The Keylight 1.2 effect options appear in the Effect Controls panel.

7 Select the eyedropper next to Screen Colour, and then sample an area of the sky near the boy's head.

Most of the sky is keyed out, but if your mask overlapped any of the shadowy areas of the buildings, they're probably affected too. You'll use Screen Balance to fix that.

8 Change the Screen Balance to **0**.

The buildings lighten up.

Screen Balance determines how saturation is measured: With a balance of 1, saturation is measured against the smallest of the other two components in the color; with a balance of 0, it's measured against the larger of the two; with a balance of 0.5, it's measured from the average of the two. Generally speaking, blue screens work best with a balance around .95 and green screens with a balance around 0.5, but it varies depending on the colors in the image. For many clips, try setting the balance closer to 0, and then closer to 1, to see what works best.

9 Click the Toggle Transparency Grid button in the Composition panel to see the keyed-out area clearly.

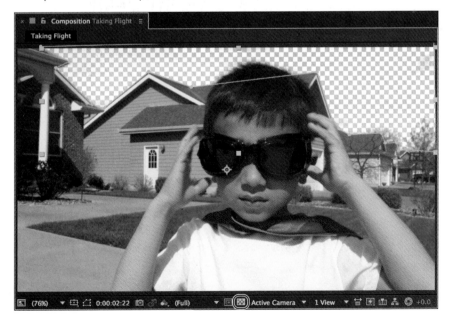

10 Expand the Screen Matte category in the Effect Controls panel, and then change the Clip White value to **67**.

The screen matte is the matte that remains when you've keyed out other parts of the image. Sometimes parts of the matte are accidentally keyed out. The Clip White value turns the gray (transparent) pixels to white (opaque).

This process is very similar to adjusting Levels for a layer. Anything above the Clip White value is considered pure white. Likewise, the Clip Black value makes anything below the value completely black.

11 Make sure Final Result is chosen in the View menu at the top of the Keylight (1.2) area in the Effect Controls panel.

12 Hide the properties for the Close Shot 2 layer.

Adding a new background

With the original sky keyed out, you're ready to add the clouds to the scene.

1 Click the Project tab to display the Project panel, and then drag the storm_clouds.jpg file to the Timeline panel, placing it below the Close Shot layer.

2 Drag the end of the storm_clouds layer to align with the end of the Close Shot layer.

Now the clouds are there, but they're not very dramatic. You'll make them larger and adjust their position.

3 Press the S key to display the Scale property for the layer, and change the amount to **222%**.

4 Press the P key to display the Position property for the layer, and change the value to **580.5**, **255.7**.

Color-correcting using Auto Levels

Although the storm clouds are dramatic, the contrast of the image and the color cast don't really match the foreground elements. You'll use the Auto Levels effect to correct that.

The Auto Levels effect automatically sets highlights and shadows by defining the lightest and darkest pixels in each color channel as white and black, and then redistributing intermediate pixel values proportionately. Because Auto Levels adjusts each color channel individually, it may remove or introduce a color cast. In this case, with the default settings applied, Auto Levels removes the orange cast and balances the shot.

1 With the storm_clouds layer selected in the Timeline panel, choose Effect > Color Correction > Auto Levels.

2 To brighten the clouds just a bit, change the White Clip value to **1.00%**.

The Black Clip and White Clip values determine how much of the shadows and highlights (respectively) are clipped to the new extreme shadow and highlight colors in the image. Setting the clipping values too high reduces detail in the shadows or highlights; 1% is as high as is typically recommended.

3 Choose File > Save to save your work.

Motion tracking the clouds

The clouds are in place, and they're looking good. But if you scrub through the clip, you'll notice that the clouds are static while the foreground moves due to camera motion. The clouds should travel with the foreground. You'll use motion tracking to solve this problem.

After Effects tracks motion by matching pixels from a selected area in a frame to pixels in each succeeding frame. Tracking points designate the areas to track.

1 Press the Home key, or move the current-time indicator to the beginning of the time ruler.

2 Select the Close Shot layer, right-click or Control-click the layer, and choose Track Motion.

After Effects displays the Close Shot layer in the Layer panel and makes the Tracker panel active.

3 In the Tracker panel, select the Position, Rotation, and Scale options.

After Effects displays two track points in the Layer panel. The outer box in each track point represents the search region (the area After Effects scans); the inner box is the feature region (what After Effects is searching for); the center "x" is the attach point.

4 Click an empty area in the inner box (the feature region) of the first track point, and drag the entire track point to the corner of the house on the left. You want to track an area with strong contrast.

5 Click an empty area in the feature region of the second track point, and drag the entire track point to the peak of the roof across from the first track point.

6 In the Tracker panel, click Edit Target. Then, in the Motion Target dialog box, choose 3. storm_clouds.jpg from the Layer menu. Click OK.

After Effects applies the tracking data to the target layer. In this case, it will track the motion of the Close Shot layer, and apply that tracking data to the storm_clouds.jpg layer so that they move in sync.

7 Click the Analyze Forward button (▶) in the Tracker panel.

After Effects analyzes the positions of the tracking regions frame by frame to track the camera movement in the clip.

8 When the analysis is complete, click Apply in the Tracker panel. Click OK to apply the data for both the x and y dimensions.

9 Switch back to the Composition panel, and scrub through the timeline. The clouds move with the foreground elements. Hide the Close Shot layer properties.

Because you selected Scale in the Tracker panel, After Effects resized the layer as necessary to sync it with the Close Shot layer. The clouds are no longer in the same position. You'll adjust the anchor point for the layer.

10 Select the storm_clouds.jpg layer in the Timeline panel, and press the A key to display its Anchor Point property. Change the Anchor Point position to **313**, **601**.

11 Press A to hide the Anchor Point property, and choose File > Save to save your work so far.

Replacing the sky in the second clip

You'll use a similar process to replace the sky in the second clip, with a few differences. You'll use the Color Range effect to key out the sky instead of the Keylight (1.2) effect.

Creating the masks

As you did with the first clip, you'll start by drawing a mask to isolate the sky so you won't key out all the blue in the image. You'll use the mask tracker to ensure the mask stays in the right position throughout the clip.

1 Go to 2:23 in the time ruler—the first frame in the second clip.

2 Hide the Close Shot, Close Shot 2, and storm_clouds.jpg layers so that you can see the full Wide Shot clip clearly.

3 Select the Wide Shot layer in the Timeline panel.

4 Select the Pen tool (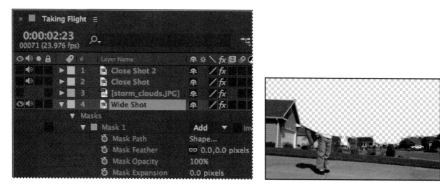) in the Tools panel, and then follow the edges of the buildings to draw a mask around the bottom of the image, omitting the sky. Make sure the boy's blue pants are entirely within the shape you draw, so they won't be keyed out with the sky.

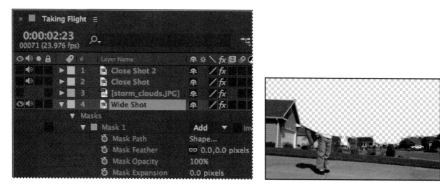

5 Select the Wide Shot layer, and then press Ctrl+D (Windows) or Command+D (Mac OS) to duplicate the layer.

A new Wide Shot 2 layer appears above the original Wide Shot layer in the Timeline panel.

6 Select the original Wide Shot layer, and press the M key twice to reveal the mask properties for the layer. Change the Mask Expansion value to **1** pixel.

The influence of the mask expands by 1 pixel beyond its outline.

7 Select the Wide Shot 2 layer, press the M key twice to reveal the mask properties for the layer, and then select Inverted.

The area that is masked in the Wide Shot 2 layer is inverted: What is masked in the Wide Shot layer is not in the Wide Shot 2 layer, and vice versa. To see this clearly, temporarily hide the Wide Shot layer and then show it again.

8 Select Mask 1 in the Wide Shot 2 layer, right-click or Control-click Mask 1, and then choose Track Mask.

9 In the Tracker panel, choose Position from the Method menu, and then click the Track Selected Masks Forward button (▶).

The mask tracker tracks the mask as the camera moves.

10 When the analysis is complete, go to 2:23 in the time ruler again. Under the Wide Shot layer, right-click or Control-click Mask 1, and choose Track Mask.

11 In the Tracker panel, choose Position from the Method menu, and then click the Track Selected Masks Forward button (▶).

12 Hide the properties for all layers.

Keying out an area with the Color Range effect

The Color Range effect keys out a specified range of colors. This key effect is especially useful where the color to be keyed is unevenly lit. The sky in the Wide Shot clip ranges in color from a deep blue to a lighter shade near the horizon—a perfect candidate for the Color Range effect.

1 Go to 2:23 in the time ruler.

2 Select the Wide Shot 2 layer in the Timeline panel, and choose Effect > Keying > Color Range.

3 Select the Key Color eyedropper, next to the Preview window in the Effect Controls panel. Then, in the Composition panel, click a midtone blue color in the sky to sample it.

The keyed-out area appears black in the Preview window in the Effect Controls panel.

4 Select the Add To Key Color eyedropper in the Effect Controls panel, and then click another area of the sky in the Composition panel.

5 Repeat step 4 until the entire sky has been keyed out.

Adding a new background

With the original sky keyed out, you're ready to add the clouds to the scene.

1 Click the Project tab to display the Project panel. Then drag the storm_clouds.jpg item from the Project panel to the Timeline panel, placing it below the Wide Shot layer.

2 With the storm_clouds layer selected in the Timeline panel, press the S key to display its Scale property, and then increase the Scale values to **150, 150%**.

▶ **Tip:** If you're typing the values, press Tab to jump between the fields.

3 With the storm_clouds layer still selected in the Timeline panel, press P to display its Position property. Then change the position values to **356, 205** or the position you prefer.

4 With the storm_clouds layer selected, choose Effect > Color Correction > Auto Levels. Change the White Clip value to **1.00%**.

Motion tracking the shot

Again, because the clip was shot without a tripod, the camera shifts. The clouds should shift with it. You'll track the motion to sync the clouds with the foreground elements, just as you did for the other clip.

1 Make sure the current-time indicator is at 2:23. Then select the Wide Shot layer, right-click or Control-click it, and choose Track Motion.

2 In the Tracker panel, select the Position, Rotation, and Scale options.

3 Click in the feature region (the inner box) of the first track point, and drag it to the right peak of the roof of the house in the center shot. Then, drag the feature region of the second track point to the peak of the house straight across from it, as in the illustration.

4 In the Tracker panel, click Edit Target. In the Motion Target dialog box, choose 6. storm_clouds.jpg from the Layer menu, and click OK. Make sure you select the second storm_clouds.jpg file, and not the first one (layer 3); you want the one that is associated with the Wide Shot layer.

5 Click the Analyze Forward button in the Tracker panel.

6 When the analysis is complete, click Apply in the Tracker panel. Click OK to apply the data to both the x and y dimensions.

7 Click the Composition: Taking Flight tab in the Composition panel to make it active. Then scrub through the clip to watch the clouds in sync with the other elements.

The clouds follow the movement of the camera, but because the layer was scaled, they may not be in the right position.

8 Hide the properties for all layers.

9 Make sure no layers are selected. Then, select the storm_clouds.jpg layer at the bottom of the layer stack, and press the A key to reveal the Anchor Point property. Adjust it so that it looks right. We used **941, 662**.

10 Make the Close Shot, Close Shot 2, and first storm_clouds.jpg layers visible again.

11 Choose File > Save to save your work so far.

Color grading

So far, the color changes you've made have been to correct inaccurate white balances or to match color between clips. You can also change color and tone to create a mood or otherwise enhance a movie. You'll make some final adjustments to give the entire movie a steely blue color, make the image soft and dreamy, and add a vignette.

Using CC Toner to map colors

CC Toner is a color-mapping effect based on the luminance of the source layer. You can map two (duotone), three (tritone), or five (pentone) colors. You'll use it to map a cold blue color to bright areas of the clip, a steely blue to the midtones, and a darker blue to darker areas of the clip.

1 Choose Layer > New > Adjustment Layer.

You can use an adjustment layer to apply an effect to all the layers beneath it at once. Because it's on a separate layer, you can also hide or edit the layer and automatically affect its influence on all the other layers.

2 Move the Adjustment Layer 1 layer to the top of the Timeline panel, if it's not already there.

3 Select the Adjustment Layer 1 layer, press Enter or Return, rename the layer **Steel Blue**, and press Enter or Return again.

4 Select the Steel Blue layer, and choose Effect > Color Correction > CC Toner.

5 In the Effect Controls panel, choose Pentone from the Tones menu. Then do the following:

- Click the Brights color swatch, and choose a cold blue color (we used R=**120**, G=**160**, B=**190**).

- Click the Midtones color swatch, and choose a darker, steely blue (we used R=**70**, G=**90**, B=**120**).

- Click the Darktones color swatch, and choose a much darker blue (we used R=**10**, G=**30**, B=**60**).

- Change the Blend With Original value to **75%**.

Adding a blur

You'll add a blur to the entire project. First you'll precompose the layers, and then you'll create a partially visible blurred layer.

1 Select all of the layers in the Timeline panel, and choose Layer > Pre-Compose.

Precomposing layers moves them to a new composition, making it easier to affect all the layers in a composition at once.

2 In the Pre-Compose dialog box, name the composition **Final Effect**, and select Move All Attributes Into The New Composition. Then click OK.

After Effects replaces all the layers in the Taking Flight composition with a single layer named Final Effect.

3 Select the Final Effect layer, and choose Edit > Duplicate to make a copy of it.

4 With the top layer selected, choose Effect > Blur & Sharpen > Fast Blur.

5 In the Effect Controls panel, change the Blurriness to **40**.

The image is too blurry. You'll reduce the opacity of the layer that contains the effect.

6 With the top layer selected, press the T key to reveal the Opacity property for the layer. Change its value to **30%**.

Adding a vignette

You'll use a new solid layer to create a vignette for the movie.

1 Choose Layer > New > Solid.

2 In the Solid Settings dialog box, do the following:

 • Name the layer **Vignette**.

 • Click the Make Comp Size button.

 • Change the color to black (R=**0**, G=**0**, B=**0**).

 • Click OK.

3 Select the Ellipse tool (◯), hidden beneath the Rectangle tool in the Tools panel, and then double-click the Ellipse tool to add an elliptical mask that is automatically sized to fit the layer.

4 In the Timeline panel, select the Vignette layer, and press the M key twice to reveal the mask properties. Change the Mask Mode to Subtract, and change the Mask Feather value to **300** pixels.

5 Press the T key to reveal the Opacity property, and change its value to **50%**.

6 Hide the properties for all layers.

7 Preview your movie!

8 Save the file.

Extra Credit

Cloning an object in a scene

You can copy an object, and then use motion tracking to ensure it remains in sync with the rest of the scene. You'll use the Clone tool to place a second light on the other side of the door in the background of the Close Shot clip. Cloning in After Effects is similar to cloning in Photoshop, but in After Effects, you can clone across the entire timeline, rather than in a single image.

1 Press the Home key, or move the current-time indicator to the beginning of the time ruler.

2 Double-click the lower Final Effect layer in the Timeline panel to open the Final Effect composition. You want to make the change to the copy of the composition that is not blurred.

3 Double-click the Close Shot layer in the Timeline panel to open it in the Layer panel. You can paint only on individual layers—not on the composition as a whole.

4 Select the Clone Stamp tool in the Tools panel.
The Clone Stamp tool samples the pixels on a source layer and applies the sampled pixels to a target layer; the target layer can be the same layer or a different layer in the same composition. When you select the Clone Stamp tool, After Effects adds the Brushes and Paint panels to the stack.

5 Enlarge the Brushes panel if necessary, and then change the Diameter to **10** pixels, and the Hardness value to **60%**.

6 Enlarge the Paint panel. Make sure the Mode is set to Normal and the Duration to Constant. The source should be set to Current Layer. Select Aligned and Lock Source Time, and make sure the Source Time Shift is set to 0 frames.

The Constant setting applies the Clone Stamp effect from the current time forward. Because you're starting at the beginning of the timeline, the changes you make will affect every frame in the layer.

(continued on next page)

Extra credit (continued)

When Aligned is selected in the Paint panel, the position of the sample point—the clone position—changes for subsequent strokes to match the movement of the Clone Stamp tool in the target Layer panel so you can use multiple strokes to paint the entire cloned object. The Lock Source Time option lets you clone a single source frame.

7 In the Layer panel, position the cursor at the top of the lamp. Alt-click (Windows) or Option-click (Mac OS) to designate a source point for cloning.

8 Click next to the left side of the door, and then click and drag to clone the light. Be careful not to clone part of the door in the process. If you make a mistake, undo and start over with a new source point.

> **Tip:** If you make a mistake, just press Ctrl+Z (Windows) or Command+Z (Mac OS) to undo the stroke, and then try again.

9 When the second light is in place, scrub through the clip.
The cloned light remains stationary while the rest of the scene moves; it isn't in sync with the side of the building. You'll use tracking data to fix the problem.

10 In the Timeline panel, expand the properties for the Close Shot layer, and then expand the Motion Trackers, Tracker 1, and Track Point 1 properties. Then, still in the Close Shot layer, expand the Effects, Paint, Clone 1, and Transform Clone 1 properties.

11 Alt-click or Option-click the stopwatch for the Transform Clone 1 Position property to turn on the expression for the property. Drag its pick whip to the Track Point 1: Attach Point property, and release it. (You may need to enlarge the Timeline panel to see both properties at once.)

The expression you created ties the position of the cloned light to the tracking data you created for the clip earlier in the lesson. The light will travel with the image. But it's in the wrong place. You'll move its anchor point.

12 Adjust the Transform: Clone 1: Anchor Point property until the light is positioned next to the door. Your values will probably be different from ours.

13 Scrub through the clip to verify that the light is positioned properly. When you're satisfied that it is, close the Close Shot tab in the Layer panel and the Final Effect composition tab in the Timeline panel. Preview the entire composition to see your work.

14 Choose File > Save to save your work.

Review questions

1 What's the difference between color correction and color grading?

2 What does the SA Color Finesse 3 effect do?

3 When would you use the mask tracker?

Review answers

1 Color correction is performed to correct errors in white balance and exposure, or to ensure color consistency from one shot to another. Color grading is more subjective; its goals are to optimize the source material, to focus attention on a key element in the shot, or to create a color palette to match the visual look the director prefers.

2 SA Color Finesse 3 is a third-party plug-in installed with After Effects CC. It performs a wide variety of color-editing effects, such as isolating a color range for enhancement. SA Color Finesse 3 affects the original layer, ignoring any effects that have already been applied to the layer.

3 Use the mask tracker when you need to track a mask that does not change shape, but that does change position, scale, or rotation through a clip. For example, you can use it to track a person in an action shot, a wheel, or an area of the sky.

11 USING 3D FEATURES

Lesson overview

In this lesson, you'll learn how to do the following:

- Create a 3D environment in After Effects.

- Look at a 3D scene from multiple views.

- Create 3D text.

- Rotate and position layers along x, y, and z axes.

- Animate a camera layer.

- Add lights to create shadows and depth.

- Export an After Effects composition to use in Maxon Cinema 4D.

- Import a Cinema 4D scene into After Effects.

This lesson will take approximately an hour to complete. Download the Lesson11 project files from the Lesson & Update Files tab on your Account page at www.peachpit.com, if you haven't already done so. As you work on this lesson, you'll preserve the start files. If you need to restore the start files, download them from your Account page.

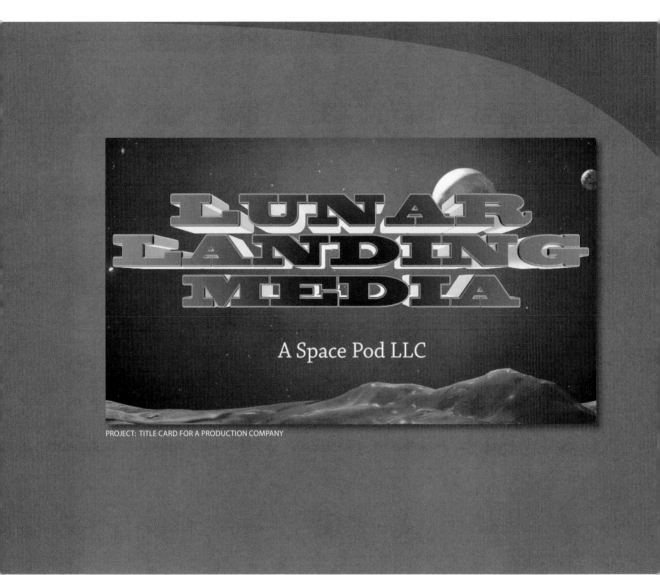

PROJECT: TITLE CARD FOR A PRODUCTION COMPANY

By clicking a single switch in the Timeline panel in After Effects, you can turn a 2D layer into a 3D layer, opening up a whole new world of creative possibilities. Maxon Cinema 4D Lite, included with After Effects, gives you even greater flexibility.

Getting started

Adobe After Effects can work with layers in two dimensions (x, y) or in three dimensions (x, y, z). So far in this book, you've worked primarily in two dimensions. When you specify a layer as three-dimensional (3D), After Effects adds the z axis, which provides control over the layer's depth. By combining this depth with a variety of lights and camera angles, you can create animated 3D projects that take advantage of the full range of natural motion, lighting and shadows, perspective, and focusing effects. In this lesson, you'll explore how to create and animate 3D layers. Then you'll use Maxon Cinema 4D Lite (installed with After Effects) to create high-end 3D text for a title card for a fictional production company.

First, you'll preview the final movie and then set up the project.

1 Make sure the following files are in the Lessons/Lesson11 folder on your hard disk, or download them from your Account page at www.peachpit.com now:

 • In the Assets folder: Lunar.mp3, Space_Landscape.jpg

 • In the Sample_Movie folder: Lesson11.mov

2 Open and play the Lesson11.mov file to see what you will create in this lesson. When you are done, quit QuickTime Player. You may delete this sample movie from your hard disk if you have limited storage space.

When you begin this lesson, restore the default application settings for After Effects. See "Restoring default preferences" on page 2.

3 Start After Effects, and then immediately hold down Ctrl+Alt+Shift (Windows) or Command+Option+Shift (Mac OS). When prompted, click OK to delete your preferences. Close the Start window.

After Effects opens to display an empty, untitled project.

4 Choose File > Save As > Save As.

5 In the Save Project As dialog box, navigate to the Lessons/Lesson11/Finished_ Project folder. Name the project **Lesson11_Finished.aep**, and click Save.

6 Click the Create A New Composition button (▣) at the bottom of the Project panel.

7 In the Composition Settings dialog box, do the following, and then click OK:

- Name the composition **Lunar Landing Media**.

- Choose HDTV 1080 24 from the Preset menu.

- Enter **3:00** for the Duration.

- Make sure the Background Color is black.

8 Choose File > Save.

Creating 3D text

In order to move something in 3D space, you need to make it a 3D object. Initially, any layer is flat, with only x (width) and y (height) dimensions, and can be moved only along those axes. But all you have to do to move a layer in three dimensions in After Effects is to turn on its 3D layer switch, which lets you manipulate the object along its z axis (depth). You'll create text, and then make it 3D. This layer will serve as a placeholder for text you'll create later in Cinema 4D.

1 Click in the Timeline panel to make it active.

2 Select the Horizontal Type tool (T) in the Tools panel.

After Effects adds the Character and Paragraph panels to the stack and opens the Character panel.

Note: If Blackoak Std is not available, install it using Typekit. Choose File > Add Fonts From Typekit, search for Blackoak Std, and sync it using Creative Cloud. Once you've synced the font, it will be available in all applications on your system.

3 Make the Character panel wider, if necessary, and then select the following settings:

- Font: Blackoak Std
- Fill Color: Black
- Stroke Color: White
- Font Size: **70** px
- Leading: **70** px
- Tracking: **20**%
- Stroke Width: **5** px
- Vertical Scale: **65**%

4 Select All Caps, and then make sure Stroke Over Fill is chosen from the pop-up menu in the Character panel. (You may need to drag the bottom of the Character panel to extend it in order to see all settings.)

5 Open the Paragraph panel, and select the Center Text alignment option.

6 Click anywhere in the Composition panel and type **Lunar Landing Media**, with each word on its own line, as in the image below.

Note: After Effects uses a different coordinate numbering convention than other 3D applications. In After Effects, the upper left corner of the composition is considered 0, 0. In many 3D applications, including Maxon Cinema 4D, the center of the world (often the screen) is the origin, or 0, 0, 0 point.

7 Select the Selection tool (➤).

8 In the Timeline panel, expand the Transform properties for the Lunar Landing Media layer, and change the Position property to **960**, **540**.

The text is centered in the composition.

9 In the Timeline panel, select the 3D Layer switch (⬡) for the Lunar Landing Media layer to give it three dimensions.

Three 3D Rotation properties appear in the Transform group for the layer, and properties that previously supported only two dimensions now display a third value for the z axis. In addition, a new property group named Material Options appears.

When the layer is selected, a color-coded 3D axis appears over the layer's anchor point in the Composition panel. The red arrow controls the x axis, the green arrow controls the y axis, and the blue arrow controls the z axis. At the moment, the z axis appears at the intersection of the x and y axes; it may be difficult to see against the black background. The letter x, y, or z appears when you position the Selection tool over the corresponding axis. When you move or rotate the layer while the pointer is over a particular axis, the layer's movement is restricted to that axis.

10 Hide the properties for the Lunar Landing Media layer.

Using 3D views

Sometimes the appearance of 3D layers can be deceptive. For example, a layer might appear to be scaling smaller along its x and y axes when it's actually moving along the z axis. You can't always tell from the default view in the Composition panel. The Select View Layout pop-up menu at the bottom of the Composition panel lets you divide the panel into different views of a single frame, so you can see your work from multiple angles. You specify different views using the 3D View pop-up menu.

1 At the bottom of the Composition panel, click the Select View Layout pop-up menu, and choose 4 Views, if your screen is large enough to display them. Otherwise, choose 2 Views - Horizontal.

With 4 Views selected, the upper left quadrant displays the scene from the top (along the y axis). There, you can see the z axis, and it's clear that the text layer has no depth. The lower left quadrant shows the view from the front. The upper right quadrant displays what the camera sees, but because there is no camera in the scene, it's the same as the front view. The lower right quadrant shows the view from the right, as if you were observing it along the x axis.

With 2 Views - Horizontal selected, the left view shows the scene from the top, and the right shows the camera's view (currently the front view).

2 Click the Front view to make it active. (Blue corner tabs appear around the active view.) Then, from the 3D View pop-up menu, choose Custom View 1 to see the scene from a different perspective. (If your Composition window displays only two views, click the Top view, and choose Custom View 1 from the 3D View pop-up menu.)

Viewing your 3D scene from different perspectives can help you align elements more accurately, view how layers are interacting with each other, and understand how objects, lights, and cameras are positioned in 3D space.

Importing a background

The text in your title card should appear to be moving in outer space. You'll import an image to use as a background.

1 Double-click an empty area of the Project panel to open the Import File dialog box.

2 Navigate to the Lesson11/Assets folder, and double-click the Space_Landscape.jpg file.

3 Drag the Space_Landscape.jpg item into the Timeline panel, placing it at the bottom of the layer stack.

4 Rename the Space_Landscape.jpg layer **Background**.

5 In the Timeline panel, select the Background layer, and then click the 3D Layer switch (◉) to convert it to a 3D layer.

6 Make sure the Background layer is selected. Then, in the Right view in the Composition panel, drag the z-axis arrow (the blue arrow) to the right to move the Background layer further behind the text. Watch the other layers as you drag to see how the layer interacts with 3D space.

● **Note:** If you're displaying only two views, select the Active Camera view, and choose Right from the 3D View pop-up menu. Then complete step 6.

7 In the Timeline panel, press the P key to display the Position property for the Background layer. Change the Position to **960, 300, 150**.

8 Choose File > Save to save your work so far.

Adding 3D lights

You've created a 3D scene, but it doesn't yet look three-dimensional from the front. Adding light to a composition creates shadows that give depth to the scene. You'll create two new lights for your composition.

Creating a light layer

In After Effects, a *light* is a type of layer that shines light on other layers. You can choose from among four different types of lights—Parallel, Spot, Point, and Ambient—and modify them with various settings. Lights, by default, are directed toward a point of interest, which is the focus area of the scene.

1 Deselect all layers so that the new layer you create will appear at the top of the layer stack.

2 Press the Home key, or move the current-time indicator to the beginning of the time ruler.

3 Choose Layer > New > Light.

4 In the Light Settings dialog box, do the following:

- Name the layer **Key Light**.

- Choose Spot from the Light Type menu.

- Set Color to a light orange (R=**255**, G=**235**, B=**195**).

- Make sure Intensity is set to **100%** and Cone Angle to **90** degrees.

- Make sure Cone Feather is set to **50%**.

- Select the Casts Shadows option.

- Set Shadow Darkness to **50%** and Shadow Diffusion to **150** pixels.

- Click OK to create the light layer.

In the Timeline panel, the light layer is represented by a light bulb icon (💡). In the Composition panel, a wireframe illustrates the light's position, with a cross-hairs icon (⊕) representing the point of interest.

Positioning the spotlight

The point of interest for this light is currently pointed at the center of the scene. Because that's where the text layer is located, you don't need to adjust it. However, you'll change the light position so the scene looks less bleak.

1 Select the Key Light layer in the Timeline panel, and press the P key to reveal the Position property for the light layer.

2 In the Timeline panel, type **955, –102, –2000** in the Position property. The light is now in front of and above the object, aiming down.

Creating and positioning the fill light

The key light gives the scene a moody look, but it's still very dark. You'll add a fill light to lighten the darker areas.

1 Choose Layer > New > Light.

2 In the Light Settings dialog box, do the following:

- Name the layer **Fill Light**.

- Choose Spot from the Light Type menu.

- Set the Color to a light blue (R=**205**, G=**238**, B=**251**).

- Set Intensity to **50%** and Cone Angle to **90** degrees.

- Make sure Cone Feather is set to **50%**.

- Deselect Casts Shadows.

- Click OK to create the light layer.

3 In the Timeline panel, select the Fill Light layer, and press the P key to reveal its Position property.

4 Change the position to **2624**, **370**, **−1125**.

The text stroke, stars, and moon highlight are all much brighter now.

5 Hide the open properties for all layers, and choose File > Save.

Casting shadows and setting material properties

The scene is looking better, with a mix of warm and cool colors. However, it still doesn't look three-dimensional. You'll change the Material Options properties to determine how the 3D layers interact with the lights and shadows.

1 Select the Lunar Landing Media layer in the Timeline panel, and press the A key twice (AA) to reveal the Material Options properties for the layer.

The Material Options property group defines the surface properties of the 3D layer. You can also set shadow and light transmission values.

2 For Casts Shadows, click the word *Off* to toggle the setting on. (Make sure it says *On*, not *Only*.)

The text layer now casts shadows based on the lights in the scene.

3 Change the Diffuse value to **60%** and the Specular Intensity to **60%** so that the text layer reflects more of the light in the scene.

4 Increase the Specular Shininess to **15%** to give the surface a more metallic shine.

5 Hide the properties for the Lunar Landing Media layer.

Adding a camera

You've already seen that you can view a 3D scene from different perspectives. You can also view 3D layers from various angles and distances using layers called *cameras*. When you set a camera view for your composition, you look at the layers as though you were looking through that camera. You can view a composition through the active camera or through a named, custom camera. If you have not created a custom camera, then the active camera is the same as the default composition view.

So far, you have been viewing this composition primarily from the Front, Right, and Custom View 1 angles. Currently, the Active Camera view doesn't let you see your composition from any specific angle. To see everything you want to see, you'll create a custom camera.

1 Deselect all layers, and then choose Layer > New > Camera.

2 In the Camera Settings dialog box, choose 20mm from the Preset menu, and click OK.

Tip: After Effects displays the wireframes for cameras by default. You can instruct After Effects to display wireframes only when cameras (or spotlights) are selected, or not at all. Choose View Options from the Composition panel menu, and then choose the options you want from the Camera Wireframes and Spotlight Wireframes menus. Then click OK.

The Camera 1 layer appears at the top of the layer stack in the Timeline panel (with a camera icon next to the layer name), and the Composition panel updates to reflect the new camera layer's perspective. The view should change slightly, because the 20mm preset shows a wider field of view than the default. If you didn't notice the scene change, toggle the visibility of the Camera 1 layer to see it, and then make sure it's visible.

3 Choose 2 Views - Horizontal from the Select View Layout pop-up menu at the bottom of the Composition panel. Change the view on the left to Right, and make sure the view on the right is set to Active Camera.

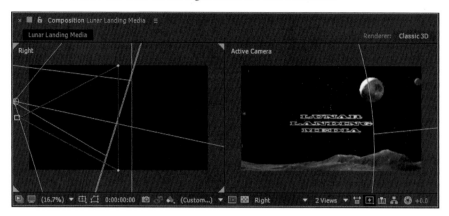

Like light layers, camera layers have a *point of interest* that can be used to determine what the camera looks at. By default, the camera's point of interest is the center of the composition. That's where your text currently is, so that point of interest works well.

4 Make sure the current-time indicator is at the beginning of the time ruler. Select the Camera 1 layer, and press the P key to reveal the Position property for the layer. Create an initial keyframe by clicking the stopwatch icon (⏱) next to the Position property.

5 Set the z-axis value to **–1000**.

The camera moves slightly closer to the text.

6 Go to 1:00.

7 Change the z-axis value to **–500.**

The camera moves much closer to the text.

8 Right-click (Windows) or Control-click (Mac OS) the second Position keyframe, and choose Keyframe Assistant > Easy Ease In.

9 Move the current-time indicator through the timeline to 1:00. As the camera moves through the scene, notice how the light reflects off the text layer, and how the overall image is influenced by the wider camera lens.

10 Hide the Position property for the Camera 1 layer, and choose File > Save.

Repositioning layers

At 1:00, the text sits low on the screen. You want to add text below it, so you'll need to make some adjustments. Also, now that the camera is in place, you'll reposition the background layer so that more of the moonscape is visible.

1 Press the Home key, or move the current-time indicator to the beginning of the time ruler.

2 Select the Lunar Landing Media layer in the Timeline panel, and press P to see its Position property. Change the y-axis value for the Position property to **470.**

3 Select the Background layer in the Timeline panel, and press P to show its Position property. Then change the z-axis value for the Position property to **700.**

4 Hide the Position properties for the Background and Lunar Landing Media layers.

5 Click an empty area in the Timeline panel to deselect all layers.

Adding a text layer

Now that there's space below the text, you'll create a new text layer to go there.

1 Select the Horizontal Type Tool (T) in the Tools panel. In the Character panel, select the following settings:

Note: If Chaparral Pro is not available, install it using Typekit. Choose File > Add Fonts From Typekit, search for Chaparral Pro, and sync it using Creative Cloud. Once you've synced the font, it will be available in all applications on your system.

- Font: Chaparral Pro
- Font Style: Regular
- Fill Color: White
- Font Size: **40** px
- Leading: **100** px
- Tracking Value: **0%**
- Stroke Width: **0** px
- Vertical Scale: **100%**

2 Deselect All Caps in the Character panel.

3 In the Composition panel, click an insertion point, and type **A Space Pod LLC**.

4 Select the Selection tool (▶) in the Tools panel.

5 In the Timeline panel, click the 3D Layer switch (⬤) for the A Space Pod LLC layer to convert it to 3D.

Note: You can use the onscreen widget to position the layer if you prefer.

6 Press the P key to display the Position property for the layer. Then type **960**, **675**, **0** for the Position property to situate the new text below *Lunar Landing Media*. Press P to hide the Position property.

7 Move to 1:04 in the timeline. Expand the A Space Pod LLC layer, and choose Opacity from the Animate pop-up menu.

8 Change the Opacity value under Range Selector 1 to **0%**.

9 Expand Range Selector 1, and make sure the Start value is 0%. Then click the stop-watch icon (⏱) to create an initial keyframe for the Start value.

10 Move to 1:12 in the timeline, and change the Start value to **100**%.

11 Manually scrub through the timeline to 1:12 to preview the animation.

12 Hide all open properties, and choose File > Save to save your work.

Working with Cinema 4D Lite

After Effects installs a version of Maxon Cinema 4D that allows motion graphic artists and animators to insert 3D objects directly into an After Effects scene without pre-rendering passes and potentially complicated file exchanges. You can import, create, and edit 3D objects in a variety of formats.

You'll use Cinema 4D Lite to create extruded text, which you'll add to the After Effects scene, replacing the initial text.

Exporting a scene file

After Effects and Cinema 4D measure coordinates from different places in a scene. In After Effects, the 0, 0, 0 position is in the upper left corner of the scene; in Cinema 4D, the same coordinates are in the center. Keep this in mind when you move between the two applications. You can open an After Effects composition in Cinema 4D without a problem, but it's easier if you line everything up initially. You'll use a null object to do that.

1 Make sure the Timeline panel is active, and then choose Layer > New > Null Object.

A null object is an invisible layer that has all the properties of a visible layer, so that it can be a parent to any layer in the composition. You'll use a null object to reposition the scene to 0, 0, 0.

2 In the Timeline panel, select the Null 1 layer, and click the 3D switch (◉) to make it a 3D layer.

3 Select the A Space Pod LLC layer, and then Shift-click the Background layer to select all the layers except the Null 1 layer.

4 Choose 1. Null 1 from the Parent pop-up menu for the Background layer.

All the selected layers are parented to the Null 1 layer. Any changes to the null object affect them all.

5 Select the Null 1 layer, and press P to reveal its Position property. Then change the x and y values to **0**.

Nothing appears to happen in the Active Camera view in the Composition panel, but in the Right view, the contents of the scene appears to shift.

6 Hide the Position property for the Null 1 layer, and then choose File > Save.

7 Select the Lunar Landing Media composition in the Project panel, and then choose File > Export > Maxon Cinema 4D Exporter.

8 In the Save As dialog box, name the file **Lesson11.c4d**, and save it in the Lesson11 folder. Click Save to export the file.

The Cinema 4D exporter exports the lights, cameras, and certain layers from your After Effects scene into a Cinema 4D file. You can also import the resulting C4D file directly into After Effects for compositing into an After Effects scene.

9 Choose File > Import > File, select the Lesson11.c4d file you just saved, and click Import or Open.

10 Drag the Lesson11.c4d file from the Project panel to the Timeline panel, placing it between the Key Light and Lunar Landing Media layers.

When you add a C4D file to the Timeline panel, After Effects opens the Cineware effect. Cineware creates and manages the link between After Effects and Cinema 4D.

While you're working with a Cinema 4D file in After Effects, you should usually choose Software or Standard (Draft) from the Renderer menu in the Cineware effect. However, when you prepare to render your final project, choose Standard (Final) from the Renderer menu.

11 Choose Standard (Draft) from the Renderer menu in the Cineware effect in the Effect Controls panel.

The Software option creates a low-resolution version of the file. The Standard (Draft) option gives you a better view of what the Cinema 4D file looks like.

12 Choose Comp Camera from the Camera menu in the Effect Controls panel.

The Comp Camera option lets you use the After Effects camera you created earlier in this composition to make any refinements to your camera motion. Cineware will automatically adjust the 3D objects from the Cinema 4D scene.

Creating 3D Text in Cinema 4D

After Effects didn't export the text layers into Cinema 4D, but it did export the background solid object, the two lights you created, and the camera layer. You will use Cinema 4D Lite to create extruded text for this project.

● **Note:** When you open Cinema 4D Lite, you may be prompted to update the application.

1 In the Project panel, select the Lesson11.c4d file, and then choose Edit > Edit Original.

The Lesson11.c4d file opens in Cinema 4D Lite.

A. Modes icon palette **B.** Viewport **C.** Tools icon palette **D.** Object Manager **E.** Material Manager
F. Timeline **G.** Coordinates Manager · **H.** Attribute Manager

2 In the Cinema 4D Timeline, change the clip length to **72** frames: Increase the value in the box on the right, and then extend the timeline to 72 frames.

3 In the Tools icon palette (below the menu bar), click and hold the triangle in the lower right corner of the Freehand icon (🐍) to display its menu, and then select the Text tool (𝕋).

A basic text spline appears in the middle of the scene.

4 In the text box in the Attribute Manager, type **LUNAR LANDING MEDIA**, with each word on its own line.

5 In the Attribute Manager, change the text settings as follows:

- Font: Blackoak Std

- Align: Middle

- Height: **70** cm

- Vertical Spacing: **−10** cm

6 Drag the playhead in the Timeline to frame 24 (1:00).

The camera moves just as it did in After Effects. There's also a 3D axis in the Viewport similar to the one in the Composition panel in After Effects.

Note: If you are unable to select the y-axis arrow, select the Move tool first.

7 Click the y-axis arrow (the green one), and drag the text object until its position is similar to the one in the image. Your goal is to make sure there's room for the other text below it.

8 In the Tools icon palette, click and hold the triangle in the lower right corner of the Subdivision Surface icon (⬡) to view its menu, and then select Extrude (⬟).

9 In the Object Manager, select the Text object, and then drag it to the middle column to the right of Extrude to parent it. You'll know you've positioned it correctly when the cursor becomes a box with an arrow pointing down (▾).

In the Object Manager, the Text object appears nested below the Extrude object, indicating the parent relationship. In the Viewport, the text is now extruded.

10 In the Object Manager, click the Extrude object to make it active (it turns bright orange).

11 In the Attribute Manager, select the Object tab, and then change the z-axis Movement value to **70** cm.

The extruded text looks much better. You'll enhance the text further by beveling the edges and making some adjustments.

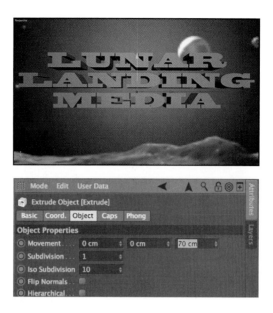

12 In the Attribute Manager, select the Caps tab, and do the following:

- Choose Fillet Cap from the Start menu.

- Increase the Steps value to **2**.

- Decrease the Radius value to **3** cm.

- Choose Concave from the Fillet Type menu.

The changes you made give the text an interesting edge.

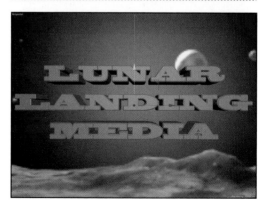

Surfacing the object

Cinema 4D Lite comes with a number of preset surfaces you can apply to 3D objects. You'll add a metallic surface to the text.

1 In the Materials Manager, click Create, and then choose Load Material Preset > Lite > Materials > Effects > Mazzie B-Blue.

2 In the Materials Manager, click the surface you just added, and drag it onto the text in the Viewport.

Note: If you see a message about version compatibility, click Yes to proceed and save the file.

3 Choose File > Save.

Updating the project in After Effects

You've made all the changes you need to make in Cinema 4D Lite, so you can now return to After Effects to see how it works in your project. As a final touch, you'll add an audio file for the title card.

1 Return to After Effects.

After Effects updates, and the Cinema 4D object appears in the Active Camera view in the Composition panel.

2 Choose 1 View from the Select View Layout pop-up menu at the bottom of the Composition panel. Choose Active Camera from the 3D View pop-up menu, if it isn't already selected.

3 In the Timeline panel, deselect the Video switch for the Lunar Landing Media text layer to hide it.

The original text layer was a placeholder for the 3D text you created in Cinema 4D Lite. You don't need it in the final project.

4 If you need to reposition the text in the Cinema 4D file, return to Cinema 4D Lite, adjust the text, and choose File > Save. Then return to After Effects again.

You can move back and forth between After Effects and Cinema 4D Lite.

5 Double-click an empty area of the Project panel, and then navigate to the Lesson11/ Assets folder. Double-click the Lunar.mp3 file to import it.

6 Drag the Lunar.mp3 file from the Project panel to the bottom of the layer stack in the Timeline panel.

7 Choose File > Save.

8 (Optional) Preview the project before you render. To cache the frames in RAM faster, expand the properties for the Lesson11.c4d layer in the Timeline panel, and click CINEWARE under Effects. Then, in the Effect Controls panel, select both No Pre-calculation and Keep Textures In RAM.

You're ready to render the file.

9 Select the Lunar Landing Media composition in the Project panel, and choose Composition > Add To Render Queue.

10 In the Render Queue panel, click Best Settings to open the Render Settings dialog box. Then choose Half from the Resolution menu. (If your system is very slow, you may want to choose Quarter or Third.) Click OK.

11 Click the blue text next to Output To, and navigate to the Lesson11/Finished_ Project folder. Then click Save.

12 Click Render in the Render Queue panel.

13 When your project has rendered, open it in QuickTime to see your handiwork!

You've only just scratched the surface of what is possible when working with a 3D scene in After Effects, as well as what you can do with the workflow between Adobe After Effects and Maxon Cinema 4D Lite.

Review questions

1 What happens to a layer when you select its 3D Layer switch?

2 Why is it important to look at multiple views of a composition that contains 3D layers?

3 What is a camera layer?

4 What is a 3D light in After Effects?

Review answers

1 When you select a layer's 3D Layer switch in the Timeline panel, After Effects adds a third axis, the z axis, to the layer. You can then move and rotate the layer in three dimensions. In addition, the layer takes on new properties that are unique to 3D layers, such as the Materials Options property group.

2 The appearance of 3D layers can be deceptive, depending on the view in the Composition panel. By enabling 3D views, you can see the true position of a layer relative to other layers in the composition.

3 You can view After Effects 3D layers from any number of angles and distances using layers called *cameras*. When you set a camera view for your composition, you look at the layers as though you were looking through that camera. You can choose between viewing a composition through the active camera or through a named, custom camera. If you have not created a custom camera, then the active camera is the same as the default composition view.

4 In After Effects, a light is a type of layer that shines light on other layers. You can choose from among four different types of lights—Parallel, Spot, Point, and Ambient—and modify them with various settings.

12 WORKING WITH THE 3D CAMERA TRACKER

Lesson overview

In this lesson, you'll learn how to do the following:

- Track footage using the 3D Camera Tracker.

- Add camera and text elements to a tracked scene.

- Set a ground plane and origin.

- Create realistic shadows for new 3D elements.

- Lock elements to planes using null objects.

- Adjust camera settings to match real-world footage.

- Remove rolling shutter distortions from DSLR footage.

This lesson will take approximately one and a half hours to complete. Download the Lesson12 project files from the Lesson & Update Files tab on your Account page at www.peachpit.com, if you haven't already done so. As you work on this lesson, you'll preserve the start files. If you need to restore the start files, download them from your Account page.

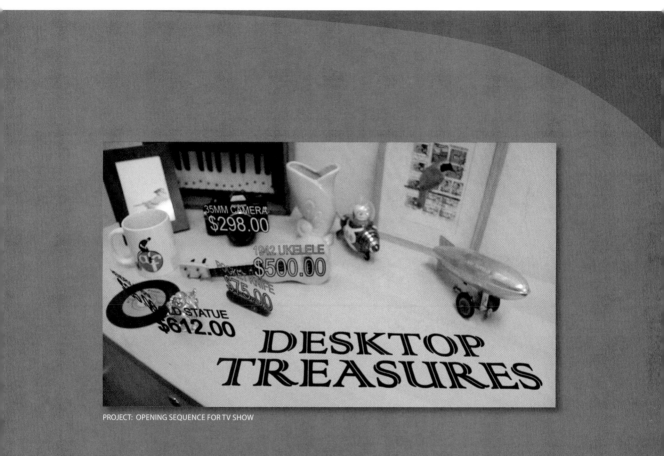

PROJECT: OPENING SEQUENCE FOR TV SHOW

The 3D Camera Tracker effect analyzes two-dimensional footage to create a virtual 3D camera that matches the original. You can use this data to add 3D objects that merge realistically with your scene.

About the 3D Camera Tracker effect

The 3D Camera Tracker effect automatically analyzes the motion present in existing 2D footage, extracts the position and lens type of the real camera that shot the scene, and creates a new 3D camera in After Effects to match it. The effect also overlays 3D track points onto the 2D footage, so you can easily attach new 3D layers onto the original footage.

These new 3D layers have the same movement and perspective changes as the original footage. The 3D Camera Tracker effect even helps create "shadow catchers," so your new 3D layers can appear to cast realistic shadows and reflections onto the existing footage.

The 3D Camera Tracker performs its analysis in the background. Therefore, you can work on other compositions while the footage is being analyzed.

Getting started

In this lesson, you'll create the opening scene for a fictional reality show that estimates the value of everyday objects found on office desks. You'll begin by importing the footage and tracking it with the 3D Camera Tracker effect. Then you'll add 3D text elements that track precisely with the scene. Finally, you'll animate the text, add audio, and enhance the footage to complete the show's introduction.

First, you'll preview the final movie and set up your project.

1 Make sure the following files are in the Lessons/Lesson12 folder on your hard disk, or download them from your Account page at www.peachpit.com now:

 • In the Assets folder: DesktopC.mov, Treasures_Music.aif, Treasures_Title.psd

 • In the Sample_Movie folder: Lesson12.mov

2 Open and play the Lesson12.mov file to see what you will create in this lesson. When you're done, quit QuickTime Player. You may delete the sample movie from your hard disk if you have limited storage space.

When you begin this lesson, restore the default application settings for After Effects. See "Restoring default preferences" on page 2.

3 Start After Effects, and then immediately hold down Ctrl+Alt+Shift (Windows) or Command+Option+Shift (Mac OS). When prompted, click OK to delete your preferences. Close the Start window.

After Effects opens to display an empty, untitled project.

4 Choose File > Save As > Save As.

5 In the Save As dialog box, navigate to the Lessons/Lesson12/ Finished_Project folder.

6 Name the project **Lesson12_Finished.aep**, and then click Save.

Importing the footage

You need to import three footage items for this lesson.

1 Choose File > Import > File.

2 Navigate to the Lessons/Lesson12/Assets folder, Shift-click to select the DesktopC.mov, Treasures_Music.aif, and Treasures_Title.psd files, and then click Import or Open.

3 Choose File > New > New Folder to create a new folder in the Project panel, or click the Create A New Folder button (📁) at the bottom of the panel.

4 Type **Footage** to name the folder, press Enter or Return to accept the name, and then drag the DesktopC. mov and Treasures_Title.psd items into the Footage folder.

5 Make sure nothing is selected. Then create another folder, name it **Audio**, and drag the Treasures_Music.aif item into it.

6 Expand the folders so that you can see their contents.

Creating the composition

Now, you will create a new composition based on the aspect ratio and duration of the DesktopC.mov file.

1 Drag the DesktopC.mov item onto the Create A New Composition button (🎞) at the bottom of the Project panel. After Effects creates a new composition named DesktopC and displays it in the Composition and Timeline panels.

2 Drag the DesktopC composition to an empty area of the Project panel to move it out of the Footage folder.

3 Drag the current-time indicator across the time ruler to preview the shot.

The camera moves around a desktop so that you can see the objects on it. You'll add labels and dollar amounts, animated in time with background music.

4 Choose File > Save to save the file.

Repairing rolling shutter distortions

Digital cameras with CMOS sensors—including video-capable DSLRs, which are becoming increasingly popular for the creation of films, commercials, and television shows—typically have what is commonly known as a "rolling" shutter, which captures a frame of video one scan line at a time. Due to time lag between scan lines, not all parts of the image are recorded at exactly the same time, causing motion to ripple down the frame. If the camera or the subject is moving, the rolling shutter can cause distortions, such as leaning buildings and other skewed images.

The Rolling Shutter Repair effect attempts to correct this problem automatically. To use it, select the problem layer in the Timeline panel, and choose Effect > Distort > Rolling Shutter Repair.

Due to a rolling shutter distortion, the pillars of the building appear to be leaning.

After applying the effect, the building looks much more stable.

The default settings usually do the trick, but you may need to change the Scan Direction or the Method being used to analyze the footage.

If you plan to use the 3D Camera Tracker effect with footage on which you've used the Rolling Shutter Repair effect, precompose the footage first.

Tracking the footage

The 2D footage is in place. Now you'll have After Effects track it and interpolate where a 3D camera should be placed.

1 In the Timeline panel, click the Audio icon for the DesktopC.mov layer to mute the audio.

You'll add a soundtrack later, and you don't want any ambient noise from this clip.

2 Right-click (Windows) or Control-click (Mac OS) the DesktopC.mov layer in the Timeline panel, and choose Track Camera.

After Effects opens the Effect Controls panel and displays its progress as it analyzes the footage in the background. When the analysis is complete, many tracking points appear in the Composition panel. The size of a tracked point indicates its proximity to the virtual camera: Larger points are closer, and smaller points are further away.

The default analysis of the footage often yields satisfactory results, but you can perform a more detailed analysis to better solve the camera position.

3 In the Effect Controls panel, expand the Advanced category, and then select Detailed Analysis.

Depending on your system, this may take a while.

After Effects analyzes the footage again. If you're working with a slower machine and you suspect you'll need a detailed analysis, you can save time by selecting Detailed Analysis while the 3D Camera Tracker is performing its initial analysis. The detailed analysis may take a few minutes, depending on your system. Because the analysis is performed in the background, you could work on other aspects of your project while it progresses.

4 When the analysis is complete, choose File > Save to save your work so far.

Creating a ground plane, a camera, and the initial text

Note: You can also add a camera by clicking the Create Camera button in the Effect Controls panel.

You have a 3D scene, but it needs a 3D camera. You'll add a camera when you create the first text element, and then you'll add a second text element related to the first.

1 Press the Home key, or move the current-time indicator to the beginning of the time ruler.

2 In the Composition panel, hover the cursor over the hole in the record on the desk until the displayed target is in line with the plane and the perspective matches. (If you don't see the track points and target, click the 3D Camera Tracker effect in the Effect Controls panel to make it active.)

Note: If the size of the target makes it difficult to see the plane, resize the target by pressing Alt or Option as you drag from the center of the target.

When you hover the cursor between three or more neighboring track points that can define a plane, a semitransparent triangle appears between the points. Additionally, a red target shows the orientation of the plane in 3D space.

3 Right-click (Windows) or Control-click (Mac OS) the plane, and choose Set Ground Plane And Origin.

The ground plane and origin provide a reference point, setting a point where the coordinates are (0, 0, 0). Though nothing appears to change in the Composition panel using the Active Camera View, the ground plane and origin make it easier to change the camera's rotation and position.

4 Right-click (Windows) or Control-click (Mac OS) the same plane, and choose Create Text And Camera.

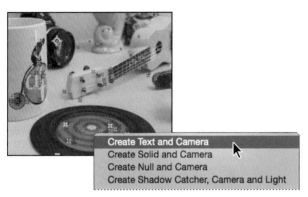

After Effects displays a large text item lying flat in the Composition panel. It also adds two layers to the Timeline panel: Text and 3D Tracker Camera. The 3D switch is enabled for the Text layer, but the DesktopC.mov layer remains 2D. Because the text elements are the only ones that need to be positioned in 3D space, there is no reason to make the background footage layer a 3D layer.

5 Move the current-time indicator along the time ruler. The text remains in position, tracking with the camera. Return the current-time indicator to the beginning of the time ruler.

6 Double-click the Text layer in the Timeline panel to add the Character and Paragraph panels to the stacked panels on the right.

7 Open the Paragraph panel, and select Center Text for the alignment. The text is centered over the record.

8 Open the Character panel. Change the font to a sans serif font such as Arial Narrow or Helvetica Light. Then change the font size to **20** px, the stroke width to **1** px, and the stroke type to Fill Over Stroke. Make sure the fill color is white and the stroke color is black (the default colors).

The text looks great, but you want it to stand on end. You'll change its location in space, and then replace it with the price of the object.

● **Note:** Instead of entering values, you could use the Rotation tool to adjust the individual axes in the Composition panel.

9 Select the Text layer in the Timeline panel to exit text-editing mode. Then, press the R key to display the Rotation property of the layer, and change the Orientation values to **0**, **350**, **0** degrees.

Any new 3D layer you create uses the ground plane and origin to orient the layer in the scene. The Text layer was originally flat, with the Orientation of 270 degrees on the x axis. When you change that value to 0, the text becomes vertical.

10 Double-click the Text layer in the Timeline panel to make it active in the Composition panel.

When the text is editable, it appears to have a light red mask surrounding it.

11 With the text selected in the Composition panel, type **$35.00** to replace it.

So far, so good. Next, you want to label the item, and the label needs to stay with the price as the camera moves. You'll duplicate the layer, modify it, and then parent one layer to the other.

12 Select the $35.00 layer in the Timeline panel, and press Ctrl+D (Windows) or Command+D (Mac OS) to duplicate it.

13 Double-click the $35.2 layer, and type **HENDRIX 45 RPM** (in all capital letters) in the Composition panel.

The text is too large; it's the same size as the price text. You'll parent it to the $35.00 layer and then scale it.

14 Select the Hendrix 45 RPM layer in the Timeline panel, and press the P key to reveal the Position property for the layer. Drag the pick whip from the Hendrix layer to the $35.00 layer.

The Position value for the Hendrix layer changes to 0, 0, 0, because its position is related to the parent layer. However, you want the Hendrix layer to appear above the $35.00 layer, not in front of it.

15 Change the y-axis position value to **–18** to move the Hendrix label above the price text.

16 With the Hendrix layer selected, press the S key to reveal the Scale property, and change the Scale values to **37.4, 37.4, 37.4%**.

17 Close the open properties, and then choose File > Save to save your work so far.

Creating realistic shadows

You've set up your first text elements, but unlike true 3D objects, they aren't casting any shadows. You'll create a shadow catcher and a light to add depth to your video.

1 Press the Home key, or move the current-time indicator to the beginning of the time ruler.

2 Select the DesktopC.mov layer in the Timeline panel, press the E key to display the 3D Camera Tracker effect, and then select the 3D Camera Tracker effect.

Note: Be sure to select the 3D Camera Tracker effect in the DesktopC.mov layer, not the 3D Tracker Camera layer.

3 Select the Selection tool (➤) in the Tools panel. Then, in the Composition panel, hover until you find the same plane you used to create the text layer.

4 Right-click (Windows) or Control-click (Mac OS) the target, and choose Create Shadow Catcher And Light.

After Effects adds a light source to the scene. The default settings are applied, so a shadow appears in the Composition panel. However, you'll need to reposition the light to match the light in the source footage. The Shadow Catcher 1 layer that After Effects adds to the Timeline panel is a shape layer that has its material options set so that it accepts shadows only from the scene.

5 Select the Light 1 layer in the Timeline panel, and press the P key to reveal the Position property for the layer.

Tip: In a real-world project, it's ideal to work with the lighting plan that was used to shoot the original 2D scene. The goal is to have the new 3D lights match the original source lighting as closely as possible.

6 Enter the following values for the Position property to reposition the light: **1900, −2500, −375**.

7 Choose Layer > Light Settings.

You can change the intensity, color, and other attributes of the light in the Light Settings dialog box.

8 Name the light **Key Light**. Choose Point from the Light Type menu, and then select a slightly red color (we used R=232, G=214, B=213) to match the slight color cast in the room. Then change the Shadow Darkness to **15%** and the Shadow Diffusion to **100** px. Click OK.

9 Select the Shadow Catcher 1 layer in the Timeline panel, and press the S key to reveal the Scale property.

10 Change the Scale value to **340%**.

Scaling the Shadow Catcher 1 layer changes the area in which shadows can appear for the light that was created with it.

Adding ambient light

The shadow looks better after the adjustments you made to the light, but it's now causing the text to appear black. You'll add ambient light to address this. Unlike a point light, ambient light creates a more diffuse light throughout the scene.

1 Deselect all layers, and then choose Layer > New > Light.

2 Name the light **Ambient Light**, choose Ambient from the Light Type menu, and change its Intensity value to **80%**. The light color should be the same as the color you selected for the point light.

3 Click OK to add the light to the scene.

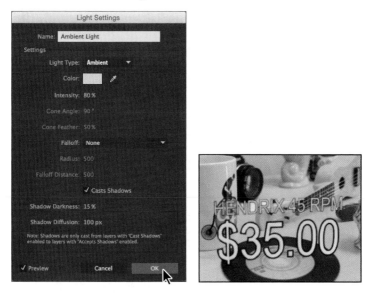

4 Hide the properties for all layers in the Timeline panel, except for the DesktopC.mov layer.

Creating additional text elements

Tip: If a 3D object should be obscured by an object in the background, duplicate the background layer, move it to the top of the layer stack, and then use the Mask tool to create masks around portions of the foreground elements. You will need to animate these masks over time, but if you do it carefully, you can create a seamless composition.

You created the label for the Hendrix record. Now you need to perform the same tasks to create labels for the camera, gold statue, pocket knife, and ukulele. You'll use the same steps to create each label, but because the objects are in different places on the table, you'll need to use different orientation and scaling values, as listed in the following chart. You'll find it easiest to attach the label for each to the correct plane at different points in the time ruler.

OBJECT	POSITION IN TIME RULER (STEP 1)	ORIENTATION (STEP 5)	PRICE (STEP 6)	PRICE SCALE (STEP 7)	LABEL (STEP 9)
camera	3:00	0, 310, 0	$298.00	3000	35MM CAMERA
statue	5:00	0, 325, 0	$612.00	2000	GOLD STATUE
knife	7:00	0, 340, 0	$75.00	2500	POCKET KNIFE
ukulele	9:00	0, 310, 0	$500.00	3000	1942 UKULELE

1 Move the current-time indicator to get a better view of the object.

2 In the Timeline panel, select the 3D Camera Tracker (under the DesktopC.mov layer) to make it active. (If you don't see the 3D Camera Tracker, press the E key to reveal it.)

Note: Make sure you select the 3D Camera Tracker effect in the DesktopC.mov layer, not the 3D Tracker Camera layer.

3 Make sure the Selection tool (➤) is selected. Then, in the Composition panel, hover over an area so that the red target is parallel to the front of the object.

4 Right-click (Windows) or Control-click (Mac OS) the target, and choose Create Text.

5 Select the Text layer in the Timeline panel, and press the R key to reveal the Rotation values. Then change the Orientation values.

6 Double-click the Text layer to make it editable, and then type the price in the Composition panel.

7 Select the price layer in the Timeline panel, and press S to reveal the Scale property. Change the Scale value.

8 With the price layer selected, press Ctrl+D (Windows) or Command+D (Mac OS) to duplicate the layer.

9 Double-click the duplicate layer in the Timeline panel, and then type the label in the Composition panel.

10 Select the label layer in the Timeline panel, and press P to reveal its Position property. Then drag the pick whip from the label layer (e.g., 35MM CAMERA) to the price layer (e.g., $298.00).

Note: If you turn on Caps Lock to type the label, be sure to turn it off again. Otherwise, you'll get unexpected results, and After Effects won't be able to update the layer name.

11 Change the y value of the Position property for the label layer to **–18** to move the label above the price.

12 Select the label layer again, and press S to reveal the Scale property. Change its Scale values to **50**, **50**, **50%**.

13 Hide the properties for the layers you just created.

14 Repeat steps 1–13 to label the additional objects, using the values in the chart on the previous page.

The labels all look good, but they may overlap in places that can make them hard to read. You can reposition them as necessary.

Note: Your labels may look different from ours, depending on where you positioned each plane.

15 If you need to adjust a label, select the price layer for the object, and then use the Selection tool to adjust its position. Because you've parented the label layer to the price layer, adjusting the price moves both text layers.

16 Choose File > Save to save your work so far.

Locking a layer to a plane with a null object

The title card for the show should be flat on the table, using the same plane you used to attach text to the record. You'll use a null object to attach the title card to that plane. The title card is an Adobe Photoshop file.

1 Press the Home key, or move the current-time indicator to the beginning of the time ruler.

2 In the Timeline panel, select the 3D Camera Tracker (under the DesktopC.mov layer) to make it active. (If you don't see the 3D Camera Tracker, press the E key to reveal it.)

3 Select the Selection tool, and then move the cursor so that the target is lying flat over the record.

4 Right-click (Windows) or Control-click (Mac OS) the target, and choose Create Null.

After Effects adds a Track Null 1 layer to the top of the layer stack in the Timeline panel. Because you know that the record is on the same plane as the desktop, you can use this null object to position the title of the show in the open area of the desk, and still have it move correctly in relation to other elements and the camera in the scene.

5 Select the Track Null 1 layer in the Timeline panel, press Enter or Return, and change the name to **Desktop Null**. Press Enter or Return again to accept the name change.

6 From the Project panel, drag the Treasures_Title.psd asset to the Timeline panel, placing it directly above the Desktop Null layer.

7 Drag the pick whip from the Treasures_Title layer to the Desktop Null layer to parent the layer.

8 Click the 3D switch for the Treasures_Title layer to make it a 3D layer.

Tip: Instead of dragging the pick whip, you could choose 2.Desktop Null from the Parent menu in the Treasures_Title layer.

Because you've parented the title layer to the null object, when it becomes a 3D layer it is automatically oriented to be flat on the desktop.

9 Move to the end of the time ruler so you can see how the title card is positioned.

You need to move the title to the empty area of the desktop, and then rotate it and resize it.

10 Select the Treasures_Title layer in the Timeline panel, and press R to reveal its Rotation property. Then change its Z Rotation value to **305** degrees.

11 Press the S key to reveal the Scale property, and change the Scale amount to **625%**.

12 With the Selection tool, move the title text into position, as in the image at the bottom of this page. If you need to resize the text, use the Selection tool to adjust the object's corner handles.

13 Click the Toggle Switches/Modes button at the bottom of the Timeline panel. Choose Luminosity from the Mode menu for the Treasures_Title layer.

14 Click the Toggle Switches/Modes button again to return to displaying switches.

15 Choose File > Save to save your work so far.

Animating the text

The 3D text elements, camera, and lighting are all complete, but you can make the introduction more interesting by animating the text to appear according to cues in the soundtrack. You'll add an audio track, and then animate the labels to appear when cash register sounds occur.

Animating the first text elements

You'll animate the record label and price to appear early in the intro, with the price cycling through characters until it arrives at the final text.

1 In the Project panel, drag the Treasures_Music.aif file from the Audio folder to the bottom of the layer stack in the Timeline panel.

2 Move the current-time indicator to the beginning of the timeline, and then press the spacebar to move the first few seconds of the composition into RAM. Press the spacebar to stop caching, go to the beginning of the time ruler, and press the spacebar again to preview what you cached.

Notice that the cash register sound occurs periodically. You'll animate the text to appear at those points.

3 Go to 1:00, and select the $35.00 layer. Press the S key to reveal the Scale property, and then change the Scale amount to **0%**. Click the stopwatch icon (⏱) to create an initial keyframe.

4 Go to 1:08, and change the Scale amount for the $35.00 layer to **3200%** so that the text is larger than its final size.

5 Go to 1:10, and change the Scale amount to **3000%**, the final value for the text.

6 Go to 1:00, and press S to hide the Scale property. Then click the arrow next to the $35.00 layer to reveal all its properties.

7 Next to the Text property, choose Character Offset from the Animate menu.

8 Expand Range Selector 1 in the Animator 1 properties. Then click the stopwatch next to Offset to create an initial keyframe, and make sure the value is **0%**.

9 Create an initial keyframe for Character Offset (under Character Range), and make sure its value is **0**.

10 Go to 1:12, and change the Range Selector 1 Offset value to **−100%**.

11 Click the word *Offset* to select both keyframes, right-click (Windows) or Control-click (Mac OS) one of the keyframes, and then choose Keyframe Assistant > Easy Ease.

12 Go to 1:17, and change the Character Offset value to **20**.

13 Preview the first two seconds of the composition.

The title of the record pops up as the text cycles through to the estimated price. The character offset values determine how the text cycles through characters to arrive at the final one.

Copying the animation to other text elements

Now that you've animated the text for the record, you can copy the animation for the other objects, placing the keyframes at the appropriate points in the time ruler.

1 Select the $35.00 layer, and press the U key to reveal only the properties that have keyframes.

2 In the time graph, drag a marquee around all the keyframes to select them.

3 Choose Edit > Copy to copy the keyframes and their values.

4 Go to 3:00, and select the $298.00 layer. Choose Edit > Paste to paste the keyframes and their values, beginning at the current time.

5 Go to 5:00, and select the $612.00 layer. Press Ctrl+V (Windows) or Command+V (Mac OS) to paste the keyframes and their values.

6 Go to 7:00, select the $75.00 layer, and press Ctrl+V (Windows) or Command+V (Mac OS).

7 Go to 9:00, select the $500.00 layer, and press Ctrl+V (Windows) or Command+V (Mac OS).

8 Hide the properties for all the layers, and then choose File > Save.

Adjusting the camera's depth of field

The intro is looking pretty good, but you can make the computer-generated elements more closely match the source footage if you adjust the depth of field for the 3D camera. You'll use the values that were used in the camera that shot the original footage, so the text that is further away from the camera appears to be more out of focus.

1. Select the 3D Tracker Camera layer in the Timeline panel.

2. Choose Layer > Camera Settings.

3. In the Camera Settings dialog box, do the following, and then click OK:

 - Select Enable Depth of Field.

 - Set the Focus Distance to **200** mm.

 - Change the F-Stop value to **5.6**.

 - Set the Focal Length to **27.2**.

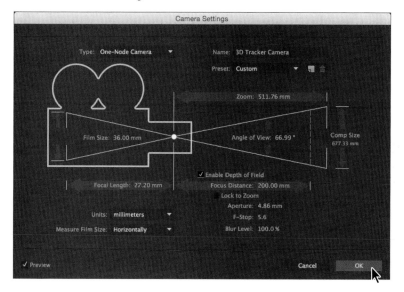

4. In the Timeline panel, select all of the layers except the audio layer. Then select the Motion Blur switch for one of the layers, applying it to all selected layers.

5. Click the Enable Motion Blur button (⊘) at the top of the Timeline panel to enable motion blur for all layers.

6. Choose File > Save to save your project.

Rendering the composition

You've done some complex work to create a scene that merges the added components with an existing tableau. To see the final results, you'll render the project. You'll learn more about rendering in Lesson 14, "Rendering and Outputting."

1. Choose Window > Render Queue to open the Render Queue panel.

2. Drag the DesktopC composition from the Project panel to the Render Queue panel.

3 Click the blue words next to Render Settings. Then, in the Render Settings dialog box, choose Half from the Resolution menu, and click OK.

4 Click the blue text next to Output Module. Then, in the Output Module Settings dialog box, choose QuickTime from the Format menu.

5 Click Format Options in the Output Module Settings dialog box. Then do the following in the QuickTime Options dialog box, and click OK:

- Choose H.264 from the Video Codec menu.

- Select Limit Data Rate To in the Bitrate Settings area.

- Change the data rate limit to **8000** kbps.

6 In the Output Module Settings dialog box, make sure Audio Output Auto is chosen in the Audio Output pop-up menu. Then click OK.

When Audio Output Auto is selected, After Effects automatically detects active audio in the composition.

7 Click the blue text next to Output To, navigate to the Lesson12/Finished_Project folder, and click Save.

8 Click Render in the Render Queue panel to render the composition.

9 When After Effects has finished rendering the composition, play the QuickTime movie to admire your work!

Review questions

1 What does the 3D Camera Tracker effect do?

2 How can you make an added 3D element look like it is the same size as elements that are farther from the camera?

3 What is the Rolling Shutter Repair effect?

Review answers

1 The 3D Camera Tracker effect automatically analyzes the motion present in existing 2D footage, extracts the position and lens type of the real camera that shot the scene, and creates a new 3D camera in After Effects to match it. The effect also overlays 3D track points onto the 2D footage, so you can easily attach new 3D layers onto the original footage.

2 To make an added 3D element appear to recede, so that it looks like it's farther from the camera, adjust its Scale property. Adjusting the Scale property keeps its perspective locked with the rest of the composition.

3 The Rolling Shutter Repair effect attempts to correct the "rolling" shutter problem that commonly occurs when you use digital cameras with CMOS sensors, which capture a frame of video one scan line at a time. Due to time lag between scan lines, not all parts of the image are recorded at exactly the same time, causing motion to ripple down the frame. If the camera or the subject is moving, the rolling shutter can cause distortions, such as leaning buildings and other skewed images. To use the effect, select the problem layer in the Timeline panel, and choose Effect > Distort > Rolling Shutter Repair.

13 ADVANCED EDITING TECHNIQUES

Lesson overview

In this lesson, you'll learn how to do the following:

- Stabilize a shaky camera shot.

- Use single-point motion tracking to track one object in a shot to another object in a shot.

- Perform multipoint tracking using perspective corner-pinning.

- Use Imagineer Systems mocha for After Effects to track motion.

- Create a particle system.

- Use the Timewarp effect to create slow-motion video.

 This lesson will take approximately two hours to complete. Download the Lesson13 project files from the Lesson & Update Files tab on your Account page at www.peachpit.com, if you haven't already done so. As you work on this lesson, you'll preserve the start files. If you need to restore the start files, download them from your Account page.

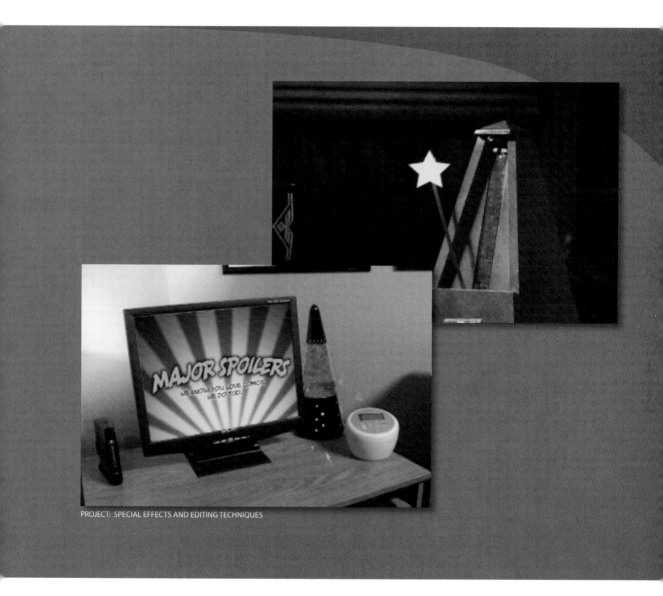

PROJECT: SPECIAL EFFECTS AND EDITING TECHNIQUES

After Effects provides advanced motion stabilization, motion tracking, high-end effects, and other features for the most demanding production environments.

Getting started

In previous lessons, you've used many of the essential 2D and 3D tools you need for motion graphics design. But Adobe After Effects also offers motion stabilization, motion tracking, advanced keying tools, distortion effects, the capability to retime footage using the Timewarp effect, support for high dynamic range (HDR) color images, network rendering, and much more. In this lesson, you will learn how to use Warp Stabilizer VFX to stabilize a handheld camera shot, how to track one object to another in an image so that their motion is synchronized, and how to use corner-pinning to track an object with perspective. Finally, you will explore two of the high-end digital effects available in After Effects: a particle system generator and the Timewarp effect.

This lesson includes multiple projects. Take a peek at all of them before beginning.

1 Make sure the following files are in the Lessons/Lesson13 folder on your hard disk, or download them from your Account page at www.peachpit.com now:

- In the Assets folder: flowers.mov, Group_Approach[DV].mov, majorspoilers. mov, metronome.mov, mocha_tracking.mov, multipoint_tracking.mov

- In the Sample_Movies folder: Lesson13_Multipoint.mov, Lesson13_ Particles.mov, Lesson13_Stabilize.mov, Lesson13_Timewarp.mov, Lesson13_Tracking.mov

● **Note:** You can view these movies all at once or, if you don't plan to complete these exercises in one session, you can watch each sample movie just before you are ready to complete the associated exercise.

2 Open and play the sample movies in the Lesson13/Sample_Movies folder to see the projects you will create in this lesson.

3 When you're done, quit QuickTime Player. You may delete these sample movies from your hard disk if you have limited storage space.

Using Warp Stabilizer VFX

If you shoot footage using a handheld camera, you will probably end up with shaky shots. Unless this look is intentional, you'll want to stabilize your shots to eliminate unwanted motion.

Warp Stabilizer VFX in After Effects automatically removes extraneous jitters. When played back, the motion appears smooth, because the layer itself is scaled and moves incrementally to offset the unwanted movement.

Bicubic scaling

When you scale video footage or an image to a larger size, After Effects must sample data to add information where none existed before. You can choose which sampling method After Effects uses when scaling a layer. For details, see After Effects help.

Bilinear sampling is the method After Effects traditionally used. However, bicubic sampling uses a more complex algorithm that typically provides better results when color transitions are more gradual, as in nearly all real-world photographic images. Bilinear scaling may be a better option for sharp-edged graphics.

To choose a sampling method for a layer, select the layer, and choose Layer > Quality > Bicubic or Layer > Quality > Bilinear. Bicubic and bilinear sampling are available only for layers that are set to Best quality. (To change a layer's quality setting to Best, choose Layer > Quality > Best.)

If you need to scale an image by a large amount while preserving details, use the Detail-preserving Upscale effect instead. The effect preserves the sharpness of sharp lines and curves. For example, you can scale up from SD frame sizes to HD frame sizes, or from HD frame sizes to digital cinema frame sizes. This effect is very closely related to the Preserve Details resampling option in the Image Size dialog box in Photoshop. Note that using the Detail-preserving Upscale effect is slower than using either bilinear or bicubic scaling for the layer.

Setting up the project

As you start After Effects, restore the default application settings for After Effects. See "Restoring default preferences" on page 2.

1 Start After Effects, and then immediately hold down Ctrl+Alt+Shift (Windows) or Command+Option+Shift (Mac OS) to restore default preferences settings. When prompted, click OK to delete your preferences.

2 Close the Start window.

After Effects opens to display a new, untitled project.

3 Choose File > Save As > Save As.

4 In the Save As dialog box, navigate to the Lessons/Lesson13/Finished_ Projects folder.

5 Name the project **Lesson13_Stabilize.aep**, and then click Save.

Importing the footage

You need to import one footage item to start this project.

1 Double-click an empty area of the Project panel to open the Import File dialog box.

2 Navigate to the Lessons/Lesson13/ Assets folder. Select the flowers.mov file, and click Import or Open.

Creating the composition

You'll start by creating the composition.

1 Drag the flowers.mov clip in the Project panel onto the Create A New Composition button (▣) at the bottom of the panel.

After Effects creates a new composition named Flowers with the same pixel size, aspect ratio, frame rate, and duration of the source clip.

2 Click the Play button in the Preview panel to preview the footage. Press the spacebar to stop the preview when you've seen the whole clip.

This clip was shot with a handheld camera in the late afternoon. A slight breeze rustles the vegetation, and the camera moves unsteadily.

Applying Warp Stabilizer VFX

Warp Stabilizer VFX starts analyzing footage as soon as you apply it. Stabilization is a background process, so you can work on other compositions while it finishes. How long it takes depends on your system. After Effects displays a blue banner while it analyzes the footage and an orange banner while it applies stabilization.

1 Select the flowers.mov layer in the Timeline panel, and choose Animation > Warp Stabilizer VFX. The blue banner appears immediately.

2 When Warp Stabilizer VFX has finished stabilizing, and the orange banner has disappeared, press the spacebar to preview the changes.

3 Press the spacebar to stop the preview.

The clip is still shaky, but it's smoother than it was initially. Warp Stabilizer VFX moved and repositioned the footage. To see how it applied changes, view the effects in the Effect Controls panel. For example, the clip's borders were scaled up (to about 103%) to hide black gaps that occur when the image is repositioned in the stabilization process. You'll adjust the settings that Warp Stabilizer VFX uses.

Adjusting the Warp Stabilizer VFX settings

You'll change the settings in the Effect Controls panel to make the shot smoother.

1 In the Effect Controls panel, increase the Smoothness amount to **75%**.

Warp Stabilizer VFX immediately begins stabilizing again. It doesn't need to analyze the footage, because the initial analysis data is stored in memory.

Warp Stabilizer VFX settings

This is a summary of the Warp Stabilizer VFX settings to help you get started. To learn more about the settings, and to read more tips for using the effect successfully, see After Effects Help.

- **Result** controls the intended result. Smooth Motion makes camera movement smoother, but doesn't eliminate it; use the Smoothness setting to control how smooth the movement becomes. No Motion attempts to remove all of the camera motion.

- **Method** specifies the most complex operation the Warp Stabilizer VFX performs on the footage to stabilize it: Position, which is based on position data only; Position, Scale, Rotation, which uses these three types of data; Perspective, which effectively corner-pins the entire frame; or Subspace Warp (the default), which attempts to warp various parts of the frame differently to stabilize the entire frame.

- **Borders** settings adjust how borders (the moving edges) are treated for footage that is stabilized. Framing controls how the edges appear in a stabilizing result, and determines whether the effect crops, scales, or synthesizes edges using material from other frames.

- **Auto-scale** displays the current auto-scale amount, and allows you to set limits on the amount of auto-scaling.

- **Advanced** settings give you even greater control over the actions of the Warp Stabilizer VFX effect.

2 When Warp Stabilizer VFX has finished, preview the changes.

3 Press the spacebar to stop playback when you're done.

It's better, but still a little rough. The Auto-scale setting in the Effect Controls panel now displays 103.7%; the effect moved the frames more dramatically, requiring more scaling to eliminate black gaps around the edges.

Rather than change the amount Warp Stabilizer VFX smooths the footage, now you'll change its goal.

4 In the Effect Controls panel, choose No Motion from the Result menu.

With this setting, Warp Stabilizer VFX attempts to lock the camera in position. This requires even more scaling. When No Motion is selected, the Smoothness option is dimmed.

5 When the orange banner disappears, preview the changes again. Press the spacebar to stop the playback.

Now the camera stays in position, so that the movement you notice is the rustling of the flowers in the wind, not the shakiness of the camera. In order to achieve this effect, Warp Stabilizer VFX had to scale the clip to about 112% of its original size.

Fine-tuning the results

The default analysis works well most of the time, but sometimes you may need to massage the end results even further. In this project, the clip skews subtly in a few places, most noticeably at about the five-second mark. Casual viewers may not notice the problem, but a keen producer will. You'll change the method that Warp Stabilizer VFX uses to remove the skew.

1 In the Effect Controls panel, choose Position, Scale, Rotation from the Method menu.

2 Choose Stabilize Only from the Framing menu.

● **Note:** Scaling a video layer up degrades the image. A good rule of thumb is to increase the layer to no more than 115% the size of the original source.

3 Increase the Additional Scale to **114%**.

4 Preview the changes.

Now the shot looks rock-steady. The only movement is that caused by the wind rustling the flowers.

5 Press the spacebar to stop the playback when you're done.

6 Choose File > Save to save your work.

7 Choose File > Close Project.

As you have discovered, stabilizing a shot is not without its drawbacks. To compensate for the movement or rotation data applied to the layer, the frames must be scaled, which could ultimately degrade the footage. If you really need to use the shot in your production, this may be the best compromise.

Tip: You can use Warp Stabilizer VFX advanced settings to achieve more complex effects, too. To learn more, see *Adobe After Effects CC Visual Effects and Compositing Studio Techniques*, available from Adobe Press.

Using single-point motion tracking

With the increase in the number of productions that incorporate digital elements into final shots, compositors need an easy way to synchronize computer-generated effects with film or video backgrounds. After Effects lets you do this with the capability to follow, or track, a defined area in the shot, and to apply that movement to other layers. These layers can contain text, effects, images, or other footage. The resulting visual effect precisely matches the original moving footage.

When you track motion in an After Effects composition that contains multiple layers, the default tracking type is Transform. This type of motion tracking tracks position and/or rotation to apply to another layer. When tracking position, this option creates one track point, and generates Position keyframes. When tracking rotation, this option creates two track points, and produces Rotation keyframes.

In this exercise, you will track a shape layer to the weighted arm of a metronome. This will be especially challenging, as the camera operator chose not to use a tripod.

Setting up the project

If you've just completed the first project, and After Effects is open, skip to step 3. Otherwise, restore the default application settings for After Effects. See "Restoring default preferences" on page 2.

1 Start After Effects, and then immediately hold down Ctrl+Alt+Shift (Windows) or Command+Option+Shift (Mac OS) to restore default preferences settings. When prompted, click OK to delete your preferences.

2 Close the Start window.

After Effects opens to display a new, untitled project.

3 Choose File > Save As > Save As.

4 In the Save As dialog box, navigate to the Lessons/Lesson13/Finished_ Projects folder.

5 Name the project **Lesson13_Tracking.aep**, and then click Save.

ADOBE AFTER EFFECTS CC CLASSROOM IN A BOOK (2015 RELEASE) **319**

Creating the composition

You need to import one footage item to start this project. You'll use it to create the composition.

1 Double-click an empty area of the Project panel to open the Import File dialog box.

2 Navigate to the Lessons/Lesson13/Assets folder. Select the metronome.mov file, and then click Import or Open.

3 In the Project panel, drag the metronome.mov clip onto the Create A New Composition button at the bottom of the panel.

After Effects creates a new composition named Metronome, with the same pixel size, aspect ratio, frame rate, and duration of the source clip.

4 Drag the current-time indicator across the time ruler to manually preview the footage.

Creating a shape layer

You're going to attach a star to the end of the metronome. First, you need to create the star. You'll use a shape layer.

1 Press the Home key, or move the current-time indicator to the beginning of the time ruler.

2 Click an empty area of the Timeline panel to deselect the layer.

3 Select the Star tool (★), hidden behind the Rectangle tool (▢) in the Tools panel.

Note: If you don't see the Fill Color swatch, make sure you don't have a layer selected. When a layer is selected, shape tools draw masks.

4 Click the Fill Color swatch, and select a light yellow such as R=**220**, G=**250**, B=**90**. Click the word *Stroke*, select None in the Stroke Options dialog box, and click OK.

5 In the Composition panel, draw a small star.

6 Use the Selection tool to position the star over the weighted end of the pendulum arm.

7 Select Shape Layer 1 to see the layer's anchor point. Use the Pan Behind tool (⊕) to move the anchor point to the center of the star shape, if it isn't already there.

Positioning the track point

After Effects tracks motion by matching pixels from a selected area in a frame to pixels in each succeeding frame. You create tracking points to specify the area to track. A track point contains a feature region, a search region, and an attach point. After Effects displays the track point in the Layer panel as it tracks.

You will track the metronome weight (the rhombus at the end of its arm) by placing tracking regions around the area that you'll track another layer to. With the star shape added to the Tracking composition, you are ready to position the track point.

1 Select the metronome.mov layer in the Timeline panel.

2 Choose Animation > Track Motion. The Tracker panel opens; increase its size if you can't see all the options.

After Effects opens the selected layer in the Layer panel. The Track Point 1 indicator is in the center of the image.

Notice the settings in the Tracker panel: Metronome.mov is selected in the Motion Source menu. The Current Track is Tracker 1, and the Motion Target is Shape Layer 1, because After Effects automatically sets the Motion Target to the layer immediately above the source layer.

Now, you'll position your track point.

3 Using the Selection tool (✹), move the Track Point 1 indicator (drag the empty portion of the inner box) in the Layer panel over the metronome weight.

Note: In this exercise, you want the star to move atop the metronome weight. However, if you wanted an object to move in relationship to the tracked area but not on top of it, you could reposition the attach point accordingly.

4 Enlarge the search region (the outer box) to encompass the area around the pendulum. Then adjust the feature region (the inner box) within the weight.

Analyzing and applying tracking

Now that the search and feature regions are defined, you can apply the tracker.

Note: The tracking analysis may take quite a while. The larger the search and feature regions, the longer After Effects takes to analyze tracking.

1 Click the Analyze Forward button (▶) in the Tracker panel. Watch the analysis to ensure the track point stays with the metronome weight. If it doesn't, press the spacebar to stop the analysis, and reposition the feature region. (See the sidebar "Checking for drift.")

2 When the analysis is complete, click the Apply button.

3 In the Motion Tracker Apply Options dialog box, click OK to apply the tracking to the x and y dimensions.

Checking for drift

As an image moves in a shot, the lighting, surrounding objects, and angle of the object can all change, making a once-distinct feature no longer identifiable at the subpixel level. It takes time to develop an eye for choosing a trackable feature. Even with careful planning and practice, you may often find that the feature region drifts away from the desired feature. Readjusting the feature and search regions, changing the tracking options, and trying again are all standard parts of digital tracking. When you notice drifting occurring, try the following:

1 Immediately stop the analysis by pressing the spacebar.

2 Move the current-time indicator back to the last good tracked point. You can see this in the Layer panel.

3 Reposition and/or resize the feature and search regions, being careful not to accidentally move the attach point. Moving the attach point will cause a noticeable jump in your tracked layer.

4 Click the Analyze Forward button to resume tracking.

The motion-tracking data is added to the Timeline panel, where you can see that the track data is in the metronome layer, but the results are applied to the Position property of the Shape Layer 1 layer.

4 Press the spacebar to preview the movie. The star not only follows the pendulum; it moves with the camera's movement.

5 When you're ready, press the spacebar to stop playback.

6 Hide the properties for both layers in the Timeline panel, choose File > Save, and then choose File > Close Project.

Motion tracking an element onto background footage can be fun. As long as you have a stable feature to track, single-point motion tracking can be quite easy.

Moving and resizing the track points

In setting up motion tracking, it's often necessary to refine a track point by adjusting its feature region, search region, and attach point. You can resize or move these items independently or in groups by dragging with the Selection tool. The pointer icon changes to reflect one of many different activities.

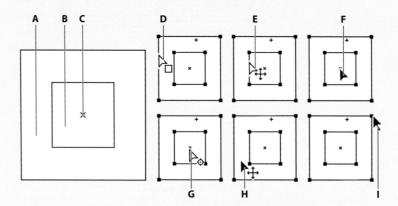

Track point components (left) and Selection tool pointer icons (right):
A. Search region **B.** Feature region **C.** Attach point **D.** Moves search region
E. Moves both regions **F.** Moves entire track point **G.** Moves attach point
H. Moves entire track point **I.** Resizes region

- To turn feature region magnification on or off, choose Magnify Feature When Dragging from the Tracker panel menu. A check mark appears next to the option when it's on.

- To move only the search region, using the Selection tool, drag the edge of the search region; the Move Search Region pointer (⬚) appears (D, above).

- To move just the feature and search regions together, Alt-drag (Windows) or Option-drag (Mac OS) with the Selection tool inside the feature or search region; the Move Both Regions pointer (⬚) appears (E, above).

- To move only the attach point, using the Selection tool, drag the attach point; the Move Attach Point pointer (⬚) appears (G, above).

- To resize the feature or search region, drag a corner handle (I, above).

- To move the feature region, search region, and attach point together, drag with the Selection tool inside the track point area (avoiding the region edges and the attach point); the Move Track Point pointer (⬚) appears.

For more information about track points, see After Effects Help.

Using multipoint tracking

After Effects also offers two more advanced types of tracking that use multiple tracking points: parallel corner-pinning and perspective corner-pinning.

When you track using parallel corner-pinning, you simultaneously track three points in the source footage. After Effects calculates the position of a fourth point to keep the lines between the points parallel. When the movement of the points is applied to the target layer, the Corner Pin effect distorts the layer to simulate skew, scale, and rotation, but not perspective. Parallel lines remain parallel, and relative distances are preserved.

When you track using perspective corner-pinning, you simultaneously track four points in the source footage. When applied to the target footage, the Corner Pin effect uses the movement of the four points to distort the layer, simulating changes in perspective.

You'll attach an animation to a computer monitor using perspective corner-pinning. The effect is similar to the Lesson 7 project, but you'll use a different technique. If you haven't already watched the sample movie for this exercise, do so now.

Setting up the project

Start by launching After Effects and creating a new project.

1 If it's not already open, start After Effects, and then immediately hold down Ctrl+Alt+Shift (Windows) or Command+Option+Shift (Mac OS) to restore default preferences settings. When prompted, click OK to delete your preferences, and close the Start window.

After Effects opens to display an empty, untitled project.

2 Choose File > Save As > Save As.

3 In the Save As dialog box, navigate to the Lessons/Lesson13/ Finished_Projects folder.

4 Name the project **Lesson13_Multipoint.aep,** and then click Save.

5 Double-click an empty area of the Project panel to open the Import File dialog box, and then navigate to the Lessons/Lesson13/Assets folder.

6 Ctrl-click (Windows) or Command-click (Mac OS) both the majorspoilers.mov and multipoint_tracking.mov files, and then click Import or Open.

7 Press Ctrl+N (Windows) or Command+N (Mac OS) to create a new composition.

8 In the Composition Settings dialog box, do the following, and then click OK:

- Type **Multipoint_Tracking** in the Composition Name field.
- Choose NTSC DV from the Preset menu.
- Set the Duration to **7:05**—the length of the majorspoilers.mov file.

9 Drag the multipoint_tracking.mov item from the Project panel to the Timeline panel. Manually preview the footage, which is shaky because it was shot with a handheld camera.

Because you're positioning the majorspoilers.mov layer on the computer monitor, it will be fairly easy to place tracking markers on the flat plane. By default, the tracker tracks by luminance, so you will use the areas around the screen that have high contrast differences for tracking.

10 Press the Home key, or move the current-time indicator to the beginning of the time ruler.

11 Drag the majorspoilers.mov footage item from the Project panel to the Timeline panel, placing it at the top of the layer stack.

12 To make it easier to see the underlying movie as you place the tracking points, turn off the Video switch for the majorspoilers.mov layer in the Timeline panel.

Positioning the track points

You're ready to add the track points to the multipoint_tracking.mov layer.

1 Select the multipoint_tracking.mov layer in the Timeline panel.

2 Choose Window > Tracker to open the Tracker panel, if it isn't open.

3 In the Tracker panel, choose multipoint_tracking.mov from the Motion Source menu.

4 Select the multipoint_tracking.mov layer again, and then click Track Motion.

The desk scene opens in the Layer panel, with a track point indicator in the center of the image. However, you will be tracking four points in order to attach the animated movie to the computer screen.

5 Choose Perspective Corner Pin from the Track Type menu.

Three more track point indicators appear in the Layer panel.

▶ **Tip:** Refer to the sidebar "Moving and resizing the track points" for help moving the track point regions.

6 Drag the track points to four different high-contrast areas of the image. The four corners of the computer screen provide excellent contrast. Use the following image as a guide. (Because the areas of high contrast are also where you want to attach the majorspoilers layer, you don't need to move the attach points.)

▶ **Tip:** It may be helpful to zoom in when placing and adjusting the track points. Zoom out again when you have finished.

Applying the multipoint tracker

You're ready to analyze the data and apply the tracker.

1 Click the Analyze Forward button (▶) in the Tracker panel. When the analysis is complete, click the Apply button to calculate the tracking.

2 Notice the results in the Timeline panel: You can see the Corner Pin and Position property keyframes for the majorspoilers layer and the track point data for the motion_tracking layer.

● **Note:** If the composition doesn't appear in the Composition panel, click in the Timeline window to move the current-time indicator and refresh the display.

3 Make the majorspoilers layer visible again, move the current-time indicator to the beginning of the timeline, and preview the movie to see the results of the tracker.

4 When you're done watching the preview, press the spacebar to stop playback.

If you don't like the results, return to the Tracker panel, click the Reset button, and try again. With practice, you will become adept at identifying good feature regions.

5 Hide the layer properties to keep the Timeline panel neat, and choose File > Save to save your work.

6 Choose File > Close Project.

mocha for After Effects

In most cases, you'll get better and more accurate tracking results using mocha from Imagineer Systems to track points in video. A version of mocha is included with After Effects. To track using mocha, choose Animation > Track In Mocha AE.

One advantage of mocha for After Effects is that you don't have to accurately place tracking points to obtain a perfect track. Rather than using tracking points, mocha for After Effects uses a planar tracker, which attempts to track an object's translation, rotation, and scaling data based on the movement of a user-defined plane. Planes provide more detail to the computer than is possible with single-point and multi-point tracking tools.

When you work with mocha for After Effects, you need to identify planes in a clip that coincide with movement you want to track. Planes don't have to be tabletops or walls. For example, if someone is waving goodbye, you can use their upper and lower limbs as two planes. After you track the planes, you can export the tracking data for use in After Effects.

mocha for After Effects uses two different spline technologies for tracking: X splines and Bezier splines. X splines may work better for tracking, especially with perspective motion, but Bezier splines work well, too, and are the industry standard.

To learn more about mocha for After Effects, choose Help > Online Help or Help > Offline Help in mocha.

We've saved some tracking data for the computer monitor in mocha for After Effects, so that you can apply it in After Effects if you'd like. To apply the data, follow these steps:

1 Create a new project in After Effects, and import the majorspoilers.mov and mocha_tracking.mov files from the Lesson13/Assets folder. Create a new composition from the mocha_tracking.mov file, and then drag the majorspoilers.mov file to the top of the layer stack in the Timeline panel.

2 Open the mocha_data.txt file (in the Lesson13/Optional_Mocha_Tutorial folder) in a text editor such as WordPad or TextEdit. (Don't use Notepad on Windows. It doesn't retain the mocha formatting, so After Effects doesn't recognize its content on the clipboard.) Choose Edit > Select All, and then Edit > Copy to copy all the data.

3 Select the majorspoilers.mov layer in the Timeline panel, and choose Edit > Paste. All the data is applied to the layer.

4 Preview the results.

Creating a particle simulation

After Effects includes several effects that do an excellent job of creating particle simulations. Two of them—CC Particle Systems II and CC Particle World—are based on the same engine. The major difference between the two is that Particle World enables you to move the particles in 3D space, rather than in a 2D layer.

In this exercise, you'll learn how to use the CC Particle Systems II effect to create a supernova that could be used as the opening of a science program or as a motion background. If you haven't already watched the sample movie for this exercise, do so now before continuing.

Setting up the project

Start by launching After Effects and creating a new composition.

1 If it's not already open, start After Effects, and then immediately hold down Ctrl+Alt+Shift (Windows) or Command+Option+Shift (Mac OS) to restore default preferences settings. When prompted, click OK to delete your preferences, and close the Start window.

After Effects opens to display an empty, untitled project.

2 Choose File > Save As > Save As.

3 In the Save As dialog box, navigate to the Lessons/Lesson13/ Finished_Projects folder.

4 Name the project **Lesson13_Particles.aep**, and then click Save.

You don't need to import any footage items for this exercise. However, you do need to create the composition.

5 In After Effects, press Ctrl+N (Windows) or Command+N (Mac OS).

6 In the Composition Settings dialog box, do the following, and then click OK:

 • Type **Supernova** in the Composition Name field.

 • Choose NTSC D1 from the Preset pop-up menu.

 • Set the Duration to **10:00**.

Creating a particle system

You will build the particle system from a solid layer, so you'll create that next.

1. Choose Layer > New > Solid to create a new solid layer.

2. In the Solid Settings dialog box, type **Particles** in the Name box.

3. Click Make Comp Size to make the layer the same size as the composition. Then click OK.

Understanding Particle Systems II properties

Particle systems have a unique vocabulary. Some of the key settings are explained here for your reference. They're listed in the order in which they appear (top to bottom) in the Effect Controls panel.

Birth Rate Controls the number of particles generated per second. The value itself is arbitrary and does not equal the actual number of particles being generated. However, the higher the number, the more densely packed the particles become.

Longevity Determines how long the particles are visible.

Producer Position Controls the center point or origin of the particle system. The position is set based on the x, y coordinates. All particles emanate from this single point. You can control the size of the producer by making adjustments to the x and y radius settings. The higher these values, the larger the producer point will be. A high x value and a y value of zero (0) result in a line.

Velocity Controls the speed of particles. The higher the number, the faster the particles move.

Inherent Velocity % Determines how much of the velocity is passed along to the particles when the Producer Position is animated. A negative value causes the particles to move in the opposite direction.

Gravity Determines how fast particles fall. The higher the value, the faster the particles fall. A negative value causes particles to rise.

Resistance Simulates particles interacting with air or water, slowing over time.

Direction Determines which direction the particles flow. Use with the Direction Animation type.

Extra Introduces randomness into the movement of the particles.

Birth/Death Size Determines the size of the particles when they are created and when they expire.

Opacity Map Controls opacity changes for the particle over its lifetime.

Color Map Use with the Birth and Death colors to shade the particles over time.

4 With the Particles layer selected in the Timeline panel, choose Effect > Simulation > CC Particle Systems II.

5 Go to 4:00 to see the particle system.

A large stream of yellow particles appears in the Composition panel.

Customizing the particle effect

You will turn this stream of particles into a supernova by customizing the settings in the Effect Controls panel.

1 Expand the Physics property group in the Effect Controls panel. The Explosive Animation setting works fine for this project, but instead of the particles falling down, you want them to flow out in all directions, so change the Gravity value to **0.0**.

2 Hide the Physics property group, and expand the Particle property group. Then choose Faded Sphere from the Particle Type menu.

Now the particles look intergalactic. Don't stop there, though.

3 Change the Death Size to **1.50**, and increase the Size Variation to **100%**.

This allows the particles to change birth size randomly.

4 Reduce the Max Opacity to **55%** to make the particles semitransparent.

5 Click the Birth Color swatch, and change the color to R=**255**, G=**200**, B=**50** to give the particles a yellow hue at birth.

6 Click the Death Color swatch, and change the color to R=**180**, G=**180**, B=**180** to give the particles a light gray hue as they fade out.

● **Note:** Even though they're at the top of the Effect Controls panel, it is often easier to adjust the Longevity and Birth Rate settings after you have set the other particle properties.

7 To keep the particles from staying onscreen too long, decrease the Longevity value to **0.8** seconds.

The Faded Sphere particle type softens the look, but the particle shapes are still too sharply defined. You will fix that by blurring the layer to blend the particles with one another.

8 Hide the CC Particle Systems II effect properties.

9 Choose Effect > Blur & Sharpen > Fast Blur.

10 In the Fast Blur area of the Effect Controls panel, increase the Blurriness value to **10**. Then select Repeat Edge Pixels to keep the particles from being cropped at the edge of the frame.

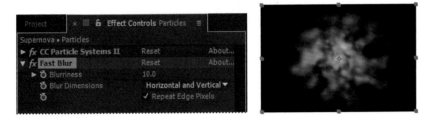

Creating the sun

You will now create a bright halo of light that will go behind the particles.

1 Go to 7:00.

2 Press Ctrl+Y (Windows) or Command+Y (Mac OS) to create a new solid layer.

3 In the Solid Settings dialog box, do the following:

- Type **Sun** in the Name box.
- Click Make Comp Size to make the layer the same size as the composition.
- Click the color swatch to make the layer the same yellow as the Birth Color of the particles (**255, 200, 50**).
- Click OK to close the Solid Settings dialog box.

4 Drag the Sun layer below the Particles layer in the Timeline panel.

5 Select the Ellipse tool (◯), which is hidden behind the Rectangle tool (▢) or the Star tool (★) in the Tools panel, and Shift-drag in the Composition panel to draw a circle with a radius of roughly 100 pixels, or one-fourth the width of the composition. You've created a mask.

6 Using the Selection tool (▸), drag the mask shape to the center of the Composition panel.

7 With the Sun layer selected in the Timeline panel, press the F key to reveal its Mask Feather property. Increase the Mask Feather amount to **100, 100** pixels.

8 Press Alt+[(Windows) or Option+[(Mac OS) to set the In point of the layer to the current time.

9 Hide the properties for the Sun layer.

Lighting the darkness

Since the sun is bright, it should illuminate the surrounding darkness.

1 Make sure the current-time indicator is still at 7:00.

2 Press Ctrl+Y (Windows) or Command+Y (Mac OS) to create a new solid layer.

3 In the Solid Settings dialog box, name the layer **Background**, click the Make Comp Size button to make the layer the same size as the composition, and then click OK to create the layer.

4 In the Timeline panel, drag the Background layer to the bottom position in the layer stack.

5 With the Background layer selected in the Timeline panel, choose Effect > Generate > Gradient Ramp.

The Gradient Ramp effect creates a color gradient, blending it with the original image. You can create linear ramps or radial ramps, and vary the position and colors of the ramp over time. Use the Start Of Ramp and End Of Ramp settings to specify the start and end positions. Use the Ramp Scatter setting to disperse the ramp colors and eliminate banding.

6 In the Gradient Ramp area of the Effect Controls panel, do the following:

 • Change Start Of Ramp to **360**, **240** and End Of Ramp to **360**, **525**.

 • Choose Radial Ramp from the Ramp Shape menu.

 • Click the Start Color swatch, and set the start color to dark blue (R=**0**, G=**25**, B=**135**).

 • Set the End Color to black (R=**0**, G=**0**, B=**0**).

7 Press Alt+[(Windows) or Option+[(Mac OS) to set the In point of the layer to the current time.

Adding a lens flare

To tie all the elements together, you'll add a lens flare to simulate an explosion.

1 Press the Home key, or move the current-time indicator to the beginning of the time ruler.

2 Press Ctrl+Y (Windows) or Command+Y (Mac OS) to create a new solid layer.

3 In the Solid Settings dialog box, name the layer **Nova**, click the Make Comp Size button to make the layer the same size as the composition, set the Color to black (R=**0**, G=**0**, B=**0**), and then click OK.

4 Drag the Nova layer to the top of the layer stack in the Timeline panel. Then, with the Nova layer selected, choose Effect > Generate > Lens Flare.

5 In the Lens Flare area of the Effect Controls panel, do the following:

- Change Flare Center to **360, 240**.

- Make sure 50–300mm Zoom is selected in the Lens Type menu.

- Decrease Flare Brightness to **0%**, and then click the Flare Brightness stopwatch icon (⏱) to create an initial keyframe.

6 Go to 0:10.

7 Increase the Flare Brightness to **240%**.

8 Go to 1:04, and decrease the Flare Brightness to **100%**.

9 With the Nova layer selected in the Timeline panel, press the U key to see the animated Lens Flare property.

About high dynamic range (HDR) footage

After Effects also supports high dynamic range (HDR) color.

The dynamic range (ratio between dark and bright regions) in the physical world far exceeds the range of human vision and of images that are printed or displayed on a monitor. But while human eyes can adapt to very different brightness levels, most cameras and computer monitors can capture and reproduce only a limited dynamic range. Photographers, motion-picture artists, and others working with digital images must be selective about what's important in a scene, because they're working with a limited dynamic range.

HDR footage opens up a world of possibilities, because it can represent a very wide dynamic range through the use of 32-bit floating-point numeric values. Floating-point numeric representations allow the same number of bits to describe a much larger range of values than integer (fixed-point) values. HDR values can contain brightness levels, including objects as bright as a candle flame or the sun, that far exceed those in 8-bit-per-channel (bpc) or 16-bpc (non-floating-point) mode. Lower dynamic range 8-bpc and 16-bpc modes can represent RGB levels only from black to white, which represents an extremely small segment of the dynamic range in the real world.

After Effects supports HDR images in a variety of ways. For example, you can create 32-bpc projects to work with HDR footage, and you can adjust the exposure, or the amount of light captured in an image, when working with HDR images in After Effects. For more information about support in After Effects for HDR images, see After Effects Help.

10 Right-click (Windows) or Control-click (Mac OS) the ending Flare Brightness keyframe, and choose Keyframe Assistant > Easy Ease In.

11 Right-click (Windows) or Control-click (Mac OS) the beginning Flare Brightness keyframe, and choose Keyframe Assistant > Easy Ease Out.

Finally, you need to make the layers under the Nova layer visible in the composition.

12 Press F2 to deselect all layers, and choose Columns > Modes from the Timeline panel menu. Then choose Screen from the Mode menu for the Nova layer.

13 Preview the movie. When you're done, press the spacebar to stop the preview.

14 Choose File > Save, and then choose File > Close Project.

Retiming playback using the Timewarp effect

The Timewarp effect in After Effects gives you precise control over a wide range of parameters when changing the playback speed of a layer, including interpolation methods, motion blur, and source cropping to eliminate unwanted artifacts.

In this exercise, you will use the Timewarp effect to change the speed of a clip for a dramatic slow-motion playback. If you haven't already watched the sample movie for this exercise, do so now.

Setting up the project

Start by launching After Effects and creating a new project.

1 If After Effects isn't open, start it, and then immediately hold down Ctrl+Alt+Shift (Windows) or Command+Option+Shift (Mac OS) to restore default preferences settings. When prompted, click OK to delete your preferences, and close the Start window.

After Effects opens to display an empty, untitled project.

2 Choose File > Save As > Save As.

3 In the Save As dialog box, navigate to the Lessons/Lesson13/ Finished_Projects folder.

4 Name the project **Lesson13_Timewarp.aep**, and then click Save.

5 Double-click an empty area of the Project panel to open the Import File dialog box. Then navigate to the Lessons/Lesson13/Assets folder on your hard disk, select the Group_Approach[DV].mov, and click Import or Open.

6 Click OK in the Interpret Footage dialog box.

Now, you'll create a new composition based on the footage item's aspect ratio and its duration.

7 Drag the Group_Approach[DV].mov file onto the Create A New Composition button (■) at the bottom of the Project panel.

After Effects creates a new composition named for the source file, and displays it in the Composition and Timeline panels.

8 Choose File > Save to save your work.

Using Timewarp

In the source footage, a group of young people approaches the camera at a steady pace. At around 2 seconds, the director would like the motion to begin to slow down to 10%, and then ramp back up to full speed at 7:00.

1 With the Group_Approach[DV] layer selected in the Timeline panel, choose Effect > Time > Timewarp.

2 In the Timewarp area of the Effect Controls panel, make sure Pixel Motion is selected in the Method menu and Speed is selected in the Adjust Time By menu.

With Pixel Motion selected, Timewarp creates new frames by analyzing the pixel movement in nearby frames and creating motion vectors. The Speed option controls the time adjustment by percentage rather than by a specific frame.

3 Go to 2:00.

4 In the Effect Controls panel, set the Speed to **100**, and click the stopwatch (⏱) to set a keyframe.

▶ **Tip:** To see the Speed keyframes, select Timewarp in the Timeline panel, and press the U key.

This tells Timewarp to keep the speed of the clip at 100% until the 2-second mark.

5 Go to 5:00, and set the Speed to **10**. After Effects adds a keyframe.

6 Go to 7:00, and set the Speed to **100**. After Effects adds a keyframe.

● **Note:** Be patient. The first time through, After Effects is caching information in RAM. The second time it plays will provide a more accurate playback.

7 Press the Home key or move the current-time indicator to the beginning of the time ruler, and then watch a preview of the effect.

The speed adjustments are rather abrupt—not the smooth, slow-motion curve you would expect to see in a professional effect. This is because the keyframes are linear instead of curved. You'll fix that next.

8 Press the spacebar to stop playback when you're ready.

9 With the Group_Approach[DV] layer selected in the Timeline panel, press the U key to see the animated Timewarp Speed property.

10 Click the Graph Editor button in the Timeline panel to display the Graph Editor instead of the layer bars. Make sure the Speed property name for the Group_Approach[DV] layer is selected. The Graph Editor displays its graph.

11 Click to select the first Speed keyframe (at 2:00), and then click the Easy Ease icon (⤸) at the bottom of the Graph Editor.

This adjusts the influence into and out of the keyframe to smooth out sudden changes.

12 Repeat step 11 for the other two Speed keyframes in the motion graph, at 5:00 and 7:00.

The motion graph is now smoother, but you can tweak it even more by dragging the Bezier handles.

▶ **Tip:** Close columns in the Timeline panel to see more icons in the Graph Editor. You can also apply an Easy Ease adjustment by pressing the F9 key.

Note: If you need a refresher on using Bezier handles, see Lesson 7, "Working with Masks."

13 Using the Bezier handles for the keyframes at 2:00 and 5:00, adjust the curve so that it resembles the following image.

14 Preview the movie again. This time, the slow-motion Timewarp effect looks professional.

15 Choose File > Save to save the project, and then choose File > Close Project.

You've now experimented with some of the advanced features in After Effects, including motion stabilization, motion tracking, particle systems, and the Timewarp effect. To render and export any or all of the projects you completed in this lesson, see Lesson 14, "Rendering and Outputting," for instructions.

Review questions

1 What is Warp Stabilizer VFX, and when do you need to use it?

2 Why might drifting occur when you're tracking an image?

3 What is the birth rate in a particle effect?

4 What does the Timewarp effect do?

Review answers

1 Shooting footage using a handheld camera typically results in shaky shots. Unless this look is intentional, you will want to stabilize the shots to eliminate unwanted motion. Warp Stabilizer VFX in After Effects analyzes the movement and rotation of the target layer, and then makes adjustments to it. When played back, the motion appears smooth, because the layer itself moves incrementally to offset the unwanted motion. You can change the way Warp Stabilizer VFX crops, scales, and performs other adjustments by modifying settings for the effect.

2 Drifting occurs when the feature region loses the feature that's being tracked. As an image moves in a shot, the lighting, surrounding objects, and angle of the object can change, making a once-distinct feature unidentifiable at the subpixel level. Even with careful planning and practice, the feature region often drifts away from the desired feature. Readjusting the feature and search regions, changing the tracking options, and trying again are all standard procedures in digital tracking.

3 The birth rate in a particle effect determines how often new particles are created.

4 The Timewarp effect gives you precise control over a wide range of parameters to change the playback speed of a layer, including interpolation methods, motion blur, and source cropping to eliminate unwanted artifacts.

14

RENDERING AND OUTPUTTING

Lesson overview

In this lesson, you'll learn how to do the following:

- Create render-settings templates for the Render Queue.

- Create output-module templates for the Render Queue.

- Output movies using Adobe Media Encoder.

- Select the appropriate compressor for your delivery format.

- Use pixel aspect ratio correction.

- Output the final composition for HDTV 1080p resolution.

- Produce a test version of a composition.

- Create custom encoding presets in Adobe Media Encoder.

- Render and output a web version of the final composition.

 The total amount of time required to complete this lesson depends in part on the speed of your processor and the amount of RAM available for rendering. The amount of hands-on time required is less than an hour. Download the Lesson14 project files from the Lesson & Update Files tab on your Account page at www.peachpit.com, if you haven't already done so. As you work on this lesson, you'll preserve the start files. If you need to restore the start files, download them from your Account page.

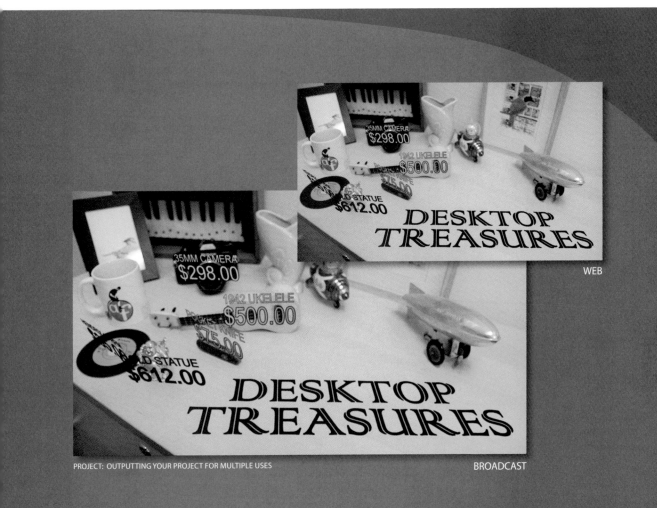

WEB

PROJECT: OUTPUTTING YOUR PROJECT FOR MULTIPLE USES

BROADCAST

The success of any project depends on your ability to deliver it in the format you need, whether it's for the web or broadcast output. Using Adobe After Effects and Adobe Media Encoder, you can render and export a final composition in a variety of formats and resolutions.

Getting started

This lesson continues from the point at which many of the preceding lessons end: when you're ready to output the final composition. In order to produce several versions of the animation for this lesson, you'll explore options available within the Render Queue panel and Adobe Media Encoder. For this lesson, we provide you with a starting project file that is essentially the final composition from Lesson 12 of this book.

1 Make sure the following files are in the Lessons/Lesson14 folder on your hard disk, or download them from your Account page at www.peachpit.com now:

- In the Assets folder: DesktopC.mov, Treasures_Music.aif, Treasures_Title.psd

- In the Start_Project_File folder: Lesson14_Start.aep

- In the Sample_Movies folder: Lesson14_Final_360p_Web.mp4, Lesson14_ Final_1080p.mp4, Lesson14_Final_lowres_Web.mp4, Lesson14_Final_ MPEG4.mov, Lesson14_HD_test_1080p.mp4

● **Note:** The Lesson14_ HD_test_1080p.mp4 file includes only the first five seconds of the movie.

2 Open and play the sample movies for Lesson 14, which represent different final versions of the movie—rendered with different quality settings—that you created in Lesson 12. When you're done viewing the sample movies, quit QuickTime Player. You may delete the sample movies from your hard disk if you have limited storage space.

As always, when you begin the lesson, restore the default application settings for After Effects. See "Restoring default preferences" on page 2.

3 Start After Effects, and then immediately hold down Ctrl+Alt+Shift (Windows) or Command+Option+Shift (Mac OS). When prompted, click OK to delete your preferences. Close the Start window.

4 Choose File > Open Project. If the Start screen opens, click Open Project in it.

● **Note:** If you receive an error message about missing layer dependencies (Arial Narrow Regular), click OK.

5 Navigate to the Lessons/Lesson14/Start_Project_File folder, select the Lesson14_ Start.aep file, and click Open.

6 Choose File > Save As > Save As.

7 In the Save As dialog box, navigate to the Lessons/Lesson14/
 Finished_Project folder.

8 Name the project **Lesson14_Finished.aep**, and then click Save.

9 Choose Window > Render Queue to open the Render Queue panel.

Creating templates for the Render Queue

When you output your compositions in previous lessons, you selected individual
render and output-module settings. In this lesson, you'll create templates for both
render settings and output-module settings. These templates are presets that you
can use to streamline the setup process when you render items for the same type of
delivery format. After you define templates, they appear in the Render Queue panel
on the appropriate pop-up menu (Render Settings or Output Module). Then, when
you're ready to render a composition, you can simply select the template that is
appropriate for the delivery format that your job requires, and the template applies
all the settings.

Creating a render-settings template for test renderings

You'll create a render-settings template, selecting settings appropriate for rendering
a test version of your final movie. A test version is smaller—and therefore renders
faster—than a full-resolution movie. When you work with complex compositions
that take relatively long times to render, it is a good practice to render a small test
version first. This helps you find any final tweaks or blunders that you want to adjust
before you take the time to render the final movie.

1 Choose Edit > Templates > Render Settings. The Render Settings Templates dialog
 box appears.

2 In the Settings area, click New to create a new template.

3 In the Render Settings dialog box, do the following:

- Leave Quality at Best.

- For Resolution, choose Third, which reduces the linear dimension of the composition to one-third.

4 In the Time Sampling area, do the following:

- For Frame Blending, choose Current Settings.

- For Motion Blur, choose Current Settings.

- For Time Span, choose Length Of Comp.

5 In the Frame Rate area, select Use This Frame Rate, and type **12** (fps). Then click OK to return to the Render Settings Templates dialog box.

6 For Settings Name, type **Test_lowres** (for *low resolution*).

7 Examine your settings, which appear in the lower half of the dialog box.

If you need to make any changes, click Edit to adjust the settings. Then click OK.

The Test_lowres option will be available on the Render Settings pop-up menu in the Render Queue panel.

Creating templates for output modules

You'll use a similar process to create a template to use for output-module settings. Each output-module template includes unique combinations of settings that are appropriate for a specific type of output. You'll create one that is appropriate for a low-resolution test version of the movie, so you can quickly see a rendered version to identify any changes you want to make.

1 Choose Edit > Templates > Output Module to open the Output Module Templates dialog box.

2 In the Settings area, click New to create a new template.

3 In the Output Module Settings dialog box, make sure the Format is QuickTime.

4 For Post-Render Action, choose Import.

5 In the Video Output area, click Format Options.

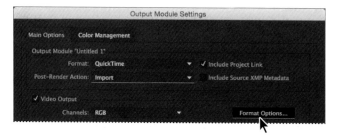

6 Select the following settings in the QuickTime Options dialog box:

- For Video Codec, choose MPEG-4 Video. This compressor automatically determines the color depth.

- Set the Quality slider to **80**.

- In the Advanced Settings area, select Key Frame Every, and then type **30** (frames).

- In the Bitrate Settings area, select Limit Data Rate To, and type **150** (kbps).

● **Note:** The IMA 4:1 compressor is commonly used when compressing audio for web or desktop playback.

7 Select the Audio tab, and choose IMA 4:1 from the Audio Codec menu.

About compression

Compression is essential to reduce the size of movies so that they can be stored, transmitted, and played back effectively. When exporting or rendering a movie file for playback on a specific type of device at a certain bandwidth, you choose a compressor/decompressor (also known as an encoder/decoder), or *codec*, to compress the information and generate a file that is readable by that type of device at that bandwidth.

A wide range of codecs is available; no single codec is the best for all situations. For example, the best codec for compressing cartoon animation is generally not efficient for compressing live-action video. When compressing a movie file, you can fine-tune it for the best quality playback on a computer, a video playback device, the web, or from a DVD player. Depending on which encoder you use, you may be able to reduce the size of compressed files by removing artifacts that interfere with compression, such as random camera motion and excessive film grain.

The codec you use must be available to your entire audience. For instance, if you use a hardware codec on a capture card, your audience must have the same capture card installed, or a software codec that emulates it.

For more about compression and codecs, see After Effects Help.

8 Click OK to close the QuickTime Options dialog box and return to the Output Module Settings dialog box.

9 Choose Audio Output On from the pop-up menu at the bottom of the dialog box. Then choose the following audio settings, from left to right:

 • Rate: 22.050 kHz

 • Use: Stereo

10 Click OK to close the Output Module Settings dialog box.

11 In the lower half of the Output Module Templates dialog box, examine your settings, and click Edit if you need to make any changes.

12 For Settings Name, type **Test_MPEG4**, and then click OK. Now this output template will be available on the Output Module pop-up menu in the Render Queue panel.

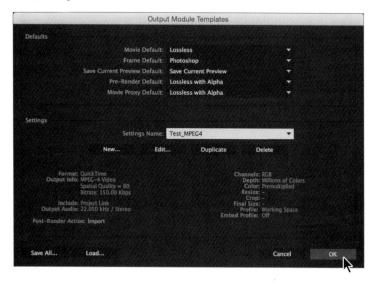

As you might expect, greater compression and lower audio sample rates create smaller file sizes, but they also reduce the quality of the output. However, this low-resolution template is fine for testing your movie before you make final edits.

Exporting using the Render Queue

Now that you have created templates for your render settings and output modules, you can use them to export the test version of your movie.

▶ **Tip:** Alternatively, you can drag the composition from the Project panel onto the Render Queue panel.

1 Select the DesktopC composition in the Project panel, and choose Composition > Add To Render Queue.

In the Render Queue panel, note the default settings in the Render Settings and Output Module pop-up menus. You'll change those settings when you select your low-resolution templates.

2 Choose Test_lowres from the Render Settings menu.

3 Choose Test_MPEG4 from the Output Module menu.

4 Click the blue words next to Output To.

5 In the Output Movie To dialog box, locate the Lessons/Lesson14 folder, and create a new folder called **Final_Movies**:

 • In Windows, click New Folder, and then type the name for the folder.

 • In Mac OS, click the New Folder button, name the folder, and click Create.

6 Open the Final_Movies folder.

7 Name the file **Final_MPEG4.mov**, and then click Save to return to the Render Queue panel.

8 Choose File > Save to save your work.

Note: You do not need to render a movie multiple times to export it to multiple formats with the same render settings. You can export multiple versions of the same rendered movie by adding output modules to a render item in the Render Queue panel.

9 Click the Render button in the Render Queue panel. After Effects renders the movie. If there were additional movies—or the same movie with different settings—in the queue, After Effects would render those, too.

When the processing is complete, the Final_MPEG4 movie appears in the Project panel.

To preview the movie, double-click it in the Project panel, and then press the spacebar to view the movie.

If you need to make any final changes to the movie, reopen the composition and make those adjustments now. Remember to save your work when you finish, and then output the test movie again using the appropriate settings. After examining the test movie and making any necessary changes, you'll proceed with outputting the movie for full-resolution broadcast.

Preparing movies for mobile devices

You can create movies in After Effects for playback on mobile devices, such as tablets and smartphones. To render your movie, add the composition to the Adobe Media Encoder encoding queue, and choose an appropriate device-specific encoding preset.

For the best results, consider the limitations of mobile devices as you shoot footage and work with After Effects. For a small screen size, pay careful attention to lighting, and use a lower frame rate. See After Effects Help for more tips.

Rendering movies with Adobe Media Encoder

Your movie is ready for final output. Adobe Media Encoder, which is installed when you install After Effects, lets you easily render your movie in multiple high-quality formats. (If it isn't installed already, install it from Creative Cloud.)

Rendering a broadcast-quality movie

First, you'll select settings to render your movie in a quality suitable for broadcast.

1 In the Project panel, select the DesktopC composition, and choose Composition > Add To Adobe Media Encoder Queue.

After Effects opens Adobe Media Encoder, and adds your composition with default render settings. Your default settings may vary from ours.

2 Click the blue link in the Preset column.

Adobe Media Encoder connects to the Dynamic Link server, which may take a few moments.

Note: If you don't need to change anything else in the Export Settings dialog box, you can change the preset using the Preset pop-up menu in the Queue panel.

3 When the Export Settings dialog box appears, choose H.264 from the Format menu, and then choose HD 1080p 23.976 from the Preset menu.

Rendering the full movie with the HD 1080p 23.976 preset may take several minutes. You'll change the settings to render only the first five seconds of the movie so that you can preview the quality. You can change the range rendered using the time ruler at the bottom of the Export Settings dialog box.

4 Move the current-time indicator to 5:00, and then click the Set Out Point button (⌐) to the left of the Select Zoom Level pop-up menu.

5 Click OK to close the Export Settings dialog box.

6 Click the blue link in the Output File column. Name the movie **HD-test_1080p.mp4**, and specify the Lessons/Lesson14/Final_Movies folder. Then click Save or OK.

You're ready to output this movie, but you'll set up a few additional movie options in the queue before you render it.

Adding another encoding preset to the queue

Tip: If you render files frequently, consider setting up a "watch folder." When you place a file in the watch folder, Adobe Media Encoder automatically encodes it using the settings you've specified in the Watch Folders panel.

Adobe Media Encoder comes with dozens of built-in presets suitable for output for traditional broadcast, mobile devices, and the web. You'll output a version of your composition ready for posting to YouTube.

1 In the Preset Browser panel, navigate to Web Video > YouTube > YouTube 480p SD Wide.

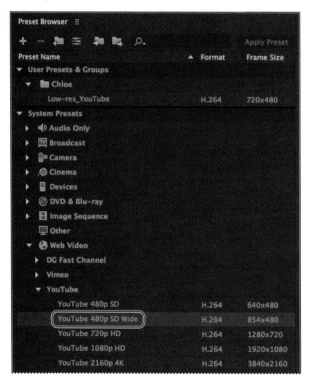

2 Drag the YouTube 480p SD Wide preset onto the DesktopC composition in the Queue panel.

Adobe Media Encoder adds another output item to the queue.

3 Click the blue link in the Output File column for the item you just added. Then name the file **Final_Web.mp4**, specify the Lessons/Lesson14/Final_Movies folder, and click Save or OK.

Rendering movies

You've set up two versions of your movie in the queue. Now you'll render and view them. Rendering is resource-intensive, and it can take a while, depending on your system, the complexity and length of the composition, and the settings you use.

1 Click the green Start Queue button (▶) in the upper right corner of the Queue panel.

Depending on your system, this may take a while.

Adobe Media Encoder encodes the movies in the queue simultaneously, displaying a status bar, and reporting the estimated time remaining.

▶ **Tip:** If you forget where you saved your encoded movies, click the blue link in the Output File column next to the finished movie. Adobe Media Encoder opens a window to show you where your files were saved.

2 When Adobe Media Encoder has finished, navigate to the Final_Movies folder in the Finder or Explorer, and double-click your files to play them.

Preparing a movie for broadcast output

The project you're rendering in this lesson is already high-resolution and appropriate for broadcast output. However, you may need to adjust other compositions for your intended delivery format.

To change the composition size, create a new composition with the appropriate settings for your final format. Then drag the project composition into the new composition.

If you converted the composition from a square pixel aspect ratio to a nonsquare pixel aspect ratio, which is used in broadcasting, items in the Composition panel may appear wider than before. To view the video accurately, enable *pixel aspect ratio correction*. Pixel aspect ratio correction squeezes the view of the composition slightly to display the image as it will appear on a video monitor. By default, this feature is turned off, but you can easily turn it on by clicking the Toggle Pixel Aspect Ratio Correction button (▤) at the bottom of the Composition panel. The quality of the pixel aspect ratio correction for previews is affected by the Zoom Quality preference in the Previews category of the Preferences dialog box.

Creating custom presets for Adobe Media Encoder

In most cases, one of the default Adobe Media Encoder presets will be appropriate for your project. However, you can create your own encoding presets if you have specialized needs. In this case, you'll create a preset that renders a lower-resolution file for YouTube more quickly than the one you just encoded.

1 Click the Create New Preset Group button (🗐) at the top of the Preset Browser panel, and give the group a unique name, such as your name.

2 Click the Create New Preset button (✚).

3 Do the following in the Preset Settings dialog box, and then click OK:

- Name the preset **Low-res_YouTube**.

- Make sure H.264 is chosen from the Format menu.

- Choose YouTube 480p SD Wide from the Based On Preset menu.

- Select the Video tab, if it's not already selected.

- For Frame Rate, deselect Based On Source.

- Choose Baseline from the Profile menu. (You may need to scroll down to see it and the following options.)

- Choose 3.0 from the Level menu.

- Make sure VBR, 1 Pass is chosen from the Bitrate Encoding menu.

- Click the Audio tab, and choose 44100 Hz from the Sample Rate menu and Medium from the Audio Quality menu.

4 Drag the Low_res_YouTube preset onto the DesktopC composition in the Queue panel.

5 Click the blue link in the Output File column. Then name the file **Lowres_YouTube**, specify the Lessons/Lesson14/Final_Movies folder, and click Save or OK.

6 Click the Start Queue button (▶).

With the settings in your new preset, the movie encodes more quickly. However, the quality isn't as high.

7 When Adobe Media Encoder has finished, navigate to the Final_Movies folder in Explorer or the Finder, and double-click the Lowres_YouTube movie to view it.

You have created both a web version and a broadcast version of the final composition.

Congratulations! You have completed all the lessons in *Adobe After Effects CC Classroom in a Book (2015 release)*.

While this book is intended to give you a good foundation for working with After Effects, it can't cover everything. To continue learning about After Effects, check out the resources described in the Getting Started section at the beginning of the book.

Review questions

1 Name two types of templates you can create for use in the Render Queue panel, and explain when and why to use them.

2 What is compression, and what are some things you should consider when compressing files?

3 How can you output a movie using Adobe Media Encoder?

Review answers

1 In After Effects, you can create templates for both render settings and output-module settings. These templates are presets that you can use to streamline the setup process when you render items for the same type of delivery format. After you define these templates, they appear in the Render Queue panel on the appropriate pop-up menu (Render Settings or Output Module). Then, when you're ready to render a job, you can simply select the template that is appropriate for the delivery format that your job requires, and the template applies all the settings.

2 Compression is essential to reduce the size of movies so that they can be stored, transmitted, and played back effectively. When exporting or rendering a movie file for playback on a specific type of device at a certain bandwidth, you choose a compressor/decompressor, or codec, to compress the information and generate a file readable by that type of device at that bandwidth. A wide range of codecs is available; no single codec is the best for all situations. For example, the best codec for compressing cartoon animation is generally not efficient for compressing live-action video. When compressing a movie file, you can fine-tune it for the best quality playback on a computer, a video playback device, the web, or from a DVD player. Depending on which encoder you use, you may be able to reduce the size of compressed files by removing artifacts that interfere with compression, such as random camera motion and excessive film grain.

3 To output a movie using Adobe Media Encoder, select the composition in the Project panel in After Effects, and then choose Composition > Add To Adobe Media Encoder Queue. In Adobe Media Encoder, select an encoding preset and any other settings, name the output file, and click the Start Queue button.

Appendix: General keyboard shortcuts

Result	Windows	Mac OS
Select all	Ctrl+A	Command+A
Deselect all	F2 or Ctrl+Shift+A	F2 or Command+Shift+A
Rename selected layer, composition, folder, effect, group, or mask	Enter on main keyboard	Return on main keyboard
Open selected layer, composition, or footage item	Enter on numeric keypad	Enter on numeric keypad
Move selected layers, masks, effects, or render items down (back) or up (forward) in stacking order	Ctrl+Alt+Down Arrow or Ctrl+Alt+Up Arrow	Command+Option+Down Arrow or Command+Option+Up Arrow
Move selected layers, masks, effects, or render items to bottom (back) or top (front) of stacking order	Ctrl+Alt+Shift+Down Arrow or Ctrl+Alt+Shift+Up Arrow	Command+Option+Shift+Down Arrow or Command+Option+Shift+Up Arrow
Extend selection to next item in Project panel, Render Queue panel, or Effect Controls panel	Shift+Down Arrow	Shift+Down Arrow
Extend selection to previous item in Project panel, Render Queue panel, or Effect Controls panel	Shift+Up Arrow	Shift+Up Arrow
Duplicate selected layers, masks, effects, text selectors, animators, puppet meshes, shapes, render items, output modules, or compositions	Ctrl+D	Command+D
Quit	Ctrl+Q	Command+Q
Undo	Ctrl+Z	Command+Z
Redo	Ctrl+Shift+Z	Command+Shift+Z
Purge All Memory	Ctrl+Alt+/ (on numeric keypad)	Command+Option+/ (on numeric keypad)
Interrupt running a script	Esc	Esc

INDEX

SYMBOLS

3D axis 267

3D cameras 273–274

 adjusting depth of
 field 308

 point of interest 274

3D Camera Tracker
 effect 290–310

3D features 262–287

3D layers

 camera layers 273

 creating in Cinema 4D
 Lite 277–285

 Position properties 185

 rotating 185

 Rotation properties 267

3D Layer switch 267

3D lights 270–272

 casting shadows with 272

 point of interest 271

3D text 265–267

3D views 267–268

A

action-safe zones 29

Active Camera view 273

adding

 blur 256–257

 transitions 237

 vignettes 190, 258

Add mask mode 246

Add Or Remove Keyframe At
 Current Time button 207

adjustment layers 137, 256

Adobe After Effects CC
 application

 After Effects Help 38

 compositions 12

 installing 2

 optimizing performance in 2

 projects 12

 workflow 11

 workspace 10

*Adobe After Effects CC Classroom
 in a Book (2015 release)*

 lesson files 3

 prerequisites 1

Adobe After Effects Help 38

Adobe Audition, editing audio
 files in 140

Adobe Bridge

 about 43

 browsing animation
 presets in 70

workspaces

 customizing 10

 in Adobe Bridge 44

 predefined 36

 saving custom 37

X

x axis 22

 in the 3D axis 267

Y

y axis 22

 in the 3D axis 267

Z

z axis 265

 in the 3D axis 267

Zoom-Bubble effect 30

zooming with touch gestures 184

Production Notes

Adobe After Effects CC Classroom in a Book (2015 release) was created electronically using Adobe InDesign CC (2015 release). Art was produced using Adobe InDesign, Adobe Illustrator, and Adobe Photoshop.

References to company names in the lessons are for demonstration purposes only and are not intended to refer to any actual organization or person.

Typefaces used

Adobe Myriad Pro and Adobe Warnock Pro as well as other Adobe typefaces are used throughout the lessons. For more information about OpenType and Adobe fonts, visit www.adobe.com/type/opentype.

Team credits

The following individuals contributed to the development of *Adobe After Effects CC Classroom in a Book (2015 release)*:

- **Writer:** Brie Gyncild
- **Illustrator and Compositor:** Lisa Fridsma
- **Copyeditor and Proofreader**: Wendy Katz
- **Indexer:** Brie Gyncild
- **Keystroker:** Megan Ahearn
- **Cover design:** Eddie Yuen
- **Interior design:** Mimi Heft
- **Lesson Designer:** Lisa Fridsma
- **Adobe Press Executive Editor:** Victor Gavenda
- **Adobe Press Project Editor:** Karyn Johnson
- **Adobe Press Production Editor:** David Van Ness

Contributors

Mark Christiansen—Author of *After Effects CC Visual Effects and Compositing Studio Techniques* (Adobe Press), Mark has created visual effects and animations for feature films, network television, computer games, and an array of high-technology companies. Recent clients include *The Orphanage* (Dimension Films), *Telling Pictures* (The History Channel), and the Couturié Company (HBO), as well as Seagate, Sun, Intel, and Medtronic. Feature credits include *The Day After Tomorrow* and films by Robert Rodriguez.

Lee Daniels—Lee is a freelance animator, illustrator, and motion graphic artist working from his home studio in South London. Following a career in magazine design and image retouch, Lee has spent the last 10 years producing bespoke animation and visual effects for a wide range of international corporate, TV, and new media clients including Channel 4, Discovery US, National Geographic, Mirror Group, Exxon Mobile, and Cancer Research. Recently, he has worked on several newly commissioned UK TV shows for the 4oD short-form comedy platform. He generously shares tips & tricks in After Effects animation with the growing subscriber community on his LeeDanielsART YouTube channel. See more of his work at leedanielsart.com.

Takeshi Hiraoka—Plucked out of paradise, Hiraoka moved to chilly San Francisco from Honolulu, Hawaii, one cold winter day in 2002. In San Francisco, he attended the Academy of Art University, graduating in May 2004. This is where Hiraoka met Sheldon Callahan, with whom he directed and produced the feature-length DV film *Origin*. In addition to being a DV producer, Hiraoka is also a 2D and 3D animator.

Stephen Schleicher—Traveling from Kansas to Georgia to California, Stephen has worked as an editor, graphic designer, videographer, director, and producer on a variety of small and large video productions. Currently, Stephen teaches media and web development at Fort Hays State University. He also works on video and independent projects for state and local agencies and organizations, as well as his own works. Stephen is a regular contributor to Digital Media Net (www.digitalmedianet.com).

Anna Ullrich—Anna is a pale but fine digital artist based in Seattle, Washington, although her heart resides in Minnesota, where her spry and brilliant Democratic grandmother lives. Anna earned a BFA from the University of Washington in Seattle and an MFA from the University of Notre Dame in Indiana (both in photography).

Special Thanks

We offer our sincere thanks to Todd Kopriva for his support and help with this project. We couldn't have done it without you!

LEARN BY VIDEO

Learn by Video is a critically acclaimed training series that offers exceptional quality high-definition video to teach the most essential creative technologies and topics. Experienced instructors and industry professionals present hours of video tutorials, complete with lesson files, assessment quizzes, and review materials.

Available in DVD and streaming formats.

To see a full list of titles go to
www.learnbyvideo.com

Add bookmarks in your video for later reference

Lesson files are included

Up to 13 hours of high-quality video training

Closed Captioning option available

Watch & Work mode shrinks the video into a small window while you work in the software

Titles

Adobe Photoshop CC Learn by Video (2015 release)
ISBN: 9780134384115

Adobe Illustrator CC Learn by Video (2015 release)
ISBN: 9780134396385

Adobe InDesign CC Learn by Video (2015 release)
ISBN: 9780134397825

Adobe Dreamweaver CC Learn by Video (2015 release)
ISBN: 9780134396378

Adobe Premiere Pro CC Learn by Video (2015 release)
ISBN: 9780134397832

**Adobe Photoshop Lightroom CC (2015 release) /
Lightroom 6 Learn by Video**
ISBN: 9780133928426

Photo Restoration Learn by Video
ISBN: 9780134096421

**Aerial Photography and Videography Using Drones
Learn by Video**
ISBN: 9780134121949

**The Photographer's Workflow - Adobe Lightroom CC and
Adobe Photoshop CC Learn by Video (2015 release)**
ISBN: 9780134384122

Peachpit **Adobe Press**

HOW TO REGISTER YOUR PRODUCT

- Go to adobepress.com/register.
- Sign in or create an account. (*If you are creating a new account, be sure to check the box to hear from us about upcoming special offers.*)
- Enter the 10- or 13-digit ISBN of your product.

BENEFITS OF REGISTERING

- A 35% off coupon to be used on your next purchase—valid for 30 days (*Your code will be available in your Adobe Press cart for you to apply during checkout. You will also find it in the Manage Codes section of your Account page.*)
- Access to bonus chapters, product updates, and/or workshop files when available
- Special offers on new editions and related Adobe Press products (*Be sure to check the box to hear from us when setting up your account or visit adobepress.com/newsletters.*)

Benefits for registering vary by product. Benefits will be listed on your Account page under Registered Products.

Discount may not be combined with any other offer and is not redeemable for cash. Discount code expires after 30 days from the time of product registration. Offer subject to change.

The fastest, easiest, most comprehensive way to learn
Adobe® Creative Cloud™

Classroom in a Book®, the best-selling series of hands-on software training books, helps you learn the features of Adobe software quickly and easily.

The **Classroom in a Book** series offers what no other book or training program does—an official training series from Adobe Systems, developed with the support of Adobe product experts.

To see a complete list of our Classroom in a Book titles covering the 2015 release of Adobe Creative Cloud go to:

www.adobepress.com/cc2015

Adobe Photoshop CC Classroom in a Book (2015 release)
ISBN: 9780134308135

Adobe Illustrator CC Classroom in a Book (2015 release)
ISBN: 9780134308111

Adobe InDesign CC Classroom in a Book (2015 release)
ISBN: 978013431000

Adobe Dreamweaver CC Classroom in a Book (2015 release)
ISBN: 9780134309996

Adobe Premiere Pro CC Classroom in a Book (2015 release)
ISBN: 9780134309989

Adobe After Effects CC Classroom in a Book (2015 release)
ISBN: 9780134308128

Adobe Photoshop Lightroom CC (2015 release) / Lightroom 6 Classroom in a Book
ISBN: 978013392482

Adobe Lightroom and Photoshop CC for Photographers Classroom in a Book (2015 release)
ISBN: 9780134288611

Adobe Acrobat DC Classroom in a Book
ISBN: 9780134171838

how to start a home-based

Business to Become a Work-At-Home Mom

how to start a home-based

Business to Become a Work-At-Home Mom

Georganne Fiumara

gPP®

Guilford, Connecticut

Editorial Director: Cynthia Hughes Cullen
Editor: Katie Benoit
Project Editor: Tracee Williams
Text Design: Sheryl P. Kober
Layout: Justin Marciano

Disclosure text on pages 42–43 courtesy of Amy Oztan
Income List text on page 47 courtesy of Maria T. O'Brien
Photograph on page 81 courtesy of Clayton McCarl
Photograph on page 84 courtesy of Lori Bergmann
Photograph on page 88 courtesy of Ralph Smith
Photographs on pages 112–113 courtesy of Michael Rogers, michaelrogersonline.com

ISSN 2162-9609
ISBN 978-0-7627-6362-7

Printed in the United States of America
10 9 8 7 6 5 4 3 2 1

With love for Jason from GiGi. You turned this Work-at-Home Mother into a Work-at-Home Grandmother . . . and I love every minute! Your special and sweet first months of life inspired me as I wrote this book.

Contents

Acknowledgments

Thank you to Mike Urban for this opportunity and a special thank you to Katie Benoit and Tracee Williams at Globe Pequot Press for your patience and support.

And, of course, thank you to the fans of HomeWorkingMom.com. I appreciate the way you've shared your hearts and your home businesses with me both for this book and throughout the years.

—G. F.

Introduction

In Grants Pass, Oregon, a woman handed the teller a note demanding cash. The note said to wait fifteen minutes before calling the police or else two children wouldn't make it home from school. It sounded like the two children were in danger, but were they? No. Instead, this bank robber mom didn't want to be late picking up her kids from school. She fled the bank with $1,300, but a tip led police to her driveway. She had just picked up her two daughters from school, and they were in the back seat happily eating ice cream.

Talk about being desperate to find a way to juggle work and family! There is no doubt that moms who are trying to earn the money they need while taking care of their children can feel that kind of deep desperation at times, but there are much better "job" choices that you will learn about in this book.

If you are a mom looking to learn more about earning money from home, there is a good chance that your interest is driven more by emotion than your deep desire to become a home-based business owner. You want to find a way to be present in your child's life while also earning the money you need. You don't want someone else to spend more time with your baby or preschooler during daytime hours than you do. Or, you want to find a way to be there when your child comes home from school and to be a "milk-and-cookies" mom. You feel a telephone call and hours of TV for the children can't substitute for you being there. If you have a teenager, the need to be at home can be as strong as, or stronger than, when the children are young. You realize that teenagers can get into trouble right under your nose . . . and when you aren't there the chances of drama increase significantly. There's a reason that the hours between three and six o'clock are called the "danger hours."

Unfortunately, you need to work to earn the money your family needs to survive and thrive. Whether you are married, a single mother, or have different

circumstances entirely, in today's world, your income matters. You want and need a reliable income that you can use to pay the bills and give your family a better life.

So, what can you do?

The dilemma of managing work and family is probably the most difficult challenge you will face as a mother. After all, you can't possibly be in two places at the same time, right? Wrong. Believe it or not, there is a way to work, earn the income you need, and be at home for your children. You can start a home-based business. Don't say it—I realize this is easier said than done. But making this a realistic possibility for you is the reason why I wrote this book.

Between 2008 and 2010 the number of moms who stay at home with their children fell from 5.3 million to 5 million. In contrast, approximately 150,000 fathers stay at home with their kids. In a shaky economy, it is evident that more and more moms will need to work to ensure the family keeps up its financial bottom line. The image of the family where Mom stays at home caring for the kids and Dad goes to work is almost extinct. In today's world Mom needs to bring in some income, but she also takes primary responsibility for her children. Since working is a necessity for today's mom, the only question is this: Will she work inside or outside of her home?

Millions of moms already do at least part of their career work at home. Some have help with child care, while others multitask and do it all by themselves. Some split child care with their husbands, and still others rely on their mothers or friends to back them up. Running a home-based business and taking care of kids at the same time is not easy. Nothing worthwhile ever is. Leaving your child so you can go to work outside your home is just as hard, if not harder.

Statistics show that between 80 and 90 percent of kids spend some time in the care of someone other than their mother by age four and a half. Kids who spent the most total time in daycare grew up to act more impulsively and to take more risks than other children, according to the *Child Development* journal study of 1,364 children who were monitored since one month of age. These children also show problems with behavior and achievement, and those problems often are carried into adulthood. Those who spent their time in "high-quality" child care were less likely to have these problems.

When I became a work-at-home mom way back in 1984, times were very different from today. There was a great controversy brewing: Should a mom stay at home and remain the primary caretaker of her children, or should she go to work and leave her children in another person's care for eight plus hours every day? In

my mind, there was a third option: I decided to work *and* take care of my kids at the same time, all under one roof. I also decided that I would let other moms know that working at home was a viable option that they could consider. That is why I started Mothers' Home Business Network and eventually my website, HomeWorkingMom .com. I have devoted over twenty-five years of my life to helping moms work at home and avoiding work-at-home scams. I'd like to help you, too.

Even though my children are grown, my work-at-home mom vision is still very clear and I completely understand what a young mom currently in the trenches is going through. As I write this book and work on my home business, my infant grandson, Jason, is spending part of his days with me. What a joy . . . I am now a work-at-home grandmother!

Today's world is a lot more complicated than when my children were young. But it is also a lot better because of the Internet. The online world has changed everything for moms who want to work at home. Online, you can start a business or promote a traditional home business to increase your chance for success. You can also get support easily from other moms who are also working at home. The world is literally at your fingertips, and you can't ask for more than that.

If I could tell you just one tip that would bring you success in the home-based business world, it would be this: Start. Start now. Start when things are not perfect. Take that first step. Everyone has to start somewhere. Forget about putting it off until you lose ten pounds, or when the kids go to school full-time, or when you buy a better computer. No matter what you see as a more perfect future time, chances are it won't be perfect. Take your first steps now and you will be so many steps closer to your dream business when you are ready to give it a full effort.

There is no valid excuse to delay. You can make excuses, or you can make money and achieve your dream. Every time you make an excuse, visualize money flying out of the window. It doesn't matter if you have a clear home business idea yet. Start working on your home business now to gain more business knowledge even before you have the perfect idea. Until you start to work, your business idea cannot grow or evolve. It doesn't cost a single penny to make plans and do research. Try a few different avenues at the same time. As you work, you will learn from your successes and gain even more knowledge from the mistakes you make. The best projects will attract more of your attention, and that will show you what direction to take. You might be surprised at how much your original idea will change after you've worked on it for a while.

This book will give you the inspiration, information, and ideas you need to help you choose the right home business for you. Even more important, as you read you will realize that my heart is with you. I understand all your feelings and how much is at stake. All my knowledge is available to you. I will give you all the facts you need to know to help you choose the business that is right for you. You will learn how to avoid the pitfalls and learn, step-by-step, how to be successful. I will also help you manage your time and efforts while working at home with children.

Let's Get Together

Because you are reading this book, I have put a special page on HomeWorking Mom.com just for you. It contains clickable links to the resources mentioned in the appendix plus direct access to ask me any questions you have about starting a home-based business. Why don't you take a look right now? I can't wait to meet you! Just go to www.HomeWorkingMom.com/wahmresources.

If you really believe that you can work at home and be the primary caretaker of your children, you can make it happen. Let go of all your "if onlys" and "somedays" and begin today. Take my hand and let's get started!

Note: You may be pregnant with your first child, or have any number of children that are boys or girls. You may be a single mom, married, or live with a significant other. You might even be a dad who wants to work at home. Grandparents can work at home with kids, too. As you can see, it is impossible to always use the pronouns that will match the particulars of your life. You may have a girl, but I might use the word *he*. You might have only one child, but I may refer to your offspring as *children*. Please understand that I have respect for your choices and circumstances, but it is too cumbersome to say he/she or child/children, and so on throughout the book. Just know that as long as you are seeking a better way to balance work and family, this book is for you.

Mothers today have a better chance than ever before to find a way to successfully manage mothering and work. All the traditional lines have blurred and each of the many work-at-home options you have can overlap. Depending on the type of work you do and who you do it for, you can be called a consultant, a freelancer, an independent contractor, a teleworker, an at-home employee, or a home-based business owner.

Can you have a home business and be a teleworker or a freelancer at the same time? Yes! The work you do could fit into many of the work-at-home categories at the same time. It is not unusual for a work-at-home mom to earn multiple stems of income from a variety of sources. This is a great way to make sure you earn enough for your family and to finance future projects. The more contacts you make, the more opportunities you will find coming your way.

Here's an example of how one fictional work-at-home mom could fit into many categories at the same time: Because she went from full-time employee to part-time teleworker, Rebecca's employer has kept her on the payroll and she has retained her previous benefits. As a freelancer, she writes articles that appear in magazines and on websites. Rebecca also writes and sells e-books, making her a home-based business owner. Once her e-book has been written and it has a sales page, Rebecca's work is done. A couple of hours of marketing online each week keep her home business going.

Having so many options can be confusing, but one thing is for sure: On the day you decide that you would like to become a work-at-home mom, an entire world of possibilities opens up for you. At home, you can be anything you want to be and do anything you want to do without waiting for someone else's permission to begin. It is your own attitude and willingness to learn and

think creatively that will determine whether or not you can succeed at home. This sounds good, but know that life does not necessarily become easier when you are in charge of your own fate. You need to find the right pathway that will take you from what is to what could be.

The Choice Is Yours

Before you can focus on the right possibilities for you and your family, there are many decisions to make. To get focused, ask yourself three questions:

Question 1: Should I Quit My Job?

Sixty-six percent of those responding to a survey on the HomeBusiness.About.com website said they think about quitting their jobs daily. It is likely that the percentage of working mothers who think about quitting their jobs every single day is a lot higher.

When real life meets wishful thinking it is difficult to give up the income and benefits you receive at your job. You need to replace that income before you can give it up, and that is not easy to do. If you are committed to working at home, it will be easier to work on your home business if you are not at your job eight hours or more each day.

There are flexible work options that could give you more quality time at home and the money you need while your home business is in the start-up stages. Some of the options you can consider include the following:

- **Job Sharing.** This option occurs when two or more workers share the work of one full-time job. Each person works part-time. Why would a company allow two employees to share one job? Increased employee morale is one reason. Retaining two valued employees who might be lost if required to work full-time is another good reason. In fact, some companies find that more skills are brought to the job when two people share it and productivity is increased because employees have a stake in making the arrangement work. Moms who share jobs often share child care too. The caregiver mom goes to the house of the mother working that day.
- **Flextime.** Flextime has been described as a full-time job with a heart. In this kind of arrangement, the employer lets the employee decide what time to start and end her day. Some may work four ten-hour days and take one day off. Others may come in early and leave late, or vice versa. Companies can benefit

because employees will be less likely to miss work. When employees work a staggered schedule, there can be a decrease in overhead, because companies save money when employees can share desk space and expensive equipment.

- **Telework.** If you have the kind of job that can be done outside of the office, you might be able to convince your company to let you telecommute to work. This option may be your best way to stay employed while also managing mothering and a home business start-up. Teleworkers do the majority of their work at home, usually on a computer that links up to their office. Some moms telecommute only one or two days each week and work in the office the remaining days.

Question 2: Is it Possible to Find a Legitimate Home Job?

Just a few years ago, I would have advised you that the only way to find a legitimate home job would be to look in your local area. Today, it is possible to find real work-at-home jobs online. However, if you want to find a job online with benefits and a regular paycheck, you might be disappointed.

The Internet has made it possible to connect with companies all over the country who are looking for people to work at home. Although there are real jobs available, many companies may still require that you live close to their office. However, if you think outside of the box and use the right search terms on major job sites like Monster.com and CareerBuilders.com you could find what you are looking for. Even if you are not a writer or an artist, check out the websites for freelancers such as Elance.com and Freelancer.com, where you can bid for a variety of projects posted by companies large and small. There are plenty of job search sites out there, so it's important to research them to find ones that fit your needs.

When you are searching for a home job, use search terms that reflect the type of work you do. Instead of just searching for the term *home job,* also search these terms: *telework, telecommute, freelance, home-based (or home based), blogger, virtual,* and *remote worker.*

There are websites that charge a fee for home job listings. Many of them are legitimate. Some just filter jobs they find from other websites, which is not necessarily bad as long as the site is updated frequently. These types of sites can save you a lot of time and trouble. One example of this type of website is HomeJobStop.com. Before you pay a fee for a job website, look to see if there is a place on the site where companies can post a job directly. Note the dates the jobs are posted.

How to Convince Your Employer

Employers can reap many benefits when part of their workforce works from home. If your company already has employees working flexible hours or teleworking, it will be easier for you to get what you want.

Your need for flexible work is important to you, but flexibility must go both ways if you want to convince your employer to let you job share, work flextime, or become a teleworker. Your employer may not go along with your request unless you can demonstrate how the company will benefit and your willingness to adapt your plan to meet the company's needs. For example, your company may be willing to let you telecommute but wants you to be in the office every Wednesday for a staff meeting. That is a compromise you should be able to accept.

Here are some dos and don'ts for convincing your employer to give you a flexible work option:

- **Do:** Put your proposal in writing. If you want to job share, write a joint proposal with your potential job-sharing partner.

- **Do:** Point out that instant messaging, text messaging, and e-mail can help you communicate with the office from home as easily as if you were in the office. You could also use Skype to attend meetings virtually.

- **Do:** Be a trusted and valuable employee. The more you contribute to your company, the more the company will try to retain you as an employee.

- **Do:** Write a proposal that demonstrates how the company will benefit if you have a more flexible work option. Increased productivity and decreased overhead expenses are just two of the areas you could write about.

- **Do:** Remind your employer that if you can telework you will be on the job in bad weather or if you or your child is ill. Business hours and time zones won't limit your work time either.

- **Do:** Suggest a trial period so that your employer will have a chance to evaluate the situation thoroughly.

- **Do:** Take note of other employees in your company who telework, job share, or work flextime. What has happened in the past can affect you, and the more informed you are the better results you will get.

- **Don't:** Press for an immediate answer. Your written proposal will continue to do your work while you wait patiently.

- **Don't:** Ignore the possible objections you might receive. Instead, be prepared to answer any of your employer's concerns.

- **Don't:** Write your proposal from your point of view. Telling your employer that you can't find a babysitter or your husband has to work late and can't be there to take care of the baby won't work.

There are some home businesses you can start that will allow you to work for a variety of companies using your specific skill set. The best example of this type of business is a virtual assistant position. I've included information about becoming a virtual assistant in chapter 5.

A more complete listing of websites where you can find work you can do at home is included in appendix B.

Question 3: Should I Start a Home Business?

Starting a home business is very similar to raising a child. Your fledgling business is new and exciting at first, but then you realize that it can only grow step-by-step, that a lot of good advice is necessary, and that the more of yourself you give it, the better it will grow and flourish. You can't be just a little committed to your baby, and your home business requires lots of hard work and attention too.

It is unrealistic to think that you can start a home business and make the money your family needs immediately. It takes an investment of time and money to build any business, whether you start it at home or not. Many moms are unwilling or unable to invest family money in a home business all at once, so they finance their idea a little at a time. While this method can help protect your bank account as you progress, it can be frustrating to try to operate without enough capital; the lack of money could also put your new business in jeopardy.

If you want to start a home-based business but you don't have a lot of money to invest, you can finance your dream without draining your family's bank account by doing other types of work at home in the start-up stages of your business. Never refinance your home to get money to start your business. If your business fails, you could lose your home, too.

If you are committed to the idea of starting a home business, you need a good idea. But additionally, and first, there are more practical matters to address:

- *How old is your youngest child?* If you have a new baby and you just realized that you don't want to leave him to go back to work, I understand. However, that is an emotional decision, not a business decision. If you can afford to take some time to plan your at-home career, great. If you need money now, you will need another income source.
- *Do other family members share your enthusiasm?* It is hard enough to start a home business without fighting against family disapproval.
- *Do you have the room for a dedicated work space?* You can be creative when designing your home office, but some space is required, especially if little hands can reach up and do damage.
- *Do you need additional space for inventory or specific equipment necessary for your business?* Anyone can fit in a laptop and a few office supplies. But carefully consider your needs if you are planning on selling a product that has to be stored in your home.
- *Will clients be coming and going from your home, or will you create noise that will attract attention in your neighborhood?* If you work online, most businesses will be acceptable in any zone. If your home business might disturb your neighbors, consider any potential zoning problems.
- *What supplies or equipment will you need at start-up, and what expenses can be delayed until you start to earn income from your business?* You need a desk, but you don't need the most expensive desk in the store. Make sure you have enough money for start-up and be frugal until you generate enough income to cover additional overhead costs.

Don't Get Scammed

When "experts" talk about work-at-home scams, they almost always warn you: "If it seems too good to be true, it probably is." I say, "If it looks too good to be true, it just

might be a great opportunity!" If you are looking for a work-at-home job or opportunity, you could miss a lot of great possibilities if you are very fearful of being scammed.

There is a new-age saying, "What you focus on expands." If you are always looking for a work-at-home scam, it will probably be all you find. My advice? As you begin developing your work-at-home plan, stop looking for scams. Instead, learn how to spot a scam and then spend your time looking for good information and real opportunities. And, if you do fall for a scam along the way, just chalk it up to experience and move on. Don't let it stop you from your mission. Chances are, the amount of money you lose will not be significant, and if you learn from your mistake it won't happen again. It would be even sadder if you lost your focus, your enthusiasm, your self-esteem, and your belief in the wonderful ways you can legitimately work at home just because you lost a few dollars.

Another old saying, "Fool me once, shame on you. Fool me twice, shame on me." This means that if you make a mistake and send in $25 to get a kit to learn how to assemble baby bibs at home and your sample is rejected (you can count on the fact that it will be), realize you were scammed and don't try it again with a different company. It is up to you to arm yourself with the correct information and learn from your mistakes.

Remember: You are not powerless against these scam artists, because, in fact, you have all of the power. Really. You can put all of the work-at-home scam artists out of business and you don't even have to make one telephone call or send an e-mail. If you and every other work-at-home hopeful ignore every sketchy offer and every promise of a secret money-making plan, scams will start to disappear.

All companies, even dishonest ones, stop paying for ads when they don't get responses. Don't visit these websites, and don't call the toll-free number you see posted on a telephone pole as you stop for a red light or that you hear in a radio ad. Instead, listen to that little voice in your head or that feeling in the pit of your stomach that tells you that this is not real. As a general rule, stay away from any ads for data-entry jobs, envelope stuffing, and assembly of toys, bibs, and so on. You will only lose money and get very frustrated.

Don't let your hope and desire for an "easy" way to earn at home overrule your good common sense. Instead, ask yourself questions and be on the lookout for the following before you respond:

- Why would a company in California want to hire workers all over the country to stuff its envelopes or assemble its toys? It wouldn't. That is why most opportunities to do overflow work for a company are local, not national.

- If you had a special "secret" to making money at home, would you sell it for $29.95? Why would you tell anyone at all? The fact is that there are no secret ways to make money or shortcuts to success.
- Are full details about the opportunity being given? If it seems a little too vague, it's probably not legit.
- Don't be fooled by a "review" of an opportunity. Although many reviews are legitimate, many reviews are just ways to sell a scam and get an affiliate payment.
- Is the company offering a salaried position or will you have to work on commission?
- Is the company offering a job or a directory of places where you can possibly find jobs? Often, directories contain old and useless information taken from other out-of-date sources.
- Is there full contact information being offered? A website address, a telephone number, and an e-mail address that includes the company's domain name are all essential.
- Don't be fooled by a .org at the end of a website address. Anyone can register a .org domain name so that it appears to be nonprofit or belongs to a large organization.
- Don't be impressed by references to large corporations. If the ad mentions companies like Walmart, Google, or Apple in a general way, it gives no value to this particular offer.
- Do you see a site that pops up after you leave another website? Often, it looks like a newspaper page with a story about a woman from your city who makes thousands of dollars each year. Close out of these kinds of sites and don't click through.
- Always read the fine print. That's where the real information can be found.
- Don't be fooled by opportunities that say they are especially for Christians or any other religious group. Making a statement doesn't make it so, and professed religious affiliation does not guarantee legitimacy.

After more than twenty-five years of protecting moms like you from work-at-home scams, I have a built-in and very accurate radar. I don't have to spend much time deciding if the job or opportunity I am looking at is a scam. With the right information, you, too, can develop the same kind of intuition.

There are some scams that can hurt you in much more serious ways that you should know about. You could lose all of the money in your bank account or even get arrested if you don't take note of the following:

- **Never** do business with anyone you don't know from Nigeria or another foreign country.
- **Never** agree to cash checks for any company for any reason. You might be told to cash the check, wire the money to the company, and keep a portion for yourself. The check will bounce and your bank account could be wiped out.
- **Never** agree to accept packages at your home for anyone (not even for someone you meet on a social networking site). The person will ask you to accept the package, inspect it, and forward it to a P.O. Box number. The scam artist may even pay you to do this. However, these are most likely stolen goods that you are accepting, which will be traced back to you, not the scammer. The postal inspector will knock on your door and accuse you of theft or possession of stolen goods.
- **Never** send money to anyone with a "sob" story on the Internet, especially someone you meet on a social networking or dating site. Even if you think he is your new boyfriend or business partner and he sends you lovely e-mails and just needs the money to get to your city, **Do Not Send Money**. Even if she says that she is a mom who needs a little money to feed her children until she finds a job, **Do Not Send Money**. Often, he or she is a scammer who lives in Nigeria or another foreign country who is posing as an American citizen, soldier, or businessperson. Even if he sends you a photo of himself, **Do Not Send Money**. These scammers have been known to take other people's photos and histories to use as their own.
- **Never** give your credit card number before you read absolutely everything. You may be offered free work-at-home information or another item and all you have to do is pay a low shipping fee. This could be true. But, you might also be agreeing to have your credit card charged much higher fees every month in the future. Check your credit card statements every month.

Note For Facebook Users: Before you share your personal information with your Facebook friends, ask yourself what would happen if that information was seen by a future employer, your competitor, a potential burglar, or an online scammer. You already know that your birth date and Social Security number should be kept

private, but did you know that your dog's name, the last school you attended, and your mother's maiden name are the answers to many security questions? Put them on Facebook and you give the scammers a head start. If you are going on a fabulous vacation, share this after you get home so that you don't notify the local thief that your house will be empty.

If you buy an e-book or other digital item that uses Clickbank or PayPal to accept your payment, there is a built-in money-back guarantee that will protect you. Clickbank or PayPal will refund your money if you request them to do so. But, if money has been automatically taken out of your account monthly because you didn't read the small print, it's not guaranteed that you will get that money back.

You have more power than you realize. It might take just a little more thought and creative energy, but you can start taking charge of your own destiny. Create your own opportunity and you will only have to trust yourself.

After considering all your possibilities, you may be thinking that you want to start a home business. Whether you already have a great idea or you are still considering your options, it is time to consider how a home business will fit into your lifestyle and whether it will really give you the extra mothering time and flexibility you are seeking.

Only you know how much money you need to earn to contribute to your family. If you don't know the amount, now is the time to figure that out. The higher the figure, the longer it will take for you to earn that amount of money in a home business.

As you figure out how much income you need, keep in mind that if you have to pay for child care, transportation, clothing, food, and other job-related costs when you work outside the home, that amount lowers your salary and may help you make the decision to work at home.

What's Your Motivation?

In a survey published on SheKnows.com, this question is posed: If money or child care were not an issue, what option would you choose? Forty percent of the respondents chose "I'd be a full-time stay-at-home mom." Thirty-five percent chose "I'd be a work-at-home mom." Twenty percent chose "I'd have a part-time job outside the home." And the remaining 5 percent chose "I'd have a full-time career outside the home." There is a good chance that the popularity of each choice here matches yours, especially if you have young children. Unfortunately, money and child care issues usually do enter into the reasons why a mom makes these choices.

Wanting to work at home so that you can spend more time with your family is a personal goal. Wanting to start a home business to earn needed income

is a business decision. Every successful business owner understands that business isn't personal. A home business is a real business, and it requires the same time and attention that any other business needs to succeed.

So what is a mother to do? Does it even make sense to start a business at home to be with your child, or will you just be adding more stress to your life? There is no question that mothering and running a home business can be hard. But leaving your child while you work outside your home is stressful too. No matter what you choose, you will soon realize that whether you are working inside or outside your home, you will be making daily—or even hourly—choices between your child and your work.

Don't misunderstand: I raised two children while running a home business and I am now taking care of my infant grandson by myself on some workdays too. It can be done. In fact, millions of mothers (and fathers) earn at least part of their income at home with their children.

Tell me that you want to be a business owner, and I will say get started now! But if your decision to start a home business is an emotional reaction to your desire to be at home with your child, I would say you need to do further research and a lot of careful thinking.

Quality of Time versus Quantity of Time

Because you might be considering a home business so that you will have more time for your children, it is important to determine how your decision could affect them. It is a controversy that started decades ago, and it continues today: What do children need more? Is it the quantity of time or the quality of time your children spend with you that is more important?

Some mothers who work outside the home will tell you that it is the quality of time that is most important. They will talk about how a stay-at-home mother may be there, but how much actual time is spent talking on the phone, watching daytime dramas on TV, cleaning the house, and so on? If you factor in a home-based business, the actual time spent on child-focused activities could be very limited.

Some stay-at-home moms disagree. They say that their simple presence in the home is comforting to their children whether or not they are interacting with them. And they believe that there is much more opportunity to mother their children when they are there all day.

Who is right? Is it the stay-at-home mom or the mom working outside the home? They are both right . . . and they are both wrong. The real answer can only be

determined by your actual family circumstances, your goals for your children, and your personality.

In 1986 I was interviewed by *Newsweek* magazine for an extensive cover article titled, "American Mothers Making It Work: How Women Balance the Demands of Jobs and Children." The article included a poll *Newsweek* conducted of working mothers. Fifty-nine percent of working mothers and 57 percent of stay-at-home moms surveyed said they thought it had become less socially acceptable for mothers to stay home full-time to raise their children. The article made the point that women were expected to be perfect mothers, wives, and homemakers while they also hold down a job outside the home. In 2008 *Newsweek* published an opinion piece titled "End the Mommy Wars." The author, Kathleen Deveny, made the point that the pressures of balancing work and family are real and mothers should stop being so defensive about their own choices and less judgmental about the choices of other mothers. I agree.

There is no doubt that children need quality one-on-one time and attention. They need to be well-nourished and stimulated in ways that will help them learn. They also need a peaceful atmosphere that allows them to thrive. But most of all, children need to be loved and feel that love every single day. These things are especially true in the first three years of life.

Burton L. White, PhD, is the author of the book, *The First Three Years of Life*. The *Detroit Free Press* called his book "the most important guide to early childhood development ever written." White has done thirty-seven years of observation and research and the result of which is a month-by-month guide to the mental, physical, social, and emotional development of infants and toddlers. He believes that the brain development that takes place from birth to three years old is the basis for the cognitive development that will take place for the rest of the child's life. If you want to do more research, it is called *synaptic pruning*.

I had the pleasure of interviewing White for an article I wrote for *American Baby* magazine. He told me, "During the first months of life, a baby needs a tremendous amount of attention. The parents or grandparents will be most likely to make sure all of the baby's needs are met." I asked him if a work-at-home mom is likely to give the proper amount of attention. He told me that a baby will have much better access to his mother if she is at home, even if she is working for part of the day.

The love and attention a child needs can be given to him by his mother or father; a grandparent, aunt, or uncle; or anyone in the baby's life who truly cares. Mothers often want to give that care themselves, and that is understandable. A father's

love is equally important but not always available. Parenting, like everything else in life, takes balance. A child who has his mother or father with him at home has the opportunity to thrive. Additional benefit can come from the love, care, and interaction with other teachers and role models who are ready and able to help. It depends on what you know, how you behave, and what you do when you spend time with your young child.

I guess you could say that as your child goes through his day, quality and quantity of excellent care are both important, but you don't have to be the only one who provides it. If you are a woman who is happier when she is working outside of her home, then that is what you should do—as long as your child is being cared for by someone who really cares. If you need to work and want to learn how to run a business but your heart is breaking as you leave your child to go to work each day, a home-based business could be your answer.

Home Business Advantages and Disadvantages for Moms

There are many wonderful benefits to starting a home business. There are also some pitfalls that you should think about before you begin. When trying to make an important decision, it is very helpful to write down the pros and cons to help you decide. Here is a list of both the advantages and disadvantages for you to consider:

Advantages

- You don't need anyone's permission to begin.
- You can create your own schedule and plan it around your kids.
- You learn business skills that can serve you for a lifetime.
- If your child is sick, you will be there to take care of him.
- If you are sick, you will be able to stay home.
- You will save money on child care, transportation, and clothing.
- You can work with your child in the room and your pet at your feet.
- You will be available for school functions.
- Your child will learn more about work than other children, and have a greater understanding of what you do.
- Your child will learn independence and patience under your watchful eye.
- You can work flexible hours anytime, day or night.
- You can work in your pajamas.

- You can automatically take orders and earn money online twenty-four hours a day.
- You can choose to do work you love.
- You will have the joy of taking an idea and making it a reality.
- You can challenge your mind and love your kids at the same time, in the same place.
- Your emotional rewards will be significant
- You can avoid working with nasty bosses or difficult coworkers. And you don't have to answer to anyone but yourself.
- You can have lunch with your kids.
- You can choose to have a baby without being judged by anyone at the office.
- You can breastfeed your baby more easily and for however long you need.
- You have the possibility of earning even more money than you could as an employee.
- You can write off your home office expenses on your taxes.
- Start-up expenses are lower than if you had to rent an office.
- Your commute time is zero.

Disadvantages

- You have no one to depend on but yourself.
- You can take sick days, but you will not be paid.
- You won't have paid vacation, health insurance, or other employee benefits.
- Your business is there twenty-four hours a day, seven days a week.
- It can be difficult to separate your personal life from your work life.
- You might feel isolated.
- It is easy to procrastinate.
- Friends and family may not take your work time seriously and interrupt you or ask for favors during those hours.
- It might take some time for you to begin earning enough money to sustain your family.
- It can be hard to concentrate when you have to stop and start your work, depending on your kids' needs.
- You can't depend on a consistent amount of money to come in each week.

Even if you've never taken a business course or don't have any idea what you would do as a home-based business owner, you can be successful at home. You don't need business experience or the perfect idea to have a home business goal. If you can read, you can teach yourself to do almost anything.

I never took a business course in college. Just by reading books, I taught myself to cook, start and run a home-based business, write magazine articles and books, market a website, raise my children, and more. I did all that when home business books were rare and before the Internet put all the information I needed at my fingertips. If you have enough self-confidence and the willingness to learn, you can find the right home business for you and make it a success. Read on and I will help you with that part of the journey.

When you make the decision to work at home, you bring a lifetime of experiences and skills with you. If you use your known talents and skills in your home-based business venture, it will be easier than trying to start from square one and learning all about an unfamiliar business. To make the right decision, you must get to your know yourself better and assess your personality, talents, and skills.

Who Are You . . . and What Do You Want?

Talents are passive traits and skills can be considered active traits. You are born with your talents; those are the things that come easily to you. A concert pianist is born with talent, but without years of practice she will not rise to her abilities, for example. Skills can be trained and developed. Your basic personality is difficult to change. The successful work-at-home mom has certain personality traits and attitudes that help her navigate the daily challenges of working at home with children. It takes a special mom to manage mothering and work all under one roof.

There are many ways that you can get to know yourself so that you can create a home business that reflects your personality, skills, and interests.

You Are Unique

No one has the same mix of talents and skills that you do. You can create a home business that not only reflects who you are but will also come more easily to you than others. That is why it will serve you to go with your strengths when choosing a home business.

You may think that you don't know much or have any talents or skills, but that is not true. Sometimes it is necessary to take a long, hard look at your life and realize you have many gifts.

Do You Think like a Successful Home Business Owner?

Take this quiz using yes or no answers. To determine if you have the right personality to become a home-based business owner, compare your answers to the ones shown below.

Questions:

1. Are you willing to learn new skills?
2. Can you communicate effectively verbally and in writing?
3. Do you believe starting a profitable home business is possible?
4. Are you ready to encounter obstacles and jump over them?
5. Are you willing to be flexible and follow wherever your idea leads, even if it is different than where you first anticipated?
6. Are you willing and able to generate the money you need to finance your business?
7. If it takes more time to earn income than you anticipated, will you persevere?
8. Will you feel isolated working at home, alone?
9. Are you a procrastinator?
10. You want a more flexible lifestyle, but can you be flexible in your work style?

Answers:

1. Yes, but it may not be necessary to learn as much as you think. As a business owner, you will need to have an overview of everything that needs to be done, but you don't have to do it all by yourself. Do the things you are good at and then outsource the others. For example, don't struggle with your taxes; hire a tax preparer instead.
2. Yes. Effective communication is key to business success. Chances are you have good writing skills or effective verbal skills. If you are lucky, you have both. You can learn the right words and techniques for marketing your business. Whatever you feel you can't do, outsource to someone else.

3. Yes. If you don't believe that you can be successful in a home business, you might as well stop reading now. To be successful, you have to believe that it will happen.

4. Yes. As I often tell my children, if it was easy, everyone would be doing it. You will encounter problems on the road to a successful home business. The way you handle those roadblocks and problems will determine whether or not you will be successful.

5. Yes. Your original business idea will grow and change as you work on it. You will begin to understand that letting it take on a life of its own will lead you to success a lot sooner. Don't blindly hold on to your original concept. Instead, follow the unexpected pathways that open up in front of you as you begin to work.

6. Yes. It is possible to start a home business with minimum start-up cash, a little at a time. But, you will need money. The more you have, the faster you will grow.

7. Yes. Only those who give up lose all their chances to succeed. In fact, many people give up when success is just around the corner. Perseverance is a personality trait you must have.

8. No. Working at home with children and no other adults can be stressful. Unproductive meetings and water-cooler conversations are not much better. Develop your work-related relationships online and satisfy your need for adult contact that way. Don't spend your valuable work time talking to friends.

9. No . . . but there is hope if you are. Just don't put off answering this question. Most procrastinators are perfectionists. If you feel that you don't want to work on your idea unless you can do a perfect job, you will need to accept that life and business are not perfect.

10. Yes. Flexibility is the best benefit a home business gives a mom. However, to get flexibility you have to be flexible. The life of a work-at-home mom can be a special experience, but it won't be quiet. Learn to concentrate with background noise. Choose work you can stop and start and work on after business hours.

Heather Wilson was a divorced mother of two with no money and even less self-esteem. She felt stuck and didn't know where to turn. Just two years later, she bought a house, lost fifty pounds, ran a marathon, and wrote and published her first book, *Life According to You* (available at www.LadyInRed.ca).

Today, Heather is a certified success coach and a "Wealth-Esteem" expert. She advises, "Trust that you already have what it takes to be successful. There is no doubt you will also need additional training and expertise—that's just good business. But the gifts you have—the core of who you are—are more than enough to achieve all your dreams and goals. Take a leap and believe it."

To get a better idea of what you have to offer, get a pen and paper and answer these questions for your eyes only. Brag if you want to:

- Have you ever worked outside of your home? If you have, you probably have skills that you learned in the workplace and can transfer to your new business. Keep these skills in mind when you are deciding what to do.
- What were your childhood dreams? What did you think you would be when you were growing up? It is likely that desire came from a special place inside of you.
- What are your hobbies? Many people have been able to turn a hobby into a business just by adjusting their perspective.
- What problems have you solved? What is it about you that makes your family and friends come to you for help?
- What accomplishments are you most proud of? What qualities do you have that allowed you to do such a good job?
- Who are your role models? What do you admire about that person? You can probably incorporate some of those traits into your life, especially if you can connect with others who exhibit those qualities.
- What energizes you? What do you look forward to doing?
- What books have you enjoyed the most? What do they have in common?

Are You Right- or Left-Brained?

You might have to do a little research to answer this question, but it could be worth the trouble. Your brain has two sides: right and left. Each side is divided by a big fold that goes from the front to the back, and the two sides are connected by lots of nerves. The right side of your brain controls the left side of your body, and vice versa. Left-brained people are usually analytic and orderly. Right-brained people are

usually more creative and unpredictable. People tend to use one side of their brains more than the other.

Right- and left-brain analysis is a lot more complicated than what I've written here, but you can see that learning which side of your brain you use most could give you clues to the type of home-based business to start.

To take a quiz that keeps score and lets you know if you are left-brained or right-brained, visit www.intelliscript.net/test_area/questionnaire/questionnaire.cgi.

Choosing the Right Home Business Idea for You

Most successful business ideas start as a problem. Learn to solve that problem and create a business to help others do the same, and you will be on your way to home business success.

Starting a home business is not easy, especially if you are home with children. You will have to work hard, make sacrifices, and keep your focus on the job at hand, no matter how many times you are interrupted.

As you begin your home business experience, please keep this in mind: There are no shortcuts to success. You need to take the time to assess your talents and skills and blend them together to help you generate home business ideas. Then you'll have to test your idea to see if others agree that you have a winning idea that will appeal to enough people to earn money.

Home Business Ideas Are All around You, All of the Time

Life is a series of ideas and the choices you make on any given day that can be very important to your future. The ideas come at unexpected times in places you would not visualize. If you keep your eyes and ears open, and a notebook and pen near you all the time, you will be able to see and record many ideas for a home business. Take note of problems you or other people have and think of ways to solve those problems. Those solutions can be made into a business.

When you spot a possible idea, don't start feeding yourself negative thoughts. And don't be afraid of what other people will say. Instead, go with the idea and visualize success. Write down everything that is going through your mind so you don't forget your inspiration. Small ideas can become big ideas with just a little bit of optimism and concentration. Take each small element of your idea and put them together in new and different ways. Get inspired and your inspiration will help you generate more ideas.

Asking the Right Questions, Getting the Right Answers

"Sometimes the questions are complicated and the answers are simple."
—Dr. Seuss

When you decide to start a home business, you'll have lots of questions that'll need answers fast. It is not unusual to fall into a black hole of confusion when you first get started. Some people never climb out of that black hole and just give up. Those who climb out and persevere begin their home business journey for real.

There are many different ways to find the answers to your questions. You can do your own research online or read industry- and category-specific books. Additionally, you can ask questions of successful home business owners who do what you want to do.

To get the right answers to your questions, you must first know what and how to ask. It is important to be as specific as possible. If your questions are vague and not well thought out, you will not get the answers you seek. If you overthink your problem, your question may be more complicated than the answer. Focus is one of the most important traits a home business owner can have.

Before you begin asking questions, ask yourself:

1. Is my question clear and concise? Write it down and then edit it so that you are using words that are powerful but focused. If you need to, ask for help.
2. Is my question creative? Will it generate the type of information I am seeking? Don't ask, "How can I start a business like yours?" Instead, ask, "What was the one best resource you used when you started your business?"
3. Do I have confidence in my question? If you don't get the answer you need, don't just give up. Have enough confidence to ask again, ask often, and, if necessary, ask more than one person.
4. Is my question sincere? Most people will be willing to answer a focused question asked by someone who sincerely needs their help. Don't disguise your wish for a free ride in a question. Show you've done your homework and really need help with this one, specific question.

Now, ask yourself if you have the courage to seek the answers you need to succeed. Go for it!

Just about every home business consultant (including me) has advised aspiring business owners to choose a business based on something that they love. Is this good advice? Maybe, maybe not. Everyone says that if you are passionate about your work and love what you do, you will try harder to succeed. But I have another point of view to consider.

When considering what type of home business to start, it makes sense to choose an idea that reflects your personal experiences. If you are a member of the potential target audience for your business, you will instinctively know how to attract that audience's attention. For example, mothers of infants know what other mothers with babies want and need. However, having a passion for your idea is not enough; you need to have a target audience that shares your passion. When starting a business, you have to consider what will attract your potential customers and what kind of business you can create that will fill a need and make them turn to you for real or perceived benefits. You can't assume that they will love the same things you do. Choosing a particular type of business based solely on your personal enthusiasm may lead you to be overly optimistic and ignore a more profitable path.

Instead of choosing a broad business category, drill your interests down so that you concentrate on one aspect of your category. If you have solved a problem in a way that others may not know about, that is a good place to start. Next, write down all the keywords associated with your business idea and type them into a search engine like Google.com. See what comes up. Go to an online bookstore like Amazon.com and type in the same keywords. You will find books on the topic and customer reviews of those books. A wealth of information and direction can be discovered here.

Obtaining advice from other work-at-home moms is also key. If you know anyone who works at home, ask her what she does and if she is happy with her choice. You will be surprised at how willing people are to share information and advice. If you hear about a business that appeals to you, ask the owner if she would like some free help in exchange for teaching you about her business. Working as an unpaid intern in a business you would like to start can be more valuable than any high-paying job that doesn't lead home.

Ultimately, if your business makes you happy and helps you work enthusiastically, that's wonderful. Building a business that makes you look forward to each workday is a good thing. But your business idea should be carefully thought out and researched, keeping your future customers' wants and needs in mind at all times.

Trying Out Ideas, Getting Help, and Connecting with Other Moms

Sometimes, you find the exact type of help you need where you least expect it. A new website, GetOutMom.com, may help you solve some of your lingering start-up questions. According to founder Cami Back, GetOutMom.com is a simple way to plug into the many talents that women have to offer. "We are providing a central place for women to market themselves in a casual way (no resumes or uploads) so they can reach others and be hired for tasks on their own terms."

The website helps the mom who wants to work or wants to hire another mom to help her with her business or her life. Current postings include a variety of skills, including home schooling and tutoring, cleaning and organizing needs, pet care help, shopping services, Mac computer training, skating lessons, and even chair reupholstering. "Launching this company was definitely driven by my desire to help women regain the person inside the mom by sharing talents and getting talented help," Cami says. "It also represents an opportunity to monetize some of that incredible talent, which, in our softer economy, can only be a plus for our moms and their families."

Want to test out an idea for a business? GetOutMom.com can help you find out if others are interested in your offering when you post it on the site. For example, if you'd like to start an organizing business, post an offer to help a mom get organized and see if you get a response. Do you need computer help and don't know where to turn? Post your need and see how other mothers respond. Want a walking partner? Post it on GetOutMom.com and find other interested women in your neighborhood.

Registered users of GetOutMom.com have their own dashboard, which provides a place to keep track of their postings, e-mails with other members, manage their jobs, etc. "In designing our website and member dashboard, we put our mom hats on and thought about what we would want to have," says Stacie Gopsill, cofounder. "We have made it extremely easy and we also thought about the importance of security, so we have features in place that are associated with each user's profile." Because of the importance of mom networking and word-of-mouth advertising, members provide testimonials and earn ratings once a particular task or job is complete.

Founder Cami is married and has two children. She is a job sharer. She teaches technology to kindergarteners through eighth graders at a local school part-time. When she decided that she'd like to teach other moms technology, she searched the Internet and could not find a casual community that would enable her to offer her talent. She decided to start a website that all moms could use to connect with each other. She teamed up with her friend, Stacie, and GetOutMom.com was born.

The women feel that this is a dream come true for them and other moms. Their community allows you to stipulate exactly how much you'd like to participate, including the hours you are

available, what you would like to get paid to do, and what your rates are (you can even barter, if you prefer). You do not have to commit to any schedule, because they understand that when you are a mom, schedules change week to week and sometimes day to day.

The women started locally to showcase how well the concept works. "Thanks to Facebook, Twitter, and other technology-based resources, we are expanding rapidly," says Cami. "Clearly the success of our concept is getting the word out to all moms to build a pool of talent and people who will hire from it." They have started to expand nationally and offer a free trial membership.

GetOutMom.com is certainly an excellent example of how moms can change the world and increase their own opportunities by following through with their ideas. "The best indication of our success will be when moms who use our website as a springboard establish their own clients and their own businesses and no longer need us," says Cami.

And remember this: You don't have to invent a brand-new concept or product in order to have a successful home business. If you see a home business that interests you, take the concept and change it, improve it, and make it your own.

In chapters 4 and 5 I present you with specific businesses to consider. And in chapter 6 I tell you how to create your own product.

Put Off Procrastination

If you really want to start a home business, but are not sure what kind of business to start, don't use that as an excuse to procrastinate. Putting your dream on the back burner will make you miserable in the long run.

It is human nature to procrastinate for a variety of reasons. Dread, anxiety, and fear play a big part in procrastination. We might put off chores we dread or hate, like cleaning out the refrigerator, cleaning out the closet, or making phone calls, as daily examples. The most common thing that people procrastinate about is working on their dreams. Dreams can come true, but it takes courage to start. For many, it is so much easier to make a wish than it is to fail trying to achieve it. Fear of failure (and sometimes even fear of success) can be a dream killer—if you let it. In a lot of ways, not acting on a dream is just as much of a failure. Instead of fearing the consequences and getting frozen in place, you need to concentrate on the possible benefits of moving forward with renewed purpose.

In a strange twist, many people procrastinate because they are perfectionists. They want everything to be perfect, so they won't work on a business idea until everything is in place and success can be assured. That means they will never do anything. Is that the way you feel?

When you get that feeling that stops you from taking action, try to figure out what is causing it. Face your fears by scheduling one small task every day until you build up some momentum. I call it the big Mo. Momentum encourages you to continue. Action sparks ideas, and the feedback you receive can keep you going. Have you ever watched a baseball game when the home team is losing? The loss of momentum slows the team; but then, one player gets a hit, another one follows, the crowd gets behind the players, and all of a sudden the game turns for the better. That's momentum.

Create a list of all the steps that will take you to your goal of starting a home business. Write down everything, even the baby steps. Then, begin to work on your dream, one (baby) step at a time.

04 Becoming an Online Infopreneur

Selling information is one of the best ways to earn money online. Everyone needs information, and you can supply it instantly or via digital delivery online. Information is one of the few products that can be purchased online and delivered immediately after a purchase is made. Instant gratification always sells.

Writers on all levels can become bloggers, write articles for content websites and article directories, and write e-books. To be successful as an infopreneur, choose your target audience first and then build a relationship with that audience using social media, a blog, and/or a website. Once you have created trust, you can enhance your relationship by offering even more information and using each method to promote the other. For example:

- Creating an e-mail newsletter. By offering a free report or e-book on your preferred topic you can get readers from your target audience to subscribe to your e-mail list.

- Provide interesting and useful free information in your e-mail newsletter that you send to your list. Then it becomes possible to promote your e-books and also send this core audience to read your blog and your articles on content websites, where your income depends on the amount of traffic you receive and how many links they click on after reading your articles.

- Become an expert. Each of these examples will help you build your own personal brand. You can also be considered an expert on your chosen topic. You are creating followers consisting of an audience that is ready and waiting for what you will tell them next. This is a very valuable commodity. You are also creating a group of followers who are interested in your work. If you write articles for residual

income, you can send your e-mail subscribers to read those articles. Tell them about new blog posts and any other offerings you have online.

I will go into detail on each one of these steps in chapter 11, but for now it is important to understand that each written product you create can be valuable on its own while also becoming part of your total marketing plan. There can be a wonderful synergy among all the written products you create. Each one can produce income while helping you market your other projects. This interconnectedness will become clear when you build a relationship with your audience and offer them exactly what they want.

As you can see, there is great power in the written word. When you put words together in just the right way, you can create a home business that has low overhead costs and a high potential for success. You can learn a lot in this chapter that will help you communicate clearly, create a successful blog, write for content sites, and write and create e-books. Effective and clear writing will also help you market your home business. If you are willing to put words together to create a money-making result, you can learn how to do that in the easiest way possible right here. Let's get started!

You Can Be Your Own Publisher Online

It is no longer necessary to be published by an established publishing company to earn money writing. It is and always has been really difficult to get a book or magazine publisher interested in publishing your work. Today we are able to write everything from articles to e-books to blogs and websites and publish them ourselves. As you will learn, it is even possible to become an unexpected millionaire by self-publishing online. There is no doubt that channeling your opinions, your emotions, your creativity, your knowledge, and your passions into words has become one of the best ways to make money online.

You don't have to be a professional writer to take part in this quiet revolution, but you do have to know how to put words together in a clear and appealing manner. It doesn't matter if you received good grades in English when you were a student. You don't need to know formal rules of grammar or be an excellent speller (although it is a good thing to learn the rules for your own education). Spelling and grammar can be checked and corrected. To earn money online, you just need to know how to put your heart and your knowledge into anything you write, communicate clearly, and learn basic article structure and marketing techniques. That's it.

A Short Course in Writing for Online Profit

You may know that I have written other books, e-books, hundreds of articles, thousands of promotional e-mails, many website pages, and more. I am a writer by trade, and that is how I make my living. What you don't know is that *everything I know about writing I taught myself*. If I can do it, you can become a do-it-yourself writer too. You can also be a do-it-yourself publisher online. The only person you need to impress is yourself.

Five Do-It-Yourself Steps

Just follow these steps and you will be able to write anything you want or need to write online:

Step 1: Read

The best way to become a good writer is to read. Read everything. If you find a writer you would like to emulate, read everything he or she has written. The more you read, the better you will get at spelling, sentence structure, and organization. It will happen automatically. As a teenager, I read every magazine available. What may have seemed a waste of time to others became my secret weapon when I started writing magazine articles. The magazine "voice" was in my head and in my soul, waiting to come out.

Step 2: Research

Here I am talking about researching how to write. When I first started, I read every book on writing that I could find. Read about how to write. Get specific books that will teach you how to do the type of writing you want to do, be it technical, medical, marketing copy, general nonfiction, and so on. Read about how to use writing to market your business. Read what successful people write for their own businesses.

Step 3: Gather Your Confidence

This is not rocket science. Chances are if you want to write, you have the skills you need to actually do it. You just need the drive, determination, and good, hard work. I graduated from the Fashion Institute of Technology in New York City with a major in communications. I was required to take a course in fashion writing. After reading one of my assignments, the petite and not very nice older woman

It is time to learn how to turn your writing into a product. If you can write a blog post, you can write an article. Turn articles into chapters and you can use the same method to write an e-book. It is easier than you think.

Just ask yourself: Why do people read? They read for the same reason you are reading this book: to get information and find answers to their questions. They also read to be inspired and motivated to do the right thing. Keeping this in mind, follow these easy steps to writing an article:

1. Choose a topic that will answer a question and/or give inspiration.

2. Choose a compelling title that contains keywords for your topic.

3. Write a list of statements or questions to be answered about your topic. Put them under your title. Arrange them in an order that will make sense to the reader. These will become the subheads for your blog post, article, or chapter. The title and subheads together will become your informal outline.

4. Do some online research. Peruse reputable websites, read articles and books on the subject, and garner your own personal knowledge. Then write the answers to the questions or explain each statement underneath each subhead.

 Your title and subheads are not engraved in stone. You can always change them during the writing process. As you do your research and begin to write, you will get ideas and discover new information you might want to include. Your project is not over until you say it is, so don't worry about making a mistake.

5. Just write. Get the words on the page.

Even Easier Ways to Write Anything

If all else fails, you can present your information using numbered or bulleted lists. Everyone can write a list, and everyone is willing to read a list, especially if she can learn what she needs to know quickly and easily. Putting information in a list format makes it easier to organize your information and write it. Put a compelling headline

on top of an informative list and you will have an article or blog post that gets the reader involved and your job done.

An attention-grabbing headline using the number of reasons, secrets, directions, or ways to do anything gives the reader a promise of what's in store if they read the article or blog post. In essence you are making the promise of valuable content in a measurable way. Take, for example, the title of the previous section: Five Do-It-Yourself Steps. It clearly states what's in store for the reader in a simple numbered way.

Think about the headlines you see on the magazine covers at the checkout counter at the supermarket. Many of them make promises that use the list format such as, "10 Ways to Becoming Clutter Free" or "Five Steps to Losing 10 Pounds in a Week." Take notice as you surf online how many list articles you see. This format is being used by experienced writers because it attracts attention. The extra benefit to you is that it is easier to write.

Remember these elements for writing in list form:

1. Attention-grabbing headline that uses a number and makes a promise

2. An introductory paragraph

3. Numbered paragraphs, each beginning with a short, descriptive sentence

4. A paragraph that recaps the information as a conclusion

Two More Fast and Easy Ways to Write

In each of these cases, include a compelling headline that promises a benefit or the answer to a problem.

- Question/Answer. It is easier to ask and answer questions than to write and organize full paragraphs. Put the questions in the natural order for revealing the topic.

- A Little of This, a Little of That: Write an introductory paragraph, give one or two tips, and one case study that proves your premise. End with a paragraph that sums up the topic.

who taught the class said to me, "You will never be a fashion writer." I guess she was half right. Every successful person has an experience like that. Don't let anyone tell you how much ability you do or do not have. If you are willing to work hard, you can do anything.

Step 4: Write

Don't think about writing. Don't plan when you will write. Just write. Write all the time—for your eyes only in the beginning, and then gradually let others see your work, once you've built up your confidence. The best thing about writing for a living is that you can do it anytime and anywhere. If all you have is a pencil and the back of an envelope, you can write. The more you flex your writing muscle, the stronger you will become. Keep the following points in mind:

- Don't use big words and long complicated sentences. Write short simple sentences that are easy to understand and allow you to easily convey your message.
- Use short paragraphs. Writing long, drawn out paragraphs is a good way to lose an online reader who has her finger ready to click away.
- Write in a conversational voice and directly to your reader.
- Let your ideas flow and do not edit yourself as you are writing initially— there's plenty of time to come back to the editing later. Put the reader first. Focus on your message.

Here's a good tip: Find an article you like and retype it. Just copy the writer's words and you will begin to get the feel of how it was written. Of course, this is an exercise for your personal use only. You cannot publish other people's writing.

Step 5: Edit

After you finish writing, take a break from it. The next day go back and read what you wrote. A clear head helps you to see corrections that are needed. Make sure that each sentence is clear. Check for organization. Ask someone else to read it and make suggestions. Or, you can read it aloud to hear how it sounds. Beyond your writing technique, did you convey your message and give the information promised? Don't get so caught up in the writing effort that you forget the reason why you want to write.

Becoming a Blogger

You hear the word *blog* all the time, and you probably have some blogs that you read on a regular basis. A blog is basically a journal that is published online and added to frequently. It can also be the basis of a website or designed to generate income.

"Can you really make money with a blog?" I often hear this question. I also hear, "You can't make money with a blog!" People will always be skeptical about things they do not understand, and if they believe that a blog will not generate income, they won't make money because they won't bother to take the time to learn how or even have anything to sell. Can you make money with a blog? The simple answer is yes.

Here are the three basic elements for a successful blog:

1. Clearly define your target audience and write directly to the individual reader, not the audience in general.
2. Create interesting (even compelling) posts that will attract readers by using a "voice" that others in your category do not.
3. Update it every day.

You can write about any topic that interests you, but make sure others share your attraction to your topic. When choosing what your blog will be about, remember the age-old question: "If a tree falls in the forest and no one is there, does it still make a noise?" If a blogger writes about a topic and no one is interested, is it really worth the effort? The answer is no. You can make a little bit of money here and there with a blog, but if you want to make a lot of money, you need to have a lot of visitors. Lots of eyes on your pages equal advertising dollars, a revenue stream, and a lot more.

Because you will be devoting a lot of attention to your blog, you should choose a topic that you have a deep interest in. You can choose a general topic such as food but then create different categories to help organize recipes and reviews of kitchen gadgets and cookbooks. Or, you can choose a much more focused topic to write about such as Crock-Pot recipes. If there are enough people who collect Crock-Pot recipes, you could become popular among them and build up a following. Before you finalize your topic, do a search at Google.com or go to www.blogsearchengine.com to see what blogs already exist.

Your blog could be a personal one that includes details of your personal life, such as how your family reacted to certain recipes or what you were doing while the Crock-Pot did the cooking. Or you could treat your topic in a professional and

impartial manner with fewer personal details and a more structured voice and blog look.

According to ebizMBA.com, the top three blogs with the most traffic are TMZ .com (gossip), thehuffingtonpost.com (Internet newspaper), and engadget.com (technology). Each of these blogs is updated frequently throughout the day and provides information people want to read. The Huffington Post is reported to have twenty-eight million unique visitors each month. Considering that each of those users will make multiple visits throughout the month, you can only imagine how much money is being made. How does this apply to you? Your success may be on a (sometimes much) smaller scale, but you can follow the examples of successful blogs and apply them to your specific topic.

You don't have to attract millions of new readers each month (called unique hits in the blog world); rather, if you learn how to create a loyal readership, this repeating audience will visit your blog frequently and stay long enough to buy whatever you are selling. You can create a loyal readership if you follow these five steps:

1. **Add value to each post.** Create an atmosphere on your blog that encourages the visitor to stay and click on links. Link your post to a few other posts you've made on a related topic.

2. **Allow comments and reply to them.** Let your readers make comments about your posts and answer or acknowledge what they write. Encouraging active responses (that you approve before they appear) gives your readers a real chance to participate.

3. **Enhance your written words.** People absorb information in many different ways, and the more senses you can stimulate, the more likely your visitors will get your message. A video of you speaking directly to the viewer will help the viewer connect with you as will photos and audio of your voice in a podcast. Take the most important points from your blog and message and use Twitter and Facebook to have a conversation (see page 142 for more information about how to use social media).

4. **Get permission.** Your blog readers come to your "home" to interact. If you can get invited to their "home" in return, it can be the beginning of a beautiful relationship. Offer something free to your devout followers, and your new friends may provide you with their e-mail address in return. Congratulations, you now have an e-mail list full of opt-in subscribers who want to know

more about you and your business. See more information about e-mail marketing and the rules you need to follow in chapter 11.

5. **Remember the *who, what, where, when,* and *how*.** When you write a blog post, you will probably give the *who, what, where,* and *when* (when applicable) but don't forget the *how*. Everyone is searching for information and wants to learn how to do a variety of things. Telling your readers how is the basis of every good information business, and it is the how that will sell your information products such as e-books and special reports.

The Mommy Blogger Model: Getting Personal

When you add the word *mommy* in front of any business word, it can be seen as a woman being minimized and classified as less than other businesspeople because she is a mom. For example, mothers who don't work as many hours as others in an office so that they can get home to their children are often said to be on the "Mommy Track." But, when you refer to a blogger as a mommy blogger, a very different impression is made.

Mommy bloggers, who blog about their home lives, are attracting attention and making money—lots of money—because they are honest women who are willing to share the details of their family lives with their readers in creative and cutting-edge ways. It is that "fly-on-the-wall," inside look into someone else's life that attracts readers and gets them clicking. The same way people love reality TV, they love to read about others' real-life trials and tribulations by reading their blog and looking at their photos. In a way, following a mommy blogger can be as compelling as watching a daytime drama or any continuing fictional story—but it is real life.

Advertisers like to work with mommy bloggers because they have a close relationship with their readers. Their opinions are valued, and they understand products for moms, children, and families.

The best way to understand exactly what attracts so many readers to mommy blogs is to read them. I have listed twenty-five mommy blogs in the appendix so that you can look at some of the best ones. As you read, take note of the attitude of the blogger and the types of things being written. Think about your own "voice" and what is different about your life that might be interesting to others. The more honest you are, the more readers you will attract.

A WORK-AT-HOME MOM'S STORY
Crystal Paine, MoneySavingMom.com

Crystal Paine almost gave up on her website, SimplyCentsible.com. She was providing money-saving tips and e-books but wasn't getting much attention. Then she got personal, and things began to change.

Crystal mentioned on her website that, at that time, she had a grocery budget of $35 per week. A barrage of questions followed, because readers wanted to know how she managed to spend so little. She started answering the questions by doing a blog series on her personal blog that she called "Supermarket Savings." Before she knew what was happening, her blog was getting 5,000 visitors per day. She wrote an e-book on the topic and then offered an online class. Both were successful, but the questions kept on coming. To meet the demand she started her current blog, MoneySavingMom.com. The blog went from 5,000 visitors per day to 10,000, then 15,000. Today, MoneySavingMom.com gets approximately 150,000 page views each day and 500,000 unique visitors each month.

Crystal agrees that sharing her personal information helped popularize her blog. She published photos of her shopping trips and posted her menu plans and financial goals. She even shared her infertility challenges as she was growing her family along with her business. Besides her personal details, Crystal also gave her readers value by sharing specific details on time-sensitive deals and money-saving ideas. So impressed were her readers that they couldn't resist telling others.

"The quick growth of MoneySavingMom.com truly showcased the beauty of viral marketing. Readers linked to me on their blogs, and their readers liked what they saw and began linking to me on their blogs. The readers began telling their friends who told their friends who told their acquaintances who told random people at the grocery store and on and on it went," Crystal explains. "I've heard quite the bizarre assortment of stories from folks as to how they first found MSM!"

Crystal runs this extremely successful blog with the help of virtual assistants. How did she accomplish it all? "With hard work and the blessing of God," she says. To read the complete story of Crystal's journey from dealing with infertility and living on a tight budget to a super-successful work-at-home mom of three, go to MoneySavingMom.com/series/becoming-a-work-at-home-mom.

Adapting the Mommy Blogger Model

You can successfully use the mommy blogger model and apply it to other categories as long as you let your readers get an insider's view of you and your topic. Julie Powell started the blog "The Julie/Julia Project: 365 Days, 524 Recipes and 1 Tiny Apartment Kitchen." Her blog did not necessarily generate a lot of income during the year that she prepared the recipes, but the attention she received ultimately became her ticket to fame and fortune. Her blog became a book and then the movie *Julie & Julia* starring Amy Adams as Powell and Meryl Streep as Julia Child, the famed cookbook author. When she started her blog, Julie did not expect all the attention she would receive. Along with blogging about her experience cooking each of the recipes in Julia Child's cookbook, she also gave an inside look into her personal life and her emotional reactions to what was happening around her. If the blog had just been a cold description of preparing the recipes, it is unlikely that she would have received nearly as much attention. Although she no longer updates it, you can still see Julie's original blog at http://blogs.salon.com/0001399/.

How to Make Money with Your Blog

"So, exactly how can I make money with my blog?" This is another question I hear a lot. You monetize a blog the same way you monetize a website. In fact, your blog can be your website. But if you are trying to create a relationship with your visitors, it is important to consider how and when you use these techniques.

It is unlikely that you will choose one way to make money that will generate exactly what you need. But if you can establish income from a variety of sources—and you can—it can really add up.

There are four basic ways to earn money with your blog. You will need to experiment and see which ones work best. It is unlikely that any one of these methods will give you significant income by itself. However, combining a few different methods can add up to a good monthly income. The amount of money you make also depends on the number of visitors you get to your blog.

1. **Contextual Ads.** Contextual ads are generated by ad systems that can be based on the keywords on the page and/or the user's recent Internet activity. In other words, the ads are "in context."

 Have you ever searched for shoes or handbags or bought clothing online and then noticed that other sites you visit just happen to have ads for shoes,

handbags, and the exact company you just bought from? This is not a coincidence. The websites you visited most likely dropped a snippet of code onto your computer through a process known as third-party hyperlinking. It is just more likely that you will click on ads based on your previous demonstrated interests. This type of advertising can be either appreciated by or annoying to the visitor, but clicks certainly happen using this method and money can be made. By signing up with contextual advertising companies, you will be able to display ads from large sponsors that will not deal with smaller sites individually.

Google Adsense is the most well-known and most used contextual ad option based on the keywords on the page. These are the small classified ads that appear on blogs and websites that say "Ads by Google." They are also called contextual ads because, when they are generated, they are supposed to be on the same topic as the content on the page. For example, if you are reading a blog about Crock-Pot recipes, the ads you see will be cooking related.

Each time a visitor to your blog clicks on one of these ads, you will receive credit to your account that can range from pennies to a few dollars for each click, depending upon the ad's category. The more Google charges the advertiser, the more you will make—but that is not the only factor that controls your payout. You will get paid more for each click that results from traffic that comes to your blog as a result of a Google.com search because Google can trust that those clicks are legitimate. Your click-through rate will also play a role. (A click-through rate, or CTR, measures the success of an online advertising campaign. It is determined by dividing the number of visitors who clicked on an ad by the total number of visitors who saw the ad.) Most website traffic is valuable, but if you are trying to increase your AdSense payout, concentrate on getting more Google-generated traffic by learning to optimize your website for search engines. You will learn more about search engine optimization, or SEO, later on page 130.

Kontera is another contextual advertising program that is easy to implement and can generate good income. After signing up for the program, all you have to do is put the relevant code provided to you on your blog. Your blog readers will see certain words highlighted in blue with two lines underneath, making them look like links to other pages. When the reader puts her cursor over the word, a small ad will appear like a bubble. The reader has the choice of clicking on the ad or moving her cursor away to make the ad disappear. The more good-quality and keyword-rich copy you write, the more money you can make from Kontera.

There are other contextual ad programs out there to use; you can find a list in appendix B. But be careful. Google does not allow some types of ads to appear on the same pages as Google AdSense so check out each program to learn the compatibility before you sign up.

2. **Paid Advertising.** If you accept paid advertising on your blog, it will usually take the form of a banner ad or a line of text. The amount of money you will be paid to put ads on your blog depends on the amount of traffic your blog receives and where the ad appears. The biggest question, however, is not how much you will make but if you should include advertising on your site at all.

 If advertising will be on your blog, it is probably best to have it there from the first day. Your readers will be used to seeing it and cannot get offended that you started advertising after they started to follow you. Will advertising stop some readers from revisiting your blog? Possibly, but most people understand that income needs to be generated in order to support a blog.

 There are different ways advertisers can pay you to display your ads. You can be paid a set amount each month for putting an ad on your blog, or you could be paid per click (CPC), per thousand views or impressions (CPM), or for each resulting sale or acquisition (CPA).

 The most popular forms of advertising that appear on many blogs are the 125 x 125-pixel ad. These are the little square banner ads that are sometimes grouped together in the sidebar and even on a separate page full of these little ads. There is limited space for words, so advertisers rely on making their ad visually attractive, which can enhance the look of your blog instead of detracting from it. This is especially true on mom blogs, because the products are often baby- or child-oriented. Because this size ad is less expensive, the number of possible advertisers interested in your blog increases.

3. **Affiliate Sales.** Affiliate programs allow you to sell products offered by another person or company. Both large and small companies offer the opportunity to become an affiliate. When you make a sale, a predetermined commission is credited to your account. The sales are tracked through special affiliate links that are assigned just to you.

 Keep your readers in mind when choosing an affiliate program. What products or services will serve their needs?

Most affiliate programs supply banner ads with your affiliate code for you to use and you could insert one or two among your little 125 x 125-pixel ads. However, unless you give editorial space to your affiliate programs you are unlikely to make many sales.

Reviews of affiliate products are a good way to bring them to the attention of your readers. Be honest in your opinions and your readers will respond in greater numbers.

4. **Create and Sell Your Own Product or Service.** This is one of the best ways to make money with your blog. Remember what I wrote at the beginning of this chapter? It is extremely important to develop a relationship with your blog readers and offer lots of good information for free. That will leave them wanting more from you and be willing to pay for it. This desire gives you an opportunity to offer information products for sale. That means special reports, e-books, and e-mail courses.

To make a sale of your own products or affiliate products, your readers need to see your offering more than once. Offer a free e-book or special report in exchange for their e-mail address. Then, mail to your list at least once each week giving good information and reminders about the items that you sell.

More Ideas for Making Money with Your Blog

Sell Blog Subscriptions on Amazon.com

This is a really neat idea that will help you earn some money and get exposure for your blog. Amazon.com sells subscriptions to magazines, newspapers, and blogs that are delivered wirelessly and automatically to Kindle users. You can submit your blog to Amazon and they will begin selling subscriptions. You will receive 30 percent of the income from subscribers. Amazon determines the subscription fee, but most blogs are priced at $1.99 per month.

The income from blog subscriptions will not make you rich, but you will be getting income from something that you give away for free. If 1,000 people subscribe to your blog, you will get almost $600 each month. Subscribers get a fourteen-day free trial, which will help attract subscribers. Subscribers will then be charged automatically if they do not cancel. Being listed for subscriptions on Amazon.com will also raise interest and increase visitors who will come to see your blog on their own for free. Signing up is easy. To get started, just go to: http://bit.ly/a9JxJW.

Once you offer subscriptions to your blog on Amazon.com you can get some free publicity if it is reviewed by any of the sites that review blogs; these sites are offered for subscription on Amazon. One of the most well-known blog review sites is the Kindle Blog Report at TheKindleReport.blogspot.com.

Paid Posts

Some advertisers will pay you to write blog posts about their products, services, and websites. There are Federal Trade Commission guidelines that say in part, "When there exists a connection between the endorser and the seller of the advertised product which might materially affect the weight and credibility of the endorsement, such a connection must be fully disclosed." This sounds ominous, but it doesn't have to be. In fact, the more honest you are with your readers, the more they will respect and believe in you. There are great resource websites that help connect bloggers with advertisers (see the appendix for a list). You can clearly state in your blog that you have been paid to write the review but then give your honest opinion.

Members-Only or Subscribers Content

Give away a lot of great information on your blog for free but then create a premium area where readers get even more. It could be direct access to you or special tools or courses that are available exclusively to members. An alternative to a membership site could be a paid subscription to an insider's newsletter. Members or subscribers are charged automatically each month until they cancel.

Honesty Is the Best Policy for Bloggers

Amy Oztan is a mommy blogger and she monetizes her blog, SelfishMom.com, using many of these techniques. She is very open and honest about what she is doing. At BehindTheScreen.selfishmom.com/public-disclosure/she provides a sample of a disclosure form that she allows others to copy as long as they give her full credit and link to her website. By reading it, you can also get a good idea how to make money with your blog, especially if you are a mommy blogger. Find her disclosure form on pages 42–43.

Compensation Levels

Compensation levels will be stated clearly at the beginning or end of any post that mentions a product, service, or location that is covered by any of the levels listed below (or possibly within a post if there are many products listed, such as a gift list). If no compensation level is listed, it is to be assumed that there was no compensation involved with the post or any products, services or locations mentioned in the post. For the purposes of these levels user does not consider transportation to and from a local event, or food consumed at an event, as compensation. Compensation refers to cash, gift certificates, products, or services.

Level 0: The blogger has no significant relationship with any product, service, or brand mentioned in this post.

Level 1: The product or service mentioned was provided to the blogger free of charge (or at a considerable discount not available to the public).

Level 2: The product or service mentioned was provided free-of-charge and the blogger was compensated to post about the product or service.

Level 3: The blogger was compensated for inserting links from a specific website into this post.

Level 4: The blogger was compensated for including a product in pictures or videos in this post.

Level 5: The blogger was compensated for attending the event mentioned in this post.

Level 6: The blogger was compensated for posting about the event mentioned in this post.

Level 7: The blogger was provided with transportation, food, lodging, tickets, and/or other incidentals for the trip mentioned in this post.

Level 8: Although not specifically compensated for this post, the blogger has an ongoing relationship with a company or person connected with a product, service, or location mentioned in this post that the blogger feels may have influenced his/her decision to post about it.

Level 9: Products or services were provided to the blogger to give away in a contest.

Level 10: Products or services were provided to the blogger to give away in a contest and to keep for his/her own use or for review.

Level 11: The blogger was compensated for administering this contest.

Level 12: The product or service mentioned advertises directly with the blogger's website.

Level 13: This is a sponsored post. The blogger was compensated to write this post. While the blogger's opinions in the post are authentic, talking points may have been suggested by the sponsor.

Level 14: The blogger is under contract with the company, product, or service mentioned in this post. While not specifically paid for this post, the blogger is paid by the company to attend events and write about the company/product/service. The blogger receives free samples of the product, special access to the company, and all of the blogger's costs are covered when attending events related to the company.

Swag

If the blogger is given free products of minimal value at a conference, event, or meeting, and these products are being given to all attendees, such as bags, books, water bottles, small product samples, coupons, etc., he/she does not consider these items as compensation and will not necessarily disclose them when talking about a product.

Sponsorships

Sponsorship deals can take many forms. A company could ask to be an exclusive sponsor in its category. Or you could run special banner advertising or put the company's logo on your site. If the sponsor is a company with a fine reputation, your association with that company can boost your image. It is unlikely that you will get a sponsorship until you can demonstrate the appeal of your blog to a large number of the sponsor's target audience.

Writing Articles for Content Websites

Just a short time ago, the only way you could earn an income writing articles was to submit a query to a traditional publisher and get an assignment. Today you can become an instant article writer in new and different ways. For the first time in history, you can write an article and have it published in just one day. Being published, however, does not guarantee that you will earn much income directly from your writing. Your payment could come in nontraditional ways, such as increased traffic to your blog, and there can be other benefits that can be as valuable as actual cash.

You always have the option to publish your own articles on your blog or website and monetize them in the ways I've explained. But, to be clear, this section is not about self-publishing.

You are about to learn about writing articles for content websites that give you the opportunity for residual income or pay you a relatively low, one-time fee. As you will see, there are benefits and drawbacks to both types of articles.

Most of the sites that pay require you to apply before they will accept articles from you. Once accepted, you are usually required to pick topics from lists that the sites provide. When you write and submit the article, you are giving up all rights to it. Demand Studios is an example of this type of site.

There are seven main benefits to writing articles for content sites:

1. **It offers residual income.** A residual-income writer writes articles for little or no upfront pay. Instead, you get the opportunity to earn income from advertising and affiliate sales that are ongoing. Because the sites that publish your articles are well established and already ranked in search engines, you can earn money more quickly than if you published them yourself, starting from scratch. This option can be worthwhile if you can write quickly and frequently. On a site like HubPages.com, you get a percentage of the AdSense and Kontera income generated from your article page and a percentage of Amazon.com and eBay affiliate sales. Realistically, you might only earn 25 cents a day or less per article, but let's take that forward. If you write 500 articles of about 400 words that earn 25 cents per day each, that would be $125 a day. That comes to $3,750 per month! So you can see that there are real income possibilities from residual article writing, and you are allowed to write about any topic. Build up an inventory of residual income

articles, promote them on your blog, website, Twitter, Facebook, and in other articles. Use keywords in your articles that will attract placement in search engines.

2. **You get a one-time payment.** Content sites like Demand Studios pay up to $20 per article, and they keep all rights, meaning you can't use your article again and they can use it any way they want to use it. It sounds unfair, and it is to a certain extent. It depends on your circumstances and what your writing goals are.

3. **Articles need to be at least 400 words.** If you can write two articles a day at $17.50 each, that would be an income of $35 a day. If you write two articles a day, every day, your monthly income could be over $1,000. That could put a lot of food on the table or even pay your mortgage. Payment is made each week so you don't have to wait to get the money you earned. You would need a lot of dedication to keep up that pace for very long, but it can be done. You would be earning a living by writing, even though some people might think that you are getting ripped off.

4. **You can pick up blog or website traffic.** If your main reason for writing articles is to generate interest in your blog or website, write only for content sites that allow you to include links. You can also increase the "link popularity" of your blog or website, which helps determine how high up your blog or website will be listed in search results. The more links from outside sources to your blog or website, the higher your link popularity will be and the better your placement in search engines will be.

5. **You can promote your products or affiliate products.** It will only be possible to promote your own products and affiliate products on sites that allow those links.

6. **You become a published writer.** I understand the longing some people feel to become a published writer. Many people have lived their lives with that desire and never achieved their goal because getting an article published in the traditional way is difficult. Publishing your articles on content sites, whether you get paid a small one-time amount or receive residual income, makes you a published writer. Put your best efforts into your writing and you will have writing samples to show higher-paying markets.

7. **You become recognized as an authority.** What better way to demonstrate your expertise than to write about your subject online? You don't have to tell people you are an expert. You can demonstrate it with your articles. Establishing a good reputation in your specialized area can be invaluable.

Many of these article content sites have an organized community that their writers can join for free. It can be a great way to learn your way around the particular site and get advice. The support and friendship of other writers could help you achieve your writing goals.

Pros and Cons of Writing for Content Sites

There are two different ways to look at writing for content sites. In fact there is a vocal group of writers online who warn aspiring writers to stay away from them. They make the argument that writers should get paid upfront and be recognized for their expertise. I agree, but I still support the idea of writing for content sites, especially for inexperienced writers. The "article snobs" say that publishing articles for content sites will not help you get higher-paying assignments. I disagree. If you write a good article, it will show your writing ability, no matter where it is published.

As a writer who has been paid a lot of money for many articles that appeared in magazines, it was originally difficult for me to accept the concept of writing for the promise of future payment or for $10 to $20 an article.

My first article was published in a free magazine that was given to expectant mothers. I was not paid for that article. However, when I was asked to provide a writing sample to *Family Circle,* I had that published article to show. It gave me the opportunity to write numerous articles for *Family Circle* at $1 per word and eventually become a book author.

If you think about it (I'm talking to you with your nose up in the air), writers are often given opportunities to write for income that will be based on sales. Book authors get an "advance" on the anticipated sales but won't make 1 cent more if their book does not sell. If an author is willing to write 60,000 words without guarantee of payment, 400-word articles are not very risky, are they?

Writers often self-publish e-books and other information products that require a lot of preparation and writing. Unless that information product sells, the writer will not make money on her writing.

Earning Thousands of Dollars per Month with Residual Income

To support my enthusiasm for this type of writing, I went to the best source I know. Maria O'Brien, who writes articles under the name WriterGig, has extensive experience writing for the residual income site eHow.com, which is run by Demand Studios. She makes thousands of dollars each month from residual income. Her success is so extensive that she wrote an e-book on the subject, *How to Earn Passive Income at eHow.com: Residual Income for Web Content Writers.*

Maria, a young mother of three with a bachelors degree in English, focuses a lot of her freelance work on writing for residual income. "For three months straight, I have earned more than $4,000 per month through my online writing, websites, and affiliate marketing," Maria reports. "My 400 articles on eHow.com provide a large portion of each month's earnings. Affiliate sales via CommissionJunction.com, Amazon.com, Clickbank.com, and Google AdSense round out my sources of income."

Previously, in November 2010, Maria earned $5,826.31 in one month. This is how she breaks it down:

- Articles on eHow/DemandStudios Revenue Share: $3,136

- Affiliate Commissions: $2,265

- Google AdSense: $342

- Articles on Bukisa: $82

"It never ceases to amaze me," Maria says, "that I can make a full-time income while working very part-time from home, where my time is spent primarily with my children and tending to the household. My writing and marketing time is somewhat limited—I wake up at 5 a.m. three days a week to write and work on my sites, and I get a little work done in the evenings sometimes. I always take off Sundays as a family day."

Maria does not have a virtual assistant or any other help. "If I can accomplish this as a work-at-home mom with several children, I truly think anyone can with enough effort and the right tools," she says. If you feel a little envious of Maria's lifestyle, then read her e-book and learn as much as you can about writing articles and marketing online. To learn more about her e-book, go to http://bit.ly/gFdwau.

Becoming an E-book Writer

E-books have changed the publishing industry. They have also changed the lives of aspiring authors. Traditional books cost a lot of money to print, produce, and send through the mail. There are virtually no production or mailing costs associated with e-books.

Anyone who wants to write a book and distribute it themselves can do so without trying to convince a publisher that her idea is worthwhile. She can publish an e-book and let the public decide if they are interested or not. Just ask Amanda Hocking, a noted "darling" of the self-publishing world.

Amanda is a twenty-six-year-old woman who lives in Minnesota. She is also a multimillionaire. One year ago she was living paycheck to paycheck. Amanda took the multiple rejections she received from traditional publishing companies and turned them into a fortune in less than a year by self-publishing her young adult paranormal romance and urban fantasy stories and selling them for just 99 cents and $2.99 each in Kindle format on Amazon.com. She has sold half a million e-books in just ten months. Amazon.com pays 70 percent commission on each e-book, and she has sold and continues to sell hundreds of thousands of copies of each title to her enthusiastic audience of young teens. When she speaks of her success, she seems stunned by it all, and who wouldn't be? If you would like to learn more about this e-book instant millionaire, you can read her blog at AmandaHocking.blogspot.com.

While Amanda is clearly the exception that proves the rule, her success shows how much the publishing industry has changed. The publishers who rejected her manuscripts recently participated in an auction for publishing rights. Even Amazon .com took part in the bidding. St. Martin's Press won the auction, paying $2 million for the series of four novels. So if you are trying to get the attention of a publisher, selling a lot of e-books could help you do that.

Beyond selling them, there are many different reasons why you might want to write an e-book. It can help establish you as an expert in your field. You can give away an e-book that is of interest to your visitors as an incentive to get them to sign up for your e-mail mailing list. The e-books you give away for free can also contain affiliate links, so you could make money if a reader buys what you recommend.

If you go to my website, www.HomeWorkingMom.com, you will see a free e-book called *Work-at-Home Job Finder for Moms*. It can be downloaded for free after the visitor subscribes to my free online newsletter, HomeWorking Mom-to-Mom. In this case, I am using the free e-book as an incentive to get subscribers, but the e-book that is being

given away has value all by itself. Giving an excellent e-book away for free gives my new subscribers a good impression of the information I have to offer, and that will give them an incentive to open up the e-mails I send to them going forward.

What Should You Write About?

If you have always wanted to write a novel and would like to try to get the type of attention Amanda Hocking is receiving, go for it. People do buy both fiction and nonfiction books to read on their Kindles, Nooks, iPads, and other e-book readers or smart phones. You could try to sell a novel. If you charge a low price or give your first edition away for free, you could attract a following that will look forward to your next book. Much of what I will write here can also be used for novels, but my focus is on nonfiction e-books.

When deciding about the topic of your e-book, first consider why people read e-books. The major benefit of an e-book is that it can be downloaded and read without delay. You don't have to wait for the book to come in the mail. You don't have to leave home to buy it. You can literally decide you want to buy it one minute and have it in your possession the next minute. This is instant gratification at its best.

You could take advantage of the instant delivery by choosing a "how-to" topic that can help people solve their problems and help them create a better life. If you have absolutely no idea where to start, consider writing about something that you know how to do.

Anything related to pets or cooking is very popular. If you choose a popular topic, you will have a lot of competition, so it is necessary to focus in on a particular niche in that category. For example, write about how to train a specific breed of dog, not dogs in general. It may seem that the more general topic will attract the most interest, but exactly the opposite is true. The more specialized and defined your topic is, the more readers you will attract. Make sure your topic is also one that generates interest by doing keyword research and searching for other e-books on the same topic; you want to make sure your e-book will be better than what is available.

Visualize Your Reader

There are two different ways your potential reader can help you decide on the topic of your e-book. The question is, what comes first, the idea or the audience?

If you let the idea come first and then look for people who are actually interested in the topic, you are taking the more difficult route. For example, you could write an

e-book about insomnia. Overtired people might be looking for information in the middle of the night and see your e-book and buy it because they can download it right away. But, how will they find your e-book? You could advertise using paid listings on search engines, but that could be very expensive.

The second option is to define your potential customer in advance, create a blog and/or an e-mail mailing list for those people, and let them get to know you. Then, write an e-book that you know will interest them. If you have the attention of young mothers, you could write an e-book about how to get your baby to go to sleep or how to potty-train a toddler. With an audience that you know will be interested in your information, it'll be easier for you to decide what to write.

Writing Your E-book

Be sure to follow all the writing tips I provided at the beginning of this chapter. And remember: If you can write an article or blog post, you can extend that kind of writing into an e-book chapter. If you still do not feel comfortable writing, you can use the list and question-and-answer format frequently throughout your e-book.

Before you start to write, create an outline that consists of the book title, chapter titles, and, most important, sub-heads throughout each chapter. Even this book follows these guidelines. Each chapter has a title and several subheads. I wrote this book the same way I am advising you to write your e-book.

Once you have your outline, you can skip around and write any part you are prepared to write. For the rest, do your research by typing your subhead words into Google.com or another search engine. Then just fill in the relevant information under each section. You can change subheads as you write to fit what you find in your research.

Write like you are speaking to a friend. If you need to, you could record yourself speaking about the subject and then transcribe what you taped. Speak or write with one specific person in mind.

As you write, think about these points:

- Are you writing for a well-defined person (a member of your target audience)?
- Are you writing to help the reader solve a problem, ease her concerns, or get something she desires?
- Are you giving your readers their money's worth?

Your E-book Needs a Title and a Cover

It is sad but true: People absolutely do judge e-books by their covers. Even though your e-book is a digital product that does not have real pages or an actual cover, it is vital that it have a keyword-rich title and very professional and appealing cover.

There are websites that help you design your own cover for a very low cost, but your cover is so important that I would suggest hiring an e-book cover designer to create the best one possible. There are a lot of bad e-book covers out there. The best e-books may not see the light of day if their covers give a bad first impression.

I've searched a lot of e-book cover websites, and one does it the right way. You can see what effective e-book covers look like and get yours done by my top recommendation, KillerCovers.com.

Title Your E-book with Care

There are very specific steps to take when giving your e-book a title:

- Keep in mind that the title should be short enough to fit in the cover design and be legible even on a very small version of your cover.
- Choose a title that tells what the book is about.
- Type the title into Google.com or Amazon.com to see what, if anything, has the same name.
- Check to see if your title is available as a domain name. If so, register it. If the name is taken, choose a different title or change it enough to allow registration.
- Add a subtitle to your title if it needs more explanation.

Choosing a Platform for Your E-book

There are a few different types of e-book formats. There is the traditional PDF that is used by most independent e-booksellers. There is also a large variety of e-readers available today. Amazon.com offers the Kindle e-reader and allows publishers to put Kindle versions of books for sale on their sites. The sales of Kindle books have bypassed paperback books on Amazon.com.

Because you are a beginner, I would suggest that you concentrate on only two e-book platforms for your e-book: PDF and/or Amazon.com Kindle.

Creating a PDF

Before there were e-readers and special e-books for them, there was the PDF. This is still a fine way to produce an e-book and sell it on your blog or website. Traditionally, e-books that are sold in this format have a higher price and some come packaged with bonuses to attract the sale.

PDF files can be read by both Mac and PC computers. Using a service like Clickbank, you can put your PDF file online for purchase and download. If you take this route, you can charge a little more for your e-book, but you will also need a domain name and a sales page that potential customers will view to make a purchasing decision.

If you write your book using Microsoft Word, it is easy to convert your document to PDF. You can also go to www.createpdf.adobe.com to create five PDF files as a free trial. Or you can pay to have a PDF file created for you.

PDF E-book Payment and Delivery

Once you have a PDF version of your e-book, and a cover, you can start selling it. You may be wondering about the logistics of accepting payment and delivering your e-book. It is not difficult.

There are many different options for accepting payment for your e-book and then offering it for download. Some options are listed in the appendix. The easiest and best option for a first-time e-book seller is Clickbank.

Clickbank is one of the leading Internet retailers of digital products like e-books. There are 50,000 digital products for sale on Clickbank right now. For a start-up cost of $49.95, you can activate your Clickbank account and Clickbank will accept payment and deliver your e-book by download for you.

The most interesting and lucrative part of Clickbank is that other Clickbank members are all potential affiliates for your e-book. This army of affiliates could promote your e-book for a fee of approximately 50 percent. That is the minimum affiliate commission you need to give affiliates for each sale if you want to attract the best. Offering a commission of 75 percent would be even more attractive. It can make sense to attract affiliates that way, because the more people selling your e-book, the more money you will make. You can also earn money by becoming an affiliate for other people's digital products through Clickbank (see pages 60–63).

When an affiliate makes a sale, Clickbank will automatically put your portion in your account and the affiliate's commission in her account. Clickbank is known

for paying on time and will deposit the money you earn in your bank account every Wednesday.

There are two downsides to working with Clickbank: The company charges $1 plus a 7.5 percent commission on every sale, which is high. It also offers a sixty-day money-back guarantee and will issue refunds to your customers without asking for your approval. This makes it possible for someone to buy your e-book, then say he is dissatisfied and get a refund. Because it is a digital product and easily copied, the customer does not have to return it. Thankfully most people are honest, and there are few returns for a good product.

In order to sell your e-book through Clickbank, you need a sales page for your e-book (see chapter 10).

Creating a Kindle

I recommend creating a Kindle above any of the other e-book reader platforms for your e-book; Amazon offers apps that allow the reader to read Kindle books on any computer or other device like a smart phone or an iPad. Kindle accepts payment and delivers the e-book for download. This means that you write the e-book, create the Kindle version, and Kindle does everything else.

Write your e-book in Microsoft Word or HTML format, get your cover done, and then go to http://bit.ly/lnu5B7 to get started publishing your Kindle. The do-it-yourself instructions are not too difficult, but you can also choose to hire someone to create your Kindle for about $100. That's what I did when I wrote my Kindle book, *Never Be Unemployed Again*. By hiring a professional, you will avoid some odd spacing problems that can occur when producing a Kindle, and the professional can link the chapters to the table of contents for you. You will decide the price of your Kindle. People purchasing Kindle books are usually looking for a good price. Remember: If you charge $9.99 or less for your Kindle, you will get a 70 percent commission from Amazon.com. If you charge more, your commission could fall to 35 percent.

05 Ten Top Home-Based Businesses for Moms

There are a lot of options to consider when starting a home-based business. Depending on the career path you choose, this may lead you to an online business or a more traditional business that has more in-person interaction. Either way, I present plenty of choices for potential home businesses in this chapter. Some of the ideas are tried and true while others may be options that you have not previously considered. You can take any of these ideas and make them your own by adding your particular point of view, talents, and skills.

Before everyone had a computer and online access, starting a profitable home business that had unlimited potential was just about impossible. Today the Internet advantage is beyond comparison. If you grew up with computers and had Internet access most of your life, it is important to fully appreciate and understand that you have a world of opportunities on your desk and under your fingertips. You buy a lot of the things you need online. You might do daily tasks—even pay your bills and do your banking—online. Or you might even have found love through the Internet. I personally know three couples who met online and got married! Because you use the Internet for a variety of things in your life, it only makes sense for you to work online as well. Today, building up an online presence is imperative. The Internet has changed every-thing for moms who want to work at home.

Whether your home business is on a website or you create a website to promote a more traditional home business, you have the ability to get an idea, attract potential customers to an e-mail mailing list, and begin promot-ing within weeks with the help of the Internet . . . and for very little start-up money. With that kind of direct, affordable access to the tools you need to grow your business and target audience, you can start many different online businesses and see what works.

About These Home-Based Businesses

The home-based business ideas in this chapter were chosen based on three criteria:

1. Popularity
2. Earning potential
3. Suitability for work-at-home moms

The amount of income you can earn with any of these businesses is up to you. I won't be giving you income ranges, because that always depends on the effort made by the home business owner. There is no minimum or maximum income for any home business. Most of the home businesses explained in this chapter have the potential to generate a very good income.

The purpose of this chapter is to give you an overview of a variety of home businesses and a springboard for your own ideas. Whenever you are trying to make a decision, it is always a good idea to get as many facts as possible and make a list of the pros and cons to get a clear picture of the choice you will ultimately make. I started that list for you under each business idea. Add your own specific advantages and disadvantages to the lists. To get you off to a good start, each idea includes start-up advice from an insider's point of view. To help you learn more about the specifics of any business idea in this book, there is a comprehensive list of on-target resources in the appendix.

If you choose a more traditional home business like child care or pet sitting, this does not mean you will be able to ignore the benefits of having an online presence. Today potential customers go online to do research before making a buying decision. Having a website and a presence on social networking sites will give your business credibility and foster communication. It will also help you connect with your customer base and attract potential customers in a way that was not possible before the Internet.

There are other benefits to doing work via the Internet. When you work online, you can continue to do business uninterrupted without worrying what else is happening around you. Your toddler can scream and your dog can bark, and it won't matter because you are communicating via e-mail. You don't have to get dressed up to impress

fellow colleagues (unless, of course, you have in-house client visits), and you can stop working at any time to share some precious moments with your family. Every moment of the day gives you a new chance to try something new. Read about a marketing idea on Twitter and apply it to your business within minutes. Or contact your e-mail mailing list soon after you get an idea or find a new affiliate program to promote. Or even try out a new business as you work on an existing one. Your home business—regardless of whether it's traditional or not—will deeply benefit with the help of the Internet.

Becoming a Virtual Assistant

A virtual assistant (VA) is a business owner who typically does work for small or home-based business owners from her own office. Because she is not in the same office as her client, work is delegated and delivered remotely via the Web, e-mail, fax, telephone, and mail. Just a few years ago, most VAs performed the duties of an administrative or executive assistant, and that continues today. Some do administrative work for any general business category while others work in a specialized area such as real estate or public relations. .

In recent years many VAs have gone beyond the basic administrative services. Some actually design websites, write articles, do e-mail marketing, or design and maintain social networking sites for their clients. Even though most virtual assistants work with online businesses, they can also do work for brick-and-mortar business owners.

You might find it easier to attract more clients if you specialize in one specific area. The more you narrow down the services you offer, the more your target audience will be attracted to using your services.

When you work as a VA, your goal is to become indispensable to your clients. This helps ensure that you get a steady stream of work. The more you learn about your client's specific business, the more valuable you become.

Training or Certification

There is a sector of the VA industry that believes you should be trained and certified before you can call yourself a virtual assistant. In my opinion, this is old-school thinking. When people first started calling themselves virtual assistants, there were very expensive schools offering certifications. Each established its own criteria. There was not and still is not any uniformity across the various schools.

You should certainly learn as much as possible about business in general, working with clients, and all the specifics about the type of business you choose.

However, you bring with you a skill set and prior experience to your VA business. You can learn about becoming a VA by reading the books and resources listed in the appendix of this book. As long as you are confident in your abilities, there is no compelling reason to spend thousands of dollars to be certified by an organization—beyond the possibility of impressing potential clients.

Even though you can start working as a VA by answering ads on job boards and freelance work sites, the most successful VAs run their own home business and create a blog or a website that gives the details of their services and establishes their expertise. Think of any assignment you get from a new client as an audition. If you do good work and meet your deadline, you increase your chances of getting more assignments.

Zarah Pimentel loves being a work-at-home mom. This mother of a five-year-old girl is living her dream. "I feel as excited and happy as a seven-year-old child working in Disneyland! I have all the things I love, and I am getting paid to do it. Sometimes I feel guilty because I have all the good things in life," she explains.

Zarah's life wasn't always so focused and enjoyable. After her daughter was born, she left her full-time job as a sales and marketing manager for a telecommunication company. A few years later she became very bored and wanted to do interesting work again. After learning about the option of working as a virtual assistant (VA), she took her skills online after receiving additional affordable training at VAClassroom.com.

She had administrative skills but little experience in Internet marketing. She joined with two other VAs and started HireAVANow.com. As they began to get clients, they didn't know whether to feel excited or afraid. "Beneath those fears, we never gave up," Zarah admits. "We did research, talked to experts, joined forums to ask questions, and read, read, and read some more to learn what we needed to know. Soon we could proudly call ourselves real experts!"

Today HireAVANow.com has a full-time staff and an unlimited pool of freelance VAs. As the clients come in, the partners coordinate with the clients and delegate the tasks to the the right VA for the job. They take a wide variety of jobs. Her most memorable one was being a virtual "nanny." A working mom hired her to help her teenage daughter do her daily homework—online! For two hours each day she watched the teenager do her homework and interacted with her on Skype. She read Zarah her books and taught her and her daughter Spanish. "My daughter loved her so much," Zarah recalls. "It was just like we were neighbors."

With her daughter now in school, Zarah works intermittently from 9 a.m. to 2 a.m., with time off during the day to spend quality time with her daughter. She also tries not to work on weekends. She and her colleagues have learned a lot about marketing online. They now have good search engine rankings do to article marketing, videos, forum postings, and directory submissions.

If you are an aspiring VA, Zarah has some advice for you: "I would suggest to start small and apply to some outsourcing and freelance websites like Odesk .com. You can put up your profile and apply for the listed jobs. Grab all of the opportunities you will get and learn from them. But never, never settle for just that. Have the thirst to learn more and do more. There are endless opportunities to earn online. You just have to know where to look."

Is This Business for You?

If you possess one or more skills that are needed by small business owners and are customer service oriented, this could be an excellent home business choice for you. You need good communication skills and to be able to adapt to work methods that your clients ask for. Most important, you need to be able to listen carefully to your clients, ask informed questions, and offer solutions to problems.

There is opportunity to earn a significant income within this profession, and you can generate consistent work from satisfied clients who come to depend on you. The start-up costs are low, and you can begin your VA business on a part-time basis. Because so many people are starting small and home-based businesses, the need for talented VAs will increase in the years to come.

Because most of a VA's work is done online, it is essential to have a website to attract clients. You will be judged not only on what your website says but also on the way it looks. It is necessary to pay to have your website designed or to do a good job designing it yourself. You also have to be willing to learn how to market your website and your business. You will learn how to do both in chapter 10.

Pros and Cons

Pros

- You can do the type of work you want to do.
- You can use skills that you previously learned in a job outside your home and probably get paid a lot more per hour.
- You don't need a lot of clients to make a lot of money. All you need is a few businesses that rely on your work and send you repeat business daily or weekly.
- If you have a computer, start-up costs are low.

Cons

- Collecting payments from clients could be a problem, especially in a difficult economy. Protect yourself by getting paid half of your fee upfront and receiving smaller payments while you work on the project. You could also offer your regular clients a chance to put you on retainer, just like an attorney. A lump-sum payment upfront will give the client priority over the needs of others. Get a business PayPal account. This will allow you to send invoices and accept payments online.
- It can become very stressful if more than one client needs work done at the same time. When your business reaches that level of success, find other VAs who can handle your overflow work and give you the opportunity to do the same for them.
- Even though you are a business owner, you will have clients with high expectations and deadlines to meet. Most clients have tunnel vision and don't want to hear about how much work you have to do for others.

Reader Q & A

Q: When starting my VA business, how do I determine what to charge my clients?
A: You can charge by the hour or by the project. To determine what to charge, look at the websites of other VAs and compare their fees. Search for one or more VAs who do the type of work you will be doing and determine what they charge. Charging less at first will help you attract your first customers, and as you gain more experience and attract more customers you can gradually increase your fees.

Becoming an Affiliate Marketer

There are products and services available online that you can sell and then receive a percentage of the sale. As you will learn, it is also possible to get paid for attracting customers (leads) who want to learn more. If you sign up to sell a product or service, you are called an affiliate. The company that creates the product or service develops an affiliate program, and each has different rules and benefits.

E-books are one of the most popular affiliate products. It is customary for affiliates to receive a 50 percent commission for the sale of each e-book. When you sign up for the affiliate program, you will be given a special link that you will use when you promote the product. Each person who clicks on your specific link and then orders the product will be credited to your account.

Affiliate marketing is an interesting choice for a home business because, while it is possible to make a full-time income as an affiliate, your efforts can easily be combined with good content to attract visitors and other money-making endeavors such as Google AdSense ads and selling your own products.

There are three basic types of affiliate programs: pay per click, pay per lead, and pay per sale.

1. **Pay per click.** Every visitor you send to the merchant's website using your link will give you a credit. Payment is usually in pennies. The only way you can make a significant amount of money is if you send a lot of traffic a merchant's way. Google AdSense is a pay-per-click program but payouts can be higher.

2. **Pay per lead.** Affiliates are paid for each person who goes to the merchant's website and completes a predetermined action such as filling out a request for more information. It is easier to get a potential customer to request information than make a sale, so if the payout is at least $1 it could add up quickly.

3. **Pay per sale.** When the customer you send to the merchant's website makes a purchase, you get a predetermined percentage of the sale. The higher the percentage, the more money you will make. Sometimes a flat fee is given instead of a percentage.

Training or Certification

You do not need any official training or certification to become an affiliate marketer. But the more you know, the better you will do. Read as much as you can and search for information online.

Is This Business for You?

Anyone can become an affiliate, but you also have to be a marketer, which takes more knowledge and effort. Affiliate marketing encompasses many different online activities and skills. Successful affiliate marketers are good researchers. You will have to create websites (and/or blogs), use social networking, use e-mail marketing, and be able to create useful content. All of these skills are important for earning money online, and they can also be applied to other online businesses.

Affiliate Marketing Start-Up Advice

Choose affiliate products and services that you personally like and believe in. They must also match the interests of your target audience. Your honest recommendation could inspire your reader to order. Always keep your eyes open for affiliate programs that are attractive but not well-known. Affiliate programs that are listed on sites like Clickbank.com and CommissionJunction.com are promoted by many people. If you see a product or service online that you want to buy, check to see if they have an independent affiliate program that they administer themselves. Look at the very bottom of the page at the little type for a link that says "affiliates" or "partners" or "associates." If you cannot find the link, e-mail the company and ask if they have an affiliate program. As I was researching this book, I uncovered many interesting and little-known affiliate programs that I signed up for. It is my personal policy to only promote affiliate programs that I carefully research and approve. On HomeWorkingMom.com I have a blog called The Real Deal where I review resources and give inspiration. The slogan on my blog is, "We buy it and try it so you can feel safe." If you want your audience to trust you, you need to carefully evaluate every affiliate product you recommend like I do.

Pros and Cons

Pros

- All of your work can be done online, so it can be done from anywhere.
- You do not have to ship products or collect payments.
- You can literally make money while you sleep.
- Anywhere you can put your affiliate code is a potential promotional opportunity.

Cons

- You can be an affiliate marketer by sending e-mails, but you need a website or blog to find real success.
- You might have to try a few different programs before you find success.

- You can't just put up a banner ad and expect to make much money.
- If you send visitors to a merchant's website, these visitors may not come back to yours. (Hint: Make affiliate links open in a new window so the visitors remain on your website, as well).

Reader Q & A

Q: Which is the best type of affiliate program?

A: In my opinion, pay per lead is one of the most reliable ways to earn affiliate money. Pay-per-lead programs with good payouts can be more lucrative, because you get paid whether the customer buys or not.

Becoming an eBay Seller

There are many opportunities for developing a home business on eBay. Selling on eBay can be a great way to test a product or develop a home business. You may have sold some items on eBay before, but to be really successful you have to find a product you can sell on a consistent basis. More than ninety million eBay users worldwide sell $1,900 worth of goods every second of the day. You could be part of all this excitement.

Selling used items is a good way to get started on eBay. You can gather items from your own home or from friends who are willing to split the profit with you. Travel in high-income neighborhoods on trash days. You could find furniture to refinish or other items to sell. You can also look for items at garage and estate sales. Another place to find products is on eBay itself. A lot of sellers don't promote products correctly. Find them and you could get some great items to resell at very low prices. Dollar stores can be a good source of products, especially if you specialize in one niche such as cosmetics. Buying for $1 and selling for $5 or more is a 400 percent profit.

Your photos and the way you write your listings are just as important as your product. Use keywords that prospective customers might use to search on eBay. Feedback really matters. Pay special attention to customer service and ask your customers to leave positive feedback. Steve Webber, the author of the book, *eBay 101: Selling on eBay for Part-time or Full-time Income,* agrees that customer service is one of the keys to eBay success. "Take care of the details and prevent customer service issues instead of reacting to problems," he says. Offering free shipping can up the appeal of your item. Make sure the price you charge also covers shipping without eating your profit."

Like any other business, you should do research and learn as much as you can. However, there is no formal training or certification required.

Is This Business for You?

If you have something to sell, there will be someone on eBay who wants to buy it at the right price. If you are a crafter or artisan who makes items that sell on Etsy.com, you could expand your business on eBay, especially at holiday time. If you like a constantly evolving business with open possibilities, this could be the business for you.

Pros and Cons

Pros

- Start-up costs are low.
- It is a great one-person business that can be done part- or full-time.
- It is a good way to get traffic to your website.

Cons

- Even if you know which products are selling on eBay, you might not be able to get those products at wholesale prices.
- Storage of products might take up too much room in your home.
- There are scammers who will try to mislead you about wholesale prices or authenticity of collectibles.

Reader Q & A

Q: I really want to start an eBay business, but I can't come up with the right concept or product to sell.

A: You can find out the best-selling items on eBay by going to Pulse.eBay.com. You will see the top ten searches on eBay right now. You can also search the subcategories.

Becoming a Wedding Planner

A wedding planning business is creative and challenging. It is also a good business for a mom because it allows for a lot of flexibility. Most wedding planners work out of their homes and do a lot of their work using the telephone and e-mail. Your in-person appointments can be scheduled at times that are convenient for you.

Because many couples are getting married later in life, they have very little time to do the planning themselves. However, they do have the funds to hire a planner to help them create the wedding of their dreams. You will coordinate every aspect of a couple's wedding and be in charge of the rehearsal, ceremony, and reception.

Most brides and grooms are emotional. You need to be the one who keeps her head when everyone else is falling apart. You can work on an hourly basis or charge by the event. Either way, a successful wedding planner can earn a good income of $3,000 to $4,000 per wedding or up to 10 percent of the entire wedding budget.

Training or Certification

Most wedding planners receive some sort of certification, but it is not required. There is no regulation by any agency. You could just call yourself a wedding planner and set up a business. However, there is a lot of specialized knowledge required, so education is important. It is possible to get your training and certification online. Or you could educate yourself by doing extensive research in every element of wedding planning. For example, study all magazines and websites for brides. Then make contacts with jewelers, bakeries, catering halls, videographers, DJs, and every other vendor needed for a wedding. Establish a good relationship with the best ones and don't be afraid to ask for a discount in exchange for using them on an exclusive basis. You can then pass on the discount to your clients or keep it as another way to increase your income. It is also possible to work out an exchange of referrals where the vendors will refer clients to you, too. An attractive business card is all you really need to get started. Use appealing graphics on your card and offer an incentive, such as a free gift, for calling or e-mailing you.

Is This Business for You?

Did you play wedding with your dolls when you were a little girl? Did you love the details of planning your own wedding?

"If you have chosen wedding planning as your dream business, you probably are creative and have a flare for design and are well organized," says Jill S. Moran, Certified Special Events Professional and author of *How to Start a Home-Based Wedding Planning Business*. "You'll want to complement these qualities with business and

Emily Bonilla is a former wedding planner and is currently the owner of Marketing ForWahm.com. She has some excellent start-up advice for aspiring wedding planners: "A mom who wants to start a wedding planning business should first work for an established planner to learn the industry. You could reach out to a wedding planner and offer your assistance in exchange for training. There are many traditions, cultures, and situations that can happen at a wedding, and your experience can help you satisfy diverse customers.

> *Once you gain experience, venture out on your own in small steps. Begin with weddings of people you know. Take photos and get testimonials from them that you can use on your website. Continuing small, begin to advertise your business through encouraging word of mouth and then free and inexpensive marketing channels. Social media marketing should focus on sharing your work. Twitter can be used to announce new blog/website updates. Post photos, videos, and written descriptions of weddings on Facebook. If you do a great job, you'll find that the majority of your business will come from recommendations. Branding will be the most important part of your marketing strategy. Make sure that you clearly set yourself apart from any other wedding planners.*

marketing savvy to build a successful and profitable business." Jill also believes that training, experience, and wise vendor selection and support are important.

Do you have experience related to any aspect of wedding planning? You may have worked for a florist, as a photographer, or as a travel agent. If you planned your own wedding or helped a friend, this is a good start and you can build from there.

You must be able to work within a budget and be very organized. If you are passionate about the wedding industry and are willing to work hard, this could be the right business for you.

Pros

- You get to help people make their dreams come true.
- There is a growing need for wedding planners.
- There can be great joy in a successful wedding day.

Cons

- Planning a wedding is a very complex project with multiple priorities.
- You will be required to meet firm deadlines.
- You sometimes have to work nights and weekends.
- You might have to work with some very fussy brides.

Reader Q & A

Q: How much does it cost to become a certified wedding planner?

A: You do not need to be certified, but becoming certified does give you a competitive edge over uncertified planners. The cost varies from course to course, but they usually start at $500 and can go over $1,000 depending on the depth of information covered.

Becoming a Medical Transcriptionist

There is a lot of interest in starting a medical transcription business because some people visualize that typing information is not difficult. They are wrong. Medical transcription requires a good understanding of medical terms. A medical transcriptionist has to accurately and quickly transcribe medical records dictated by doctors and other medical personal.

Training or Credentials

There is a lot of training necessary to become a medical transcriptionist. Training is available online. You don't have to be certified to become a medical transcriptionist, but if you do you will be able to use the letters CMT (certified medical transcriptionist) after your name. To become certified, you will have to take a test given by the American Association of Medical Transcriptionists. You will also need two years' experience before you will be certified. Take a look at the medical

transcriptionist jobs shown on mtjobs.com. Read through them and see the type of experience that is required and how many of the jobs are home based. You will see that there are home-based opportunities, but many of them require at least one year of experience.

Is This Business for You?

Medical transcriptionists need to be dedicated, disciplined, and able to meet deadlines. You need to have an interest in and be able to do research on medical terms and drug names. A basic foundation and background in medical terminology, anatomy, physiology, and laboratory tests will help you get a head start on your training. A good knowledge of English usage and grammar is also essential, as well as a strong foundation as a good typist.

Pros and Cons

Pros

- Most medical transcription jobs are work-at-home jobs.
- Once you gain experience, medical transcription can pay well.
- The more you improve your skills, the more you will earn.

Cons

- Even online medical transcription courses can be expensive. Prices are approximately $1,800, but the cost differs by course. Specific equipment such as a medical dictionary and a digital foot pedal are required.
- You are usually required to have experience to apply for independent jobs.
- It takes time to get your skills up to a professional level.

Reader Q & A

Q: If I have to have experience to start working, how do I get experience?

A: At first you may have to work on-site or find a business owner who is willing to accept you as an apprentice for half pay during your training because all your work will have to be proofed. Work that comes from private doctors' offices and walk-in clinics is easier to do than hospitals so that is also a good place to start. Some training courses offer job placement to help you get started.

Starting a Child Care Business

Child care is a huge responsibility. It can also be a good source of reliable income. Besides caring for the children, you will need to keep good records, prepare food, and create interesting activities. Home-based child care is more appealing to some parents than large day-care centers because the care can be more personal. You will have to decide what type of care you want to provide, such as full-day care, after-school care, or drop-in care.

When you sign up each new client, it is a good idea to create a contract or agreement. Include the names of the parents, the child, the time the child care will start and end, and how much will be paid each week. Include any overtime payments if parents bring the child early or pick her up late. Write in a probationary period during which either you or the parent can terminate the contract. Make two copies and have the parents sign both. Keep one copy and give the parents the other.

Training or Credentials

Every state has different requirements for training and certification. Some of it is based on the number of children in your care. For information on your state's requirements, go to nccic.acf.hhs.gov/statedata/statepro/index.html.

Is This Business for You?

If you are responsible and love children, a child care business could be a good choice. If you are a mother, a nurse, or a teacher you probably already have the necessary skills. Are you good at organizing? Are you friendly? Do you have a lot of patience? You will need adequate and appropriate space in your home. Your daily world will be filled with babies, toddlers, toys, crayons, and lots of smiles and tears.

Pros and Cons

Pros

- Child care is in high demand.
- You can take care of your own children at the same time.
- Start-up costs are low, and you will be paid every week.

Lynnrae Fors was destined to have children in her life. She is the mother of three daughters, three stepdaughters and . . . eleven grandchildren! Her career as a child care provider began after the birth of her first child. She had no idea then where that choice would lead her and how many young lives she would be able to positively affect. She is a really good example of how your home business and your career can change once you get started.

She was motivated to open a child care business in her home so she could spend more time with her newborn baby, but she didn't think things through—at first. "I unfortunately thought that the first thing I should do was get children enrolled and learn as I went along," Lynnrae remembers. "That was a mistake. I wish I had a plan before falling into being a business owner, operator, and manager!" Lynnrae eventually created a plan for her child care business and is happy to share what she learned.

"There are so many details and decisions to be made prior to having children in your home. There are many questions that need to be answered such as:

- Who is going to work with you? Will yours be a single-provider child care or a two-person child care? Do you have small children of your own who will be part of the child care count?

- What type of child care are you going to do? Will you accept all ages or infants or older children only? What type of equipment will you need, and how will that impact your own family?

- What will your hours of operation be?

- Where will you care for the children? Will you use your whole house for the business or only certain rooms? And how will that impact your own family?

- Research the licensing requirements and support organizations in your area. They do vary, and it is extremely important to be in compliance with the regulations in your area. Support groups are also a wonderful avenue of research and training.

From Child Care Provider to Expert

- How did Lynnrae progress from start-up child care provider to an award-winning child care expert? She strived to find ways that would positively impact her career, her clients, and her family. Then she concentrated on how she could also change the child care industry for the better.

- "I have set dozens of goals over the years. I reached many of them," Lynnrae says. "I entered the Provider of the Year contest offered by Providers Choice. To enter it meant writing an essay answering several questions about child care. Then several providers were chosen for an oral interview in front of a panel. I won Provider of the Year." Part of the reward was a trip to the Save the Children conference in Atlanta, Georgia. Then she helped other providers at several conferences during the following year. Lynnrae returned to the Save the Children Conference as a workshop presenter and participant on a keynote panel four more times.

- Lynnrae's life has come full circle. She spends a lot of time with her family and still uses everything she learned as a provider with her grandchildren. "I spend quality time in ways that I believe will make a difference in their lives," she explains. "There is such effectiveness in the teaching-learning process." Lynnrae wrote a book called *Moment of Peace* about fun, spur-of-the-moment games to play with children that she still uses all of the time with her grandchildren.

- All of Lynnrae's knowledge about starting a child care business is available in an entire kit contained in an e-book. *The Family Child Care Success System* is an expansive edition that covers everything from your start-up to working with parents to over fifty actual child care activities. It also contains all the forms you need to run your child care business and many other details you might not think of on your own. To get more information or to contact Lynnrae, go to her website at www.ChildCareKit.com.

Cons

- Keeping little ones and their parents happy can be difficult.
- Your own children may be jealous or possessive about your time and the toys.
- You might need to hire help.

Reader Q & A

Q: How can I determine how much to charge parents?

A: First find out what other child care providers are charging. Do they give a discount to parents with more than one child? Then figure out your expenses per child, including utilities, equipment, food, and insurance. Don't charge too much or too little. Your fees might add to a prospective parent's perception of you. If you plan to work a total of forty hours per week, multiply that by the minimum hourly wage that is acceptable. Then divide that amount by the number of children in your care.

Becoming a Personal Shopper

A personal shopper shops for someone else in a variety of different niches. If you shop for fashion, you essentially are a stylist. If you shop for the elderly or working families, you are really running an errand service. In many cases you can run a personal shopping business online, communicating with your clients by telephone or e-mail and exchanging photos. You could even shop for them online. Or you may want more personal interaction.

Really get to know your clients before you begin shopping for them. You could create a general questionnaire for them to fill out that details their likes and dislikes as well as their expectations. Don't stop there. Interview each client in person when possible.

Decide in advance how you will charge your clients. You can charge a percentage of the amount purchased, which is usually around 15 percent. Or you can charge a set fee. Some personal shoppers charge both ways.

A new option, a concierge service, gives you the opportunity to take care of all shopping and errands for your clients. If they need theater tickets or cosmetics, grocery shopping or a dress for a special occasion, you can be at their service.

According to the Small Business Association, 60 percent of home businesses are in the service industry. Personal shopping fits right into that category.

Training or Credentials

You don't need formal training or credentials to become a personal shopper. You do, however, need to know a lot about the items you will buy and how to interact with your clients. A background in retail helps. Often a personal shopper will choose to shop for a category in which she was previously employed. In other words, you do have to be knowledgeable, but you don't need anyone's permission to begin.

Is This Business for You?

If you have a sense of style or knowledge about a specialized category and you love to shop, becoming a personal shopper could be the right home business for you. When you hear the term *personal shopper,* you might think about fashion and that certainly is an option, but there are many other categories to consider. There are personal shoppers who cover many different types of purchases. Collectors of antiques, jewelry, or even memorabilia might use a personal shopper. Or, you could specialize in buying gifts for holidays and birthdays. There are also opportunities to do corporate gift buying for executives who don't have time to shop.

Although it is not essential, personal shoppers who have wholesale relationships with sources have the opportunity to make more profit. In many states, you will need a resale certificate if you buy wholesale and resell an item. This means that you will have to collect sales tax.

Pros and Cons

Pros

- A lot of groundwork and actual shopping can be done online, so you can accomplish a lot from home.
- You can often take your child with you when you go out to shop.
- Your work can be flexible, fun, interesting, and rewarding.

Cons

- Clients can be demanding and difficult to handle.
- You might be requested to shop at inconvenient hours.
- If all your clients need you at the same time, you may have to disappoint someone.

Q: I love shopping for myself. How can I tell if I will be a good personal shopper for someone else?

A: Offer your services for free to family and friends. Treat them like clients and ask for honest feedback. Evaluate what you did right and what you did wrong and then decide if you want to be a personal shopper.

Becoming a Pet Sitter

The pet industry is hot. Any home business you choose that has to do with pets has a great chance of being successful. Most people feel like they can take care of a dog or a cat, but pet sitting is not as simple as that.

Training or Credentials

As a pet sitter you will be going into people's homes when they are not there. Your potential clients need to know that you will not steal from them or ignore their pet's needs. Many unexpected situations can arise, so you need to know how to react to any problems you might encounter. For these reasons pet sitters should be bonded and insured. Certification will show that you are a serious professional. For more information contact the National Association of Professional Pet Sitters (NAPP) at petsitters.org.

Is This Business for You?

You love animals, but how good are you in an emergency? Can you give animals medicine? Are you friendly and energetic, and do you sincerely care about pets? Are you willing to clean up after dogs, cats, and birds?

Do you have contacts with at least one vet, a dog groomer, and a pet store with a bulletin board? Your very appealing business cards and flyers can be distributed through these channels, and many will be willing to recommend you when asked. Word of mouth is the best way to promote your business, but you should also have a website for people to find you online and learn more about your business.

Pros and Cons

Pros

- Pet services are in great demand.
- You will be working with animals every day.
- It is an emotionally rewarding business.

Shannon of ShannonsPetSitting.net has some wonderful advice for moms who want to start a pet-sitting service: "If you are considering this career, first find a mentor. Find a professionally established pet sitter and explain to her that you are thinking about getting into the field. See if she will let you tag along with her or possibly employ you so you can get a feel for what this job is all about. Like any job it has positives and negatives, such as walking dogs in sub-zero temperatures, driving in bad weather to get to pets, picking up dog poop, and cleaning litter boxes. It is not all playtime and cuddles. In these tough economic times, some people think they could start a pet-sitting business. Their intentions are good. However, it takes more to qualify as a 'professional' pet sitter. Not only do you have to love animals, but you also must have training and experience! You have to know how to handle a situation when it arises—and trust me they come up! For example, you need to know how to break up dog fights, how to properly walk a dog, how to read a dog's body language, what to do in case of a medical emergency, how to administer medication, and more."

You can reach Shannon by visiting her website, www.ShannonsPetSitting.net to see a good example of what a pet sitter's website looks like.

Cons

- The pets may be unfamiliar with you, and you may have some trouble coaxing them from time to time.
- You need to be bonded and insured.
- Clients can be less than honest about their pets and leave you with a big problem, like an aggressive dog or a sick cat.
- You have to deal with many different types of poop every day.

Reader Q & A

Q: How much does it cost to be certified as a pet sitter?
A: The NAPP has an online course that costs $240.

Starting a Gift Basket Business

At first look, starting a gift basket business may seem easy. Some think all you need is a basket and some interesting things to arrange inside the basket. While this is true on the surface, it is a lot more complicated that that. You have to buy baskets and their contents. You will need storage space to accommodate what you buy and the finished baskets. You will also need space for a large table to work on.

It is best to choose a niche market such as gift baskets for new babies. Then add new niche markets one at a time. You probably won't have a storefront for walk-in traffic, so hook up with businesses that do, such as florists or hospital gift shops. Think of the types of businesses that might send gift baskets to their clients such as Realtors and corporate executives.

Training or Credentials

You do not need any special training or credentials to make gift baskets. Learn all you can and possibly work with another gift basket seller to learn up close. Your work will show your skills.

Is This Business for You?

Do you have design ability? Are you a good marketer? If so, a gift basket business could be for you. Gift basket businesses are very popular, and that might mean you will have a lot of competition. However, there is strong demand for gift baskets, and there are some really good ways to get business.

Pros and Cons

Pros

- There are year-round sales opportunities.
- You can sell locally or from a website—or both.
- Gift baskets are popular because they can be a customized gift.

Cons

- You will need storage for baskets and basket contents.
- Food items are perishable and should be stored properly.
- There is a lot of competition.
- Delivery must be made either locally or by shipping.

Q: Just about anybody could want to buy a gift basket. Why should I limit my focus to one small segment?

A: While it is a good thing to sell something that a lot of people want or need, it is a mistake to market your gift basket business to a general audience. Instead, choose a niche, determine the needs of this target audience, and then develop a plan to serve them.

Becoming a Personal Chef

If you have always wanted to use your cooking and baking skills as a basis for a home business, becoming a personal chef is one option. Because there are so many health department regulations in most states, you are not allowed to cook food for sale in your own standard kitchen. You would have to rent time in a professional kitchen or a bakery. If you cook for others in their own kitchens, you can circumvent the health department rules. That is why becoming a personal chef is a good option for a food business. As a side endeavor, you could sell the components of a particular dish or bakery item with the recipe packaged in a kit. This is a good product to sell on eBay or your own website.

You could specialize in healthy options for people who want to lose weight or low-glucose options for diabetics. As with any other type of business, when you choose a niche market you have a greater chance for success. It would be a good idea to create a list of the breakfasts, lunches, and dinners your clients can choose from.

Training or Credentials

You do not need any special credentials to become a personal chef, but many do attend a cooking school. Obviously you need to be a good cook. If you have natural abilities, it would be beneficial to work in the kitchen of a restaurant or two so that you can learn from the chef and put those jobs on your resume.

Is This Business for You?

Do you have a passion for cooking? Are you always being complimented? If the answer is yes, and you can organize menus and your time, this may be a good home business for you. When you are pricing your service, anticipate the rising cost of some foods.

Pros and Cons

Pros

- All you have to do is cook. There is no serving involved.
- The need for personal chefs will increase as baby boomers get older.
- You can help people meet their dietary needs.

Cons

- Clients may not want you to cook in their homes.
- The number of clients you can cook for is limited, unless you get access to a commercial kitchen where you can cook for multiple clients at the same time.
- All food businesses are exposed to liability if a client gets sick.

Reader Q & A

Q: If, as a personal chef, I have to cook in other people's houses, how is that a home-based business?

A: You can cook multiple meals for the week all on one six- to eight-hour day for each client. You could accept a limited number of clients until you are ready to increase your hours outside the home.

Creating Your Own Product

Moms are creative. They are also inventive by nature. They have to be, because raising children calls for creative solutions all of the time. They go from repairing a little doll to fixing a dump truck without missing a beat. They solve conflict with compromise and find ways to make vegetables look appealing. They go through life with new ideas constantly flowing through their minds, but most of those ideas are lost or quickly forgotten.

This chapter is for you if you are a mom who wants to capture your ideas and turn them into inventions or beautiful creations that you can sell. Reading the stories of moms who accomplish these goals can give you the incentive you need to move ahead with your ideas, so many examples have been included here.

Creating your own product can be very simple or quite complicated. If you are a crafter, your income will be limited only by the number of pieces you can produce. Moms who invent a product that will need to be produced in a factory may have a greater chance of hitting it big, but they will also face bigger challenges and require more of an investment, especially if manufacturing is involved.

There is no better way to understand the process of bringing your own product to market than to read about other moms who are doing it. I've spoken to many and have included the best examples here for you.

It's Not Your Mother's Craft Business Anymore

Moms have been earning money at home selling their crafts for a very long time. Some would say that crafting was one of the first ways moms made money at home, but income potential used to be very limited. Even though crafting is a very traditional home business, crafters today are often able to produce artistic items that exceed previous expectations. There are many new

ways to promote your crafts that will potentially give you a worldwide audience. Moms can make real money selling their creations, and much of that potential comes from websites devoted to selling crafts.

"Online sales platforms like Etsy and Supermarket have redefined what it means to be a crafter," says Tara Gentile of ScoutieGirl.com. "No longer is there the stark divide between Grandma selling her crocheted toilet paper roll covers at a church bazaar and fine craft guild artisans selling at riverside art shows. Crafters—makers and designers—have a wide framework for creating commercially viable goods that express their inner artist. And buyers have the diversity of style, price, and skill they've craved for years."

Tara mentions Etsy.com and Supermarkethq.com as two places to sell your crafts online. There are at least ten other websites where you can sell your crafts, in addition to eBay.com (see appendix B).

There is no doubt that the beautiful and clear photos and descriptions on websites elevate the profile of each handmade item to a level that would be hard to find in person. The crafter or artist can attract shoppers looking for unique items better than ever before. Holiday shopping has never been more creative and easy to do. Everyone wins.

OK, that might be simplifying it a bit; it is not really that easy. All crafts and crafters will not necessarily find success selling online, or anywhere else. You still have to create a product that has sales appeal. Like anything else being sold, your items should be created with a target customer in mind.

Before you decide which handmade items to sell online, keep these points in mind:

- You may love making crocheted doll clothes, but is there a market for them? Study what is selling online and match your skills to the items that seem to be in demand.
- Your skills may be remarkable, but if you price your items too high they might not sell. If you target an upper-income customer who understands the time and effort that goes into your creation, you can attract sales, especially if your prices are competitive with other items in your category.
- If you want to sell in quantity, choose to create items that do not take a long time to make. If it is something that you can train others to do, you will have backup help when needed.

- Consider your cost for raw materials. To be profitable, you should price your handmade item at least double what it costs you to make. Buy in bulk at lower prices, but only if you are sure that you will use all that you buy.

Selling on Etsy.com

You can sell items in three categories on Etsy.com: handmade items you make yourself, crafting supplies, and vintage items that are at least twenty years old or older.

There is a 20 cent charge to list an item for four months. When your item sells, there is a 3.5 percent transaction fee. Fees are added up and listed in an e-mail at the end of the month. You can pay using your credit card or by PayPal.

You will need a business PayPal account to accept payment on Etsy. Payments go directly into your account.

A WORK-AT-HOME MOM'S STORY
Trisha Klein, Mama's Apron Strings

Some people might say that Trisha Klein is an accidental entrepreneur. In reality, she is an example of preparation meeting opportunity.

It all started back in 2005. Trisha was spending her days helping out her friend, Marie, who had just started a new coffee shop. Each day, she would arrive for work looking clean and nicely dressed. By the end of the day, her clothes were a mess: She was covered in coffee grounds and even found coffee beans in her belly button.

She decided to make an apron to wear. Little did she know that small decision would change the direction of her life.

"I made myself some aprons, all with coffee motifs," she remembers. "Each day I wore a different fresh and clean apron, which I would color coordinate to

whatever I was wearing." Customers began to inquire about where they could get aprons like the ones she was wearing. "People were pleasantly surprised to learn that these one-of-a-kind creations were designed and handmade by me," Trisha says. "People wanted my aprons!"

This mother of three decided to accept a few apron orders, but she did it in a very personalized way. As part of the process, she would ask her customers questions about their hobbies and other interests and then select fabric with patterns that would reflect their personalities. People loved the whole experience of talking about themselves and receiving their personalized aprons. "You'd think that I had presented them with gifts rather than something that they had purchased from me," Trisha recalls.

Trisha chooses fabrics from trusted websites and local fabric stores. She does not buy in bulk so that her inventory is ever changing. A unique fabric is used for each apron making them one of a kind. She only makes bib aprons and garden aprons. They are lined with pockets and cost $42 each. With experience, she has whittled production time for each apron down to three hours, down from six hours.

The apron orders continued to flow in, and Trisha had to cut back her hours working at Marie's coffee shop. "I lost her to her sewing machine," says Marie. "It didn't take long, because they are just so adorable."

Before becoming an apron entrepreneur, Trisha had mostly only sewed costumes for her children. However, this is where the preparation meeting opportunity comes in. She did take tailoring courses in high school and art in college. She also took numerous business courses during that time. Trisha was clearly prepared when opportunity walked into the coffee shop.

A group of business women came to the coffee shop one day to have a meeting about advertising for the Baltimore Symphony Orchestra's annual Designer Showcase, a charitable event. While placing their order, one of the women complimented her apron. She replied with her usual "Thanks, I made it myself." They asked how many aprons she had already made. She told them she had a few, and they asked to see them. She showed them a few aprons that she retrieved from the trunk of her car.

The women invited Trisha to participate in the Designer Showcase and she accepted. This event opened many doors, and Trisha began to receive invitations to sell her creations in the Kennedy Center's gift shop, the National Symphony Orchestra's Designer Showcase, the City of Baltimore's Artscape, and a wide variety of unique restaurants, wineries, kitchens, and clothing boutiques across the country. Two of her aprons even appeared on the reality show *Jon and Kate Plus Eight,* worn by Kate and one of her daughters.

Because the aprons are lightweight and the label states that they are made in Annapolis, Maryland, they are popular as gifts to be given overseas. They have been sent to South Africa, Japan, England, France, Thailand, Italy, the Philippines, and Brazil.

Even with her product's international appeal, Trisha's clientele is mostly local and her marketing is based mostly on word of mouth. Even so, she has attracted thousands of orders and is paying it forward by hiring and training another mom to help her sew the aprons when she has large orders. That mom had never sewn before and is now using the money she earns to attend college. Trisha's bookkeeper is a mom, and her graphic artist is also a mom.

Trisha recently expanded her product line and has given very clever names to her new products. She now makes shoe bags (Sole Traveler) and lingerie bags (Sacks in the City). So what is her goal for the future? Seeing her aprons sold in Whole Foods. To learn more go to www.MamasApronStrings.com.

Traditional Outlets for Selling Crafts

As you can see from Trisha Klein's story above, you don't have to sell your handmade goods online in order to be successful. Crafts have always been sold in person. Often crafters join together to create sales opportunities that will be of interest to the public. Team up with other crafters who do not compete in your category and have a home party or a garage sale. It is important to have enough tables and ways to display each craft for maximum effect.

You can also approach local stores and ask them to display your items. In a consignment agreement, the consignment store does not pay you upfront but only if the store makes a sale. When trying to make a consignment agreement or even a wholesale sale to stores, choose privately owned smaller stores that have decision

makers on the premises. Large, national chains need to be approached through their buyers at their main offices.

Think creatively when choosing stores. If you create accessories, clothing stores would be appropriate. Gifts can be sold at airport, museum, and hospital gift shops. Pot holders and other cooking-related items could sell in cookware and small appliance stores.

There are thousands of festivals and arts-and-crafts shows every year. If you think you can earn enough to warrant the registration fees, you could have fun and make contacts too. Buyers like to see crafters working on their crafts as they browse the offerings. When selling directly to the public in person, you will need a merchant credit card account. You can find out how to get a merchant account on page 119.

A WORK-AT-HOME MOM'S STORY
Lori Bergmann, Jewelry Designer

Some may call her a crafter. Others might say that she is an inventor, but that is just plain wrong. Lori Bergmann designs and produces her own bead designs made of metal or glass and transforms them into beautiful necklaces and more.

Lori started out as a graphic designer and then worked in the published scrapbooking and crafting industry for about eight years before she decided that she needed a hobby that was not her business. She was always fascinated with glass beads and jewelry making, so she decided to learn how to make her own glass beads just for fun. "After a few years honing my skills, I decided to focus more on retailing my beads and finished jewelry, since I had quickly accumulated more glass than I would ever be able to wear or give away to family and friends," Lori recalls about the start of her current business.

One Christmas, Lori gave handmade glass bottle stoppers to everyone in her family for Christmas. Her sister-in-law commissioned her to make twelve more for her family. That gave Lori the incentive she needed to open up her shop on Etsy. She named her store Ashlyn Design but says if she could name it again she would have given it a different name that would have helped brand her business. She also would have done more market research.

Despite her mistakes, Lori has created a life any crafter would love to have. "I love working from home because it affords me the ability to work around my family's schedule and I can take a 'vacation' whenever life begins to feel a little hectic," she explains. She has a separate studio space where she can have quiet time to work and keep all her tools and supplies without worrying that the kids will get into them.

Lori stays organized by making a new list every day and likes to set goals and cross them off as they are completed. Her organization extends to her studio where she makes sure she cleans everything up between projects. "It can get pretty messy during the design process," she admits. "I'm very self-motivated and constantly striving to perfect new skills and techniques to keep my work fresh."

Lori currently has over 395 craft projects, jewelry designs, and written articles that have been featured in publications such as *Better Homes and Gardens* and *Creating Keepsakes* and for Michaels Craft Stores and more.

When asked for advice for other moms who would like to follow in her footsteps, she advises, "Focus on what you love to create, set specific goals, and make sure that whatever product or service you're offering is the best quality workmanship you can possibly offer. Do your research of similar businesses and see what you love or don't like about them to help you get a better idea of the image you would like to have for your own business." Lori also suggests that you use your local library to read about business practices, get design inspiration, and learn techniques from DVDs. "Get involved in online forums and visit local businesses and/or galleries that tie into your work and might provide a mutually beneficial relationship. Attend local meetings of like-minded people who share the same love of your craft. You might even make some great, new friends!"

Whether you are a crafter or not, it is worth taking a look at Lori's intricate and beautiful designs on www.etsy.com/shop/AshlynDesign. Visit her blog at loribergmann.blogspot.com.

Are You a Mother of Invention?

There is an old saying that goes: "Necessity is the mother of invention." In recent years that has changed. Today mothers are doing the inventing and coming up with ideas for products that are missing from the marketplace. Many invent parenting-related products . . . or at least they try to. The idea is the easy part. All of the steps between idea and reality are a lot more complicated. You will need a lot of help and feedback on your journey, but, as you will find out, it can also be very rewarding. Let's start from the beginning and evaluate your product.

Is Your Product Marketable?

The journey from idea to a ready-to-sell product can be a rocky and expensive road. Before you begin, it is time to determine if there is a real market for your product idea and if it already exists. If it does not exist, is there a waiting market, or are you are the only one who is impressed? Market research is the way to find out.

What it all boils down to is this: It does not make sense to spend valuable time and money to bring a product to market that no one wants. Your market research is the most important step you can take.

If your product is of interest to moms, invite all the moms you know to tell you what they think and ask them to get feedback from the moms that are in their circle of friends. You can do this online or you can actually have a party and present your idea. Ask for an honest assessment and suggestions for improvement. This is not a time for good manners.

You could also approach potential distributors and see if you can get a purchase order. A purchase order means that they are committed to purchasing your product when it is ready. It shows that they have faith in your idea. If at some point you decide to license your idea instead of producing it yourself, a purchase order will make your idea more valuable.

Consider all the feedback you receive and then rely on your gut instinct to tell you if you should take the next step. Most of all, be realistic. Don't get so attached to an idea that you can't see its possible flaws.

Kelly Ripa has a television show called *Homemade Millionaire* on TLC. Each hour-long episode follows the competitive journey of three women vying for a chance to sell their inventions on HSN, the Home Shopping Network. A deal with HSN could change an inventor's life overnight. One woman developed a high-end clutch handbag that she named Purse Flats. Inside, leather ballet shoes are folded

HUGGIES® MomInspired™ Grant Program

How would you like to receive $1,000 to $15,000 to help you start your business?

Kimberly Clark, maker of HUGGIES® diapers, has started a grant program to help moms transform their ideas into actual businesses. In their own words, this is the reason why they decided to help: "Motherhood is a rollercoaster. To enjoy it, you have to go where it takes you—and that's exactly what inventive moms like you do. From belly flops to heart stops you enjoy the ride, embracing those chaotic moments with a smile and devising creative solutions to improve life with your little one. HUGGIES® is inspired by your ingenuity and wants to give you that extra nudge to turn those great ideas into reality."

Your idea does not have to be related to diapers or hygiene. These grants have been given out once, and other submission periods will take place in the future. To learn when the next submissions will be accepted, go to www.HuggiesMomInspired.com and add your e-mail address to "Keep me posted."

and ready to wear if your feet start to hurt on a night out. There was one flaw: After you take your high heels off, there is no place to put them except in a see-through mesh bag you had to carry separately. The inventor may not have considered that ballet-style shoes are widely available and you could fold them into your choice of handbag—one that could also accommodate your high heels. The inventor is an attorney and she invested $75,000 in her idea. We wish her good luck as she pushes on, but the moral to this story is this: Just because you have the money to invest, it doesn't mean you should.

Do You Need a Patent or a Trademark?

It is necessary to protect your idea, but spending up to $8,000 to get a patent from a patent attorney at the beginning may not be the right move. If someone tries to rip off your idea by slightly altering a feature or function, it can be expensive and difficult to enforce your patent. There are companies that exist

Moms who live in big cities have a lot in common. They usually transport their young children from place to place using a stroller and, when they leave the house, they take three things with them: a bottle of water, a diaper bag, and their phone. Walking down the street in New York City with her two young children one day, pregnant Leslie Perlman got an idea. She realized that there was a place on her stroller to store her water bottle and diaper bag, but no convenient place to put her phone for easy access. She envisioned a device that would attach to the handlebar of her stroller

and hold her smart phone up for easy viewing. Parents would no longer have to fumble around in their bag or pockets in order to locate their phone.

Instead of putting her idea in the back of her mind, Leslie made a phone call—to a patent attorney. "I hired an attorney who conducted a patent search and then filed for a provisional patent," she explains. "Then I worked with a plastics manufacturer who designed the holder and built the mold." Getting the mold built was one of Leslie's largest expenses. She reduced the expense by having the mold made in China, but she could not use a Chinese manufacturer even though it would have cut production costs. "I am a stay-at-home mom of three young kids, so flying to China to oversee production was not an option for me." The manufacturer she chose is located within an hour from her home and she can take her children with her, if necessary.

After her prototype was approved and the mold was built, Leslie began to work on the logo and the packaging. "I found the graphic designer, photographer,

box manufacturer, Velcro-strap manufacturer, etcetera either online or by recommendations," she recounts. "The entire process from just an idea to being sold in a store took one year." The end result was texthook.

During that first year, Leslie continued putting the parenting of her three children first. "My personal and business lives revolve around my children's schedule," she explains. "I work when the older kids are in school and the baby is napping and then at night when they are all asleep." Because she works in very specific time increments Leslie finds it easy to focus and work efficiently during those times.

Leslie realized that she had to get her product in front of the public. "I wish I had known how long it takes to build your brand and make people aware of your product and why they need it," she tells us. "I thought that since I developed a product that was not available on the market that I needed and used every day, that all parents would feel the same way. It takes a long time to educate your potential customers." To accomplish her goal, Leslie thought big and small at the same time. She sent out press releases and samples to magazine editors and mom bloggers. Samples and personalized letters were sent to celebrities, too. She also approached local retailers.

"I am very persistent as well as persuasive. I went into a local toy store that carried toys but not stroller accessories. I knew that most of their customers were my target market—parents with children in strollers. I convinced them to take a few units to keep by the register, and texthook™ quickly became a hot-selling item."

The product launched in December 2009. In April 2010, *The Today Show* featured texthook™ on their show during a segment about stroller accessories. A lot of website visitors and many sales resulted. It was her first big break.

Reviews of texthook™ on websites like Amazon.com revealed that parents are also using texthook™ for other purposes. "I learned that parents who exercise with their strollers love the easy access to their fitness apps, and they also keep kids entertained with music, use it for GPS purposes, and more," Leslie says. "All of these new uses have been helpful with marketing texthook™."

When asked for advice for other mom inventors, Leslie advises that you have patience: "It takes a second to have a great idea but much longer to get that idea to the marketplace!"

For more information visit thetexthook.com.

just to create copycat products. There are two alternatives to a patent that you could consider:

1. **A provisional patent.** When you have completed your market research and have a product you are almost ready to sell, apply for a provisional patent. It costs under $200. When you get a provisional patent, you are then allowed to put "patent pending" on your product. There is no patent and therefore no patent for anyone to look at. This will last for one year. You can get an eighteen-month extension by filing a Patent Cooperation Treaty (PCT) application.

2. **Register a trademark.** If you do not have enough money for a patent attorney, you could register a trademark for now. It does not cost much and it is much easier to enforce. You can start using a trademark immediately, even before you actually submit your trademark application. By placing the trademark symbol (™) next to your product's name, you begin to acquire some common law rights. Each state has different laws governing trademarks.

If yours is the first product of its kind and you can prove that you have gotten sales, you can almost always protect your idea. All of the tools and forms you need to learn what you need to know about patents and trademarks can be found on the U.S. Patent and Trademark Office's website, www.uspto.gov.

Creating a Prototype

If your invention will have to be manufactured, you need to create a handmade version first. That is your prototype. It can be very exciting to see your idea transformed into something tangible. As long as you have an accurate representation of what the real thing will look like, it is OK to use simple household items and make it yourself at first. You will eventually need a preproduction prototype, but handmade is fine for now. If the end product will be made from plastic, you can buy a product called ShapeLock (www.shapelock.com). This is a plastic that melts in hot water or in the microwave to allow you to shape it into your prototype. It is strong, safe, and reusable. Once it cools, it locks rigidly at room temperature.

Once you develop your prototype to the best of your ability, it will be time to find a prototype developer. You can find one listed online at www.tomasnet.net. This is a database of manufacturers, distributors, and many other types of help you will need on your journey. It is broken down by state.

Bringing Your Idea to Market

Every product is different. Some are easy to manufacture with few start-up costs; others require a lot of money and time. There are so many details involved in the marketing of your product that you may decide to license your product to another company. If you license it out, you will probably receive only up to 5 percent of sales as royalty fees.

If you decide to bring the product to market yourself, you can sell directly to the public online at first. Market your product and send samples and press releases to the media. Once you have created some buzz and sales, you will be able to interest large websites and stores to stock your product.

A WORK-AT-HOME MOM'S STORY
LeeAnn Piazzola, DiaperBuds™

It is a simple fact: Diapers are hard to tote around, and moms on the go don't want to be held back by bulky diaper bags. One mom asked herself, "What if you could vacuum pack a disposable diaper and make it 70 percent smaller?" That's how DiaperBuds™ was born. The diapers are individually wrapped so that they can easily be put in a pocket or a small handbag.

It was LeeAnn Piazzola's sister who had the original idea to vacuum pack diapers to lighten her load when traveling with her kids. LeeAnn and her two sisters have nine children among them, and the three decided to become partners and forge ahead with the idea to create a business, feeling sure that Diaper-Buds™ would be embraced by busy moms across the globe. They were right. Good things really do come in small packages.

After attending a trade show, the sisters received almost simultaneous orders from Amazon.com and Diapers.com, and DiaperBuds™ was on the way to success. The ABC Tradeshow in Las Vegas and several other consumer-oriented trade shows helped generate a number of leads, including Babies R Us and Buy Buy Baby. The ladies behind DiaperBuds™ continue to send out hundreds of samples to other retailers to generate interest, and they also went as far as to hire a public relations firm to generate publicity.

They had a great idea, the interest, and a strong background in sales and marketing. Next it was time to learn about sourcing materials and manufacturing. "I solved those problems by networking with people in those areas, asking tons of questions, and checking and cross-checking my facts and figures by comparison shopping," LeeAnn explains. "I cold-called every diaper manufacturer in the United States to requested samples to test." She didn't stop there. "For retail, I attended trade shows, seminars, and conferences and picked the brains of people who had successfully sold products at retail. For logistics, I called over a dozen fulfillment houses in the geographic area and comparison shopped," she recalls.

How does she handle a growing business and her five children? LeeAnn follows the "work hard, play hard" philosophy. During work hours, she focuses on building her company. When she is with her family at meals or on weekends, her attention revolves around them. "I help with homework, enjoy favorite TV shows together, and attend or participate in family events or kids activities," she explains.

Because she realizes that people are very generous about sharing what they know, LeeAnn has made it a personal policy to always be forthcoming with those who wish to follow her path. When asked for advice for moms wanting to start a home business, this is what she advised:

"Your business is off to a good start if you offer something that solves a problem and answers a need—a must-have. However, it doesn't end there. Positive thinking, dedication, and hard work are the essential ingredients for a successful business. The sacrifices you make now will pay off tenfold in the future. The most critical word of advice is to follow your gut. If it doesn't feel right, don't do it. While you should always proceed with caution, move forward letting your instincts be your guide. Don't be afraid to make minor mistakes. The only true mistakes are those we don't learn from. Take every opportunity and encounter as a learning experience. Launching a successful business is never an upward progression. There will always be delays, mishaps, and bumps in the road that can potentially derail you if you let them. Stay positive and focused."

To learn more visit www.DiaperBuds.com or @DiaperBuds on Twitter.

So what is it really like to work from home? Forget all about commuting. Forget time clocks and waking your baby up to take him to daycare. Forget salary reviews and co-workers who talk too much. In your new work-at-home life, your commute will take one minute. No one will tell you when to start working, and no one will look over your shoulder as you work.

The only chatter will come from a little one who is obsessed with dinosaurs or Barbie dolls. You can hug your child anytime you want to, breast-feed your baby when you need, or have a heart-to-heart talk with your teenager at the exact moment it will mean the most. You are living the very special lifestyle of a work-at-home mom, and, with a little planning and flexibility, you could love almost every minute.

Even though mothering and managing work at home is a great choice, there are down sides. You should be fully aware of what to expect before you take on such an all-encompassing lifestyle. It can get very intense if you are trying to get work done and be with your children at the same time. It can also be very rewarding.

Can you really work at home alone with children underfoot? Yes, you can. I know it is possible to bring up happy, involved children and work at the same time because I did it myself. In fact the majority of work-at-home moms do it every day. Yet, throughout my past twenty-five years of work-at-home experience, I have read experts stating over and over that it can't be done. All of those so-called experts are wrong, and in this chapter I'll tell you why.

Living, Working, Laughing, and Learning

As you embark on your work-at-home adventure, create a vision of how you want the balance and flow of your daily life to look. Write it down, change

it as your children grow, and refer to it often. If you want your home, your business, and your family all functioning on the highest level, you need a plan. Pay careful attention to details and your family life may become even better than your expectations.

Growing a career and a family at the same time under the same roof can be a wonderful experience. Your business may grow slowly, but your children will grow quickly. You want to keep them happy and provide them with learning experiences that only children who grow up watching a home business can have. Your home business may instill an entrepreneurial spirit in them and give them knowledge of the inner workings of a business that no formal schooling could ever provide.

Make your choice and then throw away any guilt you might feel. Parents have always worked at home with children. If you ever clean your house, pay bills, or do some gardening with your children nearby, you are working at home. You take them with you when you shop for food. A trip to the post office is no more damaging.

As your children grow, their needs change, and so should your plan. I will help you to understand what you can expect and the right techniques to use at each age range. Because so many aspiring work-at-home moms are either pregnant or have a new baby, I will detail the first year of life and then go on to the other ages and stages.

Newborn to Twelve Months

You may not have planned to start a home business, but you realize that you don't want to go back to work and leave your baby when your maternity leave is over. But you need the income and want to continue doing some rewarding work.

Even though the first months of a baby's life are joyful, they can also be very stressful. You will be sleep deprived and experiencing hormone changes that can make you very emotional. If you add a new home business to the mix, your stress level could go over the top. This is not a good time to start a new business, or anything else for that matter. So, from **one to three months,** take the time to bond with your baby and enjoy the experience. Use this time to do some business research and write down ideas. If you started doing that while you were pregnant, then take a few easy steps to get started but don't put a lot a pressure on yourself.

If you need income right away, it is unlikely that most types of businesses will bring much in the first few months, so you will have to consider other alternatives such as telecommuting or part-time work.

A baby who is raised by a work-at-home mom from an early age expects to see her mother working for at least part of the day, and that is a good thing. It makes it a lot easier to incorporate work into your daily routine as your baby grows, and that is one good reason to start working on your business within the first few months of your baby's life.

In these first few months, try to work when your baby is sleeping or try putting her in a front baby carrier. Soon your baby will associate the tapping of your keyboard, or whatever sounds you make when working, with being close to your heart.

At **four to six months**, your baby is more aware of her surroundings. Her naps will become more regular, and she will begin to sleep through the night. Let her schedule help you regulate your work time. You can get a lot of work done while she is asleep. While awake, you can put her in a swing chair or a bouncer and get short spurts of work in while she plays. She will be able to reach out for toys and begin to control her movements so she can amuse herself for a little while. Talk to her, sing songs, and don't forget to smile while you work. I am currently writing this book and doing other work at home by myself with my four-month-old grandson, Jason, here four days a week, so I am speaking from current experience. Jason is such a joy, and I consider taking breaks to feed him and cuddle him a way to recharge my energy. If this grandma can do it, you certainly can too! So plan ahead and try to schedule telephone calls and any work that requires concentration for naptime.

When baby turns **six to nine months,** he will become more mobile and self-motivated. He will be able to sit up by himself to play with toys and will be crawling before you know it. All of this exercise will probably keep him napping twice a day throughout this period of time. You can put a small play yard by your desk with his favorite toys to help you buy a little work time beyond naptime. Talk to him, sing songs, and put on some educational TV to buy a little more work time. He will be able to sit in a high chair for meals and snacking. Devise some play activities for the high chair and you can get a little work done.

You might feel like your organized day is fading away when baby gets to be **nine to twelve months.** Her mantra will be "Let me move!" and move she will. Crawling

and beginning to walk will occupy a lot of her time and attention. By this time, baby will be used to seeing you work part of your day and will expect it. So, even if you can't concentrate and don't get much work done, let her see you sitting at your desk for some time each day.

Fifteen Months to Two-and-a-Half Years

During this time, baby is walking and talking and wants to do everything by himself. This is the "no" stage. Every "no" you ever said to baby will come back at you in spades. Although he will probably take at least one nap each day, there are no guarantees. If you can afford it, this is a great time to get a little help, even if it is only a young teenager who will play with baby and follow him around the house to keep him out of trouble. Continue to let him see you work each day but try to make it the same time each day. Believe it or not, things will get easier.

Three to Four Years

The closer your child gets to three, the easier things will become. The "terrible twos" become the "terrific threes," and you have a little girl who you can have a conversation with. But this stage is not without its problems. With verbal ability comes expressed opinions, and she will have many. The good news is she will be ready to go to nursery school part-time. Continue to work at the same time each day so she expects to see you there and help her start activities you can monitor while you work. It is time to set up a mini desk next to yours and get a toy computer, toy telephone, and art supplies to let her "work" next to you. Save your junk mail and let her cut and paste to her heart's content. Give her lots of positive reinforcement, and end each work session with a child-centered activity.

Five to Ten Years

Your child is now school age! You can now count on about six solid hours of work time each day. If you use that time wisely, you will be free to spend time with your child when he gets home or needs rides to after-school activities. You can be that "milk-and-cookies" mom everyone wishes for after school and also be available to help with homework. Now is when it starts to become clear how working at home really is a benefit to your child. You are not sitting in a remote office waiting for that telephone call telling you he is home, and the TV won't be his only companion until

you get there. This is also the age when you can actually begin to involve your child in your business and give him special learning experiences. He will expect to see you working at least part of the day and won't mind the "independence" it gives him.

Eleven to Eighteen Years

There is a big difference between an eleven-year-old and an eighteen-year-old, but not as much as you might think. Eleven is the age that most girls and some boys are starting to think like young teenagers. They won't want so much attention at this age, but, believe it or not, they will need it more than they did as babies. The older the child, the more after-school supervision is needed because that is the time that trouble is most likely to happen. The hours between three and six o'clock have been called the "danger zone" for teenagers. If you are working at home, yours won't be the house where smoking, drinking, drug use, or even sexual experimentation takes place. It can be the place that is safe for interacting with friends. You will probably be one of only a few mothers in your neighborhood who is home at that time of day. You will be able to keep track of where your children are and who they are with during those hours and who they are interacting with when they're online at home.

When you are available to discuss their problems right at the time they are happening and see with your own eyes that homework gets done, your communication and cooperation with your children could improve.

Tweens and teens will probably forget everything they knew about living in a home with a business, because they are often in their own worlds. You might have to remind them why you started your home business and expect them to respect that at least part of your family's income comes from what you do. How can they show respect? They can listen to music with earphones during business hours, for example. They can have the opportunity to actually earn some extra cash by working in a business that is located in your home. If they promise to do some work, they should keep that promise. And, they shouldn't make you feel guilty if you have to work when they want you to do something else instead.

Take advantage of being your own boss, and take an afternoon off occasionally to do something special together with your children. Your tween or teen may not be that adorable baby anymore, but deep down he still needs your love and attention as much as you need his.

A WORK-AT-HOME MOM'S STORY
Robin McCoy, Inspired By Savannah, LLC

Robin McCoy of Putnam, Connecticut, was four months pregnant with her daughter, Savannah, when she got the idea for a product that would help a mom soothe her newborn baby. At that time, she was working at home as a virtual assistant providing administrative services to individuals and companies all over the world. Before that, she was a health educator who had worked in the non-profit sector for over ten years.

Robin's idea was an innovative baby sleep sack that incorporates the sound of a heartbeat the way a baby hears it while still in her mother's womb. There is a plush toy attached so that it can continue to be used even after the baby no longer needs it. You can go to her website, http://www.sootheaze.com/, to see an animation and hear the heartbeat sound.

"I thought I would have all the time in the world to work on the business when the baby was born, because I was told that babies sleep a lot," Robin recalls. It didn't quite work out that way. "I didn't factor in how tired I would be, and when she slept, I slept." Savannah's nap times were sporadic, so it was hard to create a work schedule. Now that she is seven months old, Robin reports, "I work a few hours in the morning while she is napping, maybe find an hour in the afternoon to check e-mail, and then work into the wee hours of the morning after she is sleeping."

A cancer survivor, Robin never considered giving up on her business, and she was rewarded for her efforts. In 2010 she received a $15,000 grant from the HUGGIES® MomInspired™ Grant Program (see chapter 6).

There are three components to her product: a sleep sack, a plush bear, and a programmable sound module. Because each comes from a different vendor, it became difficult to find the right people to manufacture each piece. She tried to keep the product "Made in the USA," but it was much more cost-effective to buy the pieces overseas. However, with the language barrier, different time zones, and large minimum quantities needed, selecting vendors turned out to be a time-consuming process that took over six months. She didn't give up. "I am using a manufacturer in Australia for the sleep sacks, a plush bear designer in Malaysia,

and a sound module vendor in China," she says. Once each component arrived in the United States, she had to hire a seamstress to put all the pieces together. The finished product then had to be safety tested.

McCoy has advice for new moms trying to balance working at home and a new baby. "It will be hard, and you may find yourself not able to allocate time in a given day, but don't despair," she advises. "Try to set minor goals each day, and check off each task once it is completed. I find that if I break down goals into small steps, they are easier to achieve and I don't feel so overwhelmed."

On her blog, Inspired By Savannah (ctmomreviews.blogspot.com), McCoy features other mom entrepreneurs and shares their stories of balancing work and home life.

Learning Opportunities

Technology is taking over all of our lives, and even the youngest members of the family can be affected. Today a fussy toddler is likely to be distracted with a children's video on Mom's iPhone instead of a cookie.

When reviewing the decorating show, *Ask Genevieve,* on HGTV, *Entertainment Weekly* magazine made a joke that could actually come true. The show featured expectant parents who asked how to design a playroom that could also be used as a home office. The reviewer remarked, "Well, it is important to teach kids how to use Excel as early as possible."

Our children will live in a technology-driven world as adults. The smart phones and tablet computers that dazzle us now will be relics to them. You could conclude that it is in their best interest to learn as much as they can about technology now to give them a head start.

A survey that involved 2,200 mothers of children aged two to five in the United States, Canada, Europe, Japan, and Australia offered a list of technology skills and life skills and asked which ones their child had mastered. There were some very surprising results: 69 percent of children could use a computer mouse, but only 11 percent could tie their own shoes. Fifty-eight percent knew how to play a computer game, but only 20 percent could ride a bike. Older mothers seemed to fare a little better. Mothers over thirty-five were slightly better at teaching life skills; 40 percent of their

When you are a work-at-home mom, you have to expect the unexpected. Just when you think you have everything under control, you have to deal with a new challenge. A break in your routine is not always a bad thing.

The Sounds of Summer

Summer means two whole months of no school, hot weather, and high expectations. There is no doubt that this can be a special challenge. "Can I have a drink?" "Can we go to the pool?" "There's nothing to do!" These are the sounds of summer for work-at-home moms. Some mothers hear their infant's fussy cry or the heavy silence of a toddler getting into lots of trouble. All of these sounds can feel like little pins being jabbed at you when you are trying to concentrate on an important project or just carry out your day-to-day business.

When we choose to work at home, that includes working at home during the summer. But you can arrange your day to make time for at least one interesting activity each day. Make lunch a picnic in the backyard or a park, for example. There are more daylight hours, so Dad or other special people in their lives can play ball with the kids or take the baby for a calming walk in the evening. That will give you a break and help fill the fun quotient for the day.

Lots of love and lots of hard work are a winning combination. Plan ahead for the lazy, crazy days of summer. You might not be able to take a full vacation, but you deserve to have some fun too!

Snow Days and Sick Days

You never know when your child might get sick or when school will be closed because of snow. You can pretty much count on those days to fall when you have a deadline to meet or an important client telephone call to make. If you plan ahead, you can initiate your plan instantly to keep things running smoothly.

Keep a stash of special DVDs and games that are only brought out when there is an unexpected child care glitch. I don't believe in using TV as a babysitter, but in an unexpected situation, it is a tool that can be used. And there is nothing wrong with winding down in front of an educational or entertaining show after an active day.

If your child is old enough to understand, explain your situation and encourage him to be a partner who wants to help not an inconvenience who will do everything to sabotage you. In others words, communicate. You will be rewarded for the work you are doing, so it is only right that he can share in your rewards. Celebrate at the end of the day with a special dinner and maybe even go online and buy a small toy.

Sometimes the best thing you can do is just surrender to your circumstances. Your child will recover and school will reopen. Go play in the snow or bring your ill child a tray and read stories and cuddle all day. Some of my fondest memories of my childhood include the good care my mother took of me when I was sick. If you think back to the big snowstorms and sick days of your childhood, you will remember those days. Give your child an experience that she can look back on as an adult, and she just might pass them on to her children.

kids knew how to write their own name. Only 35 percent of kids whose mothers were under thirty-five knew how.

What does this all mean? Well first, I don't think we should panic. The differences between two-year-olds and five-year-olds are great and I'm not sure they should be included in the same group. There are not many children under three who can tie their shoes whether they use technology or not. And we could blame Velcro shoe closures on lack of lacing skills. Many children don't learn how to ride a two-wheel bike until they are at least five or six, and that is not new.

The children of work-at-home moms learn life skills a lot earlier than other kids do because they get a lot of supervised independence. Here is a good example:

One work-at-home mom had a three-year-old son who repeatedly interrupted her work time with requests for a snack or a drink. Instead of getting upset, this mom created a drawer in her refrigerator that contained juice boxes, fruit, and other healthy snacks. She also kept a small basket in her work area that had small prepackaged crackers, cereal, fruit, and raisins. Her son was allowed to get his own snacks and drinks—after asking permission—and he felt very independent and proud of himself. To add to that feeling of pride, this mom also assigned her little boy "jobs" that he could do to help her each day and a child-size desk in her office where he

could "work." Instead of whining for attention and feeling ignored, he gained a sense of pride and accomplishment along with good nutrition.

There is a risk and a benefit to almost everything we do in life. It is up to each of us to create balance and an atmosphere of learning in our homes. Having the opportunity to observe a home business use technology can offer your children an insider's view of business that other children don't have available to them. There will probably be more technology in a home business household, too. And that's a good thing—so good that many children who have work-at-home moms develop a good understanding of money and entrepreneurial skills at a level beyond their years.

Working the Work-At-Home Mom Shift

When you work at home with children, you want to develop ways to weave your work into and around each child's needs instead of making him or her adapt to you. We all want our children to feel as though they are our most important priority. And these years will go by so quickly. You don't want to spend your time trying to avoid spending time with your children. You need a work plan that will give you enough time to work while caring for your children. If you leave your work time to chance, you will end up not working at all because something or someone else will always grab your attention. This may seem impossible, but it can be done.

Many work-at-home moms feel it is necessary to take care of their children by themselves 100 percent of the time, because that's why they chose to work at home. If that is the way you feel, sure, you can take care of your children yourself or only share duties with your spouse or partner. It is not easy, but it is doable. There are many different types of schedules you could use to make that choice work. If possible, you should try to keep the same work schedule every day so that your family members will get used to you working at that time. There are several different types of schedules you can try, or you can create your own by combining parts of each of these recommendations:

- **The Sleep and/or School Solution:** This technique is the one used by most mothers, especially at the beginning of their work-at-home career. You schedule your work hours for when your children are either asleep or in school. That is what I did when my children were young, and I worked many nights until 3 a.m., when the house was blissfully quiet. Some moms might choose to go to sleep early and get up at 4 or 5 a.m. to get work done. If that

sounds like a difficult day, it is. But when you are running on the adrenaline that building a business can give you, it is possible to sustain.

When my children were young, my husband also handled the hours of dinner through bath- and bedtime. I didn't feel guilty because he got to spend one-on-one time with them and develop an even closer relationship. If you don't have anyone to help you, it will be harder, but you can still follow this sleep/school work schedule.

- **The Short-Spurt Solution:** This method encourages you to look for opportune moments and use them to tend to business, not housework or anything else. Is the baby playing happily in his play yard? Use that time to send an e-mail. Grandma comes for a visit? Excuse yourself for thirty minutes and do some work. It helps if you have work you can easily start and stop at will. If you have deadlines to meet, this way of working can only be used in addition to working while the kids are sleeping or in school.
- **The Work/Play Solution:** This method involves making promises to your children . . . and keeping them. You tell your child, "Mommy is going to work until Sesame Street is over and then I promise we will go outside." Then you do exactly as you promised. When you alternate work time and playtime, it makes it easier on the kids and they will be more willing to cooperate.

When you are making the transition between work and mothering, take a few moments to put things away and make some notes to remind yourself where you left off and what you plan to do next. That way you will be able to jump right in without wasting time the next time you have an opportunity to work.

Supermom Doesn't Live Here: Getting the Help You Need

As your business grows, it may become necessary to work more hours than you originally anticipated. There is no shame if you decide to get some help with child care while you work at home. In fact it can be better for the children if there is someone who is ready, willing, and able to respond to them while you are very busy doing business. There is also no reason to tough it out when just a little help could make all the difference in your productivity and stress level. If the child care takes place in

your home, it will be easier for you to monitor what is going on with your children. You will have the opportunity to have lunch with them and interact throughout the day. And being able to closely monitor any paid help with your children will also help ease your thoughts about what kind of care your children are getting.

Some moms choose to get help with their business instead of getting help with child care, and that is a valid choice that can work. Even better, hire a mother's helper who is capable of helping with your business or your child, as the need arises. A college student who loves children and has an interest in business would be a great choice.

If it is not financially feasible to hire someone to help with your business or your children, there are alternatives. Consider the following ideas:

- Ask the grandparents, aunts and uncles, or another person who loves your children to spend time with them for one to two hours one day each week.
- Ask up to five other moms to create a reciprocal child care arrangement. Each day, one mom watches all of the children and the others get time off. This will allow you some uninterrupted time to work up to four days a week.
- Ask older children to watch younger siblings and behave themselves during a set period of time each day. Set them up with snacks and activities and put them on the honor system. Pay your child with special privileges and lots of positive reinforcement in return for being your special helper.
- Create a home-away-from-home work plan. All you really need is a smart phone, a laptop, or your favorite device. Take it with you when you take your child to the doctor, gymnastics, or another activity that will involve waiting. Use that time to make telephone calls, send e-mail, do research, or catch up on your reading.
- Do you belong to a gym that has free child care? After your workout, you can't leave the gym while your child is being cared for but you might be able to find a comfortable place to use your home-away-from-home work plan. Save up the right kind of tasks so you know exactly what to concentrate on.

Note: Make your car a phone-free zone. Even with a hands-free device, it is too distracting to drive and talk. Texting while driving is just plain dumb. You can use your car time to sing songs and interact with your children instead. For more information and to sign a no phone zone pledge, go to www.Oprah.com/packages/no-phone-zone.html.

What to Do When Things Are Not Going as Planned

You may have thought that working at home would be a wonderful way to manage mothering and work, and now everything seems to be falling apart. Your business could be suffering because you spend too much time away from it. Your children could feel ignored and are constantly whining for attention. Instead of making them feel loved, you fear that they feel rejected. What should you do?

First, don't panic. Every work-at-home mom goes through stages that make her feel like she is a failure on all levels of her life. Moms usually take on more of the child-raising responsibility and then try to work the rest of their lives around the needs of their children. It is possible to feel exasperated, whether you have a home business or not.

Moms who work outside their home and away from their children for eight to ten hours a day can feel the same kind of frustration because they are away for forty to fifty hours a week and can't spend time exclusively with their children when they get home. Mom probably has to cook dinner, clean the kitchen, wash clothes, and get ready for the next day. She might even have brought work home from the office or have important calls and e-mail to answer. Many young children are cranky at the end of their day, and when that is the only time you get to be with them, it is hard to create a meaningful connection and make up for lost time.

Let's face it: There are no easy ways to manage mothering and work. Each mother has to make the choice that feels right to her. So, unless you are willing and able to give up working completely and just stay home with your kids, compromises have to be made. I and millions of other moms believe that working at home puts all of our diverse responsibilities in one place, making it easier to manage it all. If you agree, stand proudly in your decision and learn how to make things work the way you want.

Small Changes Equal Big Results

You can influence your children and others in your life, but when you come right down to it, the only person you can truly control is yourself. Use that power to create the happy work-at-home life you really want. Here are some changes to consider:

1. Use the time you have. When you know that you will be able to work during nap time or while the kids are in school, use that time to actually work. Don't clean the house or even think about checking e-mail or looking at Facebook.

Turn off the TV. If you give work your full attention, you will get more done and your stress level will go down.

2. Plan ahead. Know exactly what you will be working on so that you can get your work started right away.

3. Prioritize. Work on the most important project when you have uninterrupted time to work.

4. Make a note. If you think about something else you have to do while you are working, write it down and then get back to work. You won't forget, and your work time won't be interrupted.

5. Be proud of your accomplishments. Don't worry about the work you haven't finished. Reward yourself for work well done.

6. Take a break. After every work period, take some time and do a child-centered activity to balance your day.

7. Stay positive. If your child sees you stressing out and acting stressed, he will model your behavior. Keep a smile on your face and let your love of working at home shine through.

8. Make a strong commitment. When things become difficult, remember your goals and the promises you made to yourself, and find a way to solve the problem. Without commitment, you might be willing to give up when the going gets tough.

9. Learn to delegate. If you try to do everything yourself, you raise your chances of burning out. Instead, delegate the work tasks you do not enjoy doing and let others help you, even if they don't do things exactly as you would like them.

10. Consider the value of one hour. Horace Mann said, "Lost between sunrise and sunset, twelve golden hours each set with sixty diamond minutes. No reward offered—they are gone forever." If you waste one hour each day, that is seven hours per week, and 364 hours in a year. How much work could you get done in 364 hours? You have more time than you think you do.

You can be a catalyst for positive change. A single shift in your behavior can positively affect what the other members of your family say and do. In the end we bring about the change that we expect. Expect a happy family and a money-making business and you will automatically make the moves that will give you exactly what you want.

Showing Moms How to Manage It All

Tara Gentile is a self-described "philosopher of creative living and DIY culture and lifestyle design expert." Her slogan is, "Empowering passionate people to produce and profit." And that is exactly what she does. I would call her an unconventional life and business coach who also writes and creates everything from websites to crafts.

If anyone can help you meet your goals and manage work and family, it is Tara. She is dedicated to helping others to live a more creative life through "a generous helping of practical philosophy, a few kicks in the pants, and a signed permission slip to reach your goals."

Asked how she manages it all, she admits that it was difficult for her at first because she considers herself a "full-time worker/full-time mom." Her husband is the primary caretaker of their two-year-old daughter as Tara works all day in her home office marketing, creating content, and coaching, among other things. She explains, "I wasn't interested in cutting back my hours and I knew my daughter would be fine even if Mommy worked. So I did. And I have." Her family spends evenings together, and then she sometimes goes back to work after her daughter goes to bed. Her business supports her family.

Tara believes that productivity is all about focus. "When I let my focus slide—maybe because I've been at my desk too long or because I've gotten sucked into the social web—I become less productive." If that happens, she looks for a change of scenery and minimizes distractions by writing lists and clear goals.

To moms who are struggling with their goals, she says, "Just get started. Forget the right way and do it your own way. You'll learn as you go—and that will serve you better than any textbook. Create and share, create and share. Follow what feels good and push yourself at the edges of your comfort."

For the inspiration you need to create the life and the business you want, visit Tara at www.TaraGentile.com. To read her blog where "creatives converse, connect, and commune" go to www.ScoutieGirl.com. See appendix B for Tara's e-books.

Reader Q & A

Q: How do I keep track of my goals and make them a reality?

A: Goals are good, but really a goal is just a wish without a plan and a deadline. To get what you want, your goals should be very specific. Don't say you want to earn money at home. Say exactly what you want to do, such as become a virtual assistant. Your goal must also be realistic. Don't say you will earn $10,000 next month if you only earned $200 this month. Give each goal a deadline and create a list of baby steps that you can do one at a time to get what you want .

Whether you have a huge home office or a little nook, you deserve to have a comfortable and inspiring place to work. The more you like your surroundings, the more productive you will be. So take a little time to plan a work space that is attractive and practical.

I share my home office with a bossy lovebird who comments on my every move and my little Havanese dog, who sleeps by my feet while I work, even though he'd rather be running around. I also have a place for my grandson to play, a recliner chair with a laptop desk, a television that is always on, and two computers. A six-foot-long work table serves as my desk. I recently added a large six-drawer bureau with modern glass-front drawers I bought at Ikea. Each drawer contains one category of items: paper and stationery in one drawer; my Kindle, my camera, batteries, and extra wires and tech-related parts in another drawer, paper and pads in another drawer and so on. My desk doesn't have drawers, so the overflow is organized in another bureau drawer. I also have shelves filled with books, pictures of my family, and some of the Raggedy Ann dolls and figurines I collect. I sometimes dream of a sleek, high-tech office with clean lines and no piles of research on my desk, but this is the home office that reflects who I am. It makes me happy, and so I am productive.

What would your perfect work space look like? It's always better if your office can be in a spare bedroom or another space that is yours alone to convert to a home office. But that is not always possible. Even if the space you have for a home office is small or nonexistent, you can dream big when you are making plans. It is possible to scale down your vision to fit your dreams.

You can create a cozy and inviting home office in many unexpected and space-saving ways such as:

- In a corner
- In a closet

- In a converted armoire
- Under a stairway
- On a fold-down shelf attached to a wall
- On a narrow table against the back of your couch

The type of business you start and the equipment you use will also influence your home office choices.

Going Wireless

All some work-at-home moms need is a laptop and a cell phone. They can work anywhere. If that is the lifestyle you want, create a tote bag and/or rolling cart to carry your office supplies. If you are at home, a mobile connection can allow you to work outside while the kids play or in the family room where your presence may be enough to create a feeling of closeness. As you will find out in the following pages, there are some surprising choices for business storage that you can use.

Do You Need It or Want It?

If your funds are limited, this is first question to ask yourself when stocking your home office: "Do I need this or do I just want it?" It's more than OK to want the coolest computer or the latest iPad to work on at the playground. Work should be fun, right? But if you are starting your business on a shoestring, you have to be realistic and only buy the items that are essential to produce the work that will impress your target audience and produce sales. As the money comes in, you can reward yourself with one of your dream items at a time. You want your office to be functional and appealing on start-up, and you can achieve that on a budget.

Style and Function on a Budget

Color and light can create the right atmosphere for working. Paint and a few accessories won't cost much and can add so much to your surroundings. Here are some tips to help you get started:

- Choose a spot with windows. If that isn't possible, include a task lamp and ambient light from other lamps. Good lighting will help prevent eyestrain and keep your spirits high.
- Color is key. Paint the walls in your favorite color and put some meaningful photos and paintings on the wall. A beautiful mug to hold pens and pencils, some flowers, or an accent rug can brighten up your surroundings.

- You don't want to risk hurting your back or developing a repetitive strain injury, so it is important to consider ergonomics, which focuses on design that fits the human body. Select your chair with care. Every expert advises that the best item to spend your money on is a good chair, and I agree. Buy the highest quality you can afford. You will be spending hours in your office chair, so it is worth a few extra dollars to be ergonomically correct and put you in a comfortable position for the work you are doing. Your chair should swivel easily and have settings for seat height and lumbar support.
- Whether you are using a laptop or desktop computer, position the screen at eye level to avoid eyestrain.

A Child-Friendly Home Office

How should you handle working at home with children? The answer: Close the door to your office and instruct the children not to bother you unless someone is bleeding or the house is on fire. In an article written by Mike Michalowicz on American Express Open (www.openforum.com/articles/13-ways-to-make-your-office-space-more-efficient-mike-michalowicz) titled "13 Ways to Make Your Office Space More Efficient," number six is: Keep the Kids Out. The author explains that you must make your office off-limits to your children because "The last thing you need is to be tripping over toys or having important work items misplaced or drawn on." It is doubtful that many work-at-home moms would share this harsh point of view.

Yes, there are other reasons to work at home besides spending more time with your children. It is more affordable and convenient to start a business at home. However, if your children are going to get an office door slammed in their faces with a warning to stay away every day of their young lives, it would be better if you worked someplace else. What these authors don't understand is that just being in the same room or even the same house as mom or dad while she or he is working has value to the child. It is not always necessary to have face-to-face interaction to create an emotionally secure atmosphere.

Clearly you don't want your child destroying your office or spending time outside your office door creating emergencies that will warrant your attention. Like everything else in life, there is a compromise point of view. Rules and regulations for being in the office are needed, and your child should to be taught *in advance* exactly what behavior is expected. It is so much easier to get good behavior in any

situation if your child is prepared and told what is expected of him *before* he is in the situation. Don't wait for bad behavior that has to be corrected. Time in Mom's office should be special and satisfying for everyone. This is easy to say, not so easy to do, especially if you don't have a dedicated office.

Safety First, Then Fun

Your office can be arranged so that you don't have to say no anymore. Try adding a designated child area equipped with a "desk" and age-appropriate supplies: paper, tape, safe scissors, discarded mail, glue, and washable markers are a good start. Add a toy computer learning game and other fun things that your child only gets access to while in the office. A DVD player with child-friendly movies to watch could also come in handy.

All of these things are helpful, but they don't address the safety of your child . . . and your equipment. Please consider the following safety tips:

- **Electrical cords.** The goal is to keep plugs plugged in and fingers or other objects out. Standard outlet inserts can do a good job with unused plugs. Try moving heavy furniture to block the view of outlets with plugs. If that is not possible, Safety 1st (Safety1st.com) makes a variety of covers for plugs and surge protectors. If you are adding outlets, it might be a good idea to put them at your desk level for easy access and to protect little fingers. Loose electrical cords are not only an eyesore but a danger. Try to keep equipment as close to the outlet as possible and use cord tubes or an organizer attached to the back of your desk.
- **Trash.** Make sure your trash can has a locking cover. Discarded objects in an office environment can be sharp and dangerous. Give your children their own trash can so they stay away from yours.
- **Data loss.** Don't let your child play with your computer even when you are not using it. You could lose important work files. Use a password to keep your screen locked. Protect CD-ROM trays from little fingers and old crackers they may want to stuff inside.

Getting Organized

Would being a little more organized simplify your life? Absolutely! The good news is that you can make just a few changes in your natural work style to help you create a home office that works for you and accommodates your needs. Organizing is accomplished from the inside out . . . and the outside in.

Professional Home Office Designs You Can Use

Luis Caicedo (LuisCaicedo.com) is a self-taught designer based in New York City who specializes in small spaces. He mixes traditional elements with modern accents put together regardless of their monetary value. "I love to pair many unique combinations as long as there is an honest dialogue between the styles and pieces," he says, "because most of us have to 'carve out' a home office from our existing dwellings."

Luis believes that, in the beginning, a home office could be as basic as a desk somewhere in a corner, but needs will change as the business grows. He uses decorative storage solutions from boxes to baskets to solve storage dilemmas so that the flow of the home is not disrupted while creating a peaceful, organized environment. He advises, "All you need is your imagination, knowing your sense of style, and how you want things to be organized. After all, this is your own space."

Here are some samples of home offices that Luis has designed with his notes. Use them to be inspired as you create your work-at-home-mom work space.

This office belongs to a mom who is a lawyer. She just gave birth to twins, so she moved her business home. Carved out of the middle of a living room, this is a more spacious office. The wall was created to separate the space from the rest of the house and provide shelving. The "window" in the middle of the installation creates a sense of openness, allowing light to come through.

A New York City mom uses this office for her work as a writer. She only needed laptop space and a few office supplies. The table and chair were discovered on Cape Cod. They were paired with custom shelving and painted in distressed white. The custom window seat and lower portion of the shelving house office supplies and a printer. This office was placed next to the window to enjoy the romantic and inspiring city view.

Quite possibly the world's smallest office, this space measures only three feet by four feet and is ten feet tall. It was a former closet. The door was removed, and the entrance was taken to the ceiling to create a sense of space. Because of its size, order is needed and not a square inch of space is left unused. There are drawers for office supplies, and recycle containers keep it all handy yet stowed away. All custom-built pieces and walls were painted the same color to make the space appear bigger. In such a small space, lighting is key. It has task lighting and a dramatic ceiling light to create a warm, inviting environment.

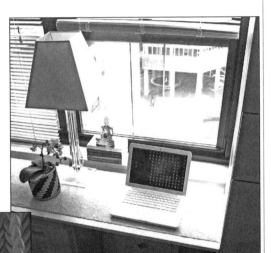

This sophisticated office was created to take advantage of the great view. A custom desk was built from wall to wall to create a surface that allows paperwork to be spread out and a laptop space. White surfaces and cabinets are used to store all the office supplies and electronics to the side and the base of the desk. Modern furnishings and ethnic accessories complement the decor so it flows with the rest of the house.

The owner of an advertising/creative business is using this office after being laid off. It is in the kitchen area of a small Manhattan apartment. The few decorative items carry some of the motifs found around the rest of the house. The desk was found at the Metropolitan Opera Thrift Shop. The shelves were custom-made.

If you have a small home office with very little floor space, use your vertical space. Put shelves or cabinets up on the wall. This is a good technique for moms with young children too, because it gives a lot of space to keep things out of the reach of little hands.

An organizing principle advocated by most organizers is simple to understand and easy to implement: Keep like things together. Just as I described my office bureau, keep all the paper, all the small electronics and parts, all the office supplies together in one place so that you will know exactly where to find what you are looking for.

When my children were little, I would take them with me to Staples, the office superstore. I would tell them that this is Mommy's toy store, and then they understood why I loved browsing the aisles. I've always told my husband that he is lucky that he has a wife who lusts after pens, notebooks, and organizers instead of jewelry and shoes. I just love office supplies and office furniture, but I've learned that no matter how much I think that new item will change my life, it hardly ever does. In fact the items I purchase often become more clutter to manage.

Organizing expert Julie Morgenstern tells her readers to get organized first, and then find the proper containers for each situation. In her classic book, *Organizing from the Inside Out*, she uses the acronym SPACE, which stands for **S**ort, **P**urge, **A**ssign a Home, **C**ontainerize, **E**qualize.

Surprising Storage Space

To keep your immediate work space free of items that you are not using on a daily basis, you can store like things together in containers out of your immediate work space. Here are some examples:

- Underneath your bed. Roomy rolling bins that fit underneath a bed provide great storage. Depending on the number of beds in your home, that might be all the storage space you need.
- Create a table. A two-drawer file cabinet is short enough to be used as a nightstand or side table. Just cover with a pretty fabric, and no one will be the wiser.
- Convert a bookshelf. Covered baskets, fabric, or leather-covered boxes can be placed on shelves in your living area without making the whole house look like an office.

You might not want to deal with recordkeeping, taxes, and business planning, but please don't skip this chapter. Home business is real business, so you should know the fundamentals. Ignoring them would be like building a house without a foundation.

Especially during your first year in business, you have nothing to fear and a lot to gain by attending to details. But don't worry, I will make it all easy to understand and even easier to do.

Choosing the Best Name for Your Business

Your business name is one of the most important decisions you have to make. The public's first perception of your business will be your business name. Cute and unusual names can give you a chuckle and attract some attention. But a cute name will not necessarily help your customers to understand what you have to offer. There are always exceptions: *Google* was a nonsensical word until it became the name of a search engine. Now it has become so much a part of the fabric of society that it is used as a verb, such as in the sentence, "You should Google him." Other companies have tried unusual or made up words as business names. Some have succeeded, like Twitter. More have failed. Also avoid puns that your think are amusing but others will not understand.

Remembering that your website address will probably be the same as your business name, it is time to start your search engines. First, write down every word you can think of that relates to your business. Many of these words will also be keywords that are so important to promoting your business. They are the words that your potential customer will type into search engines to find what you are selling. Don't think too hard as you write down your words. Just let them flow.

Take your page full of words and start to match them up and see how they look and sound together. You might even coin a new word by combining two words into one, like *infopreneur*. As you go through this process, keep in mind the image you want to convey and the wants and needs of your target audience.

When you have some possibilities, start searching for them in search engines. You might find another word or a way of phrasing that you could incorporate into your business name. You will also see similar names or titles that you may or may not like. As you come closer to choosing a name, you have more things to consider:

- Don't choose a name that is too long, confusing, or hard to pronounce.
- Choose a name that appeals to your target audience. Is there a familiar or comforting word that will give them a pleasant memory or cause them to respond on a personal or emotional level?
- Leave room for changes. You may just be selling socks today, but calling your business Sally's Socks limits your option to add other types of items.
- Before you finalize your decision, check to see if other businesses on either a local or national level have the same name.
- If you are a consultant a freelancer, using your own name as your business and domain name has some advantages. For one, you won't have to get a fictitious name or Doing Business As (DBA) certificate that is required if you use any name besides your own. You will also need a DBA in order to get a business checking account. Check with your local city or county clerk to learn the requirements where you live.

Will your business name also be the domain name for your blog or website? If the answer is yes, you have even more options to consider. Your business name is important, but your domain name can eventually become even more important, and your potential audience will be required to actually type the URL to visit your site.

Choosing the Right Domain Name

The domain name you choose for your website, blog, or sales page is very important. Here are some points to keep in mind:

- Use your business name if it works as a clear domain name.
- Your domain name should be short and easy to remember.
- Do not use hyphens.

- Choose a .com. Most people assume that a website address ends with .com (which stands for .commercial) and that is the most common suffix they will type.
- Put keywords for your topic in your domain name, and put those keywords first. However, don't just register a string of words. Your domain name should describe your site.
- Don't give up if your domain name is already taken. You can change it just enough so that it will be available to you by adding an *s* or an extra word.
- Conversely, register all of the possible options of your domain name so that others cannot register a name close to yours.

When you are ready, go to www.WonderfulWebsiteStore.com and start typing in your possibilities to see if they are available. You can register one or more domain names there for only $9.99 each, and it will be hosted for free until your blog or website is ready. Every website and blog has to be hosted. Hosting packages are very affordable there and start at $3.99 per month.

Your Graphic Image

Once you are 100 percent sure what your business name and/or domain name is, it is time to create a graphic image to enhance the words. Hiring a professional graphic artist to create a logo for your business name will give the logo extra appeal and help convey your desired image. Choosing the right artist for you is important. Remember these points:

1. The artist you choose should breathe life into your concept not try to change it. You need to come up with some ideas to discuss.
2. An artist should give you at least three possible logos to choose from and unlimited requests for changes. Don't be afraid to keep asking for changes until you get the result you want.
3. Get price quotes and a promised date for delivery up front.

One important note: You have carefully chosen keywords in your business and domain names so that the search engines will give you a good placement. Don't put your name only into a graphic image on your website or blog, because when the search engines spider your site they will skip over the graphics. If your header or logo has your business name contained within the image, make sure it is written out, too.

Your Business Structure

When you start your home business, you will have to choose from four basic forms of business ownership. Read these descriptions and you should have no problem choosing the one that is right for you.

Sole Proprietorship

This is the one used most often by home business owners. It is the easiest business structure to start and terminate. As a sole proprietor, you will have total control of all the business assets. You will also be responsible for all of the debts.

Partnership

When you first start a home business, it often feels more comfortable to have a partner to work with you. But did you know that your personal assets could be seized if your business partner makes independent decisions and puts your company into debt? In a partnership, each partner can make decisions independently. It won't protect you financially, but if you are determined to work with a partner, create a partnership agreement that clarifies each partner's role.

Corporation

This type of business structure is the most complicated to form and maintain, but it also gives you the most personal protection. A corporation is a group of people who join together to create a legal entity that is separate and can operate as one body. The only risk to the owners or shareholders is the money they initially invest. You cannot be held personally responsible for the debts or liabilities of the business, unless you sign a separate personal guarantee. More important, forming a corporation protects you from being sued personally if you have a business that creates the potential for liability.

Limited Liability Company

A limited liability company (LLC) will give you some personal liability protection without all of the requirements of a corporation. An LLC protects its members from paying the debts of the company. A single member can pay taxes like a sole proprietor. A group can be taxed like a partnership. To start an LLC, file a certificate of formation with your state.

Accepting Credit Card Payments

To be successful, a home business needs to accept credit cards. If you are selling online, there are good solutions for you. You can use PayPal for most sales. Your customers do not have to be PayPal members. They just need a credit or debit card. If you are selling a digital product like an e-book, you can still sell it directly through PayPal, or, if you use Clickbank or another fulfillment method, these companies will process the credit cards and put your share in your account.

However, if you are selling in person, by telephone, or through the mail, you need the ability to accept credit cards directly from your customer. It is difficult to get a merchant account directly from a credit card company, but there is a solution. It is called Merchant Warehouse.

Merchant Warehouse specializes in merchant accounts, and it is not difficult to be approved. You need to have a business based in the United States, a business tax ID number, and a U.S. bank account. If you have all of these things, the Merchant Warehouse approval rate is 99 percent. And you can receive your approval within twenty-four hours. But it is not just the easy and fast approval that makes Merchant Warehouse my recommendation to help you process credit card sales.

When you receive your merchant account from Merchant Warehouse, the company guarantees the lowest cost for credit card machines and credit card processing. The company was founded in 1998 on the principle that businesses should be able to operate at a reasonable rate backed by great customer service. The company's contracts are on a month-to-month basis, so you won't get caught in a long-term contract.

To get a merchant account with no application fees, set-up fees, or cancellation/termination fees, call Merchant Warehouse at (866) 761-5531 or go to www.MerchantWarehouse.com.

Easy Business Planning

There are two basic types of business plans: formal and informal. When you start a business, you definitely need a plan that you create for your eyes only. But do you need a formal business plan? If you plan to try to get funding from a bank or other loans source, you definitely need a formal business plan. There are resources online and listed in the appendix to help you write a formal plan. But don't let writing a

formal business plan stop you from moving ahead with your home business. Moms tend to bootstrap their start-ups but you don't need to get formal at the start of your business.

Forget about structure and requirements for now and just sit down and write twenty-five words that explain your business concept (sometimes known as the "elevator pitch"). Putting your business description in twenty-five words or less helps you explain it to others quickly and easily. Then write some more about your products or services and why there is a need for them. Write a description of your target customers and your plans for reaching them. What benefits will your idea give them? This will be a growing and changing plan and one you can refer to when you go off track.

When you are ready to do more formal business planning, you will have to explain how your experience and talents qualify you to run a successful business of this sort. You will also be required to project financial statements of revenue and profits or losses for the next three years. For more specific information go to the Small Business Administration's website at www.sba.gov.

Taxes Made Easy

Many uninformed people avoid starting a home business or, even worse, promoting their home business, because they are afraid of the tax implications. In actuality the tax advantages of owning a home-based business are many. In your first years in business many start-up costs are tax deductible, and you might actually pay less tax than if you were an employee who usually gets 20 to 30 percent taken off the top. As a home business owner, you are legally able to deduct every business expense. That means the cost of your new computer and cell phone could be deductible.

If you are a sole proprietor, you will file Schedule C, Profit and Loss from Business, or if your business had gross receipts of $25,000 or less and business expenses of $2,500 or less, you can file Schedule C-EZ, a simplified form. You just file your personal income taxes and attach this form. If you have profit of $400 or more, you also must file Schedule SE, Self-Employment Tax. This is a combination of Social Security and Medicare taxes.

Unless your home business is an instant sensation, it is likely that you will have enough deductions in your first year to get a refund. In fact your business expenses could even lower your personal taxes or increase your refund.

Home Office Tax Deduction

If you have a home office that you use exclusively for business you may qualify for a home office tax deduction. The question is, if you do qualify for this deduction, should you take it? You need the facts before you make this decision.

When the IRS says "exclusive use," it literally means that you cannot use your home office for any other purpose than working. However, you don't need an entire room devoted to business to qualify for the deduction. You could designate one part of a room and you don't even need to create a physical separation to qualify. The square footage of your home office in relation to the rest of your home will determine the size of your deduction. The cost of furniture, paint, and rugs can also be deducted, but your deductions cannot exceed the income from your business.

If you own a day-care business, you can deduct the business expenses for that part of your home even if you use the same space for nonbusiness purposes.

If you qualify for and take a home office deduction, should you take it? Some experts say that this deduction is a "red flag" that might trigger an audit. But even if you have no fear of an audit consider this: The amount you claim over the years will lower the amount you can claim you paid for your home when you sell it. The difference between what you paid for your home and the amount you sell your home for is taxable profit. In other words, the taxes you avoid now could increase your tax bill later.

For more information consult a tax preparer who specializes in small business taxes. You can also go to irs.gov and get Publication 587, "Business Use of Your Home," and IRS form 8829 to compute the actual amount you could deduct.

Easy Record Keeping

There are a few basic and easy financial steps I suggest you take when you start a home business.

1. You should open a business checking account and keep your personal and business funds separate.
2. Dedicate one credit card to business expenses. In the past I would have told you to open a business credit card. However, all the laws that have been

passed to protect you from credit card companies don't apply to business credit cards. If you intend to pay off your balances in full each month, you could get an American Express Card. For balances that you will carry and pay off, dedicate one of your personal credit cards to business activity only.

3. Use a planner to write down your daily expenses and income, and at the end of each week, write down the total. Besides your income and expenses, write down your marketing efforts. Make sure your calendar book is large enough and use different color ink for each type of entry so you can see it at a glance.

4. Get a monthly accordion file and file your receipts or notes to remember each month. Save your bank and credit card statements, too.

If this method seems a little primitive to you, you are correct. I feel it is important to get a real hands-on feel for your income and outflow with a hands-on system like this. If you prefer, you can keep your records online using Quicken and create spreadsheets to evaluate your business activity. Or you can use both methods in tandem.

If you do these simple things, you will have all the information you need at tax time. I strongly advise you to have a CPA do your personal and business taxes. Her fees will be tax deductible the following year. Just make sure that you choose an accountant who specializes in small business so that you know it is being done correctly. Inform yourself to make sure all tax deductions are being taken. Using a professional who knows you and your business will save you money in the long run. If you try to do your taxes by yourself, you might pay more than you need to pay.

Know Your Zone

If you live in a residential neighborhood, you need to check with your county clerk to learn the local zoning restrictions before you start your home business. If your business just involves working online, you shouldn't have a problem. However, if you do anything that outwardly lets your neighbors know that you are running a home business there could be trouble.

Answer yes or no to the following questions:

1. Will you have people coming and going during the day?
2. Will huge trucks be making frequent deliveries?
3. Will you receive enough mail to fill a mailbag each day?

4. Will you be operating an auto repair shop or a retail store? Will you have on-site employees?
5. Will you create any unusual smells or unpleasant noises?

If your answer is no to each of these questions, you probably don't have to worry about zoning regulations.

Above all, make sure you have good relations with your neighbors. You don't want one of them to report a problem with you to the zoning board. If you honor their desire to live in a pleasant, residential neighborhood, most people will not try to stop you from earning a living in your home.

10 Every Mom Needs at Least One Website

It is important for every business to have a website. The corner store, the giant retailer, the restaurant, the mom just starting a home business—each one needs a website. Any business that does not have a website today is sending the message that it doesn't care about maximizing communication with its customers.

Even if you do not sell anything online, you are selling your business image—your brand—every single day. How many times have you looked up the menu of a restaurant online before you decided where to go out to eat? How many times have you researched price and availability of an appliance before going out to shop in person? How many times have you searched for a business and, when you did not find them online, you thought a little bit less of that business?

If you don't have your own website, you have no place to send people who want to learn more about your business. Mailing them a brochure just won't cut it. Some companies (even very large ones) think that if they have a Facebook page they don't need a website. Wrong. While it is fabulous to interact with your customers on Facebook, it does not give you the prestige or the ability to sell that your own website gives you.

Suppose you own a child care business. You only take care of three children and some drop-ins. Do you need a website? Yes, you do. Current or potential clients can go to your website and be impressed at your appealing and informational content. You can have articles about the issues that most parents face when using child care, such as dealing with separation anxiety. You can post your hours. You can put your photo there and more pictures of the colorful and bright room where the children play. With parent's permission, you can show happy children playing and interacting with you. Children grow out of child care. They become school age or their family moves away. If one of the parents recommends you to a possible new client, the new client can go to your website and get the full picture immediately. Clients will know you before they even meet you. Those are only a few of the reasons why you need a website. There are more.

My Confession, Your Gain

Here it is: I am not a very technical person. Actually, I choose not to be too involved in technical issues. I'd rather be writing. I love technology and can hook up a DVD player and use my Mac computer without help, but that's about it. I don't know HTML and I don't intend to learn it. I do, however, update my own website all by myself. I was forced to learn how to do this to become more self-sufficient.

This is what happened: For the first ten years I had websites, I had a business partner who took care of all the technical aspects. I depended on her, so I did not bother to learn many of the details. I am a writer not a webmaster, I told myself. Then, she moved on. She was offered an unexpected job opportunity and was moving her entire family across the country. I was very happy for her. I really was. But I was left with websites that I could not update by myself. And I had no way to start any new websites. It just did not make sense to have to hire someone to make every little update that I needed. Instead I took up the initiative and learned what I needed to be able to update my website all on my own.

I will never be that helpless again. I've learned a lot since that day, and I have found ways to be mostly self-sufficient when I want to get information online. That is what this chapter is about. I am going to share some ways you can create a website that you can manage all by yourself.

Your home business also needs a website because:

- It is available twenty-four hours a day, seven days a week. Your website can help your business make a good impression no matter what time of day or night a potential customer starts looking for information.
- You can give immediate customer response. If they have questions, you can have the answers. Create a list of frequently asked questions (FAQ) on your site about your topic or specifically about your business. Only include positive and informative questions to answer. I have seen websites of really big companies that include "How can I get a refund?" as a question on a FAQ. Don't put negative ideas into your customers' heads. Interested people can also e-mail you from your website, which is many people's preferred way to communicate today.

- Create a personal connection. They are called personal computers for a reason. A person's close connection to her computer can transfer to good feelings about you as she reads about you online.
- It will help new customers find you. Most people search online to do research on products and services before they buy. Then they decide if they want to purchase online or go out shopping. If you have a website, people will discover your business as they search for your keywords.
- Your website can be your full-service store. It can have a shopping cart and accept credit card orders. You can set it up to answer customer questions in real time or by e-mail.
- It can be your best marketing tool. If your website makes a good impression, everyone who looks at it will trust you and your business even more. You can even put your press releases on your website.

Getting Started

In my opinion, there is nothing worse for your business image than to have a bad website. If the design is amateurish and unorganized, you will lose customers instead of gaining them. As you start your website, look around at what is out there. Make note of the websites you like and why you like them.

Decide what you want to accomplish with your website and then do what you have to do to speak to that audience through your design and your words.

The First Word You Need to Learn: WordPress

WordPress is the word that changed my online life, and it can change yours, too. Yes, WordPress is a blog platform, but it can also be the basis of your website. You will probably need a little help designing a WordPress website, but once it is up and running, you will have a beautiful site that you can manage and update on your own.

If you want to use WordPress as your blog platform, you can install a basic version on your server. I don't suggest that you host your blog on WordPress, because you will limit your options and won't have control over the server. Having your own domain name on your own server is essential. If you don't know where to start, take a look at WonderfulWebsiteStore.com. You can register your domain name and find hosting options there.

Get It Done for You

If you love the independence of being a do-it-yourself person, you will love the WP Dude. His real name is Neil Matthews. He offers free instruction for WordPress users on his website, www .WPDude.com; plus he gives courses and private coaching so you can learn everything you want to know about WordPress. And what you learn from him will be a skill you can count on forever.

What I like best of all is that Neil is available to get you out of trouble if you make a mistake while working on your WordPress website. He is a backup option that will give you the courage to get some on-the-job training. He works with fixed quotations so you don't have to worry that he will charge you any more than you expected to pay. If he can't solve your problem or you are not happy with the work that has been done, he will not charge you anything at all. He has created a short video to explain the process of working with him. You can see it at http://bit.ly/fbgYbN.

Most servers offer the option to automatically install WordPress for you. You can use the basic format for a blog, but it will look pretty boring. If you can't do it your-self, I strongly urge you to hire a WordPress website designer to help you choose a theme and tweak it to make it exactly the way you want it to be.

Free E-book Describes Another Easy Website Option

SiteSell is a comprehensive system of easy tools to help you create and maintain a website. On their website (SiteSell.com) they have a helpful community of other Site Sell owners who you can interact with. To receive a free e-book, called *WAHM-IT!: The Masters Course,* that they created just for moms who want to work online and have their own website. Go to www.wahm-masters.sitesell.com/ dreamscometrue3.html.

Create Compelling Content

I'm betting that you have a great personality. You are smart, too. You know a lot of really interesting things, and you are willing to share your knowledge. Your website visitors will have that exact impression of you when you create compelling content for your website.

Whether you are blogging or creating articles, your goal should be to teach your readers something valuable and do it in a way that will make them want more. What kind of information do they need? Answer that question and give your readers exactly what they want and need. If you do, they will be back for more.

Give your content a great headline so that your visitors will know what you have to offer and realize that they are in the right place. Have you ever clicked on a link and then looked all over and couldn't find the topic you were researching? Your visitors should see exactly what they are looking for as soon as they arrive. Effective headlines will help make that happen. Your keyword-rich headlines attract more readers and mentions on social media sites, too.

Create content that changes on a regular basis, such as a daily tip, a horoscope, or a blog that is updated frequently. Always remember to put the wants and needs of your readers first, and eventually all this good will help you make sales.

Besides your visitors, your content needs to attract search engines. Good copy that contains your keywords will do that, because search engines want their users to find relevant sites. As important as keywords are, write for the reader and not the search engines. Then, you can go back and optimize your copy.

When writing for an online audience, keep your sentences and paragraphs short. Use a lot of subheads. Lots of white space also helps make online reading easier. Write using a conversational tone and try to put at least one of your keywords in each paragraph. If that word is bolded, in italics, or linked to another page on your site, it will carry even more weight.

Dancing with Your Sales Page

Writing a sales page is like doing a dance with your potential customer, and you are in the lead. The music is made with the words you write, and there are very specific dance steps you must take. The research into what works has already been done for you.

A sales page is different from a website or blog. Its sole purpose is to sell an e-book or another product. Traditionally the sales page is one long page. Research shows that the more copy on the page, the more readers respond.

Your sales page is the destination page, where you will send your potential customers to buy your product. For example, if you are selling an e-book, you need to create a sales page before you can list it on Clickbank. All potential sales and affiliate sales will be sent to that page. You could sell your e-book directly from your blog, but it might be better to have a sales page that is written in a way that is proven to work.

The headline on your sales page is very important and needs to hit emotional triggers. A good headline engages the reader and conveys the needs of the customer and how your product provides the answers. Your sales letter headline can be more than one sentence, with the top sentence in larger type.

The first third of the sales letter presents the problem or desired benefit your potential customer is facing. You can tell a personal story or give details that tell your readers that you understand what they want and need and you are the person to give it to them.

The middle third of the page explains your product and relates once again how it will provide benefits. Don't go on and on about how good your company is. Readers are only interested in how they will benefit.

The last third of the page usually describes bonuses that the reader will receive with purchase such as free e-books or special reports. Describing all the great stuff they will "get" for "free" might be just enough to help them make their decision. Authentic testimonials from satisfied users (with photos, if possible) lets others relate how the product helped them. Offer a money-back guarantee, sign the letter, and then use a P.S. Research shows that most people read the headline and the P.S. before they decide to read the rest of the letter. Your P.S. should reiterate your biggest benefit and give a deadline that will give them a reason to buy now. The deadline could be a price increase, when a discount expires, or a bonus will be withdrawn.

Don't Stop the Music

Remember when I told you that a sales letter is a dance you do with your potential customers? That means that you will strive to get their attention and then maintain the rhythm and flow. Do not stop the band in midstream with Google AdSense ads or any other kind of ad for another product. It will stop the steps you so carefully choreographed and instead send them to another website.

Should you try to get readers to sign up for your e-mail newsletter so that you can follow up? Yes . . . and no. You could put a subscription box on your sales page, but if a person subscribes, you probably will not make a sale from her on that day. Without the subscription box, you are taking a chance that you will lose potential readers forever. You could experiment with two different pages, where one has a subscription box and the other does not.

The look of your sales letter also matters. Well-chosen stock photos depicting people doing a desired activity can be effective. The main reason for the photos is

the readers will unconsciously insert themselves into what they see to "try on" the experience. The wrong type of photos could cancel out your good words.

The best way to learn how to write a sales letter is to read a lot of them. Read good ones and make notes of the structure and phrasing being used. Read bad ones to know what to avoid. Use your own unfiltered response to guide you.

After you write your sales page, there is a way to get it designed for you and get it up and running at very reasonable rates. You can even match your e-book cover to the look of your sales page. Look for information on a Brand Pack at KillerCovers.com. A Brand Pack is what they call the service of creating a sales page and matching e-book cover.

Not So Scary Search Engine Optimization

Getting a website up and running is quite an accomplishment, but you are not finished. It is time to let the world know you are online. Most people find websites by searching in search engines like Google.com. Search engines use "spiders" that crawl the Internet to categorize and organize the information on websites. When a person types in the relevant keywords and creates a search, the search engine responds with a list of websites that meet the criteria.

Every blog or website owner knows that she needs to "optimize" to attract search engines to her site so that her website can appear on the first or second page of search results for that specific topic. But knowing and doing are two different things.

If you are learning about search engine optimization (SEO) for the first time, you will soon realize that it can get very technical. I don't know about you, but when I read words like *algorithm* and *ontology*, my eyes glaze over. The good news is that you don't have to read words like that to get the attention of the search engines. If you break down the things you need to know, you will soon realize that SEO is really about creating the best possible website.

A site that has quality content and uses the keywords associated with your topic will get good placement in search engines. If it has incoming links from well-respected (authority) websites, that's even better. Doing these things may not be enough to get on page one of Google results, but sometimes it is.

When your website is built, make sure you or the designer includes meta keyword tags and meta description tags on every page. These are HTML codes that are inserted into the header on a web page after the title tag. Meta tags sound difficult but they are not. They are keywords that communicate with the search engines so that they will be indexed correctly. Your meta description is often what you see written under your URL in search engines. You write that description in

your meta description. To see the meta tags on any website, right click and choose "view source." It is interesting to see what keywords your competition is using, and you can learn what you should choose. For more information about meta tags, go to www.metatags.org.

Getting Inbound Links

The more quality links that come from other websites to yours, the better your site will place in search engines. Some will come organically from other sites that are impressed with what you do. Others will ask to exchange links, but doing so will require you to put a link to their site on yours. You are not at the mercy of other sites, however. To create inbound links you can do the following:

- Write articles and place them on eZineArticles.com and other article directories. Link to your website in your byline at the bottom of the article.
- Place articles in content sites like HubPages.com and other sites that allow you to place a link to your website.
- Comment on blogs and use your domain name as your name or link to your domain at the end of the comment.
- Participate on message boards and forums in your business category. Create a signature that includes a link to your website.

Understanding the Importance of Keywords and Key Phrases

I've mentioned keywords a lot in this book. These are the words that relate to your topic that are searched for in search engines by potential customers. Even better than single keywords are keyword phrases of three to five words.

Keyword phrases are also called long tail keywords. Long tail keywords are used when the searcher wants to find something specific. They draw less traffic to websites than individual keywords, but the traffic is usually of higher quality. In other words, they draw people who are really interested in what you are writing about.

Some of the keywords for my website, HomeWorkingMom.com are *mom, telecommute,* and *at-home jobs.* The long tail keywords are *work-at-home mom, moms working from home, home business for moms,* and *work-at-home jobs for moms.*

If you know your category well, you might not have to do too much research to realize your keywords. However, you can do some free research.

11 Market Mom, Market!

Marketing is everything you do to promote your business. It is advertising, e-mail marketing, social networking, word-of-mouth, public relations, branding, search engine optimization, and more. Your marketing efforts can't be haphazard. You need to plan your strategy and know exactly who your target audience is and how to reach them.

As one mom to another, I know you will understand marketing and the power of persuasion if you think about how a family communicates. Consider these examples:

- When children make a request and are told no the first time, what do they do? They ask over and over again. *Your customers need to hear your message repeated at least seven times before they give you their full attention.*
- When kids do something surprising or cute, they get our attention, so they repeat the behavior. And then we tell our friends and relatives what they did. *Think of ways to surprise and delight your customers. Keep surprising them to keep their attention and get them to tell everyone they know about your business.*
- It gets our attention when children use the same words and phrases that we use when we speak to them. *When communicating with your potential customers, speak the way they speak and on a personal level. They will hear your words.*
- What makes children respond to our requests? Few of us will admit it, but we all "bribe" our kids with treats or toys to get good behavior. *Offer your customers something free or a bonus if they do what you are asking them to do.*

Emily Bonilla's passion is helping moms achieve their goals in business. Her story is a lesson in marketing, and even as she tells about her businesses and her life she gives valuable marketing tips and other advice moms need to handle work and family. "I am here for those who need me," says Emily. "The road to success is easier when you have a driver who has traveled the road before."

Emily's road to success began after she went to film school. She got a part-time job doing wedding videos and liked it so much that she decided to start her own wedding videography business. The business grew to include photography, DJs, and wedding planning. (See Emily's advice on page 66 in chapter 5, Becoming a Wedding Planner.)

The wedding business was so successful that it took a lot of time and adjustment. "I had to learn to let go and trust others to work in my business," she recalls. "I wish I had someone who had already been there and done that to coach me. I had to learn everything on my own, and it took trial and error."

Emily eventually liquidated her wedding business so that she could help other moms reach their goals using her experience and guidance. And she wanted to have more time for her two boys.

To fulfill her goal, she started the website MarketingforWahm.com. (WAHM stands for work-at-home mom.) "The most important skill any business owner can have is marketing," says Emily. "The other skills moms need are writing and computer/Internet literacy."

Asked for advice on creating a marketing plan, Emily responded: "When creating a marketing plan, several parts will play the most important roles in attaining business: branding, packaging, and a referral program. When you have a unique sales position (USP) the next step is to create packaging (a group of service or items) that reflects your position and give the customer a package that they can't resist because it is made for them. In order to create packages like this, you really need to know your customer. Creating customer profiles can help.

"Although there are many advertising options available today, the one that is your best to attract business is word of mouth. Take all your advertising options

and brainstorm how you can use that medium to encourage word-of-mouth referrals. Create a strong referral strategy that will work across all the advertising mediums that you use. Social media is a great channel for this; however, don't limit yourself to it. Be creative in using the other mediums as well.

"Paid advertising options should be used when you are making enough money to pay for it and no sooner. It can be very expensive. When paying for advertising, you should test your advertisements by comparing the numbers and improving them for best results. It is and should be a numbers game.

"When choosing where to advertise, try not to commit to a contract that doesn't give you a trial run so that you can see if it works or not. Choose magazines that also have a great marketing system including online, social media, and e-mail marketing. Create a customer management system to collect, track, and communicate with your leads gathered from your advertising efforts.

"Spread yourself wide across all marketing channels and mediums. Narrow down your efforts through testing what works best for your business' bottom line or ROI (return on investment.)"

Emily's final word of advice for work-at-home moms: "You can only do your best to please your customers. You can't please everyone. Keep your integrity and always go for a win-win situation."

To learn more about Emily and her marketing services visit her at www.MarketingforWahm.com.

Your Unique Selling Proposition

As you can see, marketing can be as easy as understanding human behavior and finding the right ways to communicate your unique selling proposition (USP) to them. Your USP shows or tells your potential customer how you are different and better than other businesses. If you break it down, it is easier to understand:

Unique: What sets you apart from your competition?
Selling: The reason why your potential customer will pay for your product.
Proposition: Your offer to your potential customer.

Your USP is also the way that you build a reputation as the business that does exactly what the customer needs. Another word for this is *branding*.

When your potential customers hear your business name and see your logo, what will they think? Brand marketing gives your business a consistent and unique image.

There are some businesses that only do brand marketing. Think about Target, for example. They run television ads that promote their brand. When you see their logo, you have a very specific image of what their business has to offer. Their slogan is "Expect More and Pay Less." That is branding.

Create your compelling USP before you do anything else to market your product. To begin, write down how your product will benefit your customer, not how good your company is. There is a marketing saying that goes, "Don't tell them how good your grass seed is, tell them how green their grass will be." Your target customer needs to feel that what you are selling will make it easier for them to be happier, get better looking, make more money, spend less money, or solve a problem. To be able to do that, you need a marketing plan.

To get an expert's point of view, read the sidebar about Emily Bonilla who specializes in helping work-at-home moms market their businesses.

Your Marketing Plan

Unless you are creating a formal business plan, you don't need a formal marketing plan as you start your home business. You do, however, need an evolving plan that will help you do the right things every day to promote your business and yourself.

The easiest way to begin is by writing one or two paragraphs that define exactly who your customers are and what benefits your business has to offer them. Be as specific as possible. It is an accepted fact that if everyone is your target market, no one is in your target market.

By focusing on a niche market, you are usually offering products and services that mainstream businesses do not. For example, the target market of my business is mothers who want to work at home. I could have focused on all the people who want to work at home, but I chose the work-at-home-mom niche. Would you be reading this book if it was aimed at a general audience instead of moms? Probably not.

Once you have defined your niche market, determine the least expensive and most effective ways to reach those in it. If your target market participates in social networking and social book marketing, you will have some very powerful tools that do not require you to spend any money at all. Your investment will be made with your time. Other free or inexpensive options are publicity, e-mail, and article marketing.

Paid advertising options can get very expensive very quickly, and there is no guarantee that they will work. Even the cost of an AdWords ad placed on Google.com can become very expensive, as you pay for each click.

Choose the marketing activities that you want to start and then create a schedule for working on each one. If you don't have a schedule, you might spend all day on one activity and then not go back for days. It is easy to lose yourself once you get started. For example, spending the day chatting on Twitter—even if it is about business—is not the best use of your time. Instead, use your schedule to develop a routine you can do for a set amount of time every day. Really focus on the activities that do the most to promote your business.

Online Marketing for Every Business

The very best marketing efforts will work together to build your brand and attract customers. Your Twitter page can help you get fans on Facebook and vice versa. Twitter and Facebook can bring traffic to your blog or website, or you can sell to your followers and fans without sending them anywhere. Collect subscribers to your e-mail newsletter on Twitter, Facebook, your blog, or your website. Then mail to your subscribers at least twice a week to give good information and promote your products or affiliate products . . . and send them back to Facebook, Twitter, or your blog/website. Register your content with Digg or another social bookmarking site and give your fans and followers a chance to read more and tell the world how much they like it. Then the cycle starts again.

Every business can take advantage of many of these promotional tools. As I've explained, every business needs a website or blog . . . and the synergy of marketing online is one of the most important reasons why.

You may be noticing by now how important it is to be able to write interesting content in order for many of these options to bring results. If you are not comfortable writing, refer back to my writing tips in chapter 4.

Marketing by E-mail

Visitors to your blog or website might be interested in what you have to offer, but once they click off they might forget about you forever. If you can get them to subscribe to your e-mail newsletter, you will have the ability to contact them over the following weeks, months, and years. You can build a relationship and provide great information. You can also sell your products and affiliate products.

When a visitor gives you her e-mail address, she is telling you that you have permission to send information directly to her. This is called permission marketing, and it is the best way to sell online. *Permission marketing* is a term first used by Seth Godin in his groundbreaking book, *Permission Marketing: Turning Strangers into Friends and Friends into Customers.* He wrote the book in 1999, but the information is still more than relevant today. Godin was not just talking about e-mail marketing. He said that when using permission marketing, the recipient should anticipate what you will send so that she looks forward to hearing from you. He also advised that the message be personalized and relevant, meaning the recipient should have a predetermined interest in your category of product. Marketing by e-mail can meet all of these qualifications.

You don't have to create a formal newsletter or e-zine to promote by e-mail, but it is easier to get subscribers if you do. Develop a concept that will appeal to your target market. At HomeWorkingMom.com, my newsletter is called "HomeWorking Mom-to-Mom Memo." Give your e-mail newsletter a name and plan the format and frequency. You can do a short newsletter or a full-fledged e-zine that accepts advertising. If you offer something free like an e-book or special report for subscribing, you will attract more new subscribers.

In your e-mail promotions you can answer questions, share information, and develop valuable relationships with your customers. Your e-mails should be formatted so that they are easy to read. Write in short paragraphs and use headings to break up the type. Send recipients to your website to read more or make them a special offer. Doing that will create traffic, more AdSense clicks, and sales of your products.

Never send unsolicited e-mail promotions. It can get you in trouble, and you could even lose your e-mail account if too many complaints are received. The Can Spam Act of 2003 requires e-mail marketers to follow specific rules. Go to www.fcc.gov/cgb/consumerfacts/canspam.html to see the guidelines.

Article Marketing

You don't have to be an experienced writer to do article marketing. There are even more ways to market with articles than you learned about in chapter 4. There are over one thousand article directories online. Articles placed in these directories are often picked up by search engines like Google.com. At the end of each article, the writer can put a resource box that includes links to the website or blog. Sometimes affiliate links are also permitted. Some article directories only cover specific topics, so

make sure that the topic of your article is appropriate before you submit your article to each directory.

The largest and most well-respected article directory is EzineArticles.com. You can search for others on Google.com. Make sure that the article directories you choose actually use your article's topic.

Getting Free Publicity

When a magazine, newspaper, website, or a high-traffic blog writes about your business, you will get a bigger and better response than if you advertise or promote your business in any other way. This is because it is always more valuable and believable when you get editorial coverage. If you learn how, getting publicity is not that difficult and your efforts could be rewarded with thousands of dollars worth of free publicity. If your target audience reads about you in a magazine or sees you interviewed on TV, the built-in endorsement of that media outlet is implied.

The media need interesting things to write or talk about. They want to tell your story, but only if it is newsworthy or interesting in some unusual way. Just asking will not get you free publicity. Your first step to getting free publicity is to write a press release.

A press release is not a letter written to the media. Rather, it is written directly to the consumer who will read the newspaper or the magazine that picks up the information. Even though large media outlets will rewrite your press release, there are some places that will pick up the press release and print it word for word.

To make sure that your press release gets used, you have to think like the media and create a message that fits them. Give them an idea that makes an interesting story and they will be knocking down your door to ask for more.

To be taken seriously, a press release must follow an expected format:

- It is always typed and double spaced, and it should be limited to one page. If you send your press release through the mail, you can use a plain piece of paper or your business letterhead.
- At the top put the contact name with a telephone number and/or e-mail address and the release date. If you want it to be published right away, put "For Immediate Release."
- Center a very interesting headline written in all capital letters. Choose your headline with care, because if it is not compelling or does not offer some

benefit to readers or viewers, your press release will probably hit the garbage can before being read.

- Write a lead paragraph. Just like the first paragraph in a newspaper article you need to cover *who, what, where, when,* and *how.* This paragraph could also send your press release to the trash can if it is not interesting.
- The body of the release should fill in the details. You should include quotes (don't be afraid to quote yourself).
- Your conclusion should contain your contact information just as you would want to see it in print.
- After the last paragraph center the symbol "###." This indicates the end of the release.

Be sure to enclose a sample of your product, if applicable, or include a fact sheet.

Distribute Your Press Release Online

Send your press release through the mail and distribute it online. Each method has different benefits.

- If you submit your press release online, the newswire service will probably provide a format that you can fill in.
- Press releases that are posted online are usually picked up by search engines and could come up in results when one of your potential customers searches for one of your keywords. This unfiltered access makes it even more important to aim your release directly at your customer. Putting keywords in your headline is a vital step for search engine optimization.

Paid Advertising

Paid advertising can be like gambling. Never spend money that you can't afford to lose. With experience and a lot of testing, you can pay for advertising, but it should not be the first way you promote your home business. If you have a limited budget, don't spend your money on advertising.

To help you decide where to advertise, consider your cost per one thousand prospects. This is referred to as CPM. This formula only makes sense if every prospect is a member of your target audience. Keep the audience in mind and choose advertising that they will be sure to see.

If you are considering an ad in a magazine or a large website, request a media kit from the magazine or website that includes the outlet's editorial calendar. That way you will know which editions will have articles of interest to your target audience. Take your time and observe how many advertisers advertise continuously. One-shot advertising simply does not work.

Radio and television advertising will not be your best choices when you are just starting up. This is especially true because the ads for both types of media have to be produced, so you are paying for more than just time. If you decide you want to try this out someday, remember that some cable television stations and radio stations have special deals for time that has not been sold.

Advertising Online

Online advertising is sometimes less expensive, and you have a wider selection of options. Here are a few of the best options:

- **Craigslist.org.** This is the only free classified advertising option that is worth-while. In recent years Craigslist has received some bad publicity for the type of ads they accepted. However, millions of people use Craigslist every day. If you have the right offer to put in front of Craigslist users, it could be a good move. Craigslist is organized by geographical location so you have to choose one at a time. Cross-promotion is not permitted. Post your ad often and choose a different city each day.
- **AdWords.** These are the ads that appear on Google.com next to the search results. They also appear on content websites, and that is the source of the AdSense ads you run on your blog or website to make money. To get started you should create an account. You then choose hundreds of keywords (the search terms that people will use that will bring up your ad). You will pay per click on your ad. You will predetermine how much you are willing to pay for each click and how much you are willing to spend each day. You will have to bid enough so that your ad appears on the first or second page of results. You need to be vigilant when you are running an AdWords cam-paign because the clicks can add up quickly. It is important to learn more before you actually try Adwords. You can find more information about Google AdWords on Google.com and in a book by the AdWords expert, Perry Marshall, listed in appendix B.

- **Advertising in e-mail newsletters and e-zines.** This is actually a good way to start advertising. Choose a newsletter that accepts advertising and is delivered directly to the members of your target audience.
- **Banner ads.** Small, square banner ads measuring 125 x 125 pixels can be affordable to have created and placed on blogs and websites. Bloggers like them because they are a good fit in the sidebar. Advertisers like them because they can put the banner ads on a few different blogs or websites for the price of one larger banner ad. Some affiliate programs offer these ads for affiliates to use. Take care to only advertise on sites that you want your business to be associated with and where members of your target market frequent.
- **StumbleUpon.com ads.** This social bookmarking site offers some advertising options that are affordable. Users register their interests, and then when they click on "Stumble" they are delivered a website that other users with similar interests rated positively. If you go to a StumbleUpon Paid Discovery, it will cost you between 5 cents and 25 cents per page delivered.

Social Networking: Making Friends to Make Money

Even if you have never sent a tweet or became a fan of a business on Facebook, you need to know about social networking. A cultural shift has taken place, and you need to be involved if you want a successful home business. Facebook, Twitter, YouTube, and LinkedIn have become part of the fabric of our society and very important tools for business owners.

Social networking has changed the way we communicate. It is about people talking to people, even when it is a business talking to its customers. All the walls dividing us have come down. It can be fun, but if you want to make money using social media, you have to do more than tweet about your kids and how good your coffee tastes. Social networking for business takes knowledge and focus first, and then you can mix in some inspiration and even a sense of humor. Your personality does matter, but you need more substance than that. And remember to check out what your competitors are doing on social networking sites to get ideas and keep up or exceed their participation.

Even if you use Facebook or Twitter for personal interactions, you still need to learn how to use them for business. The average Facebook user has 130 friends. As a business user you are not looking for friends; you want fans.

Promote your Twitter and Facebook sites in your e-mail signature, on your website or blog, and in your e-mail newsletter. Graphic buttons are available for each service. Reference them in your byline in articles you write. Put them on your business card. Promote them in every way you can think of. You could even have a T-shirt printed!

Choose One at a Time

When you learn how to harness even some of the social networking power to promote your home business, it could become the best marketing tool in your toolbox. You can have all of the marketing power that even the largest business has and even more heart. Choose the social networking site that appeals to you most and then give it your full effort. But remember: Social networking is more about listening than talking. Hear what your potential customers are saying and greet them with open arms.

Twitter.com

On Twitter, celebrities tweet and respond directly to their fans. Corporations are called to the carpet and must respond to complaints. They also have the opportunity to answer questions and show their human side.

Twitter is one of the easiest social networking sites to use. But don't let its ease of use fool you into thinking that you don't have to have a business strategy. You have 140 characters to send messages to the people who follow you.

After you register and fill in your profile, put a link to your website. If you want to, you can change your Twitter page's background at a site like TwitBacks.com. Then go to Search.twitter.com and type in words related to your business. Find interesting tweeters and follow them. There is a good chance they will follow you back. Start tweeting up to 140 characters. Send people to interesting pages on your website or blog. If you've written articles, give out the links. To shorten your links, use http://bit.ly/ (no .com). Tweet links to other interesting content online. Invite questions. Re-tweet messages sent by others.

You can find me on Twitter at Twitter.com/HowToWorkOnline.

Facebook.com

Everyone knows by now that Facebook has more than seven hundred and fifty million active users. But did you know that at least 50 percent of those users log on to Facebook

every day? Here are some more figures you may not know about Facebook, according to Facebook itself:

- People spend over 700 billion minutes per month on Facebook.
- More than 2.5 million websites have integrated with Facebook.
- More than 30 billion pieces of content such as web links, news stories, and blog posts are shared each month.

Yes, we are obsessed with Facebook. There has never been anything like it before, and no other social networking site comes close. For a business, everything on Facebook should begin with a specially designed landing page. Ask your visitors to "like" your page before looking at the next page. Offer a free e-book or a special report and capture their e-mail addresses while you are at it.

On Facebook, conversations between businesses and their customers can be read by all. We vote to "like" a business, and the consumer has power never seen before. Using Facebook for business is very much like creating a successful blog:

- Create a welcome landing page.
- Make frequent updates.
- Ask your visitors questions to start a discussion.
- Post photos and YouTube videos.
- Create a community and interact with your visitors.

Find me on Facebook at Facebook.com/HomeWorkingMom

LinkedIn

LinkedIn is a professional social network. More than Facebook or Twitter, this is a site that was created to help people connect with each other. Sign up for LinkedIn only if you will use it. Just putting up a profile without going back is not advised. Inactivity can create a bad impression instead of enhancing your reputation.

After you join LinkedIn, create a detailed profile to reassure potential networkers that you and your business are credible. Then create a plan for making connections with the people and companies whose attention you want to get. Join LinkedIn groups that contain your potential customers and participate in group discussions to get noticed.

LinkedIn done right is a great place to attract clients or find a job. Use your connections to get your questions answered or create business opportunities or to improve your status as an industry leader or answer questions to LinkedIn Q&A.

YouTube

All those YouTube videos of laughing babies and cute puppies that go viral and receive millions of views give more to their subjects than fifteen minutes of fame. You can become a YouTube sensation too. Many of these people earn thousands of dollars. Those YouTube pages contain contextual ads. YouTube has a user-partner program that gives 50 percent of the money generated by the ads on those pages to the person who submits the video. Participation in the program is by invitation from YouTube.

YouTube is also a great way to give away content to your audience. You can find "how-to" videos on every subject on YouTube, from knitting a sweater to creating a WordPress website. What can you demonstrate? If you feel comfortable in front of a camera, it can be really effective to just sit and talk about your topic or show samples of your products.

You can put your best videos right on your website or blog, too. YouTube videos from other people or businesses can also be used on your blog or website. They can also help your website to get listed by Google.com on one of the first pages of results when people search for your topic.

Social Bookmarking

As I mentioned previously in this chapter, if you have seen the links on blogs and websites that say Digg, StumbleUpon, Reddit, or Technorati, you have seen social bookmarks. There are actually more than twenty social bookmark sites, and many are listed in appendix B.

Digg.com is one of the best social bookmark sites. After registering, you can submit any of your content to be listed. Other users can "Digg" your submission and, if you receive enough Diggs, your content will move up and might make the front page for millions of Digg visitors to see. Getting those "Diggs" is the reason why you will want to put a little Digg button under your blog posts and at the end of any content that you write.

Even if you do not get many people digging your content, you still benefit. Submitting your content to a social bookmarking site like Digg.com will give you a back-link from there to your blog or website. Backlinks from "authority" sites like a social networking site will help you get better ranking on search engines like Google.com. High ranking on search engines gives you more visitors.

1. Ask your customers how you can better serve them.
2. React to your customers' suggestions.
3. Send appealing postcards with special offers. They are mini billboards that will be see by others.
4. Offer something free to get an e-mail subscriber.
5. Do one marketing activity each day.
6. Donate your product to a nonprofit organization.
7. Post comments on blogs and use your website or blog address as your user name and in your signature.
8. Submit your website to DMOZ.com (the Open Directory).
9. Provide high-quality content.
10. Track everything and analyze the results.
11. Use a signature line in your e-mails that mentions your business.
12. Get involved with social book-marketing sites.
13. Ask your customers for the sale.
14. Create an online community.
15. Always follow up.
16. Let your customers get to know you by interacting on social media.
17. Send out newsworthy press releases.
18. Write an e-book with affiliate links and give it away for free to loyal customers.
19. Offer a gift to anyone who refers a customer.
20. Always send a follow-up offer with a special discount after a customer makes a purchase.
21. Use Facebook and Twitter to make special offers and generate sales.
22. Give followers on Twitter an insider look at your business.
23. Offer your customer benefits, not products and services.
24. Co-create products with businesses that have your target audience's eyes and ears on them.
25. Use social networking to find people who need what you are selling and start a conversation with them.

More Social Networking Sites

There are two other social networking sites that you could consider after you establish your business on Facebook and Twitter.

Tumblr.com

It calls itself a free micro blogging site and says it is a place where millions of people are sharing the things they do, find, think, or create. You can create a personalized blog page and post photos, text, links, quotes, music, and videos. It incorporates a lot of features similar to Facebook and Twitter with its own twist. You can "like" a post, reblog, and ask and answer questions.

Yelp.com

Yelp is a review site where users can create locations and give details about a business, review it, and post multimedia content. There are Yelp sites for many different cities, and the businesses are often restaurants and other brick-and-mortar locations. If you put your business on Yelp, all reviews—both good and bad—stay there. Yelp allows top-quality businesses to create impressive pages.

I never could understand fear of success. Why would anyone fear being successful? Then one day I went to get my mail at my post office box and there was only a little slip of paper inside. It said to pick up my mail at the window. When I went there, I was handed a postal bin filled with envelopes and each one of them had a self-addressed, stamped envelope (SASE) with a $2 check inside.

I had written an article for *Family Circle* about starting a home-based gift basket business and offered the readers a sample of the newsletter I used to publish called "HomeWorking Mothers." The full bins continued until I had over ten thousand letters just from that article. I wrote many more articles for *Family Circle* and other national magazines. One paragraph written about working at home in *Glamour* magazine mentioned my business and another ten thousand plus envelopes and $2 checks came in over one month's time. The envelopes and checks just kept on coming.

You would think this was a good thing. I was excited that there was so much interest in my business, and the money was great. However, I had to pay for printing all those newsletters and the promotional materials that would go into the envelopes. Each envelope had to be opened. The SASE had to be removed and the rest of the contents of the envelopes saved for a mailing list. A full address had to be on them. The envelopes had to be stuffed, sealed, and stamped. Then they had to be transported to the post office, but the job was not done. Each of the names had to be added to my mailing list for follow-up.

I admit that my husband, my children, and I did a lot of envelope stuffing together in those days. We made it family time sitting around a big table, and they got paid for their work. I also transported a lot of the envelopes to other moms to stuff at home, and I hired someone to help at my house. My bank refused to process all those $2 checks, so I had to search for one that would

and change banks. Our whole lives were altered. I didn't have experience planning on how many newsletters and inserts to print, so I was either short or had excess.

I didn't have a fear of success then, but maybe I should have. I don't believe in saying no to opportunity no matter what adjustments have to be made. All of this happened from 1987 to 1995, before the Internet became what it is today. I still have the same post office box. One thing I know for sure is that people save magazines. I still get letters every week from those articles. If you would like to contact me by snail mail or send me a book or a product to review, the address is P.O. Box 423, East Meadow, NY 11554.

In 1997 I started HomeWorkingMom.com, and that changed everything for the better. The printing costs, the envelope stuffing, the postage costs all went away. Today I can communicate with thousands of moms online in as long as it takes to write the newsletter and press "send." And the costs for doing that are very affordable. If I still had to print and mail newsletters and promote through the mail, the printing and postal costs and the time-consuming work would have put me out of business a long time ago.

Being able to work online has changed everything for me . . . and it can for you, too. Working online, outsourcing, and using remote employees can make it possible to keep your business at home even if you still need help.

Can Your Business Become Too Successful?

You dream of being successful, but then success comes, and comes some more, and then you are overwhelmed. You didn't count on the added stress and responsibility, and you don't know why something so good feels so bad. Yes, your business can become too successful if you haven't planned for your success and if you are not willing to grow and change with it.

Most home business owners are used to doing everything by themselves. It is hard to admit that there is too much work to handle on your own, and you can feel a lot of conflicting emotions: elation at the extra income, fear of meeting all your obligations, determination to keep your business growing. If you have not planned for your success, it is time to make a new plan. Will you be able to enjoy your success, remain family oriented, and still keep your business on the success track? It is time to reevaluate and make a success plan.

Before you make any moves, you have to ask yourself some tough questions that only you can answer. Are you willing to consciously hold back on the growth of your

business to keep it under control? If not, in what ways are you willing to adapt the way you do business and live your life? Is this a temporary spurt of business, or did your business rise to a new and lasting higher level of operation?

Possible Problems

Here are some of the many reasons you could be contemplating moving your business out of your home:

- **You need help.** When you hire employees to work in your home, you give up your privacy and need space for them to work. Hiring employees also requires lots of paperwork, including specific tax forms and legal documents.
- **You need more space.** When you first started your business, your cozy little office was just what you needed. Now you need space for face-to-face meetings or to manufacture, store, and ship your products.
- **You feel isolated.** Talking to a two-year-old is great, but she can't give you business advice.
- **You are disturbing the neighbors.** You used to make a trip to the post office a few times a week, but now huge trucks are making deliveries and customers are coming and going all the time. If you live in a residential area, this is a problem.
- **You are endangering your children.** Dangerous equipment or boxes in the living area of your home can become hazardous to your children.
- **You just can't take it anymore.** Business-related material is spilling over into every nook and cranny of your home. You feel like you are living in your office instead of working in your home.

Possible Solutions

If you have too much work to do, but you don't want to hire people to work in your home, you do have other choices. You will be able to leverage your own skills when you give less important work to others to do. And, know your limitations. Use others to supplement your skills in tasks that you do not like to do. Think about how much more you could accomplish if you could concentrate only on the tasks that make you and your business special. The question is: How do you make that happen? It is hard to delegate if you do not have anyone to take on these responsibilities.

The answer? Use virtual assistants.

Virtual Assistants

You learned about becoming a virtual assistant (VA) in chapter 5. As you now know, a VA is an independent business owner who works remotely from her own office and communicates with business clients and delivers work by using all technology available today.

Hiring a virtual assistant can be the perfect solution when you need help with your business. We discussed how you could become a VA, but now that you have a successful home business, you can get the extra help you need by hiring one or more VAs to help with your business. Some VAs specialize in marketing, publicity, website design and maintenance, customer service, writing, and more. Other VAs offer more traditional and basic office or administrative assistant skills.

Before you choose a VA (or more than one) think about the jobs that you don't want to do or that you don't have the best skills to complete. Be honest with yourself about your shortcomings. Make an assessment of your strengths and weaknesses as well as the jobs that you just don't like to do. Would you like help answering customer service e-mails and telephone calls? Or are you looking for help with marketing and public relations? How about someone who can update your website or do keyword research for you? If you choose the right VA, she might even be able to give you creative ideas for your business and help you get started on them.

VAs can be better than employees because:

- You only have to pay for actual hours worked.
- You don't have to pay for benefits or employee regulations.
- You do not have to give up your privacy to have employees work in your home.
- They have their own business connections and resources that can be made available to you.
- Work assignments are clear, and you don't have to hover over them to make sure your work gets done.
- Because they work in their own offices, you can save on space, electricity costs, and equipment costs.

To establish good relations with your VA from the start, make sure you understand each other's expectations. Make your assignments clear and check to make sure she understands what you want. Agree on a deadline in advance. If money is an issue, decide on the number of hours that will be devoted to each task.

Your VA should work as an independent contractor so that you can avoid paying taxes and benefits and you will not be required to follow labor laws. The person you choose should be trustworthy; she will probably have access to the details of your business, such as passwords, and she will be charging you by the hour and you need to know that she reports her time accurately. Ask for references and speak with other clients before you make a final choice. If you will be giving proprietary information to your VA, it might be wise to ask her to sign a confidentiality agreement.

Reach Out to the World

You don't have to limit yourself to finding help in this country. There can be some advantages to working with people in another part of the world.

Because she will be in a different time zone, your daytime hours could be her nighttime hours and vice versa. That means that your projects may get attention while you sleep and be finished by the time you go to work the next morning. If you are interested in marketing your business to other countries, a VA or business overseas will be better able to help you. The server I use for my website, HomeWorkingMom.com, is in England and so is the wonderful woman who formatted my Kindle book, *Never Be Unemployed Again,* for sale on Amazon.com. There is a reason why large companies often outsource customer service to other countries like India: You can save a lot of money.

Outsource to Experts

Creating a team of established businesses that you use on a regular basis can take a lot of pressure off of you. You need a certified public accountant (CPA) to do your taxes, an attorney to consult with on legal issues, and business-specific resources like a printer or a fulfillment center if you mail packages to customers.

Make More Room

My office has changed rooms in my house three times since I started working at home. It started in a glorified laundry room and is now in the second-largest bedroom in the house. If you have the option of moving your home office to a bigger space, that can solve some of your space problems. Or instead of moving your office, take over another room for office work or even just a closet that is located in another room to help with storage.

If your business is really successful, you always have the option of buying a bigger house or moving to a larger apartment instead of moving your office out of your

home. Successful entrepreneurs who like to work at home have been known to buy a three-story house and use the entire third floor for office space.

You Stay, Everything Else Goes

You have the option of renting office space or storage space for your business while you continue to work in your home office. This will increase your expenses, but your productivity and profits could also rise.

Create a Home Away from Home

It can be possible to leave your home office while maintaining a close family relationship. Do you want to take advantage of the drop-in traffic a store could bring? A storefront could also give you a place to give seminars, meet with clients, and do other special events that could attract customers. Working in a store does not necessarily mean that you have to sacrifice family time. I spent much of my childhood playing in the backroom of my family's store. I spent a lot of time drawing and writing "books." In fact my family's store is where I decided I wanted to be a writer. Interacting with customers and eventually working in the store added to my self-esteem and gave me an entrepreneurial spirit. I learned to count out change, how to handle unusual personalities, and inventory management and organization—all with my parents close at hand. To this day the untraditional emotional support and skills I learned in that little store serve me well.

Playing Chicken: Should You Leave the Nest?

Ultimately the decision to transfer your business to an outside location will be determined by your personal goals. Is it possible that your increased income allows you to buy a bigger home where you can designate more work space? Does your work-at-home lifestyle mean more to you than increasing your income? You may want to consider selling your business and starting a new, less complicated option. Your business is your baby and it might be hard to let it go. But remember: Even your children will grow up someday and leave the nest. When you are willing to let go, new and different rewards could flow into your life.

No matter what you decide, I wish you all the success you can handle and a healthy and happy family!

From One Work-At-Home Mom to Another: A Personal Note

I recently went to my favorite Chinese restaurant. When I opened my fortune cookie, this is what I read: "It is time to tie up those loose ends and turn them into beautiful bows." It was the perfect message to receive as I complete this book. I've so enjoyed sharing all my knowledge about home-based business with you, and I hope that I have motivated you to follow your dreams and create the life that you and your family deserve.

I Do Have Some Closing Thoughts for You . . .

Before I became a writer, I consciously accepted the fact that my work would sometimes be rejected. I knew that I had to accept and even embrace rejection if I had any hope of being published. I told myself that every no brings me one step closer to a yes. And I decided that a rejection would probably be the opinion of one person who just might be having a bad day.

If you turn every rejection you encounter into a learning experience, it will become more valuable than anything else to help you create future success. Don't let your ego shrivel up and die because one person—or many people—tell you no. You will be tested as you work on your home-based business. This is what happened to me:

Many years ago, I sent a query to a top woman's magazine, with a circulation in the millions, to write an article about mothers working at home. My idea was accepted, and I was thrilled. I worked hard on the article, but the editor quickly sent it back with a letter detailing all the things I had done wrong. Was the editor an unpleasant hardnose? Yes. Did I think her criticisms were fair? Maybe.

I could have protected my ego and put the article in a drawer and forgotten about it. If I did, I would have lost the payment, my confidence, and

important publicity for my business. I would probably still be carrying a bad feeling about it today. So I followed the editor's suggestions, worked hard on the revision, and the article was accepted. I was proud of myself and my confidence grew instead of going away.

You have the same choices when you face rejection or a lack of sales from your new home business, and you should never give up either. Ask your potential customers for suggestions. Do research. Embrace your challenges and keep going. If you don't give up on yourself, you will succeed. I know you can do it!

In 2005 Steve Jobs, the founder of Apple, gave a commencement address to the Stanford University graduating class. He talked about turning points in his life, about how he started Apple with one other person in his parent's garage, and then when he was thirty he was voted out of the company. That started him on a very creative period of his life. He started the Pixar and Next companies and eventually, when Apple bought Next, he was back where he belonged.

Jobs said that you can't connect the dots of your life as you are going forward. It is only when you look back on your life that you can see how everything fits together. You have to trust that life will lead you in the right direction.

My message to you is clear: Do the very best you can do for your family and your business. Absorb all the knowledge you can. Love hard and work hard, and don't let anyone or anything discourage you. Trust that someday you will look back and see that life led you exactly where you are supposed to be . . . that you tied up all those loose ends and made them into beautiful, beautiful bows.

I'd love to hear from you. You can contact me at Facebook.com/HomeWorkingMom and Twitter.com/HowToWorkOnline.

Appendix A: Glossary

This glossary can serve as your guide as you work on your business idea. Not every term here is mentioned in this book, but you will encounter most of these terms on your pathway to success.

AdSense: Google runs this ad serving program that allows website owners to gain revenue by displaying ads on their websites.

Advertising: A persuasive message aimed at your target audience that appears in the media.

AdWords: Google's advertising product. AdWords offers pay-per-click advertising for text and banner ads. When advertisers use AdWords to promote their product or service, their ads appear on any related website that is using AdSense.

Affiliate: A person who is awarded a predetermined amount for every visitor, subscriber, and/or customer that is provided to the company.

Affiliate marketing: One of the most popular forms of online business. It involves selling the products and services of other companies for a predetermined commission.

Affiliate program: A revenue-sharing arrangement between an online advertiser and an e-commerce company. Payments can be based on a percentage of the sale or the number of sales, clicks, or registrations that are referred.

Article directory: Contains articles written and submitted for free to other websites as long as they publish the author's byline information. Articles that appear in article directories often are indexed by Google, which can attract more attention to a business.

Article marketing: Writing articles and submitting them to article directories and content websites and to attract attention and increase traffic to a website.

Attachment: A file that is included with an e-mail message.

Autoresponders: Automatic e-mail response programs that will send preentered e-mail messages instantly to people who request information from a website, newsletter, or online merchant.

Avatar: An icon that represents you on message boards, chat rooms, IM programs, 3-D chat rooms, and virtual worlds.

Banner exchange: A group of websites that display each other's ad banners in exchange for credits. The more impressions you display, the more credits you receive.

Blog: A shortened term for "weblog." Refers to a website where entries are made similar to a journal or diary. The entries are presented in reverse chronological order, with the newest entry on top. Although blogs were originally used like a personal journal on everyday events, they have evolved into a promotional tool.

Blogger: A blanket term for anyone who uses a blog to post information on topics that are of interest to them. Becoming a blogger is actually simpler than it might seem. As blogging has grown in popularity, many websites offer platforms to quickly and easily create a blog.

Bookmark: A tab at the top of your Internet Browser that says "Bookmarks" or "Favorites." When you are on a website that you want to bookmark, you can select "Bookmark this page" (or a similar phrase) and your web browser will save the URL information for that site.

Branding: Establishes the company's identity in marketing, and especially online marketing. Branding is the impression made as a result of an accumulation of experiences that consumers have with a particular company or product.

Brick-and-mortar: Traditional retail businesses with actual buildings. Used in contrast to dot com businesses, which exist online.

Content: Informational articles that appear on websites.

Contextual ads: Advertising that appears on website pages on the same topic as the information on the page.

Copy: Words or text written for publication, broadcast, or production.

Copywriting: Writing to persuade the reader to act somehow, whether that is buying a product, signing up for an e-course, or clicking on a link.

CPM: Cost per thousand. Used when pricing advertising.

CPO: Cost per order. A mathematical formula that divides the total cost of a mailing or advertisement by the total resulting orders.

DBA: Doing business as. A registered business name that is different from that of the business owner.

del.icio.us: A social bookmarking site. It is for storing and sharing web bookmarks with other users.

Digital products: Products that are delivered electronically. An e-book is an example of a digital product.

Domain name: The address or URL of a particular website. For example www.Google.com is the domain name for the Google search engine.

Download: Transferring a file or files from one computer to another using the Internet.

Double opt-in: A technique used in opt-in or permission-based marketing. Subscribers click a link in an e-mail to confirm they want to subscribe.

E-book: A book that can be downloaded and read on a computer or an e-book reading device such as a Kindle.

E-business: Any business that is drawing a majority of its income from selling products or a service online.

E-zine: An online magazine or newsletter distributed by e-mail.

E-mail marketing campaigns: A form of direct marketing that uses electronic mail to communicate commercial and fundraising messages.

FAQ: Frequently asked questions. Questions and answers that are related to a website, newsgroup, software, or any kind of product or service.

Forums: A place online for holding discussions. Forum members either discuss one specific topic or have a common thread among all of the members.

Forward: Redirecting e-mail from your inbox to another e-mail user.

FTP: File transfer protocol. The standard method for downloading and uploading files on the Internet. Understanding FTP is necessary if you want to create your own website.

Fulfillment: Sending information requested or products ordered.

GIF or .gif: A compressed graphics file that is used to display images online. Normally, images on web pages are in GIF format, rather than JPG format, so they will load faster.

Graphic: A photograph or still image that is generated on a computer. Graphics give websites, forums, and e-mails dimension and interest.

Hard copy: Information from a computer that has been printed out on paper.

Hit: An entry automatically registered on the web page server's log file each time someone visits a web page. The log file records the number of times that a piece of information has been requested from the server.

Homepage: The first page of a website. Also called the index page.

Host: A computer that allows other computers to access its files. Every website has a host.

HTML: Hypertext markup language. A language that was designed for the creation of web pages.

Hypertext: The code that allows you to click on a word or graphic that is linked to another place on the page, in the website, or in another website.

Independent contractor: An individual who offers a service to a number of different companies. An independent contractor is not considered an employee, making payroll taxes or other employee paperwork unnecessary. A freelancer is an independent contractor.

Internet marketing: This is also known as online marketing and web marketing. This form of marketing combines traditional marketing principles with the unique interactive elements of the World Wide Web. The purpose of Internet marketing is to promote products and services online.

Internet traffic: The term used to refer to user activity on a website.

IRT: In real time. Chat rooms allow individuals to converse IRT.

ISO: Independent sales organization. A company that offers merchant credit card processing services.

ISP: Internet service provider. A company that provides users with access to the Internet. Before you can connect to the Internet, you must first establish an account with an ISP for a monthly fee.

JPG: One of the most common types of image formats that is used on the Internet. Pronounced "jay peg."

JV: Joint venture. A business move that is made by two or more entities to the mutual advantage of each.

Keyword: A term that you type into a search engine to begin an online search. Keywords are also used in HTML to help search engines identify and index a website.

Link: A clickable reference to another document, resource, or web page.

Logo: A graphic representation of a business.

Media kit: A folder of information describing a particular advertising medium, used for the purpose of evaluating the advertising value.

Meta tags: Something used to help search engine optimization. They are part of the HTML code that makes up what you see on a website.

Multimedia: Providing information by using a combination of audio, video, text, and graphics.

Netiquette: The code of conduct and unofficial rules that govern all forms of online communication.

Newbie: Any person who is new to the online world, or a specific forum or chat room.

Niche and niche marketing: A focused and targeted portion of the market. A business that focuses on a niche market is attending to the need for a product or service that is not being addressed by the mainstream market. The niche market narrowly defines a group of potential customers.

Online: Communication between computers or people operating computers.

Opt-in subscriber: A prospective customer who gives consent to receive marketing information (normally through e-mail).

Pay per click (PPC): A method of advertising. The advertiser is charged each time a visitor clicks on the ad. AdWords is a pay-per-click advertising method.

Page views: Also known as page impressions. Page impressions refer to the number of times that a web page is requested from a server. This is the preferred method for counting traffic.

PDF: A standard format for transferring documents on the Internet.

Podcast: Refers to the publishing of audio or video files to the Internet. The files are referred to as "podcasts" or "shows" and are similar to talk radio programs or public access television shows. People who create podcasts are called "podcasters."

Post: A noun used to describe a message entered onto a blog, message board, shared e-mail list, or newsgroup.

Press release: A news story or announcement that is mailed or e-mailed to the media in the hope that the information will be disseminated to the public.

Relationship marketing: A method of marketing that pays special attention to the individual customer.

Response rate: The percentage of response received from a marketing effort.

RSS: Really simple syndications. The format used for syndicating web content.

SAM: Stay-at-Home Mom.

Search engine: A website that acts similar to a card catalog for the Internet. Search engines use spider programs to index and locate desired information. The search engine program will find information on the Internet based on the keywords entered by the user.

SEO: Search engine optimization. The process of using targeted keywords in the keywords, content, tags, and meta-tags of a website in order to gain traffic through search engines.

Signature file: Sometimes referred to as a "sig file." A short statement at the end of an e-mail message used to identify the sender and provide additional information.

Social networking: The process of meeting and networking with people through the use of specific Internet technology like Facebook, Twitter, and LinkedIn.

SOHO: Small office, home office.

Source code: The format in which a computer program or website is written. To find the source code of a web page, select "View" from the top of the Internet browser. In the "View" menu, there should be an option that says "View Source" or similar language. The source code will appear in a pop-up window.

Spider software: Used by search engines to search the Internet for new content to display in the search results.

Sub-domain name: A domain name that is part of a larger domain. If you've ever seen a web address that doesn't start with the letters *www*, then you've encountered a sub-domain.

Tag: A keyword or descriptive term associated with a piece of information, sound clip, or video on the World Wide Web. Tags have become one of the most prevalent forms of classifying information on the Internet.

Target market: The market segment to which a particular product is marketed based on similar interests, age, gender, lifestyle, or socioeconomic grouping.

Target marketing: Helps a marketer to develop a product that speaks to a certain group of people. A key step in developing a product is deciding what the target market is and how to meet the target market's needs.

Telecommute: A work arrangement in which employees have flexibility in working locations and hours. Telecommuters can work from home or from another off-site location.

Thread: A string of consecutive message postings to newsgroups, mailing lists, or forums. Threads can be organized in ascending or descending order based on the date posted. Open threads are blog posts that allow readers to comment and discuss topics relevant to the blog.

TOS: Terms of service. The rules which one must agree to abide by in order to use a service. In order to use an online service, one must read and agree to the TOS.

Tracking: Used by online businesses to tell whether or not their advertising, copywriting, and website design are converting to sales.

URL: Uniform resource locater. The technical term for any web address that you'd type into the address bar of your web browser. Using a URL will take you directly to the website you are looking for. When someone asks for the URL of a website, he wants the full address.

User name: A synonym for login name or handle.

VA: Virtual assistant.

Viral marketing: Any practice that moves a concept quickly from person to person. There are viral videos, viral jokes, viral hoaxes, and so on.

Virus: A program, spread most commonly through e-mail, that multiplies itself on computer systems and incorporates itself into shared programs. Some viruses are harmless pranks, and others can destroy computer files or disable a computer entirely.

WAHM: Work-at-home mom.

Web 2.0: The second generation of services that are available on the World Wide Web, including social networking, blogs, podcasts, and RSS syndication.

Web designer: The person who is responsible for how a site looks and feels and assures the navigation works properly.

Web hosting: The business of providing the equipment and services required to display websites. Hosting also involves maintaining files and providing fast Internet connections. If you run a website or do business on the web, you need to find a reliable host.

Webmaster: The person who maintains the content and functioning of a website.

Website: Commonly referred to as a "site," this is a place on the Internet or the World Wide Web. The term site refers to the body of information as a whole for a domain name. A website is a collection of web pages. The pages can contain text, graphics, audio or video content.

WIKI: A type of website that allows users to easily add, remove, or edit most of the content. The name comes from the Hawaiian term *wiki-wiki,* which means "fast."

ZIP File: A compressed file. ZIP is the standard technology for data compression. Larger graphics and programs are normally compressed as ZIP files before they are made available for download.

Because you are reading this book, I consider you a part of my inner circle. I have created a page on my website where you can find all of the resources listed in this chapter with clickable links. You will also find special information and updates just for you. Just go to: www.HomeWorkingMom.com/wahmresources.

Chapter 1: Focusing on Your Possibilities

Free E-book:

Work-at-Home Job Finder for Moms
Available on HomeWorkingMom.com

The Choice Is Yours

Online Resources

CareerBuilder.com

eLance.com

Flexjobs.com

Freelancer.com

HomeJobStop.com

Homeworkers.org

HomeWorkingMom.com/telecommuting

HomeWorkingMom.com/work-at-home-employee

SheLancers.com

Tjobs.com

Vworker.com

Note: Although the work-at-home job websites listed are well intended, be careful when applying for any work-at-home job. You might decide to pay for home job listing access. But never pay to apply for an actual job.

Online Resources

fbi.gov/majcases/fraud/fraudschemes.htm

fbi.gov/page2/july06/job_scams070506.htm

ic3.gov

lookstoogoodtobetrue.com/

Recommending Reading

I Got Scammed So You Don't Have To!: How to Find Legitimate Work at Home and Random Jobs in a Scamming Economy
by Bethany Mooradian
Moreradiant Publishing

Work at Home Now: The No-nonsense Guide to Finding Your Perfect Home-based Job, Avoiding Scams, and Making a Great Living
by Christine Durst and Michael Haaren
Career Press

Chapter 2: Making the Decision to Start a Home-Based Business

Online Resource

How-to-Change-Careers.com

Recommended Reading

So, You Want to Start a Business? 8 Steps to Take before Making the Leap
by Edward D. Hess and Charles D. Goetz
FT Press

The Stay-at-Home Survival Guide: Field-Tested Strategies for Staying Smart, Sane, and Connected While Caring for Your Kids
by Melissa Stanton
Seal Press

Chapter 3: The Right Home Business for You

Online Resource

Heather Wilson, LadyinRed.com

Recommended Reading

Starting a Business from Home: Choosing a Business, Getting Online, Reaching Your Market and Making a Profit (2nd edition)
by Colin Barrow
Kogan Page

What Business Should I Start?: 7 Steps to Discovering the Ideal Business for You
by Rhonda Abrams
Planning Shop

Chapter 4: Becoming an Online Infopreneur

Online Resources
HomeWorkingMom.com/infopreneur
NewbieLifeline.com

Becoming a Blogger

Online Resource
ProBlogger.net

Mommy Blogs to Sample:
alittlepregnant.com
Amalah.com
AskMoxie.org
BaconIsMyEnemy.com
Dooce.com
FiveOfMyOwn.blogspot.com
FourPlusAnAngel.com
GirlsGoneChild.net
JessicaGottlieb.com
LivingWellSpendingLess.com
Mom-101.com
MommyEnterprises.com/moms-blog.htm
NotesFromTheTrenches.com
PinkDryerLint.blogspot.com
RealLifeWithKids.com

RookieMoms.com

ScaryMommy.com

Slacker-Moms-r-us.com

StefanieWilderTaylor.com

TheLaughingStork.com

TheMommyBlog.net

WouldaShoulda.com

Crystal's Story

MoneySavingMom.com/2009/10/becoming-a-workathome-mom-its-work.html

Recommended Reading

52 Weeks of Blogging Your Passion
by Tara Gentile
ScoutieGirl.com/52-more-weeks-blogging-passion

How to Make Money with Your Blog

Ad Sites

MSN AdCenter

TextLinkAds

Yahoo Publishing Network

Connecting Bloggers with Advertisers

AdGenta.com

Blogads.com

Blogsvertise.com

Business2Blogger.com

CrispAds.com

DoubleClick.com

InteliTXT.com

Kanoodle.com

PayPerPost.com

PayU2Blog.com

Smorty.com

Contextual Ad Companies

Chitika.com

Contextweb.com

Google.com/adsense

Kontera.com

Quigo.com

Recommended Reading

52 Weeks of Blogging Your Passion
by Tara Gentile
ScoutieGirl.com/52-more-weeks-blogging-passion

The Digital Mom Handbook: How to Blog, Vlog, Tweet, and Facebook Your Way to a Dream Career at Home
by Audrey Mcclelland and Colleen Padilla
Harper Paperbacks

Google AdSense Secrets, 4th Edition
by Joel Comm
E-book

ProBlogger: Secrets for Blogging Your Way to a Six-Figure Income
by Darren Rowse and Chris Garrett
Wiley

Writing Articles for Content Websites

Article Directory

eZineArticles.com

Residual Income Article Websites

Bukisa.com

eHow.com (requires applying and having your writing approved by eHow's owner
 Demand Studios)

HubPages.com

InfoBarrel.com

Squidoo.com

Suite101.com

Xomba.com

Recommended Reading

Earn Passive Income on eHow.com and maximize online earnings through writing
web content articles: bit.ly/fevPYY

Becoming an E-book Writer

To Sell and Automatically Deliver E-books Online

Clickbank.com

Payloadz.com

eJunkie.com

Recommended Reading

*Accidental Genius: Using Writing to Generate Your Best Ideas, Insight, and Content
(2nd edition)*
by Mark Levy
Berrett-Koehler Publishers

*Content Rules: How to Create Killer Blogs, Podcasts, Videos, Ebooks, Webinars (and
More) That Engage Customers and Ignite Your Business*
by Ann Handley and C. C. Chapman
Wiley

*How to Write & Sell Simple Information for Fun and Profit: Your Guide to Writing and
Publishing Books, E-Books, Articles, Special Reports, Audio Programs, DVDs, and Other
How-To Content*
by Robert W. Bly
Linden Publishing

Make Money Online: Write & Sell eBooks Guide
by Scott Boyd
Globotic Media Publishing

Chapter 5: Ten Top Home-Based Businesses for Moms

Becoming a Virtual Assistant

Online Resources

HomeWorkingMom.com/virtual-assistant/

VirtualAssistantsGuide.com/start-a-virtual-assistant-business.html

Recommended Reading

The Road to Going Virtual: Setup, Systemize, Market and Manage Your Virtual Assistant Business
by Trena V. Stubbs
CreateSpace

The Virtual Assistant Handbook: Insider Secrets for Starting and Running Your Own Profitable VA Business
by Nadine Hill and Debbie Jenkins
Lean Marketing Press

Becoming an Affiliate Marketer

Online Resource

HomeWorkingMom.com/online-marketer

Recommended Reading

Affiliate Millions: Make a Fortune Using Search Marketing on Google and Beyond
by Anthony Borelli and Greg Holden
Wiley

The Complete Guide to Affiliate Marketing on the Web: How to Use and Profit from Affiliate Marketing Programs
by Bruce C. Brown
Atlantic Publishing Company

e-Riches 2.0: Next Generation Marketing Strategies for Making Millions Online
by Scott Fox
AMACOM

Becoming an eBay Seller

Recommended Reading

eBay 101: Selling on eBay for part-time or full-time income
by Steve Weber
Weber Books

eBay PowerSeller Secrets: Insider Tips from eBay's Most Successful Sellers (2nd edition)
by Debra Schepp, Brad Schepp
McGraw-Hill

Starting an eBay Business for Dummies
by Marsha Collier
For Dummies

Becoming a Wedding Planner

Online Resources

The American Association of Certified Wedding Planners Aacwp.org
The Association of Certified Professional Wedding Consultants BridalAssn.com
Association for Wedding Professionals International Afwpi.com

Recommended Reading

How to Start a Home-Based Wedding Planning Business
by Jill S. Moran
Globe Pequot Press

Internet Marketing for Wedding Planners: Advertising, Marketing, and Promoting Your Wedding Planning Business Online Using a Website, Google, Facebook, Search Engine Optimization (SEO) and More!
by Nick Holliday
CreateSpace

Becoming a Medical Transcriptionist

Online Resource

Medical Transcription Companies by State Mtdaily.com

Recommended Reading

The Independent Medical Transcriptionist Fifth Edition: The Comprehensive Guidebook for Career Success in a Medical Transcription Business
by Donna Avila-Weil and Mary Glaccum
Rayve Productions

Medical Abbreviations & Acronyms: Quick Reference Guide
by Corinne B. Linton
Barcharts

Medical Transcription: Techniques and Procedures (7th edition)
by Marcy O. Diehl, BE CMA-A CMT AHDI-F
Saunders

Starting a Child Care Business

Online Resources

Childcare.net
nal.usda.gov/ric/ricpubs/rural_child_care_.htm

Recommended Reading

Family Child Care Record-Keeping Guide (8th edition)
by Tom Copeland JD
Redleaf Press

How to Start a Home-Based Day-Care Business, 6th Edition
by Shari Steelsmith
Globe Pequot Press

Start Your Own Child-Care Service
by Entrepreneur Press and Jacquelyn Lynn

Becoming a Personal Shopper

Recommended Reading

The Concierge Manual: A Step-by-Step Guide to Starting Your Own Concierge Service or Lifestyle Management Company (3rd edition)
by Katharine C. Giovanni
New Road Publishing

The Elite Personal Shopper Career Training Guide
by Gillian Armour, CIP
CreateSpace

FabJob Guide to Become a Personal Shopper
by Laura Harrison McBride, Peter J. Gallanis, and Tag Goulet
FabJobs.com

Becoming a Pet Sitter

Online Resources

National Association of Professional Pet Sitters PetSitters.org
Pet Sitters International PetSit.com
Pet Sitters Associates, LLC PetSitllc.com

Recommended Reading

How to Start a Home-Based Pet-Sitting and Dog-Walking Business
by Cathy Vaughan
Globe Pequot Press

The Real Poop Scoop on Pet Sitting: Create Financial Freedom Playing with Pets!
by Bonnie Best
BookWise Publishing

Starting a Gift Basket Business

Online Resources

Gift Basket Review
Festivities-pub.com
HowToStartAGiftBasketBusiness.info

Recommended Reading

How to Start a Home-Based Gift Basket Business

by Shirley George Frazier

Globe Pequot Press

Becoming a Personal Chef

Online Resources

American Personal & Private Chef Association Personalchef.com

United States Personal Chef Association Uspca.com

Recommended Reading

How to Start a Home-Based Bakery Business

by Detra Denay Davis

Globe Pequot Press

How to Start a Home-Based Personal Chef Business

by Denise Vivaldo

Globe Pequot Press

Start & Run a Home-Based Food Business

By Mimi Shotland Fix

Self Counsel Press

Starting a Part-Time Food Business: Everything You Need to Know to Turn Your Love for Food into a Successful Business without Necessarily Quitting Your Day Job

by Jennifer Lewis

Rabbit Ranch Publishing

Chapter 6: Creating Your Own Product

Online Resources

Handmadeology.com

MomInventors.com

To Sell Crafts/Artwork Online

ArtFire.com

Bonanza.com

DaWanda.com

Etsy.com

iCraft.com

MadeIt Myself.com

Silkfair.com

Supermarket (Supermarkethq.com)

UncommonGoods.com

Recommended Reading

Etsy Success—How to Make a Full-Time Income Selling Jewelry and Other Handmade Products Online
by Kathleen Donovan and Mogul Mom
Mogul Mom Books

Everything Inventions and Patents Book: Turn Your Crazy Ideas into Money-Making Machines!
by Barbara Russell Pitts, Mary Russell Sarao, and Russ Weinzimmer
Adams Media

The Handmade Marketplace: How to Sell Your Crafts Locally, Globally, and On-Line
by Kari Chapin
Storey Publishing, LLC

How to Make Money Using Etsy: A Guide to the Online Marketplace for Crafts and Handmade Products
by Timothy Adam
Wiley

The Independent Inventor's Handbook: The Best Advice from Idea to Payoff
by Louis Foreman and Jill Gilbert Welytok
Workman Publishing Company

The Inventor's Bible: How to Market and License Your Brilliant Ideas
by Ronald Louis Docie Sr.
Ten Speed Press

The Mom Inventors Handbook: How to Turn Your Great Idea Into the Next Big Thing
by Tamara Monosoff
McGraw-Hill

One Simple Idea: Turn Your Dreams into a Licensing Goldmine While Letting Others Do the Work
by Stephen Key
McGraw-Hill

Patent, Copyright & Trademark: An Intellectual Property Desk Reference (10th edition)
by Stephen Stim
Nolo

Chapter 7: Working at Home with Kids
Online Resources
HomeWorkingMom.com/homeworking-mom-lifestyle
HomeWorkingMom.com/how-to-have-happy-kids

Recommended Reading
Making Work at Home Work: Successfully Growing a Business and a Family Under One Roof
by Mary M. Byers
Revell

Chapter 8: Creating Your Mom Work Space
Online Resources
Luis Caicedo Design
 LuisCaicedo.com
Safety1st.com

Recommended Reading

Organizing from the Inside Out: The Foolproof System for Organizing Your Home, Your Office and Your Life (2nd edition)
by Julie Morgenstern
Holt

The Smarter Home Office: 8 Simple Steps to Increase Your Income, Inspiration, and Comfort
by Linda Varone
Great Meadows Publishing

Chapter 9: Home Business Is Real Business

Merchant Warehouse
To get a credit card merchant account with no application fee, no set-up fee, and no contracts or cancellation/termination fee: call (866)761-5531 or go to MerchantWarehouse.com.

Recommended Reading

Business Plan Kit for Dummies
by Steven D. Peterson, Peter E. Jaret, and Barbara Findlay Schenck
For Dummies

Home Business Tax Deductions: Keep What You Earn (6th edition)
Stephen Fishman
Nolo

How to Write a Business Plan
by Mike P. McKeever
Nolo

Successful Business Plan: Secrets & Strategies (5th edition)
by Rhonda Abrams
Planning Shop

Chapter 10: Every Mom Needs at Least One Website

Create Your Own Website

Buildit.Sitesell.com/dreamscometrue3.html

Domain Registration, Web Hosting, and WordPress

WonderfulWebsiteStore.com

WPbeginner.com

Website Designer

KeyItUpSeo.com (mention Home Working Mom for discount)

Recommended Reading

Building a WordPress Blog People Want to Read (2nd edition)
by Scott McNulty
Peachpit Press

Content Rules: How to Create Killer Blogs, Podcasts, Videos, eBooks, Webinars (and More) That Engage Customers and Ignite Your Business
by Ann Handley, C. C. Chapman, and David Meerman Scott
Wiley

Head First WordPress: A Brain-Friendly Guide to Creating Your Own Custom WordPress Blog
by Jeff Siarto
O'Reilly Media

The Really, Really Easy Step-by-Step Guide to Building Your Own Website: For Absolute Beginners of All Ages
by Gavin Hoole and Cheryl Smith
New Holland

WordPress for Business Bloggers: Promote and grow your WordPress blog with advanced plug-ins, analytics, advertising and SEO
by Paul Thewlis
Packt Publishing

WordPress 24-Hour Trainer: Watch, Read and Learn How to Create and Customize WordPress Sites (Book and DVD)
by George Plumley
Wiley

Chapter 11: Market Mom, Market!

Distribute a Press Release Online

Business Wire.com

Free-Press-Release.com

PRNewswire.com

PRWeb.com

Managing an E-Mail Newsletter

aWeber.com

Social Bookkeeping Websites

Buzz.Yahoo.com

Delicious.com

Digg.com

Diigo.com

FriendFeed.com

Mixx.com

Reddit.com

StumbleUpon.com

Social Networking Websites

Facebook.com

Friendster.com

LinkedIn.com

MySpace.com

Ning.com

Tagged.com

Twitter.com

Recommended Reading

The Copywriter's Handbook, (3rd edition)
by Robert Bly
Holt Paperbacks

Email Marketing: A Guide to the Internet's Most Effective Marketing Tool
by Mary R. Butler
CreateSpace

Facebook Marketing: An Hour a Day
by Chris Treadaway and Mari Smith
Sybex

How to Sell with a Story: Leverage Your Story to Shape Your Business and Generate More Sales (e-book)
by Tara Gentile
Taragentile.com/tell-your-story

Inbound Marketing: Get Found Using Google, Social Media, and Blogs
by Brian Halligan, Dharmesh Shah, and David Meerman
Wiley

KaChing: How to Run an Online Business that Pays and Pays
by Joel Comm
Wiley

The Marketing Plan: How to Prepare and Implement It (4th edition)
by William M. Luther
AMACOM

The New Rules of Marketing & PR: How to Use Social Media, Blogs, News Releases, Online Video, and Viral Marketing to Reach Buyers (2nd edition)
by David Meerman Scott
Wiley

Outrageous Advertising That's Outrageously Successful: Created for the 99% of Small Business Owners Who Are Dissatisfied with the Results They Get
by Bill Glazer and Dan Kennedy
Morgan James Publishing

Permission Marketing
by Seth Goodin
Simon & Schuster

Social Media Marketing: An Hour a Day
by Dave Evans and Susan Bratton
Sybox

The Truth About Email Marketing
by Simms Jenkins
FT Press

Twitter Marketing: Promote Yourself and Your Business on Earth's Hottest Social Network
by Steve Weber
Weber Books

Web Copy That Sells: The Revolutionary Formula for Creating Killer Copy That Grabs Their Attention and Compels Them to Buy (2nd edition)
by Maria Veloso
AMACOM

Words That Sell (2nd edition)
by Richard Bayan
McGraw-Hill

Ultimate Guide to Google AdWords: How to Access 100 Million People in Ten Minutes, 2nd Edition
by Perry Marshall and Brian Todd
Entrepreneur Press

Chapter 12: Getting Bigger Every Day

Recommended Reading

A-Z Guide: The Best Ways to Work with a Virtual Assistant
Kindle edition
by Karen L. Reddick
Unity House Publishing

Conquer the Chaos: How to Grow a Successful Small Business Without Going Crazy
by Clate Mask, Scott Martineau, and Michael E. Gerber
Wiley

Hiring Independent Contractors: The Employer's Legal Guide
by Stephen Fishman and Amy Delpo
Nolo

From One Work-At-Home Mom to Another: A Personal Note

Steve Jobs commencement address to Stanford University:
YouTube.com/watch?v=D1R-jKKp3NA&eurl=

Index

About the Author

Georganne Fiumara is a home business expert and consultant and the founder of Mothers' Home Business Network and its popular website, Home WorkingMom.com. *Woman's World magazine* has chosen Georganne as one of America's Ultimate Experts on earning money at home.

More than one hundred of her articles on home business topics have appeared in national publications such as *Family Circle, Woman's Day, New Business Opportunities, Income Opportunities,* and *American Baby,* and she contributes to numerous websites. She is also the author of *Never Be Unemployed Again* and *How to Start a Home-Based Mail Order Business* (Globe Pequot Press).